The Carter Presidency

The Carter Presidency
Policy Choices in the Post–New Deal Era

Edited by Gary M Fink
and Hugh Davis Graham

University Press of Kansas

Published by the University Press of Kansas (Lawrence, Kansas 66049), which was organized by the Kansas Board of Regents and is operated and funded by Emporia State University, Fort Hays State University, Kansas State University, Pittsburg State University, the University of Kansas, and Wichita State University

Library of Congress Cataloging-in-Publication Data

The Carter presidency : policy choices in the post–New Deal era /
   edited by Gary M Fink and Hugh Davis Graham.
      p. cm.
   Includes bibliographical references (p.) and index.
   ISBN 0-7006-0895-8 (cloth : alk. paper)   ISBN 0-7006-1097-9 (pbk : alk. paper)
   1. Carter, Jimmy, 1924–   . 2. United States—Politics and
government—1977–1981. I. Fink, Gary M. II. Graham, Hugh Davis.
E872.C38   1998
973.926'092—DC21   98-9967

British Library Cataloguing in Publication Data is available.

Printed in the United States of America

10 9 8 7 6 5 4 3

The paper used in this publication meets the minimum requirements of the American National Standard for Permanence of Paper for Printed Library Materials Z39.48-1984.

Contents

Preface

The opening of the Jimmy Carter Library marked a significant turning point in the evolving historiography of the Carter administration. A stream of researchers soon found their way to the library, spending countless hours digging through the immense and remarkably rich paper record of a relatively brief administration. By the tenth anniversary of the opening of the former president's papers, the fruits of that new research began to reach print in increasing volume.

It appeared a propitious time, therefore, to consider the significance of the Carter presidency, and a conference marking the tenth anniversary of the opening of the Jimmy Carter Library and the twentieth anniversary of Carter's presidential inauguration seemed an appropriate vehicle for such an assessment. Similar gatherings at other presidential libraries have proved valuable in promoting and directing research on individual administrations.

The Carter Library had hosted a session on the Carter presidency during the 1995 Organization of American Historians' annual meeting in Atlanta. After the session, several interested scholars met in the library's seminar room to discuss the feasibility of a conference. Rather than a tightly focused assessment of Jimmy Carter and the successes and failures of his administration, however, the Atlanta conferees envisioned a broader perspective. They hoped to use the Carter administration as a lens through which to view larger changes in American government and society during the second half of the twentieth century, changes that transcended the programmatic agenda of any particular administration. From a twenty-year perspective, it appeared increasingly obvious that Carter's was a transitional presidency marking the close of the New Deal era and introducing a new age of limited government, monetarist fiscal policies, and social conservatism. Consequently, rather than evaluating the successes and failures of the Carter presidency, as such, the organizers hoped through a close examination of policy debates on a variety of issues to better understand the momentous changes that had precipitated and accompanied the demise of the "New Deal Order."

Two years later, well over a hundred scholars—historians, political scientists, economists, sociologists, psychologists, even a nuclear physicist—assembled at the Carter Library and Presidential Center, where Jimmy and Rosalynn Carter and former members of the administration joined them on the program.

William E. Leuchtenburg, the dean of American political historians, opened the conference, etching Jimmy Carter's silhouette in the increasingly dim shadow cast by the New Deal presidency. During three plenary sessions following the keynote address, invited scholars traced evolving policy decisions in specific issue areas into and through the Carter administration. These are the papers reproduced in this volume; all are original essays grounded in research conducted at the Carter Library. Not all policy areas could be covered. Such important issues as health care and education, among others, are addressed only indirectly in the following pages. The critical area of foreign policy is treated in a single essay, although, here again, related essays covering trade policy and Jimmy Carter's postpresidential years provide further insights and analyses.

Many individuals and the institutions with which they are associated assisted in this project. Donald Schewe, Martin I. Elzy, Robert Bohanan, and the staff at the Jimmy Carter Library supervised local arrangements and assisted the conference directors in countless ways. In like manner, Steven Hochman, Senior Research Associate at the Carter Center, coordinated arrangements with the Center and provided valuable assistance in other ways.

In addition to their conceptual contributions to the conference design, program consultants Betty Glad, Stanly Godbold, Robert McMath, Leo Ribuffo, Judith Stein, and William Stueck assisted in the development of individual sessions, identified and recruited participants, and, whenever called upon, offered astute advice. Numerous other colleagues and friends also rendered timely guidance and counsel. Georgia State graduate students Stephanie McConnell, Joseph Knight, Robert Woodrum, and Larry Youngs assisted with conference arrangements. Our thanks also to Ginger Carter, who directed publicity for the conference and, along with Brian Abrams, developed and maintained the conference Web page, and to Craig Kaplowitz, who prepared the index for this volume.

Professor Erwin Hargrove, political science, and Dean Madeleine Goodman joined the history department at Vanderbilt University in sponsoring the conference. David Roberts and William Stueck of the history department at the University of Georgia and Robert McMath and Craig Nobles at the Georgia Institute of Technology arranged for financial support from their institutions. Timothy Crimmins and John Matthews made graduate assistants available and committed departmental resources and staff time to this enterprise. Laura Thomson assisted with a grant from the Georgia Humanities Council, which was of critical importance in staging the conference.

Because of its impressive list of publications related to the American presidency, the University Press of Kansas seemed an obvious choice as a publisher. After our initial discussions with Fred Woodward, the director of the press, we made an early commitment to the University Press of Kansas and have never regretted it. Throughout the project, Fred has been unfailingly supportive, providing sage advice and timely encouragement while defusing occasional crankiness with good humor.

Finally, the entire project assumed a more orderly cast when Suzanne Litke assumed the role of conference manager in the fall of 1996. Suzanne joined in program discussions, corresponded extensively with participants and others, coordinated conference arrangements at the Carter Presidential Center, and assisted in editing and proofreading the essays in this volume.

Introduction

Jimmy Carter's reputation has taken a roller-coaster ride since his melancholy departure from the White House nearly twenty years ago. His stunning loss to Ronald Reagan in the 1980 election seemed to document the Washington press corps' devastating critique of his "failed" presidency, a view shared by many of the nation's opinion leaders.

Perhaps inevitably, however, Carter's stock began to rise even before his successor completed his term in office. The glowing reputations of popular presidents typically begin to tarnish soon after they leave office, while those who relinquish the White House and depart Washington with scant public approval frequently look better in retrospect. To some extent that reappraisal equates with a bookend factor where the evolving reputations of preceding and succeeding administrations influence the standing of the intervening presidency. In Carter's case, then, the relatively negative assessments of the Nixon-Ford administrations and the sharp controversies over the Reagan presidency may have prompted a more sympathetic view of the deviating Democratic administration sandwiched between two-term Republican presidencies. Finally, Carter's active, public-spirited, postpresidential career contrasted sharply with that of his Republican bookends. Indeed, John Chambers, a student of former presidents' careers and a contributor to this volume, concludes that Carter "has become one of America's greatest ex-presidents." Chambers compares Carter's postpresidency favorably to those of John Quincy Adams, William Howard Taft, and Herbert Hoover, none of whom won a second term but all of whom established impressive records of public service after being turned out of office.[1]

The early reassessments of the Carter presidency owed much to James Sterling Young and the staff of the White Burkett Miller Center of Public Affairs at the University of Virginia. Miller Center scholars, some of them commissioned by the staff to assist with particular oral histories, conducted extensive interviews with

1

the former president and members of his White House staff shortly after Carter left office. Two political scientists, Erwin C. Hargrove and Charles O. Jones, then drew on those interviews to project a different and much more positive view of the Carter administration than had been common at the time.[2]

Ten years later, an interdisciplinary gathering of scholars, journalists, and former members of the administration convened in Long Island, New York, to recall and reassess the Carter presidency at the Eighth Hofstra University Presidential Conference. The papers read during that three-day affair generally expanded upon the cautiously revisionist tone of the early literature appraising the Carter presidency.[3]

Studies of the Carter presidency by Garland Haas and a British scholar, John Dumbrell, which reached print a few years later, seemed to reinforce an emerging synthesis reviewing the Carter administration in an increasingly sympathetic light.[4] But that assessment did not go unchallenged. In the first full-scale history of the administration based largely on Carter's presidential papers, Burton I. Kaufman concluded that the "contemporary image of the Carter presidency was, unfortunately, all too accurate and helped assure a mediocre, if not failed, presidency."[5] Although acknowledging that the times were not propitious for a liberal reformist administration, Kaufman nevertheless concluded that Carter could have and should have accomplished much more than he did. In explaining that failure, Kaufman resurrected a familiar litany of complaints first sounded by Washington insiders who groused that the outsider from Georgia lacked an understanding of Washington, surrounded himself with incompetent staffers, could not work with Congress, naively tried to do too much, and then failed to assign legislative priorities. Simply put, Carter lacked the political skills, experience, and temperament to do the job.

The chapters in this volume fail to move us significantly closer to a consensus view of the Carter administration, but they do raise the level of the explication beyond the sometimes self-serving inside-the-beltway complaints of congressional, bureaucratic, and press critics. Even more to the point, however, the contributors are not particularly interested in what Bruce Schulman, in his chapter, describes as "scorecard history."[6] Rather, they focus on policy as both cause and effect of the postindustrial transformation of American society that so gripped the Carter administration.

William Leuchtenburg and Robert Zieger, in the opening chapters, establish the political and social context within which those policy debates took place. John Chambers closes the volume with an analysis linking issues that Carter addressed as president to his more selective but unusually energetic postpresidential agenda. In between, the chapters fall into three broad divisions: economic policy issues as related to labor, industrial, and energy concerns; social welfare policy, including women and minority civil rights and environmental concerns; and foreign policy.

In the opening chapter, William Leuchtenburg notes the "high expectations with which liberals contemplated the return of the Democrats to power in 1977, when, after eight years of frustration under Nixon and Ford, they could, they thought, pick up where they had left off in the Great Society era."[7] To Democrats in the 1970s, the Nixon-Ford interlude was a political fluke, the consequence of a three-party split in the bizarre year 1968, bringing the scandals of Watergate and, in its wake, swollen Democratic majorities to Congress in 1974.

Looking back from the end of the 1990s, we can see that Carter, not Nixon or Ford, was the political anomaly of the post-1960s era. His role as president, and the achievements and failures of government during his administration, must be assessed against the realities of a post–New Deal order, one whose dynamics differed sharply from those of the Great Society.

From our end-of-the-century perspective, the watershed date in postwar American political history appears to be 1968. In that tumultuous year, a realigning election signaled the collapse of the New Deal order and inaugurated a new political era of divided partisan governance. Prior to 1968, the American party systems had featured single-party control of both elected branches. Nixon was the first candidate since Zachary Taylor in 1848 to win the presidency while his party failed to carry either the House or the Senate. In the New Deal order of 1932–68, the Democrats enjoyed a majority coalition cemented by redistributionist policies on economic and social welfare issues. The social turmoil of the 1960s, however, raised new cultural anxieties related to national integration—crime and punishment, abortion, family values, the work ethic, and religious morality in education. These issues favored Republican appeals to traditional values and patriotism.[8]

The rise of cultural issues created two distinct, competing opinion majorities that failed to coincide with either class divisions or party ideology. Blue-collar workers supported liberal, redistributionist economic policies but remained traditionalists on cultural issues such as feminist challenges, antiwar protest, and racial job preferences. Conversely, affluent suburbanites who embraced tax-cutting, budget-balancing, and deregulation policies were repelled by the intrusive morality of the Religious Right. Faced with these two socially cross-cutting opinion majorities, the parties polarized: Democrats on the left on both issues, Republicans on the right. Activists used the primaries to drive both parties toward the extremes—Democrats toward McGovern and Republicans toward Reagan. Single-issue interest groups multiplied, reinforcing partisan polarization.

The electoral result of this confusing mismatch following 1968 was surprisingly rational: divided partisan government. Republicans, dominant on cultural issues of national integration, which included nationalist positions on projecting American power and values in foreign affairs, won primacy in competing for the presidency. Democrats, traditional custodians of welfare and service provision, prospered in the Congress, where constituent service and iron-triangle bargaining rewarded close ties to well-organized clientele groups and agency bureaucrats. Divided government thus increased conflict between the two elected branches, as partisan animosities compounded the normal, structural tensions and jealousies consequent to constitutional separation of powers.

The problem of the divided governance model for the Carter presidency is that it was an exception to the post-1968 rule. Given Democratic control of both the White House and Congress during 1977–81, the usefulness of the model in understanding the Carter presidency becomes problematic. For Congress during the Carter administration, Democratic control poses no problem. The literature on Congress during the 1970s describes a thriving, petri dish environment for the growth of interest group liberalism. Subcommittees and their staffs proliferated along with the inside-the-beltway network of single interest groups, lobbying organizations of every kind, and policy entrepreneurs in Congress and the agencies. Democrats, the "party of government," were aptly symbolized in Congress by House Speaker Tip O'Neill, a shrewd Boston veteran of the art of the possible.[9]

Carter, though indubitably a Democrat, marketed himself as a new kind of Democrat. Offering a fresh face from the post-1960s "New South," Carter campaigned as a racial liberal, strongly supported the Equal Rights Amendment, appealed to Hispanic voters in Spanish, and supported rigorous environmental standards. On the other hand, Carter appealed to many of the new cultural concerns that animated post-1960s voters. As an outsider, he ran against the Washington establishment. An evangelical Christian, he stressed the primacy of family values and religious morality in public life. In foreign policy, he projected abroad American constitutional values of human rights and, following the Soviet invasion of Afghanistan, strengthened national defense against communist aggression. Moreover, Carter appealed to economic conservatives by emphasizing deregulation, balanced budgets, and inflation fighting, positions traditionally championed by Republicans. Armed with the advantages of outsider status and broad centrist appeal, and competing against the uninspiring and unelected Gerald Ford against a backdrop of Watergate, defeat in Vietnam, and rising economic distress, Carter nonetheless won by a narrow margin, with 50.1 percent of the popular vote to Ford's 48.

These conflicting strains in Carter's political makeup guaranteed conflict with liberal constituencies and Democratic leaders in Congress. Yet they ill prepared him to compete successfully on economic and cultural grounds in 1980 against the conservative challenger, Ronald Reagan. Political scientist Stephen Skowronek, in his historical study *The Politics Presidents Make,* classified Carter as a "late-regime" president; like John Quincy Adams, James Buchanan, and Herbert Hoover, Carter led a party whose star was falling. "Caught between the problematic expectations of his liberal constituents and the mushrooming critique of the insurgent conservatives," Skowronek observed, "the man who had promised to make liberal government work became the leading symbol of its collapse."[10]

Such hindsight carries a distortion, however, in its implicit determinism. The Carter presidency was not doomed. And despite claims that the era of divided governance since 1968 has been characterized by policy gridlock, the Carter presidency—like the divided partisan governments that preceded and followed it—produced a substantial record of legislative activity and policy innovation.[11]

Carter's record shows the hallmarks of three different political traditions. One is the New Deal tradition, the Roosevelt-Johnson legacy of social legislation and rights expansion. For Carter, this translated to minority rights, gender equity, and environmental protection. Another anticipates the market-oriented conservatism of the Reagan era—economic deregulation, budget balancing, and anti-inflation measures. The third tradition is vintage Jimmy Carter: government reorganization, global human rights, and energy reform. In his hostility to interest group bargaining and his trusteeship style of leadership, Carter was criticized as politically naive and self-defeating. But since Jimmy Carter left the White House, what presidents or national political leaders of stature and authority have asked the American people to sacrifice current benefits to better the lives of future generations?

NOTES

1. See pp. 267–85.

2. Erwin C. Hargrove, *Jimmy Carter as President: Leadership and the Politics of the Public Good* (Baton Rouge: Louisiana State University Press, 1988); Charles O. Jones, *Jimmy Carter and the United States Congress* (Baton Rouge: Louisiana State University Press, 1988).

3. Herbert D. Rosenbaum and Alexej Ugrinsky, *The Presidency and Domestic Policies of Jimmy Carter* and *Jimmy Carter: Foreign Policy and Post-Presidential Years* (Westport, Conn.: Greenwood Press, 1994). See also Gary W. Reichard, "Early Returns: Assessing Jimmy Carter," *Presidential Studies Quarterly* 20 (Summer 1990): 603–20.

4. John Dumbrell, *The Carter Presidency: A Re-evaluation* (Manchester, England: University of Manchester Press, 1993); Garland A Haas, *Jimmy Carter and the Politics of Frustration* (Jefferson, N.C.: McFarland, 1992).

5. Burton I. Kaufman, *The Presidency of James Earl Carter, Jr.* (Lawrence: University Press of Kansas, 1993).

6. See p. 52.

7. See p. 11.

8. Byron E. Shafer and William J. M. Claggett, *The Two Majorities: The Issue Context of Modern American Politics* (Baltimore, Md.: Johns Hopkins University Press, 1995).

9. Anthony King, ed., *The New American Political System* (Washington, D.C.: American Enterprise Institute, 1978); Thomas E. Mann and Norman J. Ornstein, eds., *The New Congress* (Washington, D.C.: American Enterprise Institute, 1981); Charles O. Jones, *The United States Congress* (Baton Rouge: Louisiana State University Press, 1982); James L. Sundquist, *The Decline and Resurgence of Congress* (Washington, D.C.: Brookings Institution, 1981).

10. Stephen Skowronek, *The Politics Presidents Make: Leadership from John Adams to George Bush* (Cambridge, Mass.: Harvard University Press, 1993), 366.

11. David Mayhew, *Divided We Govern: Party Control, Lawmaking and Investigations, 1946–1990* (New Haven, Conn.: Yale University Press, 1991); Morris Fiorina, *Divided Government* (New York: Macmillan, 1992); Marc K. Landy and Martin A. Levin, *The New Politics of Public Policy* (Baltimore, Md.: Johns Hopkins University Press, 1995).

1

Jimmy Carter and the Post–New Deal Presidency

William E. Leuchtenburg

When scholars gather to consider the historiography of an American president, one can be all but certain what the keynote speaker is going to say—how dramatically interpretations of him have changed over time. Not so for Jimmy Carter. Even before he took office, observers were categorizing him as a man of the center, and that view has not altered appreciably since then. During his 1976 bid for the Democratic nomination, Carter deliberately positioned himself in the middle to carve out territory between George Wallace on the right and liberals such as Morris Udall to the left, and in his ensuing campaign for the presidency, one scholar has noted, Carter "admitted that he had to straddle both liberal and conservative positions in order to appeal to a broad spectrum of the electorate." In 1979, Bruce Mazlish and Edwin Diamond saw Carter "blurring the lines between liberalism and conservatism in his Presidency," and in 1980, Laurence Shoup not only categorized Carter as a "Centrist" but also lumped him with a number of Republican aspirants, including George Bush. In his memoir published in 1987, Tip O'Neill said that he "expected a more liberal President Carter than we got. He was progressive on foreign affairs and human rights, but on economic issues he was a lot more conservative than I was." In sum, a historian beginning work on Carter today would start out with the same assumption, in this regard, with which a scholar began two decades ago.[1]

The persistence of this leitmotif in the literature on the Carter presidency raises a number of questions, the first of which is, quite simply: Is the perception of Carter as a centrist correct? That inquiry arises because there is evidence that Carter had a more liberal record than either his contemporaries or most historians have acknowledged. In the 1976 campaign, he made enough progressive overtures to lead Senator Bob Dole to call him "Southern-fried McGovern."[2] He let it be known that he favored gun control, and he chose as his running mate one of the most conspicuous northern liberals, Fritz Mondale. Subsequently, he named as his domestic policy adviser Stuart Eizenstat, who had been associated with Lyndon Johnson's Great Society and with Hubert Humphrey's run for the White House.

When, at the end of the president's term, Eizenstat gave an exit interview, he said of Carter:

> He saved the social security system from bankruptcy. . . . He created the nation's first comprehensive urban policy. . . . He was responsible for this nation's first comprehensive energy policy. . . . Important social legislation passed like the child abuse and child welfare legislation, and . . . the farm bill of 1977 is a wonderfully innovative program. . . . I also think he did a tremendous amount in the area of youth employment. . . . We doubled the federal government's investment in employment training in the four years we were here and created a record number of jobs, well over eight million.[3]

Eizenstat's list might well be extended. Carter created the Department of Education and the Department of Energy, doubled the number of workers in public service jobs, and approved a $12.5-billion appropriation to help troubled cities. He put through measures to improve the health and safety of coal miners, and his appointees to the National Labor Relations Board were liberal enough to elicit the accusation from conservatives that they had "an anti-business pro-labor bias." He also sought to establish a new agency for consumer protection. In her exit interview, Esther Peterson, who had served under both Kennedy and Johnson, stated, "I want history to show that he was the first one, the first President that has ever really moved in and put the consumer perspective into it. . . . Had he been re-elected, . . . he would just go down in history as a superb consumer person."[4] Carter started out by recommending a tax package that denied capital gains preferential treatment, took the two-martini lunch deduction away from businessmen, and got rid of tax shelters, and when his secretary of the treasury came up with a draft, he insisted that the tax schedule be made more progressive to shift the burden from lower-income to upper-income people and to corporations. On presenting his energy program, he stipulated a windfall profits tax on the "huge and undeserved" gains that decontrol would give the oil companies.[5]

Jimmy Carter has strong grounds for claiming to be one of America's greatest presidents on the environment. When in December 1980 he overcame timber, mineral, oil, and gas interests to sign a bill preserving some one-third of the enormous state of Alaska from exploitation, he, with one stroke of the pen, doubled the entire area of the country's national parks and wildlife refuges, one of the most important pieces of environmental legislation in all our history. That same month, Carter approved a measure establishing a "Superfund" to rid the environment of dangerous chemicals that had been dumped or spilled.

Though some historians have given Carter no more than middling grades for his policies toward African Americans,[6] Bayard Rustin called him "a committed supporter of civil rights," and John Hope Franklin has said that Carter "was about as straight on the race question as we've ever seen in this country." His record on appointments was outstanding. He chose Andrew Young as U.S. ambassador to the United Nations, and also named thirty-eight blacks to judgeships. In addition, he opened up independent regulatory commissions to black appointees and doubled the number of black-owned telecommunication properties in just two years. His choice of Karen Hastie Williams as procurement director helped multiply the sum of government money going to minority enterprises. When his attorney general handed him a draft of the Department of Justice's brief supporting Alan Bakke's challenge to racial quotas and contending that the California program was unconstitutional, Carter concluded that the attorney general should back down. In the revised brief, the government declared that "a state university admissions program may take race into account." M. Glenn Abernathy has concluded, "Carter deserves considerably more credit for his civil right initiatives than has been accorded to him."[7]

Carter not only campaigned for the Equal Rights Amendment (ERA) but also originated the idea of a fund-raiser, where he was the main guest, that raised more money than any other ERA event. Sarah Weddington reports: "There were several instances . . . where he picked up on the fact that women were missing from a recommendation made to him . . . and it was something I hadn't even known . . . was going on. So . . . he was very good about that and very conscious of it." He did not understand how the National Organization for Women (NOW) could announce that it would support any candidate in 1980 save Carter when he had, he said, "appointed, I think, five or six times more women judges than all the presidents in two hundred years and really worked hard to establish women's rights."[8]

Though foreign policy entails a different set of considerations, Carter's record on foreign affairs might also have been expected to have gratified liberals in a number of respects. He pardoned Vietnam War draft evaders; sought to slow the arms race; scuttled the B-1 bomber; rallied the Senate to ratify Panama Canal treaties that marked a move away from the imperialism of the early twentieth century; pushed for aid to post-Somoza Nicaragua; and set up an agency on human rights to deal with tragedies such as the missing persons in Argentina. Carter has said that his attitude toward human rights in the world derived from his experience in seeing what the achievement of civil rights meant in the American South. He took pains to better relations with black Africa, where he arguably deserves at least some of the credit for the emergence of Zimbabwe. Overall, Raymond Moore has maintained, a "sense of decency and purpose . . . represented the main thrust of the Carter Presidency in the conduct of US foreign policy."[9]

Why, then, in view of all this, is Carter viewed as a centrist? One reason is that, to many northern liberals, he seemed an uncredentialed intruder with no connection to them or anyone else in their alliance. "When Jimmy Carter stood before the

1976 Democratic National Convention and pledged 'new leadership,' " *Time* later noted, "he had never met a Democratic President or slept in the White House." He appeared to longtime reformers to be, in the paraphrase of one of his advisers, "a sort of fluke, an ambassador from Dogpatch, at least that's what my old Kennedy friends say." Carter was, in the words of a southern columnist, "a Southern Baptist simple-talking peanut-warehousing grit-eating 'Eyetalian'-saying Cracker." A man who had served as governor of a large state with an office in a sophisticated American city, Carter was frequently depicted as a primitive rube. At the very time of his inauguration, a Washington newspaper featured, in Carter's words, "a full-page cartoon depicting an outhouse on the White House lawn, with my mother wearing a sunbonnet and smoking a corncob pipe."[10]

Little about Carter reminded liberals of his dynamic predecessors in the White House. Princeton historian Eric Goldman, who had served in the Lyndon Johnson White House, declared: "Carterism may be totally lacking in the scourging of a Theodore Roosevelt, the cathedral summoning of a Woodrow Wilson, the rollicking iconoclasm of an FDR. Carterism does not march and it does not sing; it is cautious, muted, grayish, at times even crabbed." Eugene McCarthy called Carter an "oratorical mortician" who "inters his words and ideas beneath piles of syntactical mush," and I. F. Stone wrote, "There's no music in him." Carter had kept his promise "to dismantle the imperial Presidency . . . and to restore the Presidency to the arid, nuts-and-bolts business of governing under republican forms," noted Russell Baker toward the end of 1977, and now that people had been given what they had asked for, they found it "dull, terribly dull," and were discontent. "If the Carter Administration were a television show it would have been canceled months ago."[11]

As Carter was about to leave office, a Georgia journalist wrote:

> We thought we wanted to be preached to, . . . cleansed, comforted. Then everything would be all right again. But Jimmy Carter was a mere Sunday School teacher, not a skillful preacher. More often than not, his homilies came off as self-serving rather than illuminating. There were the fireside chats on television that first February, tendentious, platitudinous embarrassments. Even Walter Cronkite could not jazz up the innate drabness of those telephone calls. They were of the same type that any night city editor gets on a Saturday evening when the moon is full.[12]

Carter's engineering mind-set alienated liberals, who charged him with approaching human problems with a slide rule mentality. "Like Hoover," Robert Dallek has written, "Carter was a moralistic progressive with an engineer's fixation on detail and an inability to inspire the electorate." When, as a counterpart of "New Deal" or "Great Society," the rubric "New Foundation" was trotted out, Mondale responded, "Frankly, it is flat; there is no drive or life in it. It doesn't make people feel good about being Americans, and it fails to leave a sharp after-image in your listeners' minds." An administration official has recalled that when, at a briefing session on urban policy, Pat Harris talked about the vicissitudes of cities, including racism, Carter was "frankly pretty bored," but when an aide presented an efficiency chart, "the President's eyes lit up." No one around him could recall his eyes ever lighting up over a program such as the Comprehensive Employment and Training Act (CETA).[13]

Liberals eyed with particular suspicion Carter's insistence that he was a foe of the Washington establishment, for those such as Edward Kennedy and Hubert Humphrey who for many years had been struggling for social justice knew they were part of that establishment. In the 1976 campaign, indeed, Humphrey had charged that "candidates who make an attack on Washington are making an attack on government programs, on blacks, on minorities, on the cities. It's a disguised new form of racism, a disguised new form of conservatism." Carter encountered a similar problem with journalists, some of them with close ties to liberal legislators. "Carter was smarter than most reporters and clearly knew it," Jody Powell has written. "They do not take kindly to being looked down upon by any politician, particularly not a peanut farmer from some piddly-ass little gnat-hole in south Georgia."[14]

Though political insiders who wished the president well counseled him to accommodate to the power brokers, Carter and his circle continued to leave the impression "that anyone who had been in Washington before the arrival of Jimmy Carter was tainted," and that disdain applied to liberals as well as conservatives. "As he left office after four years in the nation's capital," one writer commented, "Jimmy Carter remained a stranger in a strange land." Reflecting on that observation, political scientist Charles O. Jones stated, "Carter probably would not have wished it to be otherwise. He was unwilling to become a part of the Washington establishment. Indeed, as he read his mandate, to have accepted the dominant norms would violate his trusteeship." The consequences were predictable. "He is like the Cheshire cat in Alice in Wonderland," said a Democratic official in 1980. "He is disappearing into the trees, and there is nothing left but the smile."[15]

The perception of Carter as a centrist derives, too, from the high expectations with which liberals contemplated the return of the Democrats to power in 1977, when, after eight years of frustration under Nixon and Ford, they hoped to pick up where they had left off in the Great Society era. As a consequence of the close vote in 1976, liberals could claim credit for Carter's victory, and hence they believed that the new president had an obligation to satisfy their demands. "I owe the special interests nothing. I owe the people everything," Carter claimed during the campaign. In fact, he owed the "special interests," as they had come to be defined, a great deal, for he would not have won if labor unions and big-city Democrats had not gotten out the vote and if blacks had not given him the victory margin in southern states. Moreover, since a number of liberal senators had run ahead of Carter in 1976, they had reason to think that they reflected popular sentiment better than he did. They and their constituents, especially black groups and union labor, anticipated that Carter would make up for the long period of Republican neglect by enacting ambitious social welfare programs, an expectation foredoomed to disappointment.[16]

Surely, though, the most important reason for the conviction that Carter was a centrist is that, from the very beginning, his own words and actions make clear that a centrist, in truth, is what he was. It was precisely the fact that Carter was not a liberal that some found so appealing about him in 1976. James Fallows recalled, "I felt that he, alone among the candidates, might look past the tired formulas of left and right and offer something new." Hedley Donovan, asked what had initially impressed the editors of *Time* about Carter, replied, "He was not an all-out liberal by any means" but a "somewhat different political phenomenon." Stu Eizenstat has pointed out, "He was clearly the most conservative of the Democratic candidates in the 1976 campaign. He was the only one talking about balanced budgets and less bureaucracy and less red tape and themes that one associates perhaps with Republicans." Moreover, he refused to go out of his way in 1976 to cajole liberal Democrats. When Teddy Kennedy characterized Carter's position on certain issues as "imprecise," Carter responded, "I don't have to kiss his ass."[17]

After the election victory, which confirmed the belief of Carter's advisers that they had a surer feel for the pulse of the nation than did either liberals or conservatives, the president-elect's pollster, Patrick Caddell, in a lengthy memo, dismissed figures such as Kennedy, George McGovern, and Mo Udall as "traditional Democrats . . . in many ways . . . as antiquated and anachronistic a group as are conservative Republicans." He warned the incoming president against resorting "to old Democratic dogmas" and recommended that he cut "across traditional ideology" to find a path that was "neither traditionally liberal nor traditionally conservative." Carter thought the memo was "excellent," and in good part he made it the basis for his program as president.[18] Though Carter had campaigned on a promise to expand the economy to diminish the high rate of joblessness at a time when the economy was only slowly pulling out of the most severe recession since the Great Depression, eventually he concluded that the main problem he confronted as president was not unemployment but inflation and that government deficits contributed to rising prices. Faced with a choice between full employment and a balanced budget, Carter decided that having more men and women out of work was an acceptable price to pay for stability. He started out with an economic stimulus bill, but, after a short time, abandoned one of its main features, a tax rebate, as inflationary. McGovern commented: "It sometimes seems difficult to remember who won last fall."[19]

Within weeks of taking office, Carter found himself on a collision course with liberal Democrats. Labor raged at him for setting too low an increase in the minimum wage and for refusing to give ardent backing to other union demands, but it was his insistence on budget restraint, which blew to smithereens the hope for large-scale social spending, that caused the most dismay. The president, McGovern charged, was seeking to balance the budget on the backs of the poor. Carter himself has said, "Bert [Lance], Mike Blumenthal, and I were more conservative than anybody else among my advisors. We were more conservative than Charlie Schultze or Stu Eizenstat, more conservative by far than Fritz Mondale." After he left the White House, Carter told interviewers about the situation in the spring of 1977: "I wish some of you could have sat in on some of our leadership meetings and just seen the stricken expression on the faces of those Democratic leaders when I was talking about balancing the budget. John Brademas and Shirley Chisholm and Tip O'Neill, even Jim Wright. I mean it was anathema to them to be talking about balancing the budget. That wasn't something a Democratic President was supposed to do."[20]

The conflict over the budget plagued Carter through all the rest of his days in office. Early in 1978, to the distress of liberals, he submitted a "lean and tight" budget with a lower increase in government spending than at any time in Gerald Ford's tenure. That fall, when he undertook a "national austerity" program, even though it meant slashing programs helping the poor, liberals exploded. Eizenstat noted: "Spent 30 minutes with Mrs. King who says she just can't keep defending him. There is open rebellion from liberals." At a midterm party conference in Memphis in December, Carter got only a lukewarm response, whereas Senator Kennedy, when he urged vigorous resistance to these "drastic" cuts, drew a rousing ovation.[21]

Undeterred by this reaction, Carter decided early in 1979 to push ahead on his austerity course, and that resolve deepened when, in ensuing weeks, the oil crisis sent prices soaring. The president advocated cutting over $2 billion from social services and another $1 billion from Social Security and school lunches, while boosting spending by the Pentagon, a decision that led to a serious breach with the women's movement. For all his rhetoric about civil rights, Carter offered nothing to blacks, nothing to the jobless.[22] Carter continued these emphases in his last year in office. In March 1980, only weeks after he had announced a big rise in military spending, he proposed cutting another $13 billion from the budget, including taking money away from food stamps, CETA, and programs to safeguard the health of children. In the 1980 campaign, Mondale and Eizenstat sought to have Carter embrace a broad increase in social spending. If he did not do so, the vice president warned, he would go down in the history books as another Hoover. More immediately, he would jeopardize his chances for reelection by failing to inspire the Kennedy wing of the party. "We look heartless," Mondale informed Eizenstat. Carter would accept only some of this counsel, and doing even that much, he said, rubbed him the wrong way.[23]

Especially in his final years, Carter paid less heed to advisers such as Mondale and more to those who, when they envisioned the enemy, thought not of an economic royalist but of a union member. Shortly after the end of the Carter presidency, Alfred Kahn said, "I'd love the Teamsters to be worse off. I'd love the automobile workers to be worse off. . . . Unemployed automobile workers are being screwed by the employed automobile workers." To Carter appointees of this persuasion, the president's shortcoming lay in his failure to adopt an even harder line toward the New Deal constituency. A top Office of Management and Budget (OMB) official in the Carter administration reflected: "We would have been better off had we not been so infatuated with unemployment and had we dealt with inflation as an issue earlier. It seemed like every decision we made was for the 4 or 5 percent of the worst end of the spectrum and the guys that got the last consideration were the 95 percent of the people in the country who were not in some level of extraordinary disability or difficulty."[24]

Across a wide range of issues—from the firing of his secretary of Health, Education, and Welfare (HEW), Joseph Califano, to the president's promotion of an energy policy that deliberately aimed to raise prices to consumers, to his refusal to approve a costly program for health insurance—Carter antagonized liberals. Told that his plan to reform the welfare system would hurt the poor, he erupted in anger. "We don't have $5 billion to $10 billion to put in a new system," he retorted. "Why don't we just say, the hell with it!" When Califano persisted, the president, glowering, shot out, "Stop protecting those receiving welfare benefits." Carter's welfare goals, Dilys Hill has pointed out, "were similar to those of Nixon's Family Assistance Plan which sought to reduce the numbers of people eligible for, and the levels of, benefit." In an article imploring liberals to support Carter in 1980, William Attwood acknowledged, "He often seems unduly concerned with appeasing right-wingers, not realizing that it's all but impossible to outflank the Reaganites without coming out for child labor, apartheid, and the Great White Fleet."[25]

Even when Carter did embrace liberal aspirations, he often did so halfheartedly. After advocating "a complete overhaul of our nation's welfare system," Carter, one analysis has stated, "was relatively passive and inflexible," taking "little personal interest in following through." Califano has written that Carter lacked Johnson's "fire in the belly" on civil rights. "I never heard Carter speak privately with the burning conviction, much less the passion, of Lyndon Johnson about civil rights or race in America." In the Bakke dispute, he seemed curiously disengaged, and he agreed to approve the Humphrey-Hawkins full employment bill only after it had been eviscerated, and, even then, shunned the ceremony celebrating its enactment. Early in 1978, Carter noted in his diary, "In many cases I feel more at home with the conservative Democratic and Republican members of Congress than I do with the others, although the others, the liberals, vote with me much more often."[26]

In the long run, none of these issues may prove as important as Carter's leadership in deregulating the airline, banking, communications, railroad, and trucking industries, as well as oil and gas prices. Carter has called it "the greatest change in the relationship between business and government since the New Deal." To be sure, in this, as in other respects, one needs to take care not to draw too sharp a line between Carter and the liberals of the 1970s, for, as Leo Ribuffo has pointed out, one of the most forceful advocates of deregulation was Ted Kennedy, who held a joint press conference with Carter to foster trucking deregulation and stood with Carter at the ceremonial signing of the airline deregulation bill. Yet deregulation, traditional Republican party dogma, ran counter to nearly a century of reform efforts. The ninetieth anniversary of the Interstate Commerce Act of 1887, when it all began, fell in the very year that Carter took office. Though, to the disgruntlement of the left, the Progressives and the New Dealers were not Socialists, they had operated much of the time on the assumption that the more government the better; there was more than a grain of truth in the allegation of conservatives that liberals were "creeping Socialists." Now Carter was leading the country in a very different direction—toward dismantling the state and relying on the market.[27]

If Carter was, then, a centrist, how do we account for that? One explanation focuses on the man, on the belief that Carter's temperament and the ideas he brought to the White House were determinative. His proudest boast as governor had not been that he had improved social welfare, though he did make a number of modest gains, but that he had introduced zero-based budgeting to make government more cost-effective. Peter Bourne has written, "During his presidency, the aspects of his personality acquired from his mother—his general commitment to the interests of blacks, women, and the poor—were eclipsed by the cost-conscious business orientation that was his legacy from Mr. Earl."[28]

Carter paid homage to Franklin D. Roosevelt, but, though he grew up not many miles from Warm Springs, neither FDR nor the New Deal made much of an impression on him. Carter had a vivid memory of the 1936 campaign heard on a radio hooked up to a car battery on a summer night in Georgia, but he was listening not to FDR, whom his father detested, but to the nomination of Alf Landon, not everyone's favorite in the state in that depression year. When veterans of the New Deal gathered at the *Mayflower* on March 4, 1977, to commemorate FDR's first inauguration, the master of ceremonies, the columnist Marquis Childs, pointed out that there was not "a single Carter" representative at the banquet, "so in a sense this is a clean break between the past and the present." Carter did not even send perfunctory greetings to the convocation, only six blocks from the Oval Office. "Having worked several years at the White House in my youth," Arthur Schlesinger, Jr., wrote Vice President Mondale, "I know how these things operate. Every time five Bessarabians get together in Waco, Texas, and request a presidential message, they get one. How in the world do you suppose a Democratic President, on the forty-fourth anniversary of the first inauguration of the greatest Democratic President of this century, could not manage a few words expressing his sense of the occasion?"[29]

The president thought of himself as a tribune of the people, but as Mondale biographer Steven Gillon has pointed out, Carter and Mondale, while sharing "a populist disdain for wealth and a feel for the common man, . . . defined the 'common man' in different ways. For Carter the average citizen was rural, Protestant, politically independent, financially secure, and fiscally conservative; for Mondale that person was a struggling, urban, blue-collar, union member concerned about a secure job, decent wages, and education for his children." Carter, Gillon concludes, was "a Democrat who thought like a Republican."[30]

Carter asserted that, though he was a fiscal conservative, he was "quite liberal" on other matters, such as "helping people to overcome handicaps to lead fruitful lives." That remark was reminiscent of Eisenhower's statement that he was "conservative when it comes to money and liberal when it comes to human beings," a contention that led Adlai Stevenson to respond, "I assume what it means is that you will strongly recommend the building of a great many schools to accommodate the needs of our children, but not provide the money." Burton Kaufman has called Carter's claim "an untenable dichotomy," for how could he "help people overcome handicaps" without substantial federal spending? Moreover, Kaufman adds, "politically, it challenged powerful elements within Carter's own party, who denied that liberal ends could be reached by conservative means without distorting those ends—for example, if his proposals defined 'handicaps' so as to exclude people lacking basic job skills."[31]

Without doubt, Carter had to cope with the reality that the mood of the country was more conservative than in the 1960s, but it is also true that Carter fed that mood. In his second annual address to Congress, he declared, "Government cannot solve our problems. . . . It cannot eliminate poverty, or provide a bountiful economy, or reduce inflation, or save our cities, or cure illiteracy, or provide energy." If FDR had held such a view, Schlesinger commented, "we still would be in the Great Depression." Mondale told Carter that instead of hammering on what government could not do, he should be reminding the country of "the historic role of government in getting people on their feet," but to no avail. When, in the summer of 1979, "after listening to the American people" on a trip to the heartland, Carter said he had been "reminded again that all the legislators in the world can't fix what's wrong with America." Clayton Fritchey commented in the Washington Post: "If so, who passed all the progressive, social and reform legislation that, over the years, has made America such an enviable place to live?" Unpersuaded, Carter, at a press conference that fall at which he spelled out his differences with Ted Kennedy, said that the senator was "much more inclined toward the old philosophy of pouring out new programs and new money to meet a social need," whereas he stood for "much stronger defense commitments" and was "much more inclined to . . . start up new programs only when it's absolutely necessary."[32]

Carter's attitudes exasperated, and at times infuriated, liberal commentators and labor leaders. James Wieghart of the New York Daily News wrote: "The problems facing the country and the world—the energy crisis, pollution, overpopulation, structural unemployment, pervasive inflation and much more—simply did not lend themselves to solution by a weak central government which is subservient to an unfettered private sector." Asked to assess Jimmy Carter a year after his term ended, a prominent union leader said:

> As presidents go, he was on a par with Calvin Coolidge. I consider his abilities mediocre, his actions pusillanimous, and his Administration a calamity for America's working people.
>
> Since an obelisk soaring 555 feet into the air symbolizes the nation's admiration and respect for George Washington, it would seem the only fitting memorial for Jimmy Carter would be a bottomless pit.[33]

Though he did not approach this rhetorical excess, the figure who most persistently found fault with Carter was the keeper of the flame for earlier Democratic presidents, Arthur Schlesinger, Jr., who never voted for him. He explained: "I expected to vote for the Democratic candidate [in 1976], as I had always done in the past, but, once in the booth, could not bring myself to pull the lever for a man so hostile to the Roosevelt-Truman-Kennedy tradition and consequently did not vote at all for president. In 1980 I voted for John Anderson."

"The reason for Carter's horrible failure in economic policy is plain enough," Schlesinger wrote during the 1980 campaign. "He is not a Democrat—at least in anything more recent than the Grover Cleveland sense of the word." After the ballots were counted, Schlesinger denied that the returns spelled the end of a liberal era, for all that Reagan had done was defeat "an alleged Democrat" who had "won the presidency with demagogic attacks on the horrible federal bureaucracy and as President made clear in the most explicit way his rejection of . . . affirmative government. . . . What the voters repudiated in 1980 was not liberalism but the miserable result of the conservative economic policies of the last half dozen years."[34]

Another explanation for centrism concentrates less on Carter than on the changing nature of the electorate. It is true that Carter could not have won without the support of blacks and union members, but he also could not have done so without the ballots of young professionals in the suburbs and rural Protestants who had no desire to see him embark on expensive social welfare programs for the inner cities. In his postelection memo, Caddell reasoned that Democrats could "no longer depend on a coalition of economic division," for two generations of economic growth had produced more "haves" than "have-nots" and the "haves" did not speak "the old language of American politics." Hugh Davis Graham has written: "From the perspective of 1997, we can see that a sea change was transforming the American economy and political system, and Carter's presidency was caught in the middle. His administration was overwhelmed by a massive conservative revolt against taxes, militant unions, radical feminists, welfare queens and minority preferences."[35]

Carter, it should be noted, did not invent a centrist mood; he inherited it. All through the four-year period before he took office, party strategists had pointed with dismay to the consequences of running a liberal in 1972, when McGovern lost forty-nine of the fifty states, and reasoned that repeating that error was a recipe for disaster. The political editor of *Congressional Quarterly* found it "striking" at the National Democratic Issues Convention in Louisville in 1975 "to hear liberal Democrats talking about the New Deal not only as an anachronism but as a dangerous piece of ideological baggage the party will have to discard if it wants to win elections from now on." The keynote speaker, Alvin Toffler, advised the gathe ng to "throw out all the old New Deal claptrap," and a pollster warned that Democrats could not expect voters to put their party back into power "on the strength of a few newly warmed-over 1933 programs." In the fall of 1976, Gary Hart declared: "The New Deal has run its course. The party is over. The pie cannot continue to expand forever." The "mad pell-mell rush to the public trough" had to end. In like manner, a Democratic congressman from Georgia, in a 1977 address entitled "The New Deal Is Dead: May It Rest in Peace," said that the Carter presidency would be likely to be assessed by the degree to which it was "able to bid farewell to the New Deal, giving it honor but putting it to rest and moving on into a new era."[36]

Eizenstat has contended that there was not enough left of the Great Depression labor-ethnic-farm coalition capable of securing a majority with the power to govern. Union members had "become middle class taxpayers who are worried much more about how they're being taxed than about being the recipients of government programs"; their main concern was "basic middle class issues" such as how to come up with the money to send their kids to college. "Jews and Catholics and so forth don't feel that they're outside the mainstream the way they did in the '30s and '40s and perhaps even in the '50s," he went on. You could no longer count on a big block of support from farmers, for they now made up only 3 percent of the population, "and those farmers who are left are essentially corporate farmers, so they're gone." In sum, "The only ones who still vote over 85 percent Democratic are the ones who are still largely outside the mainstream and still view the government as essential to bring them in," such as racial minorities, and there simply were not enough of those.[37]

As one of the interviewers for the William Burkett Miller Center of Public Affairs at the University of Virginia, I asked Jody Powell how Carter and his circle, when they looked out at the country, determined who were their people and who were not their people. He replied:

> Our perception was that the Roosevelt coalition was still basic, and you had to have that. . . . But our perception also was that it is no longer a winning coalition in and of itself. The numbers won't add. If you go back and look at

1976, we won not just because we held together the coalition. In fact, if we had only done that, we would have lost. Go down all the big states that were close—Ohio, Pennsylvania—and you'll find that we did what a Democrat is expected to do in the big cities, in the traditionally Democratic wards and precincts and areas. We did about what Humphrey did when he lost some of those states. We won because we were able to do better than a Democrat normally does in areas that are nominally Republican.

Powell pointed out that though voters in Democratic primaries tend to be to the left of most of the electorate, Carter won the presidential nomination not just once but twice, and each time the voters understood that they had a clear choice. "Jimmy Carter didn't slip into Washington under cover of darkness and take over the government buildings and then the radio stations and announce that he was in control," Powell remarked. "He went through a long, long process," and both times the voters knew very well what they were doing. "People in '76 understood that there was a difference between Jimmy Carter and Mo Udall," just as they recognized in 1980 the clashing ideologies of Carter and Ted Kennedy.

"The crux of the problem," Powell reflected, was how you reach out beyond that Great Depression combination "without creating such chaos in your rear that you've got to turn around and deal with that before you can do more ahead." Subsequently, "the chaos in the rear did become such a problem in the person of Ted Kennedy." Powell went on, "If you looked at the demographics, . . . you knew the Democratic party had to be able, first, to have at least a decent shot at the South and second, that it also had to be able to deal with those people who used to be card-carrying members of that coalition but now . . . were not quite as dependable . . . you know, suburbs and exurbanites and all that sort of thing." In this regard, symbols came to be important, and for Carter's effort to prevail, "the balanced budget came to symbolize that."

Carter, Powell recalls, was "not the sort of person who would whip polls out of his . . . pockets and say did you see this?" but once, early in his administration, he did. "It's just great," Powell remembers him saying. What pleased the president was "that the Democrats were perceived as being more fiscally responsible and better able to handle federal spending and the taxpayer's dollar than Republicans for the first time in quite a while. And he said if we can . . . establish that point, and I think he meant . . . more than just fiscal responsibility [but] a whole range of things that fall around it, we will assure that the Democratic party is the only party in this country for the rest of our lives."[38]

Still another explanation for centrism is not political but economic: that given the economic circumstance Carter confronted, he had no reasonable choice save fiscal restraint. The deficit of over $66 billion he inherited from Ford does not sound like much today, but it seemed alarming then, for it amounted to over

4 percent of GNP, the largest proportion ever. "How easy it was to be a liberal back when there was 4.9 percent unemployment and 2 percent inflation," said one of Carter's OMB officials. "You could spend a point or two on inflation to get unemployment down. Now you just do not have the margin. You simply cannot sustain as high a level of employment without subjecting the economy to real shocks and dangers." Given rising prices and worrisome deficits, Carter did not see how he could oblige liberals with big spending packages. To be sure, tight budgets meant taking inflation more seriously than unemployment, but inflation did hurt the working class, as well as other Americans. At the end of 1978, Michael Harrington observed: "It's a weird period for liberals. In many respects this is like the calm before the storm. The problem is the conventional liberal wisdom of the past doesn't work anymore. This is like 1931. Just as the conventional wisdom of the 1920s was totally shattered by the depression, the conventional wisdom of the 1960s has been shattered by inflation." As one Carter official later said, "Traditional Democratic theology notwithstanding, we were in a period which demanded restraint."[39]

These considerations also had a political dimension. Thomas Byrne Edsall and Mary Edsall have pointed out:

> Democrats were winning in 1974 and 1976, just as the core of their traditional base among whites was crumbling. . . . In the buildup of conservative, antiliberal sentiment in the electorate, the most important development was the fact that 1973, the year the Senate set up a special committee to investigate Watergate, was also the year that marked the end of a sustained period of post–World War II economic growth. Hourly earnings, which had grown in every year since 1951 in real, inflation-adjusted dollars, fell. . . . Weekly earnings fell more sharply. . . . In a whipsaw action, the middle-class tax burden rose with inflation just as the economy and real-income growth slowed. The tax system was losing its progressivity, placing a steadily growing share of the cost of government on middle and lower-middle-class voters, vital constituencies for the Democratic party.[40]

Vice President Mondale, though he had been counseling Carter against abandoning liberal programs, recognized that the Republicans had turned the inflation issue to their advantage in the 1978 elections, the same year that California voters overwhelmingly adopted a proposition slashing property taxes that underpinned social services. Hence, he cautioned his fellow liberals at the Memphis convention that if Democrats "don't end the ever-increasing cost of living, we will be driven out of office as we were by the Vietnam War." Mondale admonished: "If we don't solve inflation, this society will suffer terribly. Everything we stand for will be eroded. Inflation can destroy everything we believe in. When we press for real income improvement, inflation burns up the increase; when we push for growth, our standard of living deteriorates; when we expand personal opportunity, inflation lays its damp hand on our dreams of a more prosperous future." Failure to curb inflation, he warned, "will mock all our efforts at social progress."[41]

There is a larger context in which these matters may be placed—the conviction that America had come to a turning point, that the long era of growth was reaching a climacteric, that the short, happy life of the U.S. empire was drawing to a close. At the time of the Silver Jubilee in Great Britain, I had the honor of being asked to give the inaugural lecture in tribute to the queen at the U.S. Embassy in Grosvenor Square, and the topic I chose was "A Sense of Limits." It was a notion that was very much in the air in 1977, the first year of the Carter presidency. In his inaugural address, Carter stated: "We have learned that 'more' is not necessarily better, that even our great nation has its recognized limits." That concept, Carter writes in his memoir, "was to prove painfully prescient and politically unpopular. . . . Americans were not accustomed to limits—on natural resources or on the power of our country to . . . control international events." He adds: "Watching the sea of approving faces [on inauguration day], I wondered how few of the happy celebrants would agree with my words if they analyzed them closely. At the time, it was not possible even for me to imagine the limits we would have to face. In some ways, dealing with limits would become the subliminal theme of the next four years and affect the outcome of the 1980 election."[42]

As Carter recognized, he paid a high price for embracing the rubric of limits. "Americans are not a people who can easily be rallied under a banner of stoical suffering," Michael Malbin has pointed out. "Americans remain a people of the Enlightenment who find it hard to accept the postmodern (or ancient) view of a world of limited possibilities." One of Carter's speechwriters noted that "the country's coming up against middle age for the first time and finding it very unpleasant and extremely difficult to live with." A Washington Post writer, in a summing up two days before Carter's presidency came to an end, observed: "He preached to us constantly about sacrifice and limitations, which none of us wanted to hear."[43]

When Carter sought to arouse the nation to the gravity of the energy crisis by borrowing a phrase from William James, critics jeered that the acronym for "Moral Equivalent of War" was MEOW. In 1979, the young governor of Arkansas was one of many who raised objections to the president's statements on energy. Carter sounded, said Bill Clinton, like a "17th century New England Puritan [rather] than a 20th century Southern Baptist."[44]

In these circumstances, Carter's defeat in 1980 came as no surprise. As one historian has written, "Whatever Reagan did, many Americans felt, would be better than the hand wringing, sermons, and demands for sacrifice of the last four years." Jimmy Carter, said an aide, told a television audience, "In order to be a good

American . . . , you've got to drive cars you don't like . . . and turn up the thermo-
stat in the summer and down in the winter. . . . You're a pig, you've been using
too much energy all your life and you've got to change." Ronald Reagan, on the
other hand, announced, "If you want to be a good American, . . . call your congressman and demand a tax cut for yourself, dial yourself a tax cut." Carter, the
British historians Dilys Hill and Phil Williams have concluded, was "a victim of
the age of limits."[45]

Carter's reliance on limits struck me at the time, and still does, as understandable but problematic. In my address in London in 1977, I quoted from Carter's
energy speech, in which, employing a line from Chicken Little, he warned, "The
sky is falling." I acknowledged that in a range of areas—from the environment to
population growth to the temptation to embark on "grandiose ventures in foreign
policy"—limits was a counsel of wisdom. But I went on to say:

> Still, "limits" will not always be the best choice. . . . It must be remembered
> that Americans have long been, in David Potter's phrase, "people of plenty."
> The United States has traditionally lifted its citizens out of poverty not
> by redistributing income but by economic growth, so that while the rich
> were getting richer the poor were moving into the middle class. In a static
> economy, America would be directly confronted for the first time by the
> question of which shares of the national income should go to which classes,
> and I'm not sanguine about the prospect that we would deal with that situ-
> ation well.[46]

If in one sense little has changed over twenty years in our perception of Carter as
a centrist grappling with limits, in another sense it is well that we reconsider him
two decades later, because Carter can be seen now not as idiosyncratic but as the
first in a line of post–New Deal/Great Society Democratic presidents or presidential contenders. When Fritz Mondale, the man who had been Carter's vice president, ran for president in 1984, I was asked to provide quotations for his acceptance
address. I sent a good number, especially statements such as that of FDR's in 1936:

> Governments can err, Presidents do make mistakes, but the immortal Dante
> tells us that divine justice weighs the sins of the cold-blooded and the sins of
> the warmhearted in different scales.
>
> Better the occasional faults of a Government that lives in a spirit of charity
> than the consistent omissions of a Government frozen in the ice of its own
> indifference.

But the only one Mondale used was from Harry Truman: "A President cannot
always be popular. . . . He has to be able to say yes and no, and more often no to
most of the propositions that are put up to him by partisan groups and special
interests who are always pulling at the White House for one thing or another."
Mondale was anxious to demonstrate not that he was a liberal but that he could

stand up to interest groups, and "interest groups" no longer connoted greedy corporate moguls but organizations such as teachers' unions.[47]

Mondale's response in 1984 foretold what was to follow. Four years later, Michael Dukakis's acceptance address was said to "signal a final break with the party's New Deal, big government past," for he "offered virtually none of the traditional promises of federal spending for the poor," and for the rest of the campaign Dukakis backpedaled away as fast as he could from being identified with "the dreaded L-word." After the Democrats were returned to power in what has been called "in many ways our national apology to Jimmy Carter," Bill Clinton's declaration that "the era of big government is over" could be seen as the predictable culmination of Carter's centrism.[48]

To his champions, Carter has never been given enough appreciation for his hardihood in the face of misfortune or for his vision. As caustic a critic as John Connally conceded, "He suffered from almost unending bad luck," while a scholar has alluded to "the tyranny of circumstances" that made Carter's presidency "a fated one." "Since FDR," observed a Carter official, "every Democratic President has been operating . . . on the assumption that there is a larger slice of the pie to be divided up among traditional constituency groups all the time. Carter was the first Democrat who didn't have that situation. And to his everlasting credit, he tried to come to grips with it in a responsible fiscal manner." Erwin Hargrove has praised him as "one of the first to see that the Democratic policy agenda was depleted of ideas and that new issues were on the horizon"; John Dumbrell has esteemed him as a leader who "sought to adjust liberalism to post-liberal conditions"; and Louis Koenig has said, I think rightly, that "Jimmy Carter is the last serious president that we have had in the United States." From this perspective, Carter may be regarded not as a failed liberal but as one of a number of world leaders—ranging across a spectrum from Margaret Thatcher in Great Britain to the former Eastern bloc legatees seeking to create a civil society—who sought to guide their nations away from the leviathan state toward a new polity.[49]

Other writers, however, deny that the situation the thirty-ninth president faced was so intractable, and they deplore the consequences of the turn that Carter and the Democrats took in the 1970s. "I am not convinced that the nation was as ungovernable as some of Carter's defenders contend," Burton Kaufman has written, and Kenneth Morris has challenged the familiar notion that Carter was trapped in a conservative tidal wave. "Economic liberalism . . . remained strong through most of the 1970s," he has asserted. Somewhere in the 1970s, a number of commentators have said, Carter and the Democrats took a wrong turn. Carter, his critics charge, blazed the trail that came to a cul-de-sac with Clinton's signing of a welfare bill that abandoned millions of poor children.[50]

As we enter the third decade of thinking about the Carter presidency, our base point remains centrism with its stress on limits. But how we evaluate these emphases (Were they inevitable? Were they unfortunate? Were they prudent?) and how we place the Carter years in the history of the twentieth century, not only in

America but in the world—these questions continue to command our interest and to challenge us.

NOTES

1. Michael J. Krukones, "The Campaign Promises of Jimmy Carter," *Presidential Studies Quarterly* 15 (Winter 1985): 137; Bruce Mazlish and Edwin Diamond, *Jimmy Carter: A Character Portrait* (New York: Simon and Schuster, 1979), 231; Laurence Shoup, *The Carter Presidency and Beyond* (Palo Alto, Calif.: Ramparts Press, 1980), 215; Tip O'Neill, with William Novak, *Man of the House: The Life and Political Memoirs of Speaker Tip O'Neill* (New York: Random House, 987), 313. Carter's straddling of ideological positions in the 1976 campaign led the comedian Pat Paulsen to say that there was a movement to put Jimmy Carter on Mount Rushmore, "but they didn't have room for two faces" (Martin Shram, *Running for President 1976: The Carter Campaign* [New York: Stein and Day, 1977] , 12). For the perception that Carter combined "the three main types of southern politicians in the one man," see William C. Havard, Jr., "Southern Politics: Old and New Style," in *The American South: Portrait of a Culture,* ed. Louis D. Rubin, Jr. (Baton Rouge: Louisiana State University Press, 1980), 56.

2. Steven M. Gillon, *The Democrats' Dilemma: Walter F. Mondale and the Liberal Legacy* (New York: Columbia University Press,1992), 174.

3. Stuart Eizenstat, Exit Interview, 10 January 1981, pp. 18–20, Jimmy Carter Library (JCL).

4. Sam Church, Jr., to Kenneth Kline, January 12, 1982, Ken Kline Collection, JCL; James A. Gross, *Broken Promise: The Subversion of U.S. Labor Relations Policy, 1947–1994* (Philadelphia: Temple University Press, 1995), 242; Esther Peterson, Exit Interview, [Date?], 12, 19, JCL.

5. Burton I. Kaufman, *The Presidency of James Earl Carter, Jr.* (Lawrence: University Press of Kansas, 1993), 58–59; Gillon, *Democrats' Dilemma,* 253.

6. Harvard Sitkoff, *The Struggle for Black Equality, 1954–1980* (New York: Hill and Wang, 1981), 225–26; Steven F. Lawson, *In Pursuit of Power: Southern Blacks and Electoral Politics, 1965–1982* (New York: Columbia University Press, 1985), 257.

7. Bayard Rustin, "For President Carter," August 27, 1980, Rustin MSS, Box 16, Library of Congress; Frye Gaillard, "Carter: A New Look at an Unfinished Presidency," *Charlotte Observer,* July 11, 1985; Louis Martin, Exit Interview, December 10, 1980, pp. 9–10, JCL; Gillon, *Democrats' Dilemma,* 194; Lincoln Caplan, *The Tenth Justice: The Solicitor General and the Rule of Law* (New York: Knopf, 1987), 44; M. Glenn Abernathy, "The Carter Administration and Domestic Civil Rights," in *The Carter Years: The President and Policy Making,* ed. M. Glenn Abernathy, Dilys M. Hill, and Phil Williams (New York: St. Martin's Press, 1984), 120.

8. Sarah Weddington, Exit Interview, January 2, 1981, 13–14, JCL; Jimmy Carter Interview, November 22, 1982, William Burkett Miller Center of Public Affairs, University of Virginia Project on the Carter Presidency, Transcripts (hereafter cited as Miller Center), 46, JCL.

9. Raymond A. Moore, "The Carter Presidency and Foreign Policy," in Abernathy, Hill, and Williams, *Carter Years,* 72; William V. Shannon, "Score 10 for Carter," *Boston Globe,* November 4, 1981. Of course, other foreign policy developments, such as Carter's

overreaction to the Soviet invasion of Afghanistan and his decision to admit the shah, cut in a contrary direction.

10. *Time,* August 18, 1980, 11; Louis Martin, Exit Interview, December 10, 1980, 4–5, JCL; Roy Blount, Jr., *Crackers: This Whole Many-Angled Thing of Jimmy, More Carters, Ominous Little Animals, Sad-Singing Women, My Daddy and Me* (New York: Knopf, 1980), 4; Jimmy Carter, *Keeping Faith: Memoirs of a President* (New York: Bantam, 1982), 23.

11. *New York Times,* March 10, January 26, 1978, A15; Russell Baker, "The Jimmy Carter Show," *New York Times,* December 18, 1977, sec. 6, 12. An aide has acknowledged that he was "on television, blah," and that "even at a Christmas party, when we went through, it was a little cold" (Al McDonald Interview, March 13–14, 1981, Miller Center, 127, 89, JCL). Even his friend Griffin Bell remarked jocularly that Jimmy Carter was "about as good a President as an engineer can be." (Griffin Bell with Ronald J. Ostrow, *Taking Care of the Law* [New York: William Morrow, 1982], 47).

12. Phil Garner, "The Carter Enigma: Now That His Era Is Over, What Did It All Mean?" *Atlanta Weekly,* January 18, 1981, 24. For the shortcomings of Carter as a speechmaker, see Gaddis Smith, "Carter's Politicals Rhetoric," in *The Carter Presidency: Fourteen Intimate Perspectives of Jimmy Carter,* ed. Kenneth W. Thompson (Lanham, Md.: University Press of America, 1990), 202–3.

13. Robert Dallek, *Hail to the Chief: The Making and Unmaking of American Presidents* (New York: Hyperion, 1996), 193; Gillon, *Democrats' Dilemma,* 252; Bruce Kirschenbaum Interview, April 17–18, 1981, Miller Center, 11, 53, JCL.

14. Peter Carroll, *It Seemed Like Nothing Happened: The Tragedy and Promise of America in the 1970s* (New York: Holt, Rinehart and Winston, 1982), 194; Jody Powell, *The Other Side of the Story* (New York: William Morrow, 1984), 207.

15. Gaddis Smith, *Morality, Reason, and Power: American Diplomacy in the Carter Years* (New York: Hill and Wang, 1986), 246; Irwin B. Arieff, "Carter and Congress: Strangers to the End," *Congressional Quarterly Almanac,* 96th Cong., 2d sess. (Washington, D.C.: Congressional Quarterly, 1980), 5; Charles O. Jones, *The Trusteeship Presidency: Jimmy Carter and the United States Congress* (Baton Rouge: Louisiana State University Press, 1988), 200; *Time,* August 18, 1980, 11.

16. Address of September 13, 1976, in U.S. Congress, House, Committee on House Administration, *The Presidential Campaign, 1976* (Washington, D.C.: Government Printing Office, 1978), vol. 1, pt. 2, p. 727. For the importance of black ballots in the South for Carter in 1976, see Lawson, *In Pursuit of Power,* 254–56; Harry S. Ashmore, *Civil Rights and Wrongs: A Memoir of Race and Politics, 1944–1994* (New York: Pantheon, 1994), 264; Henry Paolucci, *"The South and the Presidency": From Reconstruction to Carter, a Long Day's Task* (Whitestone, N.Y.: Griffin House, 1978), 10.

17. James Fallows, "The Passionless Presidency: The Trouble with Jimmy Carter's Administration," *Atlantic,* May 1979, 35; Hedley Donovan, Exit Interview, August 14, 1980, 2, JCL; Stuart Eizenstat Interview, Miller Center, January 29–30, 1982, 10, JCL; Leo Ribuffo, "'I'll Whip His Ass': Jimmy Carter, Edward Kennedy, and the Latest Crisis of American Liberalism" (paper presented at the annual meeting of the Organization of American Historians, April 15, 1994, 7). As Ribuffo remarked dryly, "The posterior motif entered their relationship early." Subsequently, when Kennedy contemplated seeking the Democratic nomination, Carter responded, "I'll whip his ass."

18. Kaufman, *Presidency of James Earl Carter,* 24.

19. Leonard Silk, "Carter's Economics," *New York Times,* July 14, 1976; Ann Mari May, "Fiscal Policy, Monetary Policy, and the Carter Presidency," *Presidential Studies Quarterly* 23 (Fall 1993): 706; "The Liberals and Carter," *Progressive* 91 (July 1977): 5. See, too, George McGovern, "Memo to the White House," *Harper's,* October 1977, 33–35.

20. Jimmy Carter Interview, November 29, 1982, Miller Center, 12, 69, JCL.

21. Gillon, *Democrats' Dilemma,* 198–99, 206–7.

22. Seymour Melman, "Jimmy Hoover?" *New York Times,* February 7, 1979; Susan M. Hartmann, *From Margin to Mainstream: American Women and Politics since 1960* (Philadelphia: Temple University Press, 1989), 151–52.

23. Gillon, *Democrats' Dilemma,* 277–78, 287; Chet Fuller, *I Hear Them Calling My Name* (Boston: Houghton Mifflin, 1981), 252. His election-year budget for fiscal 1981 stated bluntly, "Desirable new programs have been deferred" (Timothy B. Clark, "Carter's Election-Year Budget—Something for Practically Everyone," *National Journal,* February 2, 1980, 184).

24. Alfred Kahn Interview, December 10–11, 1981, Miller Center, 41–42, JCL. Hubert Harris in James McIntyre Interview, October 28–29, 1981, Miller Center, 26, JCL.

25. Joseph A. Califano, Jr., *Governing America: An Insider's Report from the White House and the Cabinet* (New York: Simon and Schuster, 1981), 336, 230; Lester M. Salamon, *Welfare: The Elusive Consensus—Where We Are, How We Got There, and What's Ahead* (New York: Praeger, 1978), 214–15; Dilys M. Hill, "Domestic Policy," in Abernathy, Hill, and Williams, *Carter Years,* 19; William Attwood, "Why I Support President Carter," *New Republic,* August 16, 1980, 32.

26. Laurence E. Lynn, Jr., and David Whitman, *The President as Policymaker: Jimmy Carter and Welfare Reform* (Philadelphia: Temple University Press, 1981), 44, 275; Califano, *Governing America,* 230; Diary, January 19, 1978, in Carter, *Keeping Faith,* 102. For contrary evidence on Carter's commitment to Humphrey-Hawkins, see Stuart Eizenstat and Frank Moore to Carter, n.d., Domestic Policy Staff (DPS)-Eizenstat, JCL.

27. Stuart Eizenstat, Exit Interview, January 10, 1981, 20, JCL; Ribuffo, " 'I'll Whip His Ass,' " 10, 14.

28. Peter G. Bourne, *Jimmy Carter: A Comprehensive Biography from Plains to Postpresidency* (New York: Scribner, 1997), 369. "The reforms Carter sponsored during his governorship did not encompass bold, new innovative programs but rather sought to make existing programs operate more efficiently, economically, and justly," the foremost authority on Carter's governorship has written. But he adds: "While essentially conservative in character, many of these reforms carried with them the possibilities for far-reaching social change. Many Georgians . . . viewed zero-based budgeting as a unique opportunity to re-slice the economic pie" (Gary M. Fink, *Prelude to the Presidency: The Political Character and Legislative Leadership Style of Governor Jimmy Carter* [Westport, Conn.: Greenwood Press, 1980], 167).

29. Jimmy Carter, *Turning Point; A Candidate, a State, and a Nation Come of Age* (New York: Times Books, 1992), 5–6; William E. Leuchtenburg, *In the Shadow of FDR: From Harry Truman to Bill Clinton* (Ithaca, N.Y.: Cornell University Press, 1993), 190–91; Joseph P. Lash, *Dealers and Dreamers: A New Look at the New Deal* (New York: Doubleday, 1988), 3–4; "New Deal Dinner, 1977–1978," Rexford G. Tugwell MSS, Box 17, Franklin D. Roosevelt Library, Hyde Park, New York; David Broder, "It Was a Shame Carter Couldn't Come," *Washington Post,* March 9, 1977.

30. Leuchtenburg, *In the Shadow of FDR,* 179; Gillon, *Democrats' Dilemma,* 171, 161. After Carter returned from "mixing with the people" in Bardstown, Kentucky, a *Washington Post* writer remarked, "Although the United States today is overwhelmingly an urban society, the president seems to favor rural or smalltown America when he sets out to rub elbows with real folks" (Clayton Fritchey, "Carter: Misreading the Grass Roots," *Washington Post,* August 13, 1979).

31. William E. Leuchtenburg, *A Troubled Feast: American Society since 1945,* updated edition (Boston: Little, Brown, 1983), 88; Kaufman, *Presidency of James Earl Carter,* 29.

32. Arthur Schlesinger, Jr., "The Great Carter Mystery," *New Republic,* April 12, 1980, 21. Gillon, *Democrats' Dilemma,* 252; Ribuffo, "'I'll Whip His Ass,'" 15–16; Fritchey, "Carter."

33. Arthur Schlesinger, Jr., "The End of an Era?" *Wall Street Journal,* November 20, 1980; William R. Winpisinger (president of the International Association of Machinists and Aerospace Workers) to Kenneth Kline, January 7, 1982, Ken Kline Files, JCL.

34. Carroll Engelhardt, "Man in the Middle: Arthur M. Schlesinger, Jr., and Postwar American Liberalism," *South Atlantic Quarterly* 80 (Spring 1981): 141; Schlesinger, "Great Carter Mystery," 21; Schlesinger, "End of an Era?"

35. *Atlanta Constitution,* February 19, 1997; Gillon, *Democrats' Dilemma,* 178. For the view that the New Deal system gave way to a new political paradigm in the 1960s, see Byron E. Shafer, "The United States," in *Postwar Politics in the G-7: Orders and Eras in Comparative Perspective,* ed. Bryon Shafer (Madison: University of Wisconsin Press, 1996).

36. Alan Ehrenhalt, "Last Hurrahs for the New Deal," *Washington Monthly* 7 (1976): 56–57; *Denver Post,* October 10, 1976, clipping, Gary Hart MSS, Box 197, University of Colorado, Boulder, Colo.; Jack W. Germond and Jules Witcover, *Wake Us When It's Over: Presidential Politics of 1984* (New York: Macmillan, 1985), 28. One scholar has written bluntly, "The New Deal collapsed in the 1960s" (Jonathan Rieder, "The Rise of the 'Silent Majority,'" in *The Rise and Fall of the New Deal Order, 1930–1980,* ed. Steve Fraser and Gary Gerstle [Princeton, N.J.: Princeton University Press, 1989], 243).

37. Eizenstat Interview, Miller Center, 62, JCL.

38. Jody Powell Interview, Miller Center, December 17–18, 1981, 33, 94–95, 91, JCL.

39. Stephen Woolcock, "The Economic Policies of the Carter Administration," in Abernathy, Hill, and Williams, *Carter Years,* 35; W. Bowman Cutler, quoted in James Fallows, "Is It All Carter's Fault?" *Atlantic,* October 1980, 47–48; Bourne, *Jimmy Carter,* 431; Bruce Kirschenbaum Interview, Miller Center, 31, JCL. See, too, Van Ooms in James McIntyre Interview, Miller Center, 17, JCL.

40. Thomas Byrne Edsall with Mary D. Edsall, *Chain Reaction: The Impact of Race, Rights, and Taxes on American Politics* (New York: Norton, 1992), 105.

41. Walter F. Mondale, Address to Democratic Mid-Term Convention, December 10, 1978, Box 132, Gary Hart MSS.

42. Carter, *Keeping Faith,* 21.

43. Michael J. Malbin, "Rhetoric and Leadership: A Look Backward at the Carter National Energy Plan," in *Both Ends of the Avenue: The Presidency, the Executive Branch, and Congress in the 1980s,* ed. Anthony King (Washington, D.C.: American Enterprise Institute for Public Policy Research, 1983), 239; Gordon Stewart in Hendrick Hertzberg, Miller Center Interview, December 3–4, 1981, 141, JCL; Edward Walsh in *Washington Post,* C1.

44. *Washington Star,* July 9, 1979. As early as his first year in office, a news magazine reported: "Carter has been rather at odds with the temper of his time—the bearer of bad news and belt-tightening programs to a nation unprepared to believe . . . that an energy crisis even exists" (Peter Goldman, "The President Learning," *Newsweek,* December 26, 1977, 26).

45. Michael Schaller, *Reckoning with Reagan: America and Its President in the 1980s* (New York: Oxford University Press, 1992), 33; William H. Cable Oral History, JCL; Dilys M. Hill and Phil Williams, "Conclusion: The Legacy," in Abernathy, Hill, and Williams, *Carter Years,* 218.

46. William E. Leuchtenburg, "The Jubilee in the Bicentennial Era: A Sense of Limits," in *Britain and the United States: Four Views to Mark the Silver Jubilee,* ed. William E. Leuchtenburg, Anthony Quinton, George W. Ball, and David Owen (London: Heinemann, 1979), 1–21.

47. Samuel I. Rosenman, ed., *The Public Papers and Addresses of Franklin D. Roosevelt,* 13 vols. (New York: Random House, Macmillan, Harper, 1938–50), 5:235; Harry S. Truman, *Memoirs,* 2 vols. (Garden City, NY: Doubleday, 1956), 2:196.

48. Leuchtenburg, *In the Shadow of FDR,* 257; John Dumbrell, *The Carter Presidency: A Re-evaluation* (Manchester, England: Manchester University Press, 1993), 216; William Jefferson Clinton, "Address before a Joint Session of the Congress on the State of the Union (January 23, 1996)," *Weekly Compilation of Presidential Documents,* January 29, 1996, 32: 90–98.

49. John Connally, with Mickey Herskowitz, *In History's Shadow: An American Odyssey* (New York: Hyperion, 1993), 291; Edward R. Kantowicz, "Reminiscences of a Fated Presidency: Themes from the Carter Memoirs," *Presidential Studies Quarterly* 16 (Fall 1986): 651; Richard Moe, Miller Center Interview, 132; Erwin C. Hargrove, "The Carter Presidency in Historical Perspective," in *The Presidency and Domestic Policies of Jimmy Carter,* ed. Herbert D. Rosenbaum and Alexej Ugrinsky (Westport, Conn.: Greenwood Press, 1994), 21, 26; Dumbrell, *Carter Presidency,* 224; Louis Koenig in Rosenbaum and Ugrinsky, *Presidency and Domestic Politics,* 415. Carter's former speechwriter James Fallows, who had written one of the most devastating critiques early in the administration, stated in 1980, "My view is that Carter is the scapegoat for, not the cause of, our worst political dissatisfactions, and . . . to expect they will be relieved if he is expelled is to think that a train's burst boiler will be repaired if we shoot the engineer" (Fallows, "Is It All Carter's Fault?" 45). His earlier article was "The Passionless Presidency," *Atlantic,* May 1979, 33–47. For the perception that Carter was a "late-regime" president, see Stephen Skowronek, *The Politics Presidents Make: Leadership from John Adams to George Bush* (Cambridge, Mass.: Harvard University Press, 1993), 361–406.

50. Kaufman, *Presidency of James Earl Carter,* 3; Kenneth E. Morris, *Jimmy Carter: American Moralist* (Athens: University of Georgia Press, 1996), 210. Erwin Hargrove has reported: "One of the reviewers of my book accused both Carter and myself of being "neoliberals," as if this were a crime. The criticism reflects a widely shared view that Carter was a traitor to the New Deal–Great Society legacy of the Democratic party" (Hargrove, "Carter Presidency," 21). He was alluding to *Jimmy Carter as President: Leadership and the Politics of the Public Good* (Baton Rouge: Louisiana State University Press, 1988).

2

The Quest for National Goals, 1957–81

Robert H. Zieger

In 1960 and again in 1979, a beleaguered president appointed a commission whose task it was to review the state of the nation, rearticulate its fundamental goals and purposes, and identify the most serious challenges facing the American people. The activities and reports of these two bodies remain of interest for three main reasons. First, the very existence of these commissions is suggestive of the world-view of significant segments among U.S. policy making and politically defining classes at two key junctures in modern U.S. history. Second, each produced analyses of important features of American life that remain instructive and thought-provoking. Finally, both initiatives illuminate, in a distinctive twentieth-century idiom, the theme of what Sacvan Berkovitch calls "the American Jeremiad," a mode of discourse that warns of a fall from grace, validates established values, and establishes ever-changing and ultimately unrealizable agendas for the future.[1]

RESPONDING TO CRISIS

The President's Commission on National Goals (PCNG) was appointed in January 1960 and delivered its report to the president ten months later. The President's Commission for a National Agenda for the Eighties (PCNA) came into existence in October 1979 and delivered its report in January 1981. Before 1960, both Congress and the president had often resorted to special commissions to investigate specific public issues, but these two initiatives remain unique because of the timing of their creation, the general nature of their briefs, and the prestige and visibility of their memberships.[2]

Both commissions owed their existence to widespread expressions of public concern about the state, direction, and viability of the American project. In the case of the Eisenhower commission, the Soviet launching of an earth satellite, dire reports of American military vulnerability issued by presumably authoritative bodies such as the Gaither commission, and pervasive questions about the nation's spiritual, moral, and political health formed the immediate backdrop to the president's call in his January 11, 1959, State of the Union Address for the creation of a commission consisting of "a group of selfless and devoted individuals." Their deliberations and reports would serve as "long term guides" toward "goals that must stand high." The commission would study particular problems of economic performance, international relations, and social concern, but above all its deliberations were designed "to inspire every citizen to climb always toward mounting levels of moral, intellectual and material strength . . . [and to] spur pride in individual and national achievements." Powerful and prosperous, the country appeared too often to lack direction and common purpose. Declared the president, "We Need a National Goal."[3]

In the case of the Carter commission, the president's stunning July 15, 1979, speech, questioning the country's moral fiber and spiritual health, provided the immediate impetus. The sense of national doubt and aimlessness in the late 1970s was, if anything, more pervasive than in the late 1950s, and, in retrospect, more legitimate as well. In the early 1960s, little basis existed in fact for alarmist concerns about America's military power, technological performance, or ability to compete with the Soviet Union and the People's Republic of China in economic performance. True, critics did raise legitimate questions about the country's priorities and overall public values, but these chronic concerns hardly merited the apocalyptic language of the post-*Sputnik* years.

By the late 1970s, however, a stronger case for sober reassessment of the American project had arisen. Defeat in Vietnam, the ongoing energy crisis, Watergate, omnipresent racial tensions, and a new surge of Soviet initiatives in the Third World made the seventies a decade of doubt and confusion. Underlying these disparate insecurities and setbacks was the seemingly inexplicable phenomenon of stagflation. Through the late 1970s, the American economy, the symbol and substance of national superiority, faltered and flagged. Annual rates of inflation approached 20 percent, while unemployment—supposedly inversely related to inflation—remained stuck at double previous recession rates. Neither private enterprise nor the government seemed to have any answer. Living standards, the steady rise of which had come to seem an American birthright, leveled off and even began to decline among lower-income citizens. Pollsters and pundits, the Carter commission staff noted, consistently reported "a spreading sense of pessimism regarding the nation's future."[4]

These anxieties and dilemmas peaked in the late 1970s, and of course the incumbent administration bore the brunt of the blame. Moreover, the administration's response, instead of reassuring or distracting a nervous populace, fed the sense of crisis. Indeed, the administration's more attractive qualities—its openness to diverse ideas, its self-criticism, the expressed desire of President Carter and his spokesmen to speak with frankness and candor to the American people—added to the sense of public dismay.

This was, of course, not the intent of the administration. Indeed, the president's summoning of a wide variety of public leaders, social critics, and moral and academic exemplars to Camp David in the early summer of 1979 was intended to launch a serious public dialogue. Certainly, this was the sense that President Carter's remarkable July 15 speech attempted to convey. Carter's address—and especially the press reaction to it—had highlighted the nation's underlying "crisis of spirit," or, in a phrase not actually used by Carter but quickly and pervasively attached to it, a "national malaise."[5]

In the fall, the White House made explicit the link between the anguished reassessment of national purpose and performance of the summer and the creation of a presidential commission. On October 24, a press release announced the establishment of the President's Commission for a National Agenda for the Eighties, which, it declared, "is a direct outgrowth of the President's extensive discussions at Camp David this summer." At the conference, adviser Donovan and commission chair William McGill stated that the commission's work would not be confined to making specific studies of such problems as inflation, productivity, and energy but would look "ahead to broader questions of . . . the general temper and spirit of the country." Referring indirectly to the Eisenhower commission, Donovan told reporters that "President Carter felt that the country really suffered from a lack of a sense of vision and goals and purpose."[6]

The similarities and differences in the composition, deliberations, and final reports of these two commissions reveal much about the state of public discourse in the country at these two moments of perceived crisis. The Eisenhower commission consisted of ten white males, all but one of whom lived and worked along the Northeastern corridor. Brown University president emeritus Henry Wriston chaired the commission. Half of the members had direct ties to the scientific-military-industrial complex; two—former Harvard president James Bryant Conant and Du Pont president Crawford Greenewalt—had played major roles in the Manhattan Project. All vocally supported the main tenets of postwar American foreign policy. Little ideological conflict divided the commissioners, with AFL-CIO president George Meany and University of California chancellor Clark Kerr representing the "left" end of the narrow spectrum and Greenewalt and his brother-in-law, former Virginia governor Colgate Darden, holding down the "right." The commission's staff director, William Bundy, a consummate Washington insider and organizer, was between stints as director of the CIA's Office of National Estimates and deputy secretary of defense under John Kennedy.[7]

In contrast, the Carter commission eventually consisted of forty-five members. Columbia University president William J. McGill chaired the body, whose members included social commentator Daniel Bell; poet Gwendolyn Brooks; television producer Joan Ganz Cooney; Children's Defense Fund director Marian

Wright Edelman; NAACP president Benjamin Hooks; AFL-CIO president Lane Kirkland; former secretary of commerce Juanita Kreps; religious scholar Martin Marty; former Pennsylvania governor William Scranton; and scientist Lewis Thomas. Two Carter commission members had been closely involved with the Eisenhower panel: John Gardner, who had written the chapter on education for its report, *Goals for Americans;* and Frank Pace, Jr., former secretary of the army and CEO of General Dynamics, who had served as vice chairman of the Eisenhower commission. Thirteen of the Carter commission members were women, four were African American (including two women), two were of Hispanic background. Four labor union officials served, as did representatives of religious bodies, environmental organizations, and consumer and public interest groups. The business representatives on the Carter board were drawn from both major corporations and banks and smaller specialty firms, with substantial representation among management, technology, and productivity experts from both business and academic backgrounds. No one from the military served on the Carter commission, and only Texas Instruments head Fred Bucey was from a distinctively defense-oriented corporation.[8]

By design, both commissions projected an image of wise deliberation by thoughtful and public-spirited leaders at times of national crisis. In reality, both functioned in their organization and procedures as variations on a peculiar bureaucratic construct, the generic presidential commission.[9] In view of the short time allotted for issuance of a final report and the extensive scope of their briefs, both commissions exhibited more in the way of hasty and at times even frantic intellectual negotiation than calm, deliberative counsel. This especially held true for the more diverse and contentious members of the Carter panel, whose deliberations often reflected extreme frustration at the knottiness of social problems in a period of relative scarcity. Thus, at a session charged with developing language for the final report, one commissioner, faced with the prospect of having to say something about education, threw up his (or her) hands, admitting that "we don't know what the hell to do about it. . . . it's a zoo out there and nobody knows what to do about it." Remarked a veteran observer of bureaucratic life, social commentator Amitai Etzioni, "More than anything else, commissions are part of government by fire-brigade."[10]

The Eisenhower effort was privately funded, in accordance with the president's hopes that it could be free of partisan or official influences. Eisenhower and his staff spent considerable time in the year between announcement of the project, in January 1959, and its actual launching a year later trying unsuccessfully to get funding from the Ford Foundation and other large private donors. Eventually, the president, perhaps embarrassed by frequent questions about the phantom commission at news conferences, turned to his mentor in the ways of academic politics, Henry Wriston. After his departure from Brown in 1955, Wriston had become head of the American Assembly, a public service adjunct of Columbia University that Eisenhower had established during his university presidency with funding initially from the Harriman family estate.[11] Under Wriston's energetic direction, the American Assembly arranged for foundation grants to finance the project (now somewhat scaled down in scope and ambition from the plans initially circulating in administration circles), supplied staff and secretarial support for the commission's work, and, in January 1960, initiated its commission's deliberations.[12]

In contrast, Carter's initiative was a government project, its funding coming from the budgets of the Executive Office and the executive departments. Its senior staff of about twenty consisted largely of younger academics and veterans of other governmental agency and congressional staff assignments. Neither of its codirectors had the cachet or connections of which Bundy could boast, and the senior staff lacked his intimacy and social familiarity with commissioners. Nonetheless, the senior staff, while operating in a more bureaucratic milieu than Bundy and his aides, significantly shaped the Carter commission's month-to-month agenda and had much influence in selecting expert witnesses, arranging for public forums, and shaping the panel studies that were at the heart of the published report.[13]

The two panels functioned in broadly similar ways. In each case, staff members, in consultation with the chair, translated the president's various statements relating to the project into a series of discrete topics for investigation and report. Both commissions identified the economy, technology, urban policy, the workings of the political system, and social welfare programs as discrete topics. Likewise, both considered foreign policy, with special emphasis on economic aspects; neither, however, subjected defense policy to separate scrutiny, a more surprising omission in the Goals report in view of the debate raging through the late 1950s and into 1960 over the so-called missile gap.

The agendas of the two commissions did differ. The Eisenhower group did not award separate consideration to race relations, which in contrast was at the heart of the Carter commission's Panel on Government and the Advancement of Social Justice. Conversely, Carter's panel gave little consideration to artistic expression and cultural enterprise, in contrast to its predecessor, whose discussion of "The Quality of American Culture" was a significant stepping-stone toward creation of the National Endowment for the Arts and the National Endowment for the Humanities. And more generally, the Carter commission members and staff shunned broad, speculative considerations of national purposes, focusing instead on concrete problems and institutions. From the inception of the Eisenhower counterpart, however, Wriston was at work on a broad introductory essay that he intended as a philosophical statement about the relationship of the individual to the American social order in the modern age.

Once early meetings of the commissioners had established these agendas, staff members set about organizing discussion of specific topics. The Eisenhower body undertook its deliberations largely free from public scrutiny. Bundy and his assistants spent the first two months on the road, conferring with academics, policy experts, and public officials (though rarely with representatives of advocacy groups) and selecting authors and committee members for the specialized essays. In consultation with Wriston, Bundy drew up a list of experts to be commissioned to write authoritative papers on such subjects as agricultural policy, foreign economic policy, economic organization, education, health and welfare, and other broad areas. Each author was to be guided by a small committee of fellow experts in the field. The full commission was to meet periodically to review the work in progress and to formulate a separate statement of goals at its final meeting in November.[14]

At this session, the panel adopted a twenty-three-page statement that Bundy had prepared, encapsulating the ongoing deliberations. Although the energetic and authoritative Wriston worked hard to gain consensus among his colleagues, lingering differences in emphasis, especially between Greenewalt and Meany, ensured that the final report would contain "additional statements," if not formal dissents, from some members.

In the published report, titled *Goals for Americans* and issued by Prentice-Hall two weeks after the presidential election, the statement of goals and these mildly dissenting "additional statements" were followed by the expert-written essays. These occupied almost three hundred pages of text. The tone and tenor of these papers broadly conformed to the statement of goals, but the commission carefully informed readers of *Goals for Americans* that the papers were provided only as "interesting and relevant discussions of vital issues," not expressions of views endorsed by the commission, whose "own position is set forth solely in its own Report," that is to say, the twenty-three-page statement of goals preceding these essays.[15]

More of the work of the Carter body occurred within the nine separate panels, each of which consisted of several commissioners with particular expertise or interest in its subject matter. Thus, for example, General Motors chief economist Marina von Neumann Whitman headed the panel on economic growth, while the NAACP's Benjamin Hooks presided over the social policy panel. Senior staff were assigned to each of these panels, which were expected to spend the first half of the commission's existence gathering information and absorbing expert opinion. Staff members played a key role in enabling the panels to accomplish their information-gathering functions. They read and summarized a wide range of material, preparing briefs and synopses for the panel members to review and discuss at their periodic meetings. In more public sessions, panel members participated in forums or conferences at which experts presented papers or less formal testimony and engaged in cross talk with the commissioner-panelists. In some cases, panel chairs gave the senior staff wide latitude in setting up these meetings, relying heavily on them for the identification and recruitment of speakers and witnesses.[16]

Although in theory the full PCNA met on several occasions, in practice its large size and diversity precluded authoritative common sessions. An executive committee appointed by McGill and chaired by Cal Tech economist Roger G. Noll met periodically to hash out the commission's overall direction and eventually to oversee the drafting of its final report. Several commissioners, notably Whitman and religious scholar Martin Marty (serving on the Quality of American Life Panel) exerted influence through shaping the panel reports and by providing succinct and authoritative advice to the harassed McGill. The senior staff handled the "technical" problems of expert recruitment, logistics, rapporteuring, and preparation of documents. Inevitably, however, in view of the diversity of the commission and the busy public schedules of its members, much of the original drafting of position papers and reports also fell to the senior staff. In a process surprising only to the bureaucratically uninitiated, commissioners, having in effect delegated authority, often now sought to influence the staff in its production of interim papers and, finally, of the panel reports.[17]

The small size, relative homogeneity, and quasi-secretiveness of the Eisenhower commission encouraged the notion of the nation's Olympian solons hard at work ruminating on the country's plight. Wriston and Bundy carefully guarded their work from public scrutiny. No leaks occurred, and despite the divisions in opinion that surfaced in *Goals for Americans,* neither the commissioners nor the staff sought to appeal directly to the public through the press. The few press reports that did appear were respectful, accepting without apparent skepticism the official view of the commission as a council of wise men, cogitating in disinterested fashion about the state of the nation.[18]

The composition, organization, and format of the Carter commission, however, did not lend itself to such restraint and decorum. The Carter assemblage, even more than its earlier counterpart, spoke frequently of the need for consensus, for unified national response to the challenges the country faced. But ten white males sharing similar educational, historical, and even personal experiences found it easier to invoke consensus than forty-five highly visible public advocates, many of them selected precisely because they represented competing ethnic, sectoral, or social groups. In addition, each panel held some sort of public meeting. While often bland affairs featuring experts presenting their views and being questioned by commissioners and staff members, a few sessions turned into lively and even disputatious public encounters, laying bare some of the raw social tensions that had surfaced during a decade of uneven economic performance.[19]

GOALS FOR AMERICANS

The reports themselves reflected the different times in which they were drafted and published. That of the Eisenhower commission, published in 1960 by Prentice-Hall as *Goals for Americans,* was a far more unified and coherent document than *A National Agenda for the Eighties* (1980), also published by Prentice-Hall. It was also, for all the atmosphere of crisis that preceded the appointment of the Goals commission, a far more positive and optimistic document.

Indeed, *Goals for Americans,* while dutifully cataloging the challenges and difficulties facing the country, was programmed from the start to strike a positive note. For all the tribulations of the latter years of his presidency, Eisenhower still commanded vast public respect. As a military man, he stood above the partisan battles and fractional disputes and had commanded a diverse, even polyglot, army in a fashion that seemed to combine democratic simplicity with vast personal authority. The press, and implicitly the public, trusted him to appoint commissioners who shared his general perspective while at the same time plausibly claiming that they were men of individual principle and integrity. Thus, the PCNG was *Eisenhower*'s commission in a way in which the PCNA could never be *Carter*'s, for many men and women of the latter body, in everything except the most formal sense, reported not to the president but to the constituencies they represented.

Given his prestige and reputation for disinterestedness, Eisenhower could choose like-minded men who plausibly assumed the persona of disinterested sages. The only commissioners remotely representing constituencies were Meany and Greenewalt. Once the president had tapped Wriston to head up the project, the former Brown president, along with Bundy, had a free hand in choosing the expert authors of the discussion chapters. They operated within the tight world of the Ivy League universities, the Council on Foreign Relations, and the liberal cold war consensus. John W. Gardner, executive director of the Carnegie Foundation, wrote the chapter on education, while Warren Weaver of the Rockefeller Foundation wrote the chapter on science. Thomas Watson of IBM wrote on technology, and Kerr himself authored a chapter on economic organization. Among the more notable contributions were the essays by Cornell political scientist Clinton Rossiter on "The Democratic Process" and the essays by Herbert Stein and Edward F. Denison on employment and economic growth and August Heckscher on American culture. Historian William L. Langer, a key figure in the Office of Secret Services, the World War II predecessor to the CIA, surveyed foreign policy, while veteran foreign and defense policy practitioner John J. McCloy contributed the chapter "Foreign Economic Policy." Wriston himself produced an introductory essay titled "The Individual," and Bundy concluded the volume with his reflections, "A Look Further Ahead."

A more skeptical later generation might have considered the heavy CIA–national defense orientation of so many of the principals in the Goals commission as suspect, perhaps even sinister. Commissioners Conant, Killian, Gruenther, Pace, and Greenewalt had been central figures in the defense industry, weapons development, nuclear research, and military life. Moreover, Bundy and his aide Guy Coridan came to the commission directly from the CIA, while the authorship of the chapters on foreign policy by Langer and McCloy strengthened the military-intelligence cast of the enterprise.

In the late 1950s, however, virtually no one even commented on the apparent military-defense orientation of the commission's principle figures. So complete was the pre-Vietnam cold war consensus that the press and the broad public made little distinction between pressing domestic problems and problems relating to military and foreign policy affairs. The raging debate over educational standards and performance, for example, was largely couched in terms of education's contribution to America's place in the world arena.[20] Widespread criticisms of rampant consumerism, public complacency, and selfishness were usually expressed in terms of undermining the nation's ability to project its virtue and its power in the contest against communism. Was a national highway system needed? Did higher education require enhanced support? Then Congress would pass a National Defense Highway Construction Act and a National Defense Education Act.

Few challenged the primacy of military and related foreign policy questions. Indeed, in the late 1950s the Eisenhower administration fell under heavy attack for the perceived weakness of U.S. foreign and military policy. In 1957, a blue-ribbon panel, appointed by Eisenhower and chaired by Ford Foundation executive H. Rowan Gaither, Jr., confounded the administration by producing a report that depicted the United States as virtually at the mercy of Soviet missiles. Along with the launching of the Soviet earth satellite that fall, the Gaither Report fueled charges that under Eisenhower the country had become complacent and lethargic. The war hero president was clearly on the defensive, with the sometimes barely loyal opposition calling aggressively for further militarization of American life. No public body appointed in 1960 that presumed to articulate national goals and purpose could dare bypass those who had won World War II, faced down the Soviets, and played central roles in building the vast U.S. military establishment.[21]

And just as the activities of the Eisenhower commission were pre-Vietnam, they were also pre-Watergate. Even the politically moderate members of the Goals commission were predisposed to view the federal government as a central, dynamic, and positive force in domestic as well as foreign affairs. These people had come of age during the depression and World War II. Commissioners Greenewalt and Darden apart, few associated with the project doubted that government should play an expanded role in education, management of the economy, civil rights, and social policy.

A positive view of government action appeared throughout the twenty-three-page statement of goals. To be sure, the commissioners sought to buttress the "free enterprise" system, but they held that "increased investment in the public sector is compatible with this goal." They called for drastic increases in expenditures in education, public health, social welfare, and housing. *Goals for Americans* urged "further urban renewal programs, costing as much as $4 billion per year," and a doubling of educational expenditures by 1970 to $40 billion a year, noting diffidently that "the federal role must now be expanded." Though the commission paid homage to voluntarism and private enterprise (the word *capitalism* made no appearance in the statement of goals), it made no apologies for the current level of federal activity. It pledged the country to sustaining a growth rate of from 3.4 percent to 5 percent annually and to steady progress "toward our goal of full employment," which entailed finding jobs for 13.5 million entrants into the labor force in the 1970s, all the while improving living standards, boosting competitiveness, and avoiding inflation. All this, they believed, could be achieved "without extraordinary stimulating measures."[22]

In foreign affairs also, the Goals panel posited an expanded governmental presence. It urged dramatic expansion of U.S. foreign aid and a more vigorous U.S. presence, especially in the Third World. Here the commission's report revealed that distinctive mix of moral confidence and practical uncertainty that characterized foreign policy elites of the late 1950s. On the one hand, no hint of doubt appeared in *Goals for Americans* regarding the inherent superiority of the American way of life or of the superiority of Western values and institutions generally. "We must never lose sight of our ultimate goal," intoned the report, which was "to extend the opportunities for free choice and self-determination throughout the world."[23]

Yet there could be no denying the physical power and exemplary appeal of the Soviet Union and the People's Republic of China. "It will be a major task to prevent their expansion in the coming decade," warned the commissioners. Soviet economic advances, scientific achievements, and military strength, along with communism's constant threat of internal subversion, especially in developing nations, required that "we must be ready to make the sacrifices necessary to meet the rising costs of military" preparedness. And it was likely that "over the next decade, Communist China may be more aggressive than the U.S.S.R."[24]

The combination of moral certitude and practical vulnerability was particularly obvious in the commissioners' remarks on the developing world. The legacy of Western colonialism, along with miserable living conditions, made the Third World uniquely vulnerable to the superficially attractive designs of Moscow and Peking. Through the example of our superior domestic institutions and achievements, and through generous public and private investment abroad, the commissioners hoped, the advance of communism might be stemmed. Fixated on the U.S.-Soviet rivalry, they conveyed little sense that the choices and policies of developing countries responded primarily to their own cultural, political, and economic concerns and not to the dictates of great power rivalry. In the final analysis, their blend of righteousness and doubt posited the distinct possibility of a future world order increasingly inhospitable to U.S. and Western interests and values. After all, "The United States, while omnipresent, is not omnipotent," they cautioned, and "Whether nations will prefer freedom to totalitarianism" was by no means clear.[25]

But this uncertainty was rare in *Goals for Americans*. Apart from these doubts as to how other, presumably less steadfast and sophisticated, peoples might act, the commissioners repeatedly reaffirmed their faith in the American way and the American people. To be sure, they acknowledged the concerns that had, at least indirectly, given birth to their efforts. Wriston, for example, in his overview essay "The Individual," noted the persistent "mood of doubt regarding our system."

Clinton Rossiter added that "time and space are closing in on us" and that "the quiet times are gone forever." Government had made mistakes. Soviet advance in outer space underlined the need to revitalize American institutions.[26]

Despite these concerns, however, *Goals for Americans* radiated optimism. Observed Wriston, "The characteristic historical tone of American life has been optimistic." Rossiter little doubted the country's ability to achieve "a new order of imagination all through the structure of democracy." Yes, the introduction to the report acknowledged, "the nation is in grave danger," a danger primarily posed by the military power and meretricious appeal to the worlds dispossessed by communism. But the commissioners confidently concluded, "We can continue to improve our own way of life, and at the same time help in the progress of vast numbers in the world." In the final analysis, "our past performance justifies confidence that [even the most lofty goals] . . . can be achieved."[27]

A NATIONAL AGENDA FOR THE EIGHTIES

The report of the Carter commission, in contrast, stressed challenges, limits, and dilemmas. Indeed, *A National Agenda for the Eighties* rather enviously contrasted the Carter panel's task with that of its predecessor. "As the nation entered the 1960s, we believed that we could do almost anything," it observed. "*Goals for Americans* . . . reflected the optimism of an entire nation, and a belief in the government's ability to address and solve its problems." But the "principal task" of the Agenda commission was "to draw national attention to the necessity of choice and to clarify the implications and consequences of the difficult choices before us."[28]

A National Agenda contained no soaring vision as found in the essays by Wriston and Rossiter. Its first chapter, titled "A Decade of Choices," presented a fourteen-page overview of the themes on which the commission members had concentrated, stressing the difficulty of their task and the complex nature of national problems. Though it did contain a two-page summary statement of overall conclusions, unlike its predecessor, it failed to advance a set of goals or even general precepts. "While we encourage people to think about moral questions," the commissioners declared, "we strongly believe it is not the business of government or governmental commissions to endorse a specific set of moral virtues." Another contrast lay in the area of arts and culture, with *Goals for Americans* featuring an important paper by Twentieth Century Fund Director August Heckscher titled "The Quality of American Culture," while *A National Agenda for the Eighties* specifically avoided consideration of culture and "the humanities," along with any invocation of "the human spirit."[29]

It was the charge of *this* commission to bring the country back to reality. Its predecessor had the luxury of assessing the country's prospects from the perspective of seemingly limitless (and costless) economic growth. But the American people now faced "a world that is not as much in our control as it once was," in good part because "the resources are not there to do everything in the coming decade."[30]

The language of limits, choices, and warnings dominated the report. The era of unchallenged U.S. economic supremacy, based as it was on unparalleled access to world markets, cheap energy, and limited competition, was over. The stagflation of the 1970s, the steep increases in oil prices, and the emergence of aggressive competition from Germany, Japan, and other modernizing economies posed unique challenges for a U.S. economic order that had been experiencing lowered rates of growth and productivity. Moreover, mounting environmental concerns reinforced the theme of limits, trade-offs, and the need for hard choices. The severe economic and environmental challenges, the report argued, made greater social and political cohesion imperative.

Yet even as the need for consensus became ever more obvious, in the real world of American political and social life dissensus seemed the order of the day. Even as the need for common effort to revitalize the economy deepened, political institutions had atrophied and special interest groups had mushroomed. Thus, in a chapter on demographic developments, the report warned of increasing intergenerational conflict as age-groups competed for scarce resources. All sorts of advocacy groups based on ethnic, racial, gender, sectoral, regional, and lifestyle interests posed "a significant danger to our democracy" that made common approaches to crucial problems of productivity and energy difficult. And this at a time when "new vocal elements" and widespread cynicism about the country's political institutions were leading to "an increasing inability . . . to form effective coalitions for the common good." The commissioners detected abroad in the land a political psychology that is "self-, and not community-, centered."[31]

Occasionally, bold ambitions did surface. Thus, in the area of social justice, it posited as "goals for which we should strive in the Eighties—a guaranteed minimum income, a coherent urban policy, an effective educational system, universal health insurance, and the advancement of civil rights." Yet here, too, the motif was less the *possibilities* of achieving these desiderata than, once again, "the theme of hard choices, [which] applies to the social justice and urban policy areas just as it does to the other segments of public policy."[32]

In education, health policy, social welfare, and urban policy, the commissioners stressed repeatedly the dilemmas of attempting to combine equity, compassion, and hardheaded calculation of resources. "The goal of ending poverty," they declared, "appears to be too distant to reach in the decade ahead." They placed emphasis on efficiency of operation and outcome in regard to health and education.[33]

Recommendations for a new urban policy proved the most controversial in the entire report.[34] Offering "New Perspectives on Urban America," the commission urged the adoption of federal policies designed to help people, in place of those designed to rescue older urban centers. The decay of the great, older conurbation was, to be sure, distressing and even poignant. But new technologies, along with shifts in living patterns, regional distribution of population, and economic functions dictated in part by international trends, made the decline of some great cities inevitable. Let us, the commission urged, not attempt endlessly to re-create the cities of our nostalgic imagination, to attempt "to preserve under glass" the historic industrial city. Regarding the so-called urban renaissance of the 1970s with skepticism, it advocated shifts in federal funding to enable *people* to escape declining environments and to build new lives in more viable locales, presumably the suburbanizing areas and new highway cities. To continue federal programs premised on the notion of attempting to revitalize once thriving but now moldering (and mostly northern) cities would be to deprive people now trapped in those dead-end places of the resources they needed to relocate, retrain, and participate fully in the emerging new economy.[35]

Responding to the call of Jeremiah, the commissioners by no means, however, embraced the role of Cassandra. The United States had great strengths. "America," they insisted, "is not facing an era of inevitable economic decline and diminished capacity." It was "still a nation of relatively plentiful resources and opportunity." But the age of limits had arrived, and it was time for the American people to realize that they lived in "a land of limited wealth that cannot do everything simultaneously."[36]

The brief foreign affairs section of the report reflected this sense of limits as well. Gone was the strident clarion call of the Goals commission for the defense of freedom against a ruthless and puissant foe. Instead the Carter body advanced a far more limited view of the world, in terms of both the capabilities of America and the evil incarnated in the Soviets. Whereas the men of the Eisenhower commission had seen "Sino-Soviet" power and appeal as an awesome and at times seemingly irresistible tide, the Carter panelists took a much more skeptical look at Soviet success. True, many Americans believed that since the early 1970s, the USSR had enjoyed a favorable "correlation of forces." But *A National Agenda for the Eighties* implicitly acknowledged the role of the Sino-Soviet split in undermining the notion, widely accepted in the late 1950s, of an irresistibly advancing red tide. The Soviet Union was a powerful and resourceful foe, but its threat to America, and indeed even to the unaligned nations, lay in its tangible power, not its magnetism.

Moreover, the commissioners insisted, reports of U.S. weakness and vacillation had been greatly exaggerated. We may have had to share economic and diplomatic power with rising centers, for clearly our virtually unrivaled political, diplomatic, and economic hegemony of the period 1945 to 1970 was "unnatural and inherently transient." But neither friend nor foe should be mistaken: "We are not a crippled giant inevitably destined to lumber off to a kind of elephant graveyard for declining nations." Our nuclear power was vast; the U.S. economy was still the world's strongest, and "we produce more than 20 percent of the world's real output and are the largest single center of enterprise in research and development"; our natural resources and technological capacities were huge. American agricultural wealth still led the world. The people of the world still looked to the United States for moral and political leadership, even if new times required a lower profile in its exercise. "In the last analysis," the report concluded, "the United States is in an excellent position to engage the U.S.S.R. in a worldwide competition of ideas and systems."[37]

The harsher language of doubt and perplexity, however, trumped these occasional expressions of faith and confidence. The commissioners repeatedly cited the omnipresent "mood of discontent and pessimism," pointing to polls that revealed that 70 percent of the American people expressed at best minimal confidence in their government. They even invoked the dreaded "M" word, referring to "the impression of malaise, of pervasive discontent with the quality of life today." Gone were the heroic opportunities for wide-front advance posited in the Eisenhower commission report, which held out the message that "we could do almost anything." "The task of the Eighties," however, was a more thankless and more difficult one, for it was to find ways to "cope with the tensions between high expectations and the realities of an era of resource constraints and somewhat slower growth rates."[38]

AFTERMATH

The work of the Eisenhower commission had a much longer half-life than did Carter's. By October 1962, over two hundred thousand copies of *Goals for Americans* had been sold or otherwise distributed, and the report remained in print through the 1960s. It served as a text in innumerable civic forums, adult education classes, and college classes. Through an arrangement with the Advertising Council, the Goals report received much publicity. One handsomely produced, widely distributed poster in 1961 featured full-face portraits of Dwight Eisenhower and John F. Kennedy, with the headline above declaring "We Are Challenged as a People[—]We Are Summoned as a Nation." Newspapers awarded the initial report extensive coverage, and the follow-up forums and assemblies generated much local press attention. Commission members appeared in a series of television documentaries aired by public stations. These broadly distributed films provided the basis for organized public discussion in towns and cities around the country.[39]

A particular feature of the Eisenhower body's work was the follow-up activity coordinated by the American Assembly. Through the early 1960s, the Assembly, with funds provided by the Johnson Foundation and other private groups, held elaborate regional meetings at which hundreds of business, labor, religious, academic, and civic leaders used *Goals for Americans* as the basis for forums that typically extended over a three-day period. Local sponsorship was usually provided by a university or public affairs group, such as the Town Hall of Los Angeles.

The tone of these meetings, organized and overseen by Wriston's bright, earnest aides at the American Assembly, was sober and diligent, with the participating community leaders generally sharing the worldview of the prestigious commissioners. Even so, local participants sometimes challenged what they saw as the bland and establishment tone of *Goals for Americans*. The most notable example occurred at an assembly held at Duke University in May 1961, at which civil rights activists criticized the report's failure to highlight racial injustice and secured adoption of strong civil rights statements.[40]

Another offshoot of the Eisenhower commission's activities was the stimulus it gave, through the American Assembly, to the creation of separate goals projects in communities across the country. The most notable of these was the Goals for Dallas project, launched in December 1965 with the advice of the American Assembly, now headed by Wriston's successor, Clifford Nelson. This initiative brought together eighty-seven prominent Dallas citizens under the leadership of Mayor Erik Johnson to develop detailed projections of the city's future trajectory. By now, however, the goals concept had shed much of its Eisenhower-era concern with broad questions of public purpose and moral agenda. Johnson, who as a Texas Instruments executive had directed similar corporate efforts, made sure the Texas city's report stressed concrete issues and specific programs.

Goals for Dallas provided the one tangible link between the work of the Eisenhower and Carter commissions. When Jimmy Carter assumed the governorship of Georgia in 1971, one of his first acts was to launch Goals for Georgia, which was explicitly modeled on the Dallas experience. Directed by Sam Nunn, this program quickly developed into a vehicle for Carter's gubernatorial program of governmental reorganization, regional development, and environmental concern, as he used the ostensibly nonpartisan project as a means of direct appeal to the public, bypassing recalcitrant legislative and bureaucratic opponents.[41]

In contrast to the relatively dynamic aftermath of the Eisenhower study, the National Agenda Commission soon sank from public sight. When the report was issued in January 1981, of course, President Carter was about to leave the White House. To be sure, *Goals for Americans* was also issued during a partisan change in administrations. But in that case, the political consensus was so widely shared that the Goals panel's recommendations were fully compatible with the agenda of the new administration. The easy transition of William Bundy—the "Republican" Bundy brother—from staff director of the project to a subcabinet position in the new administration symbolized the sense of common understanding prevalent in public policy in the early 1960s. Indeed, after Kennedy's election, Bundy urged the new president to read *Goals for Americans,* whose combination of vigorous domestic advocacy and tense cold war resolve meshed closely with the perspective of Kennedy and his principal advisers.[42]

But on virtually every score, the Agenda report would have been anathema to the incoming Reagan administration. Despite its caution and language of constraint, *A National Agenda for the Eighties* still insisted on a positive role for government. Even its very language of limits, making do, and hard choices contrasted with the up-tempo tone of the new Republican regime. With a total lack of resonance within the incoming administration and with no in-place structure for further dissemination such as that enjoyed by the Goals commission through the American Assembly, the work of the Agenda participants soon sank into oblivion.

Indeed, only one feature of the Agenda report created any public interest. Reporters pounced on the urban policy recommendations in which the Carter commission urged a refocusing of federal efforts away from attempts to revitalize older industrial cities. A *Washington Post* story painted the commission's urban recommendations in bold strokes: "The United States," it paraphrased the Agenda report's careful language, "must accept the inevitable decline of cities in the Northeast and Midwest and adopt a radically new urban policy." The *New York Times* and the wire services followed suit, and for the next month controversy raged as urban politicians, editorialists, and leading columnists weighed in. Just before leaving office, Carter repudiated the urban recommendations, declaring that "we cannot abandon our older urban areas." On February 4, in one of its last acts, the commission sponsored a "public seminar" on its urban policy recommendations, but by then the new administration was in full swing, and it attracted little attention. The so-called Sunbelt Report quickly faded into oblivion.[43]

Such, too, was the fate of the overall report, *A National Agenda for the Eighties.* Whereas observers in 1961 could easily regard *Goals for Americans,* with its activist orientation, as translatable into an agenda for the incoming administration, little in the Carter commission report appealed to the triumphant Reaganites.[44] It was the economic analysis of Jude Wanniski and the alarmist reports of the Committee for the Present Danger that inspired the men and women of the new administration as they set about restoring American optimism and squaring off against the Evil Empire.[45] Apart from occasional references by commission watcher–historians such as Hugh Davis Graham and Edward Berkowitz—who served as a member of the senior staff—the work of the Carter commission has seemingly gone down the memory hole.

It has deserved a better fate. As the chapters in this volume attest, the combination of declining public confidence in government, a "rights revolution" that emboldened a wide range of interest and advocacy groups, and stark environmental, international, and economic realities presented the Carter administration with unprecedented dilemmas. Eschewing quick-fix solutions and fantastic formulas for painless plenty, the Carter commission attempted to articulate a sober and mature agenda suitable for a drastically changed economic, social, and physical environment. If it struck a pessimistic note, in contrast with the ebullience of *Goals for Americans,* it nonetheless balanced calls for fiscal restraint, diminished expectations, and regulatory curtailment with an understanding that positive public action remained essential. Its recognition that economic growth brought with it environmental and social costs posed questions that remain unaddressed, and its cautious, but clear, warnings about the dangers of American hubris in a suddenly multipolar world now seem wise, if not prescient.

FALLING APART, WINDING DOWN, FALLING AWAY

The establishment, activities, and reports of both presidential commissions reenacted, in a distinctive post–World War II idiom, the central features of the American Jeremiad. As explicated by Sacvan Berkovitch, the American Jeremiad had its origins in Puritan New England in the latter half of the seventeenth century and has remained a central strand of American political and social discourse since. It involves an explicit but internalized commitment to high ideals, indeed, to a sense of mission or purpose. It further features the periodic warning, often in stark and even despairing terms, of the nation's falling away, the apostasy of the people, on the part of prophetic voices. But the Jeremiad is not a single, enclosed wail of despair; rather, it is an ongoing discourse, elaborating the nation's sins and, eventually, articulating a strategy—invariably requiring sacrifice and renewed dedication—for stopping the decline, renewing the original commitment, and, in a distinctively American twist, promoting (in Berkovitch's words) the "release of the restless 'progressivist' energies required for the success of the venture." It reminds the people of the strength and virtue of their heritage but does so within a context of chronic unfulfillment. In Berkovitch's summary of the American Jeremiahs' resolution of the crisis, "The future, though divinely assured, was never quite there. . . . Denouncing or affirming, their vision fed on the distance between promise and fact."[46]

In *The Pursuit of American Character,* Rupert Wilkinson holds that throughout American history cultural guardians and civic spokesmen have regularly questioned the ability of the nation to fulfill its destiny. With remarkable consistency, for over two hundred years they have uttered their lamentations in terms of four fears: the fear of being owned, the fear of falling apart, the fear of winding down, and the fear of falling away. The late 1950s and the late 1970s were two periods in which what Wilkinson calls "the rich tapestry of American anxiousness" was particularly evident. In the mid-1950s and again in the mid-1970s, Soviet strength seemed on the ascendant, while America's appeared diminished and uncertain. In both cases, the country seemed to be falling away from the faith of the Fathers. America seemed perhaps to be winding down, drifting from the high standards of endeavor and achievement her Founders had established. And this seemed to be true no less during times of prosperity than in times of economic tribulation. Indeed, it seemed to some that affluence, with its corrupting and becalming effects, might be the greatest danger of all. Thus, in *The Affluent Society,* a paradigmatic book of the late 1950s, John Kenneth Galbraith depicted a country clogged with wealth, adrift in a sea of plenty.[47] Declared John F. Kennedy in 1960, "A nation replete with goods and services, confident that 'there's more where that came from,' may feel less ardor for questioning" and be less eager for noble adventure. In 1979, it was President Carter himself—the most explicitly ministerial of all our chief executives—who in his July 15 speech sounded the tocsin. These American Jeremiahs drove home the message: we were in danger of falling away, coming apart, winding down.[48]

The presidential commissions fulfilled the second part of the Jeremiah's task. They reformulated the warnings into a middle-class idiom. They subjected the charges of apostasy, betrayal, and enfeeblement to sustained scrutiny. They issued reports that, while echoing the prophets' warnings, stressed the nation's strengths and its special role. But in the distinctive discourse of the American Jeremiah, they advanced ambitious agendas, the fulfillment of which alone could validate the national project.

They did these things, of course, in sharply differing idioms. The Carter commission issued a report that was more subdued and less capacious than that of its predecessor. But even in its admonitions about limits, constraints, and difficulties, *A National Agenda for the Eighties* set out a challenging platform for the American people, one based on the assumption that only through continued change and development could the country keep faith with its heritage and carry the errand into the future.

In more mundane terms, these two presidential commissions serve as reminders of both the ruptures and continuities of recent American history. In form, process, and function the two commissions evidenced clear similarities, a fact reinforced by the frequent references made to the Goals commission in the deliberations and publications of the Agenda commission. Likewise, both initiatives revealed the faith shown by chief executives in the ability of elites—however broadly defined in the seventies—to formulate meaningful agendas for public action in a society that otherwise discourages planning, explicit goal setting, and formal social direction. The report of the Carter commission, however, serves as a rough register of how much had changed in the post-Vietnam, post-Watergate, and post-Keynesian world of the late 1970s. Readers of *Goals for Americans* might well be reminded of a world we have lost. Those perusing *A National Agenda for the Eighties* would encounter the world we have found.

NOTES

The author wishes to express his indebtedness to Ron Formisano, Bob McMahon, and, especially, Ed Berkowitz, for their thoughtful comments on earlier drafts of this chapter.

1. Sacvan Berkovitch, *The American Jeremiad* (Madison: University of Wisconsin Press, 1978), 3–30 and passim. See also Rupert Wilkinson, *The Pursuit of American Character* (New York: Harper and Row, 1988).

2. John W. Jefferies, "The 'Quest for National Purpose' of 1960," *American Quarterly* 30 (Fall 1978): 451–70; James L. Baughman, "The National Purpose and the Newest Medium: Liberal Critics of Television, 1958–1960," *Mid–America* 64 (April–July 1982): 41–55; Edward D. Berkowitz, "Commissioning the Future," *Reviews in American History* 11 (June1983): 294–99; Edward D. Berkowitz, "Jimmy Carter and the Sunbelt Report: Seeking a National Agenda," in *The Presidency and Domestic Policies of Jimmy Carter,* ed. Herbert D. Rosenbaum and Alexej Ugrinsky (Westport, Conn.: Greenwood Press, 1994), 33–44; Hugh Davis Graham, "The Ambiguous Legacy of American Presidential Commissions," *Public Historian* 7 (Spring 1985): 5–25.

3. *Public Papers of the Presidents of the United States: Dwight D. Eisenhower, 1959* (Washington, D.C.: Government Printing Office, 1959), 10–11, 757. Commentary on the perception of crisis and the activities of the Eisenhower commission is found in Douglas T. Miller and Marion Nowak, *The Fifties: The Way We Really Were* (Garden City, N.Y.: Doubleday, 1977), 17–18; William L. O'Neill, *American High: The Years of Confidence, 1945–1960* (New York: Free Press, 1986), 285; Charles C. Alexander, *Holding the Line: The Eisenhower Era, 1952–1961* (Bloomington: Indiana University Press, 1975), 268–71; and Wilkinson, *Pursuit of American Character,* 104–7.

4. "Energy and National Goals: Address to the Nation, July 15, 1979," in *Public Papers of the Presidents of the United States: Jimmy Carter* (Washington, D.C.: Government Printing Office, 1980), book 2 (1979), 1235–41; Staff to Commissioners, January 31, 1980, Background Paper: Summary of Public Opinion Trends, Box 1, President's Commission for a National Agenda for the Eighties (PCNA) Papers, Jimmy Carter Library (JCL). The chapters by Bruce Schulman, Melvyn Dubofsky, and Judith Stein, in this volume, ably outline the central economic policy dilemmas of the Carter administration.

5. Berkowitz, "Jimmy Carter and the Sunbelt Report," 34; Burton I. Kaufman, *The Presidency of James Earl Carter, Jr.* (Lawrence: University Press of Kansas, 1993), 144–45.

6. Background paper and news conference, October 24, 1979, Box 1, PCNA, Papers, JCL. Later in the same press conference, Donovan backed away from the word *goals* as being too suggestive of detailed planning. See also Hedley Donovan, Exit Interview, August 14, 1980, JCL.

7. In addition to Wriston, Kerr, Meany, Darden, and Greenewalt, the commissioners were Frank Pace, Jr. (Truman's secretary of the army and CEO of General Dynamics); James R. Killian (Eisenhower's science adviser and president of the Corporation of Massachusetts Institute of Technology); General Alfred Gruenther (former NATO chief and, in 1960, head of the American Red Cross); James Bryant Conant (former president of Harvard University, high commissioner to the Federal Republic of Germany, and analyst of the U.S. educational system); and Erwin Canham, editor of the *Christian Science Monitor* and outgoing president of the U.S. Chamber of Commerce. Federal Judge Learned Hand was also appointed, but the eighty-nine-year-old jurist resigned from the commission in October, citing health problems.

8. For a roster, along with brief biographies, of the members of the commission, see United States, President's Commission for a National Agenda for the Eighties, *A National Agenda for the Eighties: Report of the President's Commission on a National Agenda for the Eighties* (Englewood Cliffs, N.J.: Prentice-Hall, 1980), 199–207 (hereafter *Agenda*). See Berkowitz, "Jimmy Carter and the Sunbelt Report," 34–35, on the diversity of the commission's membership.

9. Elizabeth Drew, "On Giving Oneself a Hotfoot: Government by Commission," *Atlantic Monthly,* May 1968, 45–49; Frank Popper, *The President's Commissions* (New York: Twentieth Century Fund, 1970).

10. Etzioni in the *Wall Street Journal,* July 8, 1968, as quoted in Popper, *The President's Commissions,* 25. The words quoted here appear in the transcript of the executive committee meeting of November 11, 1980, Box 5, PCNA Papers, JCL. These lengthy transcripts rarely identified speakers.

11. On the American Assembly, see Travis Beal Jacobs, "Eisenhower, the American Assembly, and 1952," *Presidential Studies Quarterly* 22 (Summer 1992): 455–68. For the difficulties in getting the Goals commission in motion, see Eisenhower to Ellis Slater, June 15, 1959; Wilton D. Persons to Robert W. Woodruff, December 9, 1959; Alfred Gruenther to Eisenhower, May 27, 1959; Robert E. Merriam memorandum for the record, April 2, 1959, all in Box 941, Central Files, Official File (Files of the President's Commission on National Goals), Dwight David Eisenhower Presidential Library; Henry T. Heald to the Trustees [of the Ford Foundation], September 22, 1959, Box 18, James R. Killian Papers, Massachusetts Institute of Technology Library.

12. "Henry Merritt Wriston," *Current Biography* (1952): 654–56; "Henry Wriston Dies, Brown Head, 1937–55," *New York Times Biographical Service,* March 9, 1978. On Wriston's relationship with Eisenhower, see Robert D. Schulzinger, *The Wise Men of Foreign Affairs: The History of the Council on Foreign Relations* (New York: Columbia University Press, 1984), 82, 137–41. The beginnings of the commission's work are indicated in, for example, President's Commission on National Goals, "Current Statement of Mission," ca. February 15, 1960, copy in Erwin Canham Papers, Archives of the First Church of Christian Science, Boston, Massachusetts; minutes of the [first] meeting of the President's Commission on National Goals, February 16, 1960, vol. 1, American Assembly Papers, American Assembly office, New York.

13. There are brief biographies of the codirectors and senior staff in *National Agenda for the Eighties,* 209–14. On the Carter commission's mode of operation, see Berkowitz, "Jimmy Carter and the Sunbelt Report," and note 17.

14. Minutes of the meeting of the PCNA, February 5, 1980, Box 1, PCNA Papers, JCL.

15. President's Commission on National Goals, *Goals for Americans* (Englewood Cliffs, N.J.: Prentice-Hall, 1960), 33 (hereafter *GFA*).

16. Berkowitz, "Jimmy Carter and the Sunbelt Report"; Edward Berkowitz to Robert H. Zieger (e-mail), ca. November 1, 1996 (in author's possession).

17. The materials in, for example, Box 6, PCNA Papers, JCL, dealing with the Panel on Energy, Natural Resources, and the Environment, and Box 7, dealing with the American economy, are the bases for the characterization of the commission's mode of operation contained in this paragraph. The report-writing process is outlined in McGill's remarks, Transcript of Full Commission Meeting, November 17, 1980, Box 5, JCL, and in an undated, unsigned staff memorandum, Box 2, JCL. See also Berkowitz, "Jimmy Carter and the Sunbelt Report."

18. See, for example, William Miller, "Provocative Goals for a Hard Decade," *Life,* December 12, 1960, 108–16.

19. See, for example, Berkowitz, "Jimmy Carter and the Sunbelt Report," 33–34; Addie Wyatt response to question, Transcript of Social Justice Panel Press Conference, Chicago, July 22, 1980, Box 9, PCNA Papers, JCL.

20. Robert A. Divine, *The Sputnik Challenge* (New York: Oxford University Press, 1993), 93, 159–61.

21. Ibid. 35–41, 78, 172–78, 185; Peter L. Roman, *Eisenhower and the Missile Gap* (Ithaca, N.Y.: Cornell University Press, 1995), 33; Stephen E. Ambrose, *Eisenhower,* vol. 1, *The President* (New York: Simon and Schuster, 1984), 434–35.

22. GFA, 3–15; quotes on pages 10, 13, 7, 10–11.

23. Ibid., 15–22; quote on page 18.

24. Ibid., 18.

25. Ibid., 15. The almost pathological concern of U.S. policy makers over Soviet initiatives in the Third World is discussed in Robert J. McMahon, "The Illusion of Vulnerability: American Reassessments of the Soviet Threat, 1955–1956," *International History Review* 18 (August 1996), 591–619.

26. Henry M. Wriston, "The Individual," 51; Clinton Rossiter, "The Democratic Process," 64–65; both in *GFA.*

27. Wriston, "The Individual," 51; Rossiter, "Democratic Process," 76; "Introduction," 1–2; all in *GFA.*

28. *Agenda,* 1. These themes permeate the essays by Schulman, Dubofsky, and Stein, cited earlier, and are prominent in those on welfare policy, by James Patterson, housing and urban policy, by Thomas Sugrue, and environmental policy, by Jeffrey Stine, all in this volume, as well.

29. The quotes in this paragraph are drawn from Chairman William McGill's unpaginated "Statement," which is included in *Agenda.*

30. Ibid., 1, 4.

31. Ibid., 10, 11. The furious debates over women's issues waged within the administration (see Susan M. Hartmann's chapter in this volume), and the administration's stance with reference to labor law reform, as explicated in Martin Halpern, "Arkansas and the Defeat of Labor Law Reform in 1978 and 1994" (paper presented at the conference "The Carter Presidency: Policy Choices in the Post–New Deal Era," Jimmy Carter Library and Presidential Center, Atlanta, February 22, 1997), illustrate the Carter administration's difficulties in responding to the claims of key elements in the Democratic party's electoral constituency.

32. *Agenda,* 57–58.

33. Ibid., 57–90; quote on page 76. See also James T. Patterson's chapter in this volume.

34. Thomas J. Sugrue's chapter in this volume provides an excellent overview of the conflicting forces within the administration on urban policy.

35. *Agenda,* 64–71. See also Berkowitz, "Jimmy Carter and the Sunbelt Report."

36. Berkowitz, "Jimmy Carter and the Sunbelt Report," 5–8.

37. Ibid., 115–26.

38. Ibid., 187–92, 1–14; quotes on pages 191, 188, 1, 7–8.

39. The American Assembly subsidized the sale and distribution of *Goals for Americans* as an element in its follow-up and outreach projects. Some of these follow-up activities are indicated in Henry M. Wriston to John E. Stipp, March 29, 1961, American Assembly Papers, vol. 3. The Ad Council's efforts are detailed in a report enclosed in Theodore S. Repplier to Henry M. Wriston, August 30, 1961, American Assembly Papers.

40. There is much material, including transcripts of several assemblies, relating to these Goals-related forums and assemblies in the American Assembly Papers, vol. 3, which also

contains an undated list of the universities and civic groups with which the Assembly collaborated in the holding of assemblies. My oral history interviews with Clifford Nelson, Mystic, Conn., June 20, 1993, and Paul Eisele, San Francisco, July 21, 1994, provided additional material.

41. On the origins of Goals for Dallas, see James H. Berry to W. E. Cushen, January 15, 1968, American Assembly Papers, vol. 5. See also *Goals for Dallas* (Dallas: Goals for Dallas, 1966), and interview with Clifford Nelson, June 20, 1993. For the Dallas-Georgia link and Carter's use of Goals for Georgia, see Mattie S. Anderson, "Governor Jimmy Carter: Idealist or Realist? A Study of Carter's Commitment to Citizen Participation and Planning in the Goals for Georgia Program" (Master's thesis, Georgia State University, 1979); and Gary M. Fink, *Prelude to the Presidency: The Political Character and Legislative Leadership Style of Governor Jimmy Carter* (Westport, Conn.: Greenwood Press, 1980), 12, 17–18, 109, 171.

42. Robert H. Zieger interview with William Bundy, Princeton, N.J., June 18, 1993.

43. Berkowitz, "Jimmy Carter and the Sunbelt Report" (*Washington Post* quoted on pages 42–43); Edward Berkowitz to Robert H. Zieger (e-mail), March 28, 1997 (in author's possession); Robert Pear, "Panel on National Goals Proposes U.S. Aid for Migration to Sun Belt," *New York Times,* December 27, 1980, 1; "Tomorrow's City: Worth Arguing About," editorial, *New York Times,* December 31, 1980; John Herbers, "President Opposes Report Urging Shift to Sunbelt," *New York Times,* January 17, 1981, 1; Robert J. Gallivan, City Clerk, Hartford, Connecticut, proclamation, January 26, 1981, Box 2, PCNA Papers, JCL; statement of PCNA Commissioner Robert Benson, February 4, 1918, Box 2, PCNA Papers, JCL. See also Sugrue, "Jimmy Carter's Urban Policy Crisis."

44. Indeed, *The Economist* (December 12, 1960) titled its coverage of the PCNG report "An Agenda for Kennedy."

45. Committee on the Present Danger, *Alerting America: The Papers of the Committee on the Present Danger,* ed. Charles Tyroler II (Washington, D.C.: Pergamon-Brassey's, 1984), ix–xi, xv–xxii; Ronald Reagan, *An American Life* (New York: Simon and Schuster, 1990), 217, 294–95; Jerry W. Sanders, *Peddlers of Crisis: The Committee on the Present Danger and the Politics of Containment* (Boston: South End Press, 1983), 277–83; Jude Wanniski, *The Way the World Works: How Economies Fail—and Succeed* (New York: Basic Books, 1978); David Stockman, *The Triumph of Politics: How the Reagan Revolution Failed* (New York: Harper and Row, 1986), 44–99.

46. Berkovitch, *The American Jeremiad,* 3–30; quote on page 23. Berkovitch cites Clinton Rossiter, author of the *Goals for America* essay on "The Democratic Process," on the distinctively middle-class character of the American "errand."

47. Wilkinson, *Pursuit of American Character,* 72–80; John Kenneth Galbraith, *The Affluent Society* (New York: Viking, 1958).

48. Wilkinson, *Pursuit of American Character,* 53–81, 113–15; quotes on 72, 80–81 (Kennedy, *Life,* September 26, 1960); Berkovitch, *American Jeremiad,* 3–30.

3

Slouching toward the Supply Side: Jimmy Carter and the New American Political Economy

Bruce J. Schulman

"Are you better off than you were four years ago?" With that pointed question, Ronald Reagan defined the 1980 presidential election as a referendum on Jimmy Carter's economic policies. "Is it easier for you to go and buy things in stores than it was four years ago?" Reagan asked at the dramatic climax of the presidential debate. "Is there more or less unemployment?"[1] For several weeks the Carter campaign had successfully focused the nation on Reagan's apparent extremism, raising doubts about the Californian's fitness for office that had narrowed his once overwhelming lead in the opinion polls. But Reagan's devastating queries redirected attention to Carter's dismal economic record, to a "misery index"—a combination of the inflation and unemployment rates—that had swollen from 12 to nearly 20 percent. Carter's momentum stalled, Reagan picked up endorsements from labor and African American leaders, and the Republican went on to win a historic victory.[2]

Reagan's questions about Carter's economic leadership not only shaped the 1980 election, they set the terms of debate for scholarly and journalistic evaluations of the Carter presidency. Early assessments reiterated Reagan's appraisal of Carter's failures. Dubbing him "Jimmy Hoover," contemporary commentators suggested that Carter had made "his own name a synonym for economic mismanagement," compiling so bleak a record as to rival "Herbert Hoover's dawdling at the onset of the Great Depression." Even former administration officials lambasted Carter's presidency as inept, passionless, confused. A 1983 survey of historians ranked Carter twenty-fifth on a chart of presidential greatness; among twentieth-century chief executives, only Nixon, Harding, and Coolidge earned poorer grades.[3]

By the mid-1980s, however, a more sympathetic historical evaluation of the Carter presidency had emerged. Stressing the crushing economic conditions Carter faced and the political constraints under which he operated, this second wave of

51

studies credited the administration with significant achievements. In the light of Reagan's massive deficits, Carter's efforts to balance the budget won renewed respect. One econometric analysis even asserted that Carter's economic policy record compared favorably with that of almost every previous postwar president. Rather than directionless flip-flops, the administration's apparently inconsistent fiscal policies represented a stable, consistent response to prevailing economic conditions. On subsequent presidential surveys, Carter moved up several notches.[4]

Many of these favorable reassessments emphasized the tensions between fighting unemployment and controlling inflation, between expanding social programs and balancing the budget, between satisfying influential constituencies in the Democratic party and appealing to a more conservative national electorate wary of special interests. The portrait of President Carter emerging from these accounts is one of a Clintonian "New Democrat" arrived sadly before his time—before a decade of tight monetary policy had ironed inflation out of the American economy and before twelve years of conservative Republican presidencies had trimmed the power and tamed the demands of Democratic interest groups. Carter's tenure represented a "transitional Democratic presidency, in which the old politics weren't really working . . . and nobody had really defined the new ones yet."[5]

Most recently, the tide has begun to turn again, with the latest studies conceding the difficulties Carter faced but finding failing or mediocre marks justified.[6] Still, even these nuanced accounts remain obsessed with scorecard history, with rating the Carter presidency as a success or failure. Such is only to be expected in assessing the presidency, when opinion polls and academic surveys constantly track presidential reputations. Narrow scorecard history is particularly rife in assessing Carter's economic policy; unforgiving numbers—the Consumer Price Index (CPI), the unemployment rate, the budget deficit—offer clear bases for measurement.

But scorecard history often obscures more than it reveals; the obsessive interest in success or failure neglects the broader significance of presidential action. Carter's economic policies marked a decisive watershed in American political economy—the emergence of a post–New Deal orthodoxy in the conception of economic policy and of new popular attitudes toward business, government, and the market. They also laid the blueprint for the distinctive American response to the international crises of welfare state financing and double-digit inflation in the 1970s and 1980s.

ECONOMIC POLICY IN THE CARTER WHITE HOUSE: A BRIEF REVIEW

Jimmy Carter entered the White House during a major crisis in American economic life, amid the disintegration of the long, sweet summer of postwar prosperity. Unprecedented in its size, scope, and duration, that boom had touched nearly every American; it lifted blue-collar workers and their families into comfortable middle-class homes, it stimulated laggard regions, it made possible the liberalism of John F. Kennedy's New Frontier and Lyndon Johnson's Great Society. During the 1970s, the bubble burst. Economic growth and productivity advances slowed. A new term, *stagflation,* entered the lexicon, signifying a virtually inconceivable combination of galloping inflation with anemic growth and tenacious unemployment.[7]

Stagflation defied the reigning economic orthodoxy. It left many policy intellectuals, including Charles Schultze, the future chairman of Carter's Council of Economic Advisers (CEA), scrambling to explain the seemingly impossible conjuncture of joblessness and inflation without throwing overboard their basic faith in neo-Keynesian fiscal management. At the same time, OPEC (Organization of Petroleum Exporting Countries) oil shocks, wild international currency fluctuations, and the first serious peacetime shortages in the nation's history made it seem that Americans no longer controlled their own economic destiny.[8]

Faced with the seemingly intractable challenges of stagflation, Carter entered the White House with additional commitments to a wide range of social and macroeconomic policies—deregulation, energy conservation, minimum wage increases, national health insurance—that crosscut his basic objectives to restrain inflation and prevent recession. In the short run, for example, decontrolling energy would raise prices and threaten layoffs in the automobile industry. A comprehensive national health insurance program would torpedo the balanced budget. Civil service reform required the support of public employee unions, tempering the administration's efforts to cap federal workers' pay raises in the fight against inflation. "One always knew that he wanted to spend as little money as possible," domestic policy adviser Stuart Eizenstat recalled, "and yet at the same time he wanted welfare reform, he wanted national health insurance, he wanted job training programs." Carter and his key economic advisers attempted to balance these extensive, crosscutting commitments by keeping a quick trigger finger on the policy controls—creating a tendency to zigzag between stimulus and contraction as economic conditions changed. So often did the administration submit austere March revisions to more expansive January budget proposals that one wag discerned a pattern of holiday cheer followed by Lenten repentance.[9]

Staff chaos increased this appearance of vacillation and confusion in economic policy. The administration began with a large, unwieldy Economic Policy Group (EPG), containing several cabinet members, the Office of Management and Budget (OMB) and Domestic Policy Staff (DPS) directors, the vice president, and the CEA chairman. Some meetings assembled as many as forty people. The group rarely reached consensus; EPG memos presented the president with too many options and discordant points of view. The lack of coordination on economic policy led to embarrassing contradictions in public statements, and nearly all key policy makers felt frustrated by their lack of influence. In the summer of 1977, Carter took steps to coordinate economic policy making and dissemination, but the confusion continued. Feeling like a fifth wheel, inflation czar Alfred Kahn wanted to resign in 1979 and was shocked to discover that he was really a "seventh wheel," that both CEA chairman Charles Schultze and Domestic Policy Adviser Stuart Eizenstat also felt out of the loop on economic policy decisions.[10]

Despite the apparent confusion, Carter's economic record formed a clear pattern. The economy boomed during the Carter years, experiencing three years of rapid growth. Real per capita income rose, and unemployment, while remaining high, was lower than in the Ford or Reagan years. Still, the rapid growth proved unhealthy. Like a cancer, the boom carried with it staggering inflation, a deteriorating dollar, and finally a severe election year recession.[11] Carter's economic policies fell essentially into three periods: 1977, when the administration focused on economic stimulus to combat the Ford recession and relieve unemployment; the battle against inflation in 1978–79; and the recession and run-up to the election in 1980. Over the course of these three policy regimes, the Carter administration shifted gradually away from neo-Keynesianism to monetarist and supply-side thinking, from an emphasis on growth and unemployment to an all-out attack on inflation, from short-term fiscal management to long-term structural change. Carter's economic policy shoved aside the legacies of the New Deal and the Great Society and laid the groundwork for the conservative "Reagan Revolution."[12]

THE 1977 STIMULUS

At the beginning of the Carter presidency, fiscal stimulus topped the administration's economic priorities. During the campaign, unemployment had been the nation's most pressing concern. A November 1976 Gallup poll reported that 31 percent of Americans ranked joblessness as the most important problem facing the nation; five months later, 39 percent listed unemployment as their chief concern. During the transition, Carter's advisers raced to develop a stimulus program, which the president sent up to Capitol Hill immediately after he took office. The package included small permanent tax reductions, a public service jobs program, stepped-up spending for public works, and a one-time-only fifty-dollar rebate to every taxpayer. CEA chairman Charles Schultze defended the package in Keynesian terms, blaming the recession on insufficient demand and suggesting that boosting consumer spending would speed economic recovery. With unemployment still high, Schultze assured the House budget committee that Carter's economic proposals would not reignite inflation. The nation suffered from "momentum inflation," Schultze asserted, and "this kind of inflation has not been and will not be cured by a policy of sluggish recovery, high unemployment, and idle plant capacity. Equally important, it will not be accelerated by a prudent policy of economic stimulus that restores a steady and sustainable rate of economic recovery."[13]

Carter's stimulus fell short of returning to the liberal economic policies of the Kennedy and Johnson years. The president tried to hold spending for public works and public service employment well below the levels desired by congressional Democrats. He tried to devise automatic triggers that would shut off program funding as soon as unemployment fell. He fought organized labor and congressional Democrats to moderate increases in the minimum wage. Most important, in April 1977, Carter withdrew the proposed fifty-dollar rebate, which had been intended as a single concentrated dose of economic stimulation. The president had harbored doubts about the proposal from the beginning, and as the economy improved and the need for such medicine diminished, he decided to change course. Budget cutters in OMB thought it a "wise and courageous decision," but the withdrawal unleashed a "firestorm of criticism from Capitol Hill," angering congressional leaders who had shepherded the proposal through the House of Representatives despite their own reservations. The rebate cancellation also made Carter appear a waffler on economic policy, creating an image that he never would shake.[14]

Nonetheless, the thrust of economic policy during Carter's first year pointed in a traditional Democratic direction. Carter signed the minimum wage bill in November 1977, with a very strong liberal speech designed to please organized labor. The president never mentioned the need for restraint in wage demands nor his efforts to temper the bill's inflationary effects. In January 1978, Carter's State of the Union Address and economic report continued to name a "high employment economy" as the administration's number one economic priority. Reducing inflation ranked third, below relying on private investment to lead economic expansion and job creation.[15]

As the first anniversary of Carter's inauguration approached, the OMB produced a summary of first-year domestic accomplishments. The stimulus package featured largely in this official reckoning. Noted achievements included $4 billion in public works programs, creating about 200,000 jobs, a $1-billion increase in countercyclical revenue sharing, 425,000 new slots in public service employment and training programs, and a major youth employment program. "As a result, in part, of the stimulus package," the first year summary concluded, "the economy *has* improved" (emphasis in original).[16]

These "accomplishments" would soon come to haunt Carter's economic policy makers. Analysts continue to debate the direct inflationary effects of the stimulus programs—even OMB director James McIntyre and his chief economist Van Ooms disagreed on this point. But the emphasis during the first year on unemployment and recovery featured a combination of policies that heated up the inflationary spiral and became apparent only in later years. During the stimulus phase, the administration made inflationary commitments on farm price supports, public service jobs, and the minimum wage. More important, first-year policies created expectations for employment programs and other budgetary goodies; they failed to teach the constituencies the need for restraint, making such sacrifices a tougher sell in years ahead.[17]

The final months of Carter's first year in Washington, however, featured a shift in emphasis for domestic policy. The economy replaced the energy crisis as the administration's principal focus. At the same time, inflation gradually supplanted unemployment as the nation's number one economic problem. To be sure, President Carter had closely monitored rising prices and wages during his first months in the White House. Inflation had slowed steadily during the last two years of the Ford administration, but rapid fuel and food price jumps in the winter of 1977 almost doubled the prevailing rate and neared double-digit levels in January 1977. Carter opened an April press conference with an announcement of mild, voluntary anti-inflation measures. Still, he refused to commit himself to an all-out war on inflation: "We have not been willing to control inflation by deliberately dampening the economy nor holding down employment." Responding to questions, Carter rejected the suggestion that his cancellation of the rebate and concern about inflation indicated he was "leaning in the conservative direction" and mimicking his predecessor's fiscal conservatism.[18]

By the fall of 1977, inflation fears had mounted. Pat Caddell's tracking polls revealed that "energy has declined and inflation and unemployment are back up to numbers 1 and 2" as major issue concerns of the American people. Carter's economic advisers nixed more expansive proposals to continue the stimulus program and developed a series of options for a voluntary incomes policy. But public statements reflected a continued unwillingness to move too boldly. In September letters to Senators John Tower and Robert Byrd, the administration went on record against both mandatory wage and price controls and formal numerical guidelines for voluntary compliance. The threat still seemed manageable. Within the White House, Charles Schultze predicted that without vigorous action, the inflation rate would hover around 6.5 percent.[19]

As the first year closed, the staff discussed priorities for 1978. Vice President Mondale suggested that the president make the economy the administration's premier issue by delivering a short, punchy State of the Union Address entirely devoted to economic issues, but Carter's domestic policy staff splashed cold water on Mondale's proposals. The administration's own economic projections suggested that Carter could compile no better than a C record on the economy, with inflation and unemployment holding steady. "I do not think the President sees himself as, or will want to run for reelection as, a 'man of the economy,'" DPS staffer Bob Ginsburg argued. "I expect he will want to offer a broad gauged record of accomplishment (including a number of areas in which our performance is likely to be better than it will be on the economy)." Most likely, Ginsburg concluded, "we would *not* want to face an up or down vote from the public on the crucial issues of inflation, unemployment, and the budget deficit."[20] (emphasis in original)

Carter rejected Mondale's suggestion to focus narrowly on economic issues, even though he did declare that "our main task at home is the nation's economy." With inflation threats mounting, he warned that his new budget would be "tight and lean" but promised it would remain compassionate enough to meet the nation's most pressing social needs. In fact, the inflation-fighting overtures remained largely symbolic. The budget included increased spending requests for domestic programs and a $25-billion tax cut. Of course, Carter's team neither understood the long-term decline in productivity growth nor predicted the OPEC price increases that would send the CPI spiraling out of control. In the opening salvo of the war on inflation, the president had fired blanks.[21]

THE BATTLE AGAINST INFLATION

The failed battle against inflation was not simply a matter of misjudging the threat. From the start, Carter and his top officials understood the intractability and political dangers that inflation posed. In fact, Carter himself, given his native fiscal conservatism and desire to balance the budget, seemed more alert to inflation dangers than his principal economic and domestic policy advisers. And, even before he took office, the president's confidant, fellow Georgian Bert Lance, warned that Carter's reelection hopes hinged on bringing down inflation.

Nor did Carter's inflation fighters suffer from a lack of imagination. They developed and considered a panoply of weapons for the battle against the insidious wage-price spiral: fiscal restraint, including the promise of a balanced budget; pressuring the Federal Reserve for monetary contraction; jawboning labor and business leaders; regulatory reform; incomes policy; procurement controls and repeal of the Davis-Bacon Act, which set wage standards for federal contractors; cuts in federal government employment and salaries; aggressive enforcement of the antitrust laws; credit controls; and a wide variety of tax measures, including a federal buyout of state and local sales taxes, real-wage insurance for workers, and investment incentives for business.

President Carter also received a broad range of policy advice. At one end of the spectrum, the Treasury Department, the OMB, and loyal Georgians like Jody Powell and Jerry Rafshoon insisted on an all-out attack on inflation. They recommended tightening the budgetary screws, even if doing so stalled the economy or antagonized key Democratic constituencies. OMB director James McIntyre wanted the president to send up a balanced budget in January 1978, taking the political heat and the inevitable recession early in his term and appealing to fiscally conservative middle America. McIntyre and Powell both advocated a tougher stance vis-à-vis organized labor.[22] At the other end of the spectrum, the Labor Department, the Department of Health, Education, and Welfare (HEW), the Environmental Protection Agency (EPA), and the congressional liaison staff sought more expansionary policies. They touted the needs and values of specific spending programs, warned against offending unions, farmers, and other crucial constituencies, and fought efforts to reduce environmental, health, and safety regulations.[23]

Between these factions sat middle-of-the-roaders like CEA chairman Charles Schultze and Domestic Policy Adviser Stuart Eizenstat. They wanted to restrain inflation without causing a contraction (Schultze's emphasis) or unduly alienating key constituencies (Eizenstat's). This group included Robert Strauss, the president's first Special Counselor on Inflation, and, reluctantly, Special Inflation Adviser Alfred Kahn. Kahn personally favored a harder line on government spending and deregulation than his fellow middle-of-the-roaders but found himself forced to compromise. "When you have Doug Fraser of the United Auto Workers in your office saying that if you ever deregulated gas or crude oil, we could kiss goodbye any chance that the Automobile workers would comply with the [wage and price] guidelines, obviously I found myself dragging my heels on deregulation." These moderates won out, not out of any coherent strategy of splitting the difference but by a less conscious series of incremental decisions, following the path of least resistance.[24]

Carter's initial sallies against inflation came amid the energy and stimulus focus of the spring of 1977. Federal Reserve chairman Arthur Burns urged Carter to take extreme steps, confessing that some were politically unpalatable; Eizenstat scribbled "No!" on recommendations like lowering the minimum wage for teenagers and repealing the Davis-Bacon Act. Instead, Carter opted for Schultze's milquetoast program of jawboning, promised economies, and regulatory review, rejecting even the clear targets for voluntary wage and price standards that Eizenstat and the DPS recommended. No one could dispute Eizenstat's conclusion that *"this is not a tough anti-inflation program,"* (emphasis in original).[25]

The administration stepped up its efforts in 1978. Carter announced firm voluntary guidelines in January and appointed Robert Strauss as special counselor on inflation three months later. Calling upon his formidable skills as a lobbyist and wheeler-dealer, Strauss set up an impressive "jawboning" operation. At the same time, President Carter spurned more serious proposals, such as McIntyre's plan for draconian budget cuts, because 1978 was an election year and congressmen needed to bring home the bacon to their constituents. The president also rejected recommendations to suspend meat import quotas and to veto the tax bill Congress had passed, one quite different from the tax reform he had proposed.[26]

Carter's tepid policies failed to restrain inflation. In August 1978, chaos in international currency markets dropped the dollar to a new low against the German mark and the Japanese yen. The inflation rate hurtled upward. George Meany denounced an agreement with the postal workers that kept pay increases within the administration guidelines, assuring that the rank and file would reject the contract and infuriating President Carter. In that atmosphere of crisis, Jerry Rafshoon, Carter's "image maker" and communications adviser, sent the president an impassioned alarm. "It is impossible to overestimate the importance of the inflation issue to your presidency," Rafshoon warned. "It affects every American in a very palpable way. It causes insecurity and anxiety. It affects the American Dream." Rafshoon insisted that the nation remained favorably disposed toward Carter but wanted a "President who is 'in control.'" Failure to "demonstrate some control over inflation will make it very difficult for most Americans to be enthusiastic about your Presidency." Rafshoon recommended the toughest possible anti-inflation program; "it would be difficult to err on the side of too tough a program." Such staunchness, however, would cast down "the gauntlet with George Meany—if not the whole labor leadership. The business community won't be happy either." Rafshoon suggested that Carter immediately request national television time for a bold assault on inflation. The president returned the memo with a handwritten note—"Jerry OK."[27]

But it was not to be. Eizenstat convinced the president to delay the announcement, leaving time for his staff to devise a program and to prepare the ground for the announcement with congressional leaders, agency heads, and key interest groups. Nearly two months of internal debate and negotiations ensued. The administration also undertook a program of briefings and outreach on the inflation package.[28]

This tortuous process culminated in Carter's October 24, 1978, address from the Oval Office. Carter's speech was characteristically modest. He confessed to not having all the answers to the inflation problem and called on the American people to join together in the fight, challenging "those that say . . . that we have lost our ability to act as a nation rather than as a collection of special interests." Carter also announced a series of new initiatives. He promised to cut the federal budget deficit for fiscal year 1980 to $33 billion, a hard-and-fast commitment that cheered budget hawks in his administration. He rejected Rafshoon's call for a federal hiring freeze but promised to fill only one of every two vacancies in the national service. He established new wage and price guidelines, and limited federal procurement to contractors who obeyed those standards. He also endorsed Schultze's proposal for real-wage insurance, a program guaranteeing workers who accepted contracts under the guidelines that their income would at least keep pace with inflation.[29]

That speech represented a genuine turning point in administration policy. Until then, most of Carter's advisers, including Schultze and Eizenstat, had underrated the seriousness of inflation. They thought they could still control it while fighting unemployment and pursuing other goals. After October 1978, nearly everyone in the White House accepted the need for real restraint. Carter signaled this new discipline in the weeks after his speech by vetoing four pieces of legislation, a dramatic change for a president who eschewed the veto during his first year in office.[30]

Carter also appointed Alfred Kahn as his Special Adviser on Inflation and chairman of the Council on Wage and Price Stability. The outspoken former professor and expert on the economics of regulation had won wide acclaim as the architect of airline deregulation. He brought instant credibility to the president's battle against inflation. One journalist described Kahn as "the rumpled professor with the thick stack of briefing papers seemingly sewn to his arm, the man whose combination of self-deprecating wit and breathtaking, almost pathological, candor caused him to say (it sometimes seemed) whatever unedited phrase happened to pop into his head." Kahn accepted the role of inflation czar despite serious reservations about the potential effectiveness of the president's program. Inflation, Kahn believed, "was not just an economic problem but a profoundly social problem—a sign of a society in some degree in dissolution, in which individuals and groups seek their self-interest and demand money compensation and government programs that simply add up to more than the economy is capable of supplying." The position of inflation czar offered only an "unmanageable, amorphous, social, economic, political, inspirational task" with insufficient authority. But the president's request was "irresistible."[31]

The new urgency led the White House to reconsider measures previously rejected as too draconian—rollback of the minimum wage, strict regulatory control, buyouts of state and local sales taxes, antitrust squeezes on the food industry, and credit controls. But the administration never adopted a coherent policy, articulated it effectively, or stood by it against countervailing pressures. Instead, it abandoned a federal pay cap because it interfered with civil service reform, and it refused to tangle with milk and sugar producers. Tough options remained on the drawing board when OPEC launched a new round of oil price increases.[32]

OPEC's action combined with other factors to produce double-digit inflation. The inflation rate, 6.5 percent in 1977 and 7.7 percent in 1978 despite Carter's best efforts, careened out of control. For 1979, the annual rate was 11.3 percent, cracking the double-digit barrier. The administration appeared powerless to deal with it. OPEC's hikes ensured the failure of the voluntary guidelines; management lacked the resolve to refuse pay increases, and labor declined to moderate its demands. The administration then negotiated a "historic Accord" with organized labor, the inevitable inflated adjective and capital "A" disguising a retreat, an attempt to purchase labor's cooperation by raising the approved level for pay increases from 7 to 9.5 percent. Cabinet departments failed to cooperate with Kahn's inflation council. When the OMB graded departments on their regulatory reform efforts, it passed out mostly Cs and Ds.[33]

Polls showed that an overwhelming majority of Americans regarded runaway inflation as the nation's most severe problem. Failure to rein it in was most often reported as the administration's major failure. At the same time, Carter sank to record lows in the approval ratings; the mark of 33 percent approval he registered in a June 1979 *New York Times*–CBS poll scored lower than even the troughs for Gerald Ford and Lyndon Johnson. Carter's attempts to stop the hemorrhaging with the "malaise" speech and his cabinet reshuffle failed.[34]

After that fiasco, the focus of the inflation fight turned to the Federal Reserve and its new chairman, Paul Volcker. The White House, of course, only exerts indirect control over monetary policy through appointments to the board and its powers of persuasion with Federal Reserve governors. In March 1977, Carter had replaced the sitting chairman, Arthur Burns, with G. William Miller, whose stewardship of the board remained very much in sync with the general thrust of Carter's economic policies. Although the Federal Reserve under Miller responded to mounting inflation by raising interest rates, Miller opposed any extreme actions to shrink the money supply or contract the economy. Unsurprisingly, Miller failed to slow monetary expansion; the money supply, so-called M1, grew faster during the first three years of Carter's presidency than at any time since World War II. Economic analysts, particularly those of the monetarist persuasion, blamed this uncontrolled monetary expansion for the too rapid growth and crippling inflation of the late 1970s. After the cabinet reshuffle brought Miller into the Treasury, Carter reassured the financial markets by appointing Paul Volcker chairman of the Federal Reserve. Volcker immediately prescribed bitter medicine; rather than manipulating interest rates, he sought to slow monetary growth directly by controlling banks' reserves. Schultze and top White House officials opposed the move. They expected monetary restraint from Volcker but feared the recession his extreme approach would bring during an election year. In the end, Carter acquiesced, accepting an election year downturn and promising not to criticize Volker. As Schultze later put it, in a period of high inflation, the Federal Reserve "is the only game in town." The president "can't afford to tangle with them." Interest rates immediately skyrocketed to 15 percent, the dollar stabilized, and the economy stalled.[35]

1980: RECESSION AND "REVITALIZATION"

As the nation waited for the expected recession, Carter unveiled his fiscal year 1981 budget in January 1980. Printed in green on white, the Carter-Mondale campaign colors, the economic report represented the administration's final attempt to have it both ways. The budget included the steep defense increases President Carter had promised NATO leaders and a number of favors for Democratic constituencies in health, education, and employment spending. But the budget also stressed fiscal restraint; Carter eschewed a recession-avoiding tax cut and projected a $16-billion deficit, less than half that of earlier estimates. The plan pleased no one. The budgetary goodies hardly satisfied liberal Democrats rallying around Senator Ted Kennedy's challenge to Carter's renomination. The nation's leading newspapers and media outlets condemned Carter for his timidity; a *New York Times* editorial conceded that Carter's "decision to take a recession in an election year may be unusual" but concluded that "the nation should be at war against inflation. The President is still toying with a pea shooter." Worst of all, the financial community panicked upon learning that the president would renege on his long-announced commitment to a balanced budget. Inflation accelerated, reaching 18 percent in February 1980, the bond market collapsed, and interest rates approached a usurious 20 percent. The expected recession arrived in force.[36]

Carter responded with a revised budget and an intensified anti-inflation program. "Present high inflation threatens the security of our nation," Carter warned a national audience. "Since my economic and budget reports were made to the Congress and to the people in January rapid changes in world events and economic prospects have made it necessary to intensify our anti-inflation fight." Carter introduced a new, balanced budget with steep spending cuts, "not just cutting the bureaucratic fat" but painful "cuts in good and worthwhile programs." He ordered a freeze on federal civilian employment, a ten cent per gallon gasoline conservation fee, and stepped-up monitoring of the voluntary wage and price controls. While both Senator Kennedy and Republican contender Ronald Reagan promised tax cuts, Carter offered only targeted tax relief for investment "after fiscal discipline is achieved." He also announced temporary controls on consumer credit and asked Americans to stop buying goods and services with borrowed money.[37]

The new program offered the right medicine at precisely the wrong time. The credit controls worked all too well; Americans responded beyond expectations to the president's call for discipline. Consumer spending plummeted. The second quarter of 1980 showed the steepest drop in GNP in American history. The recession caused chaos in the Carter White House. Despite the administration's best efforts to hold the line on federal spending, which alienated some Democratic constituencies, the downturn threw the budget out of balance, leaving a bigger deficit than when Carter took office. That allowed Republicans to attack Carter as a free-spending liberal despite his considerable economic and political sacrifices on the altar of fiscal restraint. Meanwhile, the staff struggled to develop antirecessionary measures without upsetting the inflation program. Its frustration was palpable. DPS staffers concluded a list of recession-fighting options for Stu Eizenstat by suggesting "a program to provide muzzles for economists working in Politically-distressed areas." Eizenstat marked it with an exclamation point.[38]

As the "quickie recession" dragged into the election season, the administration devised a new long-term "economic revitalization plan" for the fall campaign. While some aides believed they had developed "a political economic strategy that could neutralize the economic issue this Fall," the plan announced in August rounded up the usual suspects of limited tax incentives, extended unemployment benefits, and modest new social welfare initiatives. The plan got little traction with the media or the electorate, and Carter trailed badly as long as the economy remained the principal issue. The Carter campaign focused instead on Reagan's fitness for office, a strategy that gained ground until Reagan reminded Americans that they were not better off than they had been four years earlier.[39]

TOWARD A NEW ORTHODOXY

Carter's economic policies starkly revealed the dilemmas for Democratic policy makers in the post–New Deal era. Carter fashioned economic policy as the nation embarked on a new economic regime, adjusting to the end of the long postwar boom and the end of unquestioned U.S. international hegemony. The 1970s saw a thorough internationalization of the U.S. economy. In that decade, reliance on imports and exports, measured as percentages of GNP, more than doubled. American overseas investment and foreign investment in the United States nearly tripled. Carter faced not only a radically altered economic situation but also a transformed political landscape. He was the first Democrat to win the presidency after the demise of the New Deal coalition. Carter's economic policies negotiated these transitions by defining a distinctive American response to an international economic crisis and by ushering in a new conservative orthodoxy in American political economy.[40]

President Carter and his top advisers understood they were dealing with an international crisis. Throughout the industrialized world, economic stagnation, slowing productivity advances, and escalating demands for government spending had produced vicious trade-offs. Western governments could no longer finance their welfare states, relieve unemployment, and restrain inflation. In many respects, Carter's incomes policy and fiscal restraint produced better results than similar efforts in Great Britain, Italy, and Japan. Even in Germany, where the ghosts of Weimar made fighting inflation the top priority, the rate exceeded 13 percent in early 1980. The late 1970s and 1980s, then, witnessed a worldwide crisis of the welfare state. Economic decline and global competition precipitated political realignments throughout the Western world, but whichever party proved victorious at the polls, fiscal conservatism and retrenchment of social programs proved the order of the day.[41]

The administration suffered the same pressures and the same political fate of many other governments in the late 1970s and early 1980s. Reagan's election in 1980 and his politics of retrenchment echoed the victories of conservative parties in Britain (1979), Germany (1982), Canada (1984), and Sweden (1976 and 1979). Even those nations that reversed decades of rightist rule and elected socialist presidents in the early 1980s embraced fiscal conservatism and tightened the belt on social spending.[42]

Carter's policies and the subsequent "Reagan Revolution," however, revealed more than a few peculiar local implications of a global political shift. They displayed certain signature features that distinguished the American experience from the Western European norm. First, only the United States diverted a larger portion of public resources to defense during the late 1970s and 1980s. Other nations' military budgets swelled temporarily—Great Britain's in the wake of the Falklands War, for example. But by the end of the decade even Mrs. Thatcher allotted defense a skimpier share of government spending. During the early 1970s, the United States had avoided large deficits by running down the defense budget. Carter initially continued this practice. When he revised Ford's final budget in March 1977, Carter further reduced budget authority for defense by $2.7 billion. After crises in Afghanistan, Latin America, and Iran, Carter reversed field. He promised the NATO allies and delivered real growth in Pentagon spending. Reagan continued this trend.[43]

Second, most European governments compensated for the whittling away of their welfare states by redirecting public resources toward the needy. As these governments slimmed down, they shifted resources away from defense and education, slightly increased but basically held steady the share of outlays dedicated to health care, and boosted resources for welfare and social security.[44] They thus cushioned broad-based cutbacks to some extent by protecting benefits for the most downtrodden. Even Margaret Thatcher concentrated her attacks on the universalistic components of British income security programs. Thatcher's government relied more heavily on means-tested programs targeted to the very poor.[45]

In the United States the poor bore the brunt of welfare state retrenchment without the cushion that Europeans had provided. Carter never forgot the downtrodden altogether: his initial tax reform package pressed for progressivity; he stabilized Social Security financing and slowed its drain on the federal budget; and he cared more than his successor about job training and other programs for the needy. Still, political and budgetary constraints ensured that efforts to reduce the deficit would center on social welfare programs. OMB official Van Ooms assumed, probably correctly, that a second Carter administration would have been less harsh on the working poor than Reagan's, but Carter's final budgets initiated the trend—a stark contrast from the European pattern.[46]

Finally, neither Carter nor Reagan ever prescribed the harsh medicine of fiscal conservatism that prevailed, however reluctantly, on the Continent.[47] Alone among conservative budget- and benefit-cutting regimes, Reagan's America embraced the palliative sugar pill of supply-side economics. President Reagan insisted that lower taxes would generate higher revenues—that he could increase defense spending and balance the budget with few painful economies. During the 1980 election, Carter vociferously attacked Reagan for his irresponsible embrace of the "economics of joy." He repeatedly lectured Americans to face the reality of limits and the need for a balanced budget. But Carter could never build the case for fiscal restraint or resist the temptations of tax cuts, program enhancements, and other fiscal stimuli. While small by subsequent standards, Carter left behind a budget shortfall larger than when he took office, despite three years of boom in which to close the gap. Neither Democrat Jimmy Carter nor his Republican successor proved willing or able to practice the fiscal restraint they preached.[48]

To be sure, Carterism represented a milder version of all three distinctive features. Lacking the messianic anticommunism of Reagan, Carter would have controlled defense expenditures more than Reagan and tempered cuts in social spending. He likely would have generated smaller budget deficits. But the differences remain matters of degree rather than kind, for Carter pioneered a new approach to economic policy. Long before the Reaganites entered the White House, the Carter administration had already rejected the neo-Keynesian orthodoxy that had governed economic policy making in the United States for a generation and was slouching toward a new one, toward monetarism and supply-side economics.

Carter came to power at a time when established views within the economics profession were very much under challenge. During the Kennedy and Johnson years, confidence in Keynesian fiscal management reached its apex. Most economic policy makers had assumed that a deft touch on the fiscal levers could offset downturns in the business cycle and maintain full employment. Neo-Keynesians assumed a clear trade-off between inflation and unemployment along the so-called Phillips curve and blamed the inflation of the late 1960s and early 1970s on chance exogenous events, changes in the labor market, and an improper application of the fiscal controls. By 1970, however, monetarist economists challenged these notions. Led by Milton Friedman, monetarists tied changes in economic activity principally to fluctuations in the money supply and emphasized the importance of long-term expectations, including expectations about the direction of economic policy, to sustaining inflation and an inflationary psychology. The monetarist critique not only explained a simultaneous upward trend in both prices and joblessness but also suggested real limits in government's ability to relieve unemployment over the long term. The new thinking placed a premium on monetary policy as the instrument to control inflation and on long-term growth over short-term fiscal management.[49]

Nonetheless, when the Carter administration took office, a chastened neo-Keynesianism remained the dominant viewpoint. Charles Schultze, the chief economic adviser, had served in the Johnson administration and believed in working the fiscal levers to minimize unemployment. In July 1977, Schultze laid out alternate economic strategies for the president and recommended "a balanced high-employment budget strategy," one in which "the fiscal dials are set to produce a balanced budget in 1981 only if the economy returns to high employment—that is a 4 and ¾ percent unemployment rate." Schultze's assumptions—that the administration could "set the fiscal dials"—and his willingness to run a deficit for the sake of full employment revealed the continued hold of the old orthodoxy. Vice President Mondale, Stuart Eizenstat, the majority of the cabinet, and much of the White House staff shared this view.[50]

Over the course of Carter's presidency, that confidence dissipated. The late 1970s economy emphatically confirmed the long-term upward trends in both unemployment and inflation. Whatever short-term reductions in joblessness an expansive fiscal policy offered soon vanished. Whatever breaks from inflation temporary controls and recessions provided failed to ground the wage-price spiral. Even the administration's most committed liberal Keynesians lost faith. DPS staffer Al Stern concluded that either "we are following the wrong policy [or] our announced policy has been irrelevant" to economic performance. "We look like either fools or villains." Stern's boss, Stuart Eizenstat, concurred. In a 1980 address at the University of North Carolina, Eizenstat conceded that "traditional Keynesian economics was ill-equipped to deal with this dual problem" of simultaneous inflation and recession. By 1980, a new orthodoxy had emerged within the Carter White House and throughout the American policy-making establishment—a consensus about the need for fiscal restraint, the primacy of monetary policy in controlling inflation, the value of deregulation, and the necessity of tax relief.[51]

The growing importance Carterites attached to cutting taxes and removing debilitating regulations testified to their acceptance of supply-side thinking. In his North Carolina speech, Eizenstat declared that the "economic policy of the 1980s must place *greater emphasis on the supply side of our economy*" (emphasis in original). The Carter administration, Eizenstat maintained, had initiated and hoped to complete "a transition from economic policies which focused largely on controlling demand [Keynesian fiscal management] to ones which place more—though not exclusive—emphasis on the supply side of our economy." In June 1980, the OMB's "Report on Growth and Inflation" criticized the supply-side extremism of Ronald Reagan's tax cut proposals but carefully defended a more tempered version of supply-side economics.[52]

The new economic orthodoxy reflected more than the triumph of abstruse economic theories or a revised set of assumptions for economic policy. It reflected an entirely different attitude about the role of government and the centrality of private business in American life. In what amounted to a direct rebuke to Lyndon Johnson and a generation of Democratic politics, President Carter stressed the limits of government action: "Government cannot eliminate poverty or provide a bountiful economy or reduce inflation or save our cities or cure illiteracy or provide energy." Carter and his advisers repeatedly asserted that private investment must lead economic recovery, that the market must restore productivity and high employment. Criticism of business and the free market gradually dropped out of mainstream American political discourse. Carter certainly found business more amenable to his program than labor, more willing to respect voluntary inflation controls and applaud regulatory reform.[53]

The growing idolization of the market in the 1970s emerged out of the mounting discontent with government that a decade of scandal, military defeat, and economic distress had produced. Conservatives and business interests did not merely exploit this vague mistrust and aversion; they transformed negative impressions into enthusiastic affirmation, popularizing the ideas of a cohort of conservative economists and shrewdly organizing for more effective political lobbying. Business groups spearheaded battles against labor legislation, environmental restrictions, safety regulations, and corporate taxes. Large corporations also began underwriting conservative foundations and intellectuals. The Heritage Foundation financed monetarist guru Milton Friedman's TV show and Reaganite policy analyst Charles Murray's research; the Olin Foundation, led by economic libertarian William Simon, sponsored the work of supply-side proselytizer Jude Waninski.[54]

Free market ideas triumphed, also, for lack of opposition. To be sure, the Democratic party had never been truly hostile to business. Even as Franklin D. Roosevelt assailed the forces of privilege arrayed against his New Deal, he had relied on strong currents of business support. John F. Kennedy and Lyndon B. Johnson had maintained even friendlier relationships with business interests. They believed that sustaining the economic prosperity and the political will to build the Great Society depended on the willing cooperation of big business. Nonetheless, from the 1930s through the 1970s, the Democratic party remained the center of efforts to restrain business, and to protect the rights and safety of workers and consumers from the excesses of untrammeled free enterprise. During the Carter years, the Democratic party muted its criticism of business, a trend that accelerated in the 1980s when the Democratic National Committee redoubled its efforts to collect campaign contributions from business interests.

Furthermore, the Carter years turned Americans, previously conservative in their financial dealings, into a nation of entrepreneurs, speculators, and investors. The age of inflation simply altered Americans' relations with money; to let savings sit in a bank was to lose everything. Inflation czar Alfred Kahn concluded that "the ten years of inflation that we have experienced have given rise to a permanent change in our attitudes toward savings." Americans spent more, borrowed more, and, when they did save, demanded higher returns than regulated bank deposits would allow. Financial institutions gradually slipped through the regulatory net, offering a whole new range of products—credit cards arriving in the mail from anonymous institutions far from home, cash management accounts and money market funds, discount stock brokerages and direct-marketed mutual funds. A brave new world of personal finance, with all its attendant opportunities and dangers, had arrived.[55]

Jimmy Carter's presidency reinforced these transitions in economic policy, attitudes, and behavior. Carter's policies inaugurated a new era in American public life, an era of unpopular government in perpetual budgetary duress. What appeared like inconsistency, vacillation, and malaise in fact revealed the first tentative, reluctant steps into a brave new world of political economy, in which the national government and the Democratic party would have to renegotiate the New Deal compact made half a century earlier.

NOTES

1. *New York Times,* October 29, 1980, A29.

2. Burton I. Kaufman, *The Presidency of James Earl Carter, Jr.* (Lawrence: University Press of Kansas, 1993), 205; Garland A. Haas, *Jimmy Carter and the Politics of Frustration* (Jefferson, N.C.: McFarland, 1992), 164–66.

3. Sidney Weintraub, "Carter's Hoover Syndrome," *New Leader,* March 24, 1980; Seymour Melman, "Jimmy Hoover?" *New York Times,* February 7, 1979; James R. Fallows, "The Passionless Presidency," *Atlantic Monthly,* part 1 (May 1979): 33–48, and part 2 (June 1979), 75–81; Joseph Califano, Jr., *Governing America: An Insider's Report from the White House and the Cabinet* (New York: Simon and Schuster, 1981); R. K. Murray

and T. H. Blessing, "The Presidential Performance Study," *Journal of American History* 70 (December 1983): 443–55; Clark Mollenhoff, *The President Who Failed* (New York: Macmillan, 1980).

4. Ann Mari May, "Fiscal Policy, Monetary Policy, and the Carter Presidency," *Presidential Studies Quarterly* 23 (Fall 1993): 699–711. Prominent examples of second-wave reassessments include Erwin C. Hargrove, *Jimmy Carter as President: Leadership and the Politics of the Public Good* (Baton Rouge: Louisiana State University Press, 1988); and John Dumbrell, *The Carter Presidency: A Re-evaluation* (Manchester, England: Manchester University Press, 1993). In a 1995 presidential survey, Carter placed nineteenth, ahead of both Ronald Reagan and Gerald Ford (William J. Ridings, Jr., and Stuart B. McIver, "1990's Presidential Poll," in Ridings, letter to participants, February 1, 1995 [in author's possession]).

5. Van Ooms, James McIntyre Interview (including Hubert Harris, Van Ooms), October 28–29, 1981, 88, William Burkett Miller Center of Public Affairs, University of Virginia Project on the Carter Presidency, Transcripts (hereafter cited as Miller Center), Jimmy Carter Library (JCL); Kaufman, *Presidency of James Earl Carter,* 24; Hargrove, *Jimmy Carter as President,* 43–44.

6. Kaufman, *Presidency of James Earl Carter,* 3, 75, passim; Robert Dallek, *Hail to the Chief* (New York: Hyperion, 1996), 31–37; Mark A. Peterson, *Legislating Together* (Cambridge, Mass.: Harvard University Press, 1990), 17–19.

7. For the Carter administration's understanding of prevailing economic conditions in the 1970s, see Speech, Stuart Eizenstat, "A Non-Economist's Look at Economic Policy for the 1980s," Alumni Forum, University of North Carolina, Chapel Hill, May 10, 1980, Box 5, James McIntyre Papers, JCL.

8. Charles Schultze, "Has the Phillips Curve Shifted? Some Additional Evidence," *Brookings Papers on Economic Activity* (1971), 452–67.

9. Harrison Wellford to James McIntyre, March 20, 1978; Frank Moore to Les Francis, March 20, 1978, Domestic Policy Staff (DPS)-Eizenstat, Box 144, JCL; Stuart Eizenstat Interview, Miller Center, JCL, 101–2; David Calleo, *Imperious Economy* (Cambridge, Mass.: Harvard University Press, 1982), 143.

10. Alfred Kahn, Exit Interview, Tape 1, Side 1, JCL; Eizenstat to Carter (with handwritten comments by Carter), June 2, 1977, Box 194, DPS-Eizenstat, JCL; Henry Owen to Carter, July 20, 1979, Box 191, JCL; Hargrove, *Jimmy Carter as President,* 72–76.

11. May, "Fiscal Policy," 700; Calleo, *Imperious Economy,* 139.

12. For similar portraits of Carter as precursor to Reagan, see the chapters in this volume by Thomas Sugrue, James Patterson, and Melvyn Dubofsky.

13. Charles Schultze, "Testimony before the House Budget Committee," January 27, 1977, Box 192, DPS-Eizenstat, JCL; May, "Fiscal Policy," 706–7; Hargrove, *Jimmy Carter as President,* 88–89.

14. Charles Schultze to EPG, January 24, 1977, and Gene Godley to Michael Blumenthal, February 18, 1977, Box 192, DPS-Eizenstat, JCL; Hargrove, *Jimmy Carter as President,* 81–83; Kaufman, *Presidency of James Earl Carter,* 28–31; McIntyre Interview, Miller Center Interview, 18, passim.

15. James Fallows to Carter, October 31, 1977, "Remarks at Signing Ceremony for Minimum Wage Bill," Jimmy Carter, November 1, 1977, Box 11; "Signing Statement Draft," January 19, 1978, Box 17; all in Staff Offices Files, Speechwriters Office—Chronological File (hereafter Speechwriters Chronological File), JCL.

16. "Summary and Outline of First-Year Domestic Accomplishments," December 17, 1977, McIntyre Papers, Box 7, JCL.

17. McIntyre Interview, Miller Center, 4, 48–49.

18. "Press Conference No. 5 of the President of the United States," April 15, 1977, Box 144, DPS-Eizenstat, JCL. For the early emphasis on energy issues, see President Carter's Fireside Chat on November 8, 1977, which described economic woes, such as the struggles of an unemployed Detroit steelworker, as rooted in the energy crisis ("Fireside Chat," November 8, 1977, Box 12, Speechwriters Chronological File, JCL).

19. "DNC Field Survey, Summary of Issue Concerns of the American People, 1500 Interviews," August 31 to September 12, 1977, Box 33, Staff Offices, Chief of Staff—Jordan (hereafter Jordan Papers), JCL; James McIntyre to Carter, October 28, 1977, and Charles Schultze to Carter, October 7, 1977, Box 194, Al Stern to Eizenstat, May 20, 1978; Briefing Book, "Inflation: Challenges and Responses for 1978 and Beyond," December 8, 1977; Eizenstat to John Tower and Robert Byrd, September 19, 1977; Barry Bosworth to Blumenthal, Eizenstat, and Schultze, November 25, 1977; and Schultze to Blumenthal, November 11, 1977; all in Box 144, DPS-Eizenstat, JCL. On the administration's failure to appreciate the inflation threat in 1977, see also McIntyre Interview, Miller Center, 48–49.

20. Bob Ginsburg to Eizenstat, December 7, 1977; Eizenstat to Mondale, December 7, 1977; Mondale to Eizenstat, December 7, 1977, Box 194, DPS-Eizenstat, JCL; Kaufman, *Presidency of James Earl Carter,* 73–74.

21. Eizenstat, "A Non-Economist's Look."

22. Eizenstat, Schultze, and Alfred Kahn to Carter (with handwritten note to Eizenstat from Jody Powell), December 6, 1978, Box 143, DPS-Eizenstat, JCL; McIntyre Interview, Miller Center, 6, 59.

23. Joseph Califano to Carter, September 18, 1978, Box 145; Gus Speth to Carter, August 20, 1980, Box 192, DPS-Eizenstat, JCL.

24. Schultze to Blumenthal, November 11, 1977, Box 144, DPS-Eizenstat, JCL; Kahn, Exit Interview, Tape 3, Side 1, JCL.

25. Schultze to Carter, March 29, 1977; Eizenstat and Ginsburg to Carter, April 7, 1977; Arthur Burns to Carter, March 31, 1977, Box 144, DPS-Eizenstat, JCL. On regulatory review in 1977, see Schultze to Carter, October 7, 1977, Box 194, DPS-Eizenstat, JCL.

26. Esther Peterson to Robert Strauss, June 1, 1978, Box 144; Strauss to Eizenstat, September 6, 1978; "Briefing Materials," June 1978, Ginsburg to Eizenstat, July 31, 1978, Box 143, "Address, Jimmy Carter to the American Society of Newspaper Editors," April 11, 1978, Box 144, DPS-Eizenstat, JCL; Stuart Eizenstat, Exit Interview, 17–18; McIntyre Interview, Miller Center, 6.

27. Jerry Rafshoon to Carter, September 1, 1978, Box 145, DPS-Eizenstat, JCl; Kaufman, *Presidency of James Earl Carter,* 101.

28. Schultze to Carter, September 24, October 5, 1978; Califano to Carter, September 18, 1978; McIntyre to Carter, n.d.; Stern to Eizenstat, September 8, 1978; and "Briefing/Outreach Materials" collected in Folder "Anti-Inflation 9/78 [2]"; all in Box 145, DPS-Eizenstat, JCL.

29. "Fact Sheet on Anti-Inflation Program," October 24, 1978; "Speech, Jimmy Carter," October 24, 1978; Memorandum, Jerry Rafshoon for distribution, October 23, 1978, Box 145, DPS-Eizenstat, JCL.

30. "Presidential Statement, Jimmy Carter," November 11, 1978, Box 144, DPS-Eizenstat, JCL; Hargrove, *Jimmy Carter as President,* 100; Haas, *Jimmy Carter and the Politics of Frustration,* 72.

31. Kahn, Exit Interview, Tape 1, Side 1; Joseph Nocera, *A Piece of the Action* (New York: Simon and Schuster, 1994), 173.

32. Orin Kramer to Eizenstat, December 4, 1978; William D. Nordhaus to Schultze, November 27, 1978, Box 143, DPS-Eizenstat, JCL; "Report on Reforming Social Regulation," n.d.; Dept. of Treasury to EPG Steering Committee, November 27, 1978; Bill Johnson to Eizenstat, November 29, 1978; Don Haider to Roger Altman, December 15, 1978; Curt Hessler to EPG Steering Committee, November 20, 1978; all in Box 191, DPS-Eizenstat, JCL; Robert S. Greenberger, "Odd Man Out," *Wall Street Journal,* January 10, 1980, 1, 36.

33. Kahn to Carter, April 25, 1979, Box 143; Kahn to Carter, January 24, 1979; and Memo, Ralph Schlosstein to Eizenstat, January 4, 1979, Box 229, "Minutes of June 28, 1979, Meeting of Inflation Working Group," Box 191, DPS-Eizenstat, JCL; Kahn, Exit Interview, JCL; Greenberger, "Odd Man Out," 1, 36; "Regulatory Review Grade Sheets," Box 1, McIntyre Papers, JCL.

34. Cambridge Survey Research to DNC, February 1979, May 25, 1979; and Patrick Caddell to Carter, June 11, 1979, Box 33, Jordan Papers, JCL.

35. Charles Schultze Interview, Miller Center, January 8–9, 1982, 105–8, JCL; Calleo, *Imperious Economy,* 145–47; May, "Fiscal Policy"; Herbert Stein, *Presidential Economics* (New York: Touchstone, 1985), 218–30; Nocera, *A Piece of the Action,* 181–82.

36. "Press Summary," February 1980, Box 21, Domestic Policy Staff Files, Special Projects–Al Stern (hereafter DPS-Stern), JCL; *Economic Report of the President,* 1981 (Washington, D.C.: Government Printing Office, 1981), 158–62; Hargrove, *Jimmy Carter as President,* 86, 102; Stein, *Presidential Economics,* 231.

37. Charles D. Ravenal to Eizenstat, February 26, 1980, Box 143; "Address on Economic Policy, Jimmy Carter," March 14, 1980, Box 192, DPS-Eizenstat, JCL.

38. Bert Carp to Eizenstat, n.d., Box 143; Stern to Eizenstat, June 18, 1980, Box 192, DPS Eizenstat Papers, JCL; Hargrove, *Jimmy Carter as President,* 104–5; May, "Fiscal Policy," 701.

39. "Press Release, White House Press Office Inflation Report," August 28, 1980, Box BE20, White House Central Files (WHCF)–Subject File, JCL; "Briefing Material, Carter vs. Reagan Economic Programs," n.d., Box 6, Eizenstat to Carter, August 23, 1980; Al From to Robert Strauss, May 27, 1980; Eizenstat to Carter, n.d., in Box 192, DPS-Eizenstat, all in JCL; Eizenstat, Exit Interview, 12.

40. James M. Cypher, "Monetarism, Militarism, and Markets," *MERIP Reports* 14 (November–December 1984): 10.

41. "Speech, Carter," March 14, 1980; Schultze to Carter, August 31, 1980, Box 194, DPS-Eizenstat, JCL; Van Ooms, quoted in McIntyre Interview, Miller Center, 10–11; Hargrove, *Jimmy Carter as President,* 86.

42. Gosta Esping-Andersen, *The Three Worlds of Welfare Capitalism* (Princeton, N.J.: Princeton University Press, 1990); Peter Baldwin, *The Politics of Social Solidarity* (New York: Cambridge University Press, 1990); Paul Pierson, *Dismantling the Welfare State?* (New York: Cambridge University Press, 1994); Hugh Heclo and Henrik Madsen, *Policy and Politics in Sweden* (Philadelphia: Temple University Press, 1987).

43. Ooms, quoted in McIntyre Interview, Miller Center, 10; Haas, *Carter and the Politics of Frustration,* 42; "Economic Report of the President, 1981," passim. For the international comparisons, see Bruce J. Schulman, "The Reagan Revolution and American Exceptionalism" (paper presented at the annual meeting of the Organization of American Historians, Chicago, April 1996 [in author's possession]). Data for the comparisons derive from Organisation for Economic Cooperation and Development (OECD), *National Accounts,* vol. 2, *Detailed Tables,* 1979–1991 (Paris: Organisation for Economic Cooperation and Development, 1993), passim; U.S. Census Bureau, *Statistical Abstract of the United States 1995,* (Washington, D.C.: Government Printing Office, 1995) 337–38, and *Statistical Abstract of the United States 1991* (Washington, D.C.: Government Printing Office, 1991), 316–17; and OECD, *National Accounts,* vol. 2, *Detailed Tables,* 1977–1989 (Paris: Organisation for Economic Cooperation and Development, 1991), 39. See also Peter Saunders, "Recent Trends in the Size and Growth of Government in OECD Countries," in *The Growth of the Public Sector,* ed. Norman Gemmell (Aldershot, England: Edward Elgar, 1993), 18–21.

44. OECD, *National Accounts,* vol. 2, *Detailed Tables,* 1979–1991, passim. France presents the exception to this rule, both in the data it reported and in its spending pattern.

45. Pierson, *Dismantling the Welfare State?* 144–45.

46. Income Security programs shrank from 14.9 percent of federal outlays in 1977 to 13.1 percent in 1979, returning to 14.6 percent in 1980. The steep initial drop reflects the exaggerated effect of the stimulus and rapid economic growth; the rapid return stemmed from the onset of recession. Nonetheless, the secular trend pointed toward reduction over time, a trend continued during the 1980s. See *Statistical Abstract of the United States 1992,* 317. Ooms, quoted in McIntyre Interview, Miller Center, 61.

47. U.K., Central Statistical Office, *Annual Abstract of Statistics 1995* (London: HMSO, 1995), 259; Charles Dellheim, *The Disenchanted Isle* (New York: Norton, 1995), 180–81, 199–200; Peter Jenkins, *Mrs. Thatcher's Revolution* (Cambridge, Mass.: Harvard University Press, 1988), xi–xx; Hugh Heclo and Henrik Madsen, *Policy and Politics in Sweden* (Philadelphia: Temple University Press, 1987), 64–74.

48. Stein, *Presidential Economics,* 232–33.

49. Calleo, *Imperious Economy,* 35–40, 144, 230; Stein, *Presidential Economics,* 223–25.

50. Schultze to Carter, July 7, 1977, Box 191, DPS-Eizenstat, JCL.

51. Stern to Eizenstat, April 4, 1978, Box 144, DPS-Eizenstat, JCL; Eizenstat, "Non-Economist's Look."

52. Eizenstat, "Non-Economist's Look"; "Report, OMB Director's Report on Growth and Inflation," June 1980, Box 7, McIntyre Papers, JCL; "Overview of Revised Tax Reform," November 25, 1977, Box 191, DPS-Eizenstat, JCL.

53. "Economic Report of the President, 1978"; Kahn, Exit Interview; Kaufman, *Presidency of James Earl Carter,* 72; Dumbrell, *Carter Presidency,* 22; Thomas Ferguson and Joel Rogers, *Right Turn* (New York: Hill and Wang, 1986).

54. Ferguson and Rogers, *Right Turn.*

55. Kahn to EPG Steering Committee, May 17, 1979, Box 146, DPS-Eizenstat, JCL; Nocera, *A Piece of the Action.*

4

The Locomotive Loses Power: The Trade and Industrial Policies of Jimmy Carter

Judith Stein

The subject of this paper may seem an oxymoron. In his memoir, President Jimmy Carter ignored both trade and industrial questions.[1] One would never suspect that Carter agreed to rescue Chrysler from bankruptcy, contemplated an industrial policy, struggled to manage a stagnant world economy, and negotiated a GATT Round in Tokyo in 1979. At the root of his silence was the incompatibility of the nation's past ideas and practices and the new conditions the president confronted.

Carter, a Georgia farmer and small-town entrepreneur, possessed the free trade ideas and suspicions of big business typical of his sector and region. Special Trade Representative (STR) Robert S. Strauss recalled that Carter was "almost puritanical" in his opposition to "protectionism" and conjured up "visions of Senate conspiracies to make a protectionist of me, and in turn, out of him."[2] Nevertheless, these liberal ideas differed little from the trade and industrial policies the president inherited.

Postwar policy makers of both parties had assumed that domestic manufacturers were strong enough to share the American market with goods produced by U.S. allies. But the stagflation of the late 1970s sharpened conflicts between domestic and international interests, which had been manageable during the years of global growth. An examination of the president's broad foreign economic policy and his response to steel crises in 1977 and 1980 illustrates these conflicts and his response to them. During this period, his macroeconomic policy shifted from expansion to restraint, but Carter's foreign economic and industrial policies remained constant.

In the end, Carter favored international over domestic objectives and macroeconomic policies when sectoral measures in manufacturing were needed. His choices prepared the way for the more radical Republican policies that transferred labor and capital from manufacturing to nontrading service sectors. Politically, they weakened links between the Democratic party and its core constituency.

U.S. FOREIGN ECONOMIC POLICY

Carter inherited a foreign economic policy shaped by the cold war. Although Presidents Franklin D. Roosevelt and Harry S. Truman believed that economic nationalism had been a cause of World War II and preferred free trade, the cold war subordinated domestic economic interests and trade liberalization itself to maintaining strategic alliances.[3] This meant the economic resurrection of Europe and Japan, and then of other allies—South Korea, Taiwan, Mexico, Brazil. The untrumpeted corollary of that goal was opening U.S. markets to the exports of allies. Americans became global consumers of first and last resort. Conversely, the U.S. government tolerated foreign trade barriers limiting U.S. exports. The policies raised the cost of domestic investment and encouraged offshore production.

The Bureau of the Budget articulated the policy in 1950: "Foreign economic policies should not be formulated in terms primarily of economic objectives; they must be subordinated to our politico-security objectives and the priorities which the latter involve."[4] The more old-fashioned Eugene Grace of Bethlehem Steel observed that we are "deindustrializing the United States."[5] Scholars have agreed with Grace. Stephen Krasner concluded that the "United States used its power . . . to promote general political goals rather than specific economic interests." It "was prepared to allow discrimination against its own exports to alleviate the strain of involvement in international trade for its allies." Gerard and Victoria Curzon concluded in 1976 that "postwar trade liberalization has been a beneficial exercise for America's trade partners. . . . [I]f any country could be said to have 'lost' . . . it was the United States itself."[6]

These results were intentional, not inadvertent. Truman's assistant secretary of state for economic affairs mused, "The great question is . . . whether the country is willing to decide in the broader national self-interest to reduce tariffs and increase United States imports even though some domestic industry may suffer serious injury." Republicans answered yes. A trade negotiator of the 1950s acknowledged, "We did make some big tariff cuts and didn't get any reciprocity. It was quite deliberate." The head of President Dwight D. Eisenhower's Council on Foreign Economic Policy recalled, "There was no general recognition of the need to relate foreign economic conditions and policies with similar factors of the domestic economy." George Ball, undersecretary for economic affairs in the Kennedy State Department, assumed that the nation could afford "some temporary sacrifice of commercial interests."[7]

President John F. Kennedy called such sacrifices responsibilities, but the stagnant economy of the early 1960s led some to question U.S. policy and forced the president to act. British Laborite Harold Wilson told Senator Hubert H. Humphrey that American foreign economic policies simply "suck in imports and kill exports," producing the unemployment and balance-of-payment problems that distinguished the U.S. from European economies.[8] Senator William Proxmire, no friend of the steel industry, was horrified when a State Department official complacently accepted European discrimination against American steel.[9]

Kennedy's Trade Expansion Act of 1962 promised to reverse the balance-of-payments deficit by reducing European trade barriers. The negotiations ending in 1967 lowered tariffs on manufactured goods but failed to touch other protective devices. U.S. imports grew much faster than exports.[10] The imperatives of the cold war, the ideology of the affluent society, and then the stimulus of the tax cut and Vietnam spending masked industrial problems until 1971, when the United States registered its first merchandise trade deficit. The AFL-CIO attempted but failed to alter trade and investment policy in the early 1970s.[11] President Richard M. Nixon's devaluations eased problems temporarily, but they returned with a vengeance after the oil and commodity inflation in 1974 unleashed a global recession.[12]

Carter assumed that the United States could restore global growth by accepting more imports. To enhance his credentials for the 1976 presidential campaign, he joined David Rockefeller's Trilateral Commission, a private organization of leading figures from Japan, Europe, and the United States. During commission meetings, Carter met Zbigniew Brzezinski, whom he later chose to head his National Security Council (NSC). Brzezinski believed Americans had three tasks: repairing relations with Europe and Japan that had been damaged by the unilateralism of the Nixon-Ford years, integrating Third World nations into the global economy by providing them access to Western markets and capital, and reaching some accommodation with the Soviet Union.[13]

In line with trilateral thinking, economists at the Brookings Institution and Organisation of Economic Cooperation and Development (OECD) urged the United States, Japan, and Europe to stimulate their domestic economies to become "'locomotives' for global recovery," an international Keynesianism. The big powers should run trade deficits to provide markets for the weaker oil importers, Third World nations who "have already exhausted their ability to finance oil related trade deficits." Carter followed the script, announcing his $30-billion stimulus on February 2. He urged Japan and Germany, which enjoyed trade surpluses despite oil imports, to follow the U.S. example by increasing domestic consumption and accepting more imports. At the London economic summit in May 1977, it became clear that Japan and Germany would build their recovery on exports, not domestic expansion.[14] Brzezinski was not deterred: "The United States would have to do more than our allies, unpalatable as this may seem to some sectors of our public. If we could demonstrate fortitude and commitment, if we were prepared to undertake the necessary sacrifices," Japan and Europe would "emulate our commitment."[15]

The American trade deficit was an example of the necessary sacrifice. It jumped from $9.5 to $31.1 billion between 1976 and 1977. At the same time, Japan, despite its dependence on foreign oil, increased its trade surplus from $9.8 to $17.2

billion.[16] Every relevant government body was unconcerned. The White House consensus in April 1977 was that "relatively free access to U.S. markets is a matter of ranking importance for our allies and almost all the developing countries of the world." The Treasury Department opposed taking "measures that would attempt to improve our trade balance at the expense of our trading partners," Europe and Japan. Richard N. Cooper, in charge of international economics at the State Department, feared that any talk of an American balance-of-payments problem would lead to protectionism. Alan Wm. Wolff, Strauss's deputy, warned that "other countries will take the position that the relative strength of the U.S. economy requires a clear exhibition of our self-restraint on trade issues if the U.S. is to take the lead (and no one else is in a position to do so) in avoiding a general resurgence of trade restrictive actions." Legitimate trade relief, for instance, should be weighed against the goals of supporting the economies of newly industrializing countries like South Korea, Mexico, and Brazil and effecting a successful Tokyo Round of the Multinational Trade Negotiations (MTN). Because Europeans were reluctant to commit themselves to "a major negotiating effort," the United States should not stringently enforce existing American law against them.[17] Thus, President Carter rejected International Trade Commission recommendations for import restraints on shoes and television sets and publicly reaffirmed the American commitment to liberalizing trade.[18]

By 1978, Secretary of the Treasury W. Michael Blumenthal finally recognized the consequences of the policy. Blumenthal told Carter that, "adjusted for inflation, U.S. exports have not grown since 1974; the volume of U.S. manufactured goods has actually declined. The rest of the world, by contrast, has seen a 12 percent growth in export volume since 1974." Council of Economic Advisers (CEA) head Charles Schultze discovered the same truth, telling the president that the trade deficit rose despite the decline in oil imports.[19]

At home, Carter attributed the trade deficit to oil imports and pressured Congress to pass his energy legislation.[20] But at the Bonn economic summit in July 1978, he told a Japanese reporter that "most of our trade balance now comes from the purchase of manufactured goods, not oil. Of course, the nations like Japan and Germany, who sell a lot of manufactured goods to us, like to talk about our oil imports, but they don't deplore the fact that we also buy large quantities of manufactured goods from your country and others." Again he urged Japan and Germany to stimulate their economies.[21]

Both nations resisted and continued to register surpluses, even after the second oil shock.[22] The U.S. recipe for restoring the 5 percent global growth rates of the postwar period had failed. Under current conditions (2 percent), trade became a zero-sum game. Nevertheless, foreign policy imperatives shored up the beliefs that dollar depreciation could reverse the manufacturing shortfalls and that the U.S. economy was sound. This strategic purpose permitted Carter to continue to find virtue in rising imports.

IMPORTS AND ANTI-INFLATION: STEEL

If imports were crucial tools to manage the world economy, they "can play an important role in the fight against inflation," Carter stated in April 1977.[23] He reiterated traditional postwar Democratic doctrine that attributed inflation to the monopolistic practices of big business. According to macroeconomic theory, an open trading system encouraged imports and competition, thereby producing lower inflation rates.[24] In the real world, energy and housing items accounted for nearly 90 percent of the increase in the Consumer Price Index (CPI) from 1977 to 1980.[25]

At the president's request, STR Strauss prepared a memorandum, "Trade Measures to Increase Supply of Foreign Steel in the U.S. Market."[26] Strauss, who had plenty of political experience but no trade expertise, was unaware that foreign steelmakers were helping him. When rising steel imports began to register in the middle of the year, Schultze and Office of Management and Budget (OMB) chief Bert Lance blithely told Carter that imports would keep domestic steel prices down.[27]

Like his Democratic predecessors, Carter focused on the macroeconomy, the presumed effect of steel prices on the economy, not the health of the steel industry. The assumption that steel wages and prices were a key cause of inflation was an article of faith in postwar policy.[28] Schultze led Carter's version of jawboning. Government advocacy reduced a rise in the price of carbon steel to 6 percent in May. White House aide Stuart Eizenstat and Schultze acknowledged that rising oil, ore, and coal prices might justify the price increases. In April, Nippon Steel, the price leader of the Japanese industry, had raised domestic prices 8 percent. Nevertheless, Eizenstat repeated the words of previous American leaders: "The sacrifices which must be made in the fight against inflation must begin somewhere, and price increases such as this in the steel industry will have a ripple effect throughout the economy."[29]

While Carter focused on prices, the industry eyed imports, which reached a record 20 percent of the market. The year 1977, the third-highest year for steel consumption in U.S. history, found American mills operating at only 78 percent of capacity. The "locomotive strategy" had sectoral effects because the crisis in the European and Japanese steel industries simply became another American import.

The recession had come at a bad time for the European and Japanese steel industries. *Fortune* magazine crowned the American steel industry "king among the crippled" because the U.S. industry, concentrating on modernization, had expanded less than the others. The capacity of the nations of the European Community (EC) had grown from 127 million tons in 1970 to 169 in 1976, the Japanese from 103 to 151; American capacity grew only from 155 to 159. European utilization rates plummeted from a comfortable 87 percent in 1974 to a profitless 65 percent for the rest of the decade, falling to 57 percent in 1982. Although the Europeans closed mills after the oil crisis, they failed initially to reduce capacity. Governments and steel companies shut down older, inefficient facilities and expanded the new ones.[30] The EC subsidized closures, extended loans for new mills, financed research and worker retraining, set minimum prices, and negotiated import quotas. It effectively excluded foreign steel by imposing antidumping levies on Japan, Canada, South Korea, Spain, and East European countries. Whatever their political complexion, governments subsidized unprofitable steel operations.[31]

Japan was not immune to the crisis. After 1975, its Ministry of Trade and Industry (MITI), which had projected growing world demand, reversed gears. Tokyo established recession cartels and provided credit to firms that closed underused plants and absorbed weaker companies. In 1979, when steel imports threatened to take 3 percent of the domestic market, MITI suspended the preferential tariff the United States had forced Japan to extend to developing countries. Now it could no longer afford to help.[32]

European and Japanese domestic measures were insufficient. A good part of their growing steel capacity had been earmarked for export, mainly to the United States. From 1970 to 1974, European exports rose from 11 to 29 percent of production; Japanese exports rose from 32 to 54 percent. Then, as domestic economies contracted in the wake of the oil crisis, foreign markets became even more critical. One scholar characterized Tokyo's policy as "the greatest supply-oriented export phenomenon" in its history. In 1976, Japanese steelmakers reduced their export prices 32 percent, even though companies lost over $15 per ton shipped. European shortfalls were greater. In 1977, the Germans lost $42 and the French $76.[33]

U.S. Steel's Edgar Speer charged foreign steelmakers with countercyclical exports to compensate for depressed domestic demand. In 1976, the American Iron and Steel Institute had filed suit under the 1974 trade act, arguing that the EC-Japan agreement of 1976, limiting Japanese steel imports to the EC, diverted steel to the U.S. market, where it sold below home prices. Japanese imports into the United States were 37 percent higher in 1976 than in 1975, constituting 55.9 percent of imported steel. The determination of dumping is not a science, but Japanese newspapers documented it. As domestic demand fell in 1975, MITI mandated production cuts, price rises at home, and an export drive abroad. Fearing retaliation, the government pulled back, however, in the wake of foreign protests. Now MITI urged steelmakers to cease "offering their products for exports at cheaper prices than for domestic customers for whom they have recently raised the price." In 1976, Japan negotiated quota and price agreements with Australia and Canada as well as the EC.[34] The Carter administration did nothing.

The cacophony of presidential jawboning on price and industry trade suits forced a summit. Blumenthal, Barry Bosworth, the executive director of the Council on Wage and Price Stability (CWPS), and officials from Treasury and Commerce met with the heads of the largest companies in August 1977. Speer told them that the steel men wanted to cooperate. He said that the industry could compete on everything—quality, service, and costs—but not price because foreign producers, aided by their governments, dumped steel.[35]

Although he was not a steel expert, Bosworth was skeptical. The U.S. industry suffered from high labor costs, he opined, and questioned whether Japanese export prices were lower than those in their home market. Armco Steel's William Verity told the group that it was not simply Japan. Verity had pledged to meet Japanese prices in the Gulf Coast region. Within three months British Steel, a particularly inefficient producer, came in thirty dollars below the Japanese. Then the South Africans undercut the British. Speer said that the only permanent solution was sectoral negotiations at the MTN. Without immediate government action on dumping, he warned, some very big mills, even whole companies, would go under.[36]

But necessary remedies conflicted with Carter's domestic and international economic policies. The president told steelmakers, "I can't single out an industry, even when it is as important as yours, and make a decision . . . that might escalate enormous inflationary pressures."[37] Carter compartmentalized his thinking. He knew that the EC had restricted first Japanese and then South Korean, Spanish, and South African steel, which would likely end up in the U.S. market. Earlier in February, Alan Wolff informed him that the EC's allocation of domestic shipments "has a reasonable likelihood of resulting in the dumping of EC steel in the U.S. market." A CIA report had warned that the Japanese imperative to produce at full operation, when combined with European protection, "leaves only the U.S. and possibly Canada as potential major outlets for surplus Japanese steel." The president acknowledged that the Japanese method of ending its recession through exports undermined global recovery, but he refused to apply that insight to the steel industry's problems. Goals of repairing international relations and furthering the MTN negotiations preserved the view that the industry's difficulties were unrelated to the global crisis.[38]

Thus, the many government bodies, reflecting earlier U.S. industrial history, set out to work with their traditional missions unchanged. The CWPS surveyed prices, the Federal Trade Commission examined competitive practices, the Justice Department began a preliminary antitrust investigation, and a White House task force examined trade policy. Marching to its own drummer, the Export-Import Bank approved a $17.9-million loan to South Korea's Pohang Iron and Steel Company to finance equipment for a new mill. Adding up the action and inaction, the United States continued to promote competition at home and more capacity abroad.[39]

SOLOMON PLAN

Thus, Carter was at a loss when confronted with a wave of mill closings in August and September. More than fourteen major steel mills shut down, and companies curtailed operations at many others. At least twenty thousand steelworkers lost their jobs, joined by thousands of others affected by the closures.[40]

Carter could not ignore the subsequent insurgency. George Pino, an operator at the closed Campbell works of Youngstown Sheet and Tube, said, "I feel stabbed in the back. We gave him [Carter] our votes, and now he's not helping." Charles A. Vanik of Ohio, chair of the House Ways and Means Subcommittee on Trade, told Strauss that legislators would not passively watch the closure of steel mills. Former Kennedy aide Ted Sorensen underscored the political imperative: "The coalition that elected Carter—blacks (disproportionately hurt by steel layoffs because of their higher proportion among recent hires), urban and industrial areas, labor, ethnics—" demanded some response.[41]

The *Wall Street Journal* captured the president's dilemma: "Caught off balance without a steel policy, the administration is scrambling to develop one." Yet the government clearly found the elimination of some mills desirable; imports had a role to play in disciplining prices, and the United States did not need a steel policy. CEA member William D. Nordhaus said, "The federal government is not in the business of telling industry not to shut down, when to shut down or where to shut down." Richard Heimlich, Strauss's assistant, perfectly summarized postwar policy when he explained that the trade office did not approach its work "from the standpoint of what our industry should be like." The president hedged, telling reporters that "large steel imports . . . are legitimate and needed . . . to ensure competition. But we certainly do not want to have illegal sales of foreign steel."[42]

Forced to act, the president invited politicians, steel executives, and labor leaders to a White House Conference on Steel on October 13. Carter created the Special Task Force on Steel, headed by Under Secretary of Treasury Anthony Solomon, who announced he would address all of the problems facing the industry.[43] Despite the brave talk, the White House favored a minimal trade solution. Relevant cabinet secretaries served on the committee, but the Treasury Department, which then enforced the antidumping law, ran the task force. The decision effectively isolated Commerce secretary Juanita Krups and labor secretary F. Ray Marshall. It also excluded Robert Strauss by design. Strauss now agreed "that the surge of Japanese exports to us was basically the result of dumping and strong demand conditions here as compared with other markets." He wanted to stay as far away as possible from the steel issue until concluding the MTN negotiations. The United States sought to promote agricultural and high-technology exports by ending European subsidies, procurement preferences on telecommunications, and other nontariff barriers. Keeping the steel question off the MTN table would help U.S. negotiators.[44]

Members of the administration debated whether the Japanese dumped steel, but all agreed with the U.S. industry that the Europeans were selling far below home prices. EC Commissioner Etienne Davignon acknowledged the dumping, although he observed that after looking the other way for a long time, enforcing the law in effect created new rules. Still, Davignon was prepared to accept a minimum price structure, some rules on capacity expansion, and temporary quotas. American trade negotiator Alan Wolff now agreed and advocated a global steel pact.[45] Carter was dead set against it, however, and would accept only some mechanism on fair prices. He opposed either voluntary or mandatory restraints, which Presidents Johnson and Nixon had employed. (The theory behind such measures was that short-term market developments, such as import surges, reduced profits, which thwarted the financing of long-term adjustments.) The Europeans and Japanese, fearing stronger measures, would have accepted either. Carter's opposition to quantitative limits amazed Japanese officials.[46] Had he agreed to discuss steel capacity and market shares, the subsequent history of the industry would have been different.[47]

Thus, Carter's feeble solution warred with the Solomon Report's conclusion that the industry had been injured by dumping. Solomon stated that foreign producers had lowered prices to maintain output and employment, sending record tonnage to the United States. The reduced steel earnings made it difficult for the industry to raise capital for modernization and antipollution investments. To meet the situation, Carter proposed a minimum price system, called the "trigger price mechanism" (TPM), based on Japanese costs of production, at that time the lowest in the world.[48] The government would initiate dumping investigations if prices fell below benchmark levels. By allowing everyone to sell at the Japanese price, which was below their own costs of production, Carter had acted against runaway dumping, but not dumping. Summing up the effect of the policy, the Congressional Budget Office in 1987 concluded that the TPM "essentially gave less efficient firms in other countries a license to dump."[49]

Anti-inflation and foreign policy purposes still dominated Carter's steel policy. He believed that reducing imports would simply benefit the companies by producing "greatly increased prices, which would have to be paid for by the American consumers." He accepted minimal trade relief, which he rejected in other sectors, because Solomon had told him that the new price structure would help the European steel industry even more than the American. Had the industry's suits proceeded, "the bulk of steel imports from Europe" would have been excluded. By preserving an American market for the Europeans, the TPM would help stem European social unrest, which the government believed was fueling Eurocommunism. The Japanese were pleased, too. They had accepted quantitative limits imposed by many countries. Though the TPM did not limit them, some evidence exists that Tokyo restrained exporters.[50]

Unlike other steel-producing nations, Carter focused on consumption, not production. He had rejected supply-side measures proposed by Secretary of Labor F. Ray Marshall. Marshall had advocated tax credits for pollution-control equipment, investment incentives for marginal plants, and rebuilding rail and water networks in coal and steel areas. This kind of program won support in Congress. Congressman Vanik argued that although infrastructure expenditures and tax incentives would cost money, it would be better to spend "to modernize the steel industry" than "sprinkle $20 billion in tax cuts throughout the economy which could only be financed by increased public borrowing and additions to the budget deficit and the public debt." Vanik was referring to the $20-billion tax cut currently making its way through the Congress in 1978. The investment provisions lowered capital gains taxes and the minimum tax on individuals claiming high deductions and exclusions. The cut reflected the traditional macroeconomic approach to the American economy, relying on the market to allocate resources. Vanik advocated more targeted interventions.[51] Another member of Congress observed, "We are not getting the same rate of return for each dollar of tax reduction as far as dollars returned to the economy are concerned."[52] Imports trumped Keynesian techniques. If consumers used the increased purchasing power resulting from government deficits to buy foreign goods—clothes, electronics, or steel—it weakened the multiplier, imparting an inflationary tilt to a given level of government spending.

The president was deaf to such suggestions. Carter stated that his "comprehensive program" for steel required "no specific legislative measures and can be implemented quickly." Existing programs would help. As a result of the advocacy of the United Steelworkers of America (USWA), he authorized the Economic Development Administration (EDA) to offer loans to firms having difficulty obtaining funds in the capital market for modernization and antipollution. The president had initially resisted this modest measure. Even so, the EDA was hardly the agency to decide steel questions. Operating at the margins of the economy, it handled $5- to $10-million projects, mainly in rural areas. Its intellectual shortcomings and vulnerability to political influence fed the growing popular view that government could do little. Similarly, Marshall had persuaded Solomon to create a tripartite committee to discuss steel questions, which the president initially opposed and mostly ignored.[53] This kind of bargaining, the essence of social democracy, was incompatible with Carter's self-conception as a president above the interests.

Solomon had failed to address the capital needs of the industry as a whole. By authorizing small sums to small firms, government actions assumed that the industry could generate enough funds for modernization, even though the Solomon report stated that the entire industry had been injured. The report was silent on size and structure. It skirted the question of whether the plan would or should preserve the firms pressed in the current crisis. Specifics on depreciation schedules, pollution standards, and antitrust were sent to the relevant departments for study. The White House opposed modifying antitrust laws to permit joint ventures, which could cheapen the costs of modernization. It reluctantly accepted Solomon's recommendation to shorten depreciation write-offs. The Treasury had just completed a study that contemplated increasing the guideline from eighteen years to twenty! It took two years, a sign of its low priority, for the Treasury to reduce the time to fifteen, still much higher than in foreign nations.[54]

Carter, less assertive on what the Solomon plan would do than what it would not, stated it would have little impact on inflation and the federal budget, it would not violate antitrust laws or pollution standards, and it would not foster industrial concentration. Strauss warned that the report "will be read as insufficient."[55] Ending runaway dumping and the falling dollar halted the import surge, however, even though it ignored investment shortfalls. A leading Wall Street "bear" became bullish on the industry, concluding that "the worst is over and that the industry outlook [was promising] into 1981." Though dissatisfied with the Carter package, the steel men acted confidently. Speer planned to upgrade equipment at many facilities. He had been the guiding light behind the decision to build a new greenfield plant on the shores of Lake Erie at Conneaut, Ohio, an old dream of Andrew Carnegie. Board chair David Roderick, who would cancel the project during the steel crisis in 1980, was a big booster in 1978. Once the corporation got over what he called "the capital punishment" of financing the facility, the Conneaut plant would produce steel with 35 percent less energy and 30 to 50 percent less labor.[56]

The one dissenter was the USWA. By March 1978, the union demanded a full-blown industrial policy. Most of the growth of steel capacity since World War II "has come about because of planned programs of the governments involved," stated a union press release. "These programs have normally involved direct grants, guaranteed loans, or some other form of assistance." Estimating that the steel companies could generate only $48 billion of the $82 billion needed to modernize over the next twelve years, the Union urged the Congress to provide $2.5 to $3 billion a year in guaranteed loans to the industry.[57] The proposal went nowhere.

1980 CRISIS

Because the administration had ignored fundamental questions in 1977, a steel crisis (joined by one in the automobile industry) returned in 1980. Carter, confronting a recession and a new round of oil price rises, waffled. The response to the first oil crisis had been expansionary; now, led by the new chair of the Federal Reserve Board, Paul A. Volcker, austerity became the order of the day.

A new surge of steel imports beginning at the end of 1979 stemmed from yen-dollar currency changes, which reduced the minimum price of steel even while Japanese and European costs rose. The system of floating currencies begun in the Nixon years injected new instability into global trade. Although it took over six months for Carter to act, another deal was struck, raising the minimum to compensate for the currency changes. Like the earlier one, the 1980 agreement aimed to protect European steelmakers as well as American steelmakers. Carter had decided to ignore European steel subsidies and trade diversions, like the EC-Japan agreement of 1976. If these violations of the recently negotiated Tokyo Round had been pursued, the American government could have imposed countervailing duties on European steel. The Europeans explained, however, that although illegal, the subsidies were temporary and would result in less capacity. Foreign policy imperatives in Iran and Afghanistan guaranteed U.S. acquiescence.[58]

If the priorities of foreign affairs and inflation made Carter complacent about 50 percent operating rates in steel, others chafed. Steel was not unique. One million jobs ended between January and July 1980. Fed chief Volcker's monetary stringency had produced a recession, without significantly reducing inflation. The GNP fell in 1980, the unemployment rate rose to 7.2 percent, but the inflation rate remained at 13.5 percent. The failure of macroeconomic remedies opened space for new policies. The government already had put together an "industrial policy" to save Chrysler from bankruptcy in 1979, think tanks around the nation studied industrial innovation, and coalitions of businessmen, mayors, governors, and labor in the hard-hit Northeast and Midwest added political weight to the idea that the nation required a new recipe for growth.[59]

According to the new thinking, government needed to do more than ensure everyone a piece of the pie; it had to bake a larger one. Ezra Vogel's *Japan as Number One* had been a best-seller in 1979. Vogel attributed Japanese potency to its national strategy. In 1980, business leaders, including the National Association of Manufacturers and Bethlehem Steel chair Lewis Foy, advocated a "competitive business strategy," the *New York Times* ran a five-part series, and a congressional committee held hearings on industrial policy. *Business Week* published a special issue called "The Reindustrialization of America." Although skeptical, the editors of the *Wall Street Journal* acknowledged that the talk about "sectoral solutions reflects an explicit claim that the problems of U.S. industry cannot be solved solely by macroeconomic policy."[60]

Sober statistics propelled the talk. Workers' after-tax income, which rose 34 percent in the 1960s, increased only 7 percent in the 1970s and actually declined 5.5 percent in 1980. Only 5 percent of the new jobs produced in the 1970s were in manufacturing. Manufacturing workers composed 38 percent of the workforce in 1960 but only 28 percent in 1981. No longer could this decline be attributed to automation. Productivity had slowed from over 3 percent to an annual average of 1.6 percent in the period 1966 to 1975; in 1979 it was −2.0 percent.[61]

The decline of manufacturing had been observed earlier but was deemed natural, even desirable. In 1966, Harvard economist Raymond Vernon updated the theory of comparative advantage with the idea of the "product cycle." One nation pioneered a manufacturing process, which then migrated to low-wage countries. The initiator went on to new industries.[62] The state should only ameliorate resulting distress through unemployment insurance and retraining. While painful, change ensured progress in the long run.[63] In 1973, Daniel Bell, writing in a more popular vein, announced that the United States was now a "post-industrial society." Bell argued that mature nations naturally moved to a postindustrial phase in which new service industries replaced traditional employment. The various "green" movements added environmental arguments, depicting the demise of polluting industries, such as steel, as a social gain.[64]

Vernon, Bell, and their followers had assumed that the United States would prosper in a postmanufacturing regime. Little evidence existed to support this claim in the 1970s. GNP fell from a 4 percent annual growth rate in the 1960s to 2.5 in the 1970s.[65] Apparently the nation faced economic as well as industrial decline. The complacent could find specific problems in textiles, shoes, electronics, autos, and steel. Together, the record suggested more basic problems. Many explanations were offered: oil was too expensive, lazy workers received too much money, the rate of savings had declined, the baby boomers diluted the stock of experienced workers, and the government spent and taxed too much.[66]

Nevertheless, some academics, business and labor leaders, and politicians believed manufacturing decline was neither inevitable, desirable, nor irreversible. What if the public value of a sector exceeded its private benefit, the judgment most of the world had made about the steel industry? Global trade was now dominated by items that reflected not "comparative advantage" but state decisions to promote sectors that produced high returns, had positive spillover effects, and thus promoted the general welfare.[67] Although some connected trade policy with the condition of manufacturing, they stressed domestic solutions and targeted, sectoral interventions.

Industrial policy divided intellectuals, regions, and classes. In the academy, institutional economists, with labor sympathies, supported it. Orthodox Keynesians and monetarists, the mainstream of the economics profession, fashioned the arguments for the opposition.[68] Because industrial policy focused on manufacturing, Sunbelt politicians usually opposed it. Those from the Frostbelt supported it; yet even there, the middle-class segment of the baby-boom generation resisted such New Deal–type solutions. Baby boomers may have started out antibusiness in the 1960s, but in the economic crisis of the 1970s they muted their critique, often becoming antilabor.[69] Meanwhile, foreign policy, and racial, gender, and environmental issues still dominated New Left politics. Assuming that growth was inevitable and part of the problem, the New Left initially had little to contribute.[70]

Industrial policy divided Democrats, who were its primary advocates, more than Republicans. Within the Carter administration, Keynesians held the key economic positions on the CEA and at the OMB and the Treasury. Industrial policy advocates could be found in Commerce and Labor, departments with less clout on economic matters. When the Economic Policy Group was reorganized in the fall of 1977, Marshall had been excluded from the steering committee, signaling the White House rejection of his supply-side solutions to the steel crisis. Arnold Packer, assistant secretary for policy at the Department of Labor, was not optimistic about converting White House "economists, who believe the market, high interest rates and investment tax credits will solve all our problems." He was right. The CEA thought "the potential for a successful massive program is low, for a large embarrassment, high." Peter Solomon at the Treasury scoffed at the notion of "a plan to pick or fund winners" or, he added, "supporting losers."[71]

As rising unemployment rates and forecasts of a deeper recession made the president's reelection uncertain, however, some of his advisers embraced industrial policy as a means of political revitalization. In May 1980, Eizenstat told Carter,

"We are now in a balanced budget box." The administration's economic policy was "viewed solely as one of austerity, pain and sacrifice, with few positive aspects." By making anti-inflation and a balanced budget the linchpin of his economic policy, the president was vulnerable to Republican candidate Ronald Reagan's promised across-the-board tax cut and the traditional Democratic agenda of Senator Edward M. Kennedy, who challenged Carter in the presidential primaries. Eizenstat believed that a plan to reindustrialize "would excite workers disillusioned with the administration and offer the Nation hope that our basic industries will remain competitive." He suggested distinguishing the short-term measures in place from "long term structural solutions to inflation," which would also reduce unemployment. "If we are to continue to champion free trade and avoid import restrictions, a positive thrust to our troubled industries is necessary."[72]

Eizenstat had been talking with the AFL-CIO's Lane Kirkland and Felix Rohatyn, the investment banker who had been instrumental in resolving the New York City fiscal crisis of 1975. Both advocated a Reconstruction Finance Corporation–type bank, with private and public funds, for investment in infrastructure and manufacturing technologies. The AFL-CIO proposed putting $600 billion of employee pension funds in the bank, a financial contribution ensuring that "the labor movement" was "a partner, not a special interest." By creating a consensual instrument with capital resources, the government role in growth would be direct. Kennedy and the Senate Democratic caucus had already signed on to the proposal. Carter drew closer to the labor movement as the election neared, and Lane Kirkland assumed more of the functions of the aging George Meany, but the president nonetheless rejected a bank.[73]

On August 28, Carter presented his program to a diverse group of cabinet, government, business, and labor leaders. He promised to create a tripartite, economic revitalization advisory board to mobilize public and private resources to restore industrial development and create jobs in areas affected by economic dislocation. Carter named Irving Shapiro, head of the Du Pont Company, and Lane Kirkland cochairs of the board. Kirkland had agreed to serve even though he thought that the penniless board "only guarantees inaction."[74]

The rest of Carter's program was as vacuous, though larded with the lingo of industrial policy—structural, long-term, partnership. The president properly distinguished the initiative from macroeconomic policies. It "is neither a traditional stimulus program nor a general tax cut proposal." But he advocated no new institutions, and his specifics amounted only to a series of tax cuts for business and individuals. Carter promised public investment "in crucial areas like energy, technology, transportation, and exports." He cited "a vast new synthetic fuels industry." Carter had opted for an industrial policy for energy, which had a long history of government regulation. His plan proposed to "fund winners"—synthetic, liquid, and gaseous fuels from coal. He had recently signed a law that created a new corporation and offered loans, loan guarantees, and price and market guarantees to private firms building the plants.

But the market, not the state, held center stage. Carter celebrated the deregulation of the airlines, trucking, rail, banking, and communications industries, covering a much greater swath of the economy. The president told the Democratic convention that his proudest achievement was ending "government regulations to put free enterprise back into the airlines, the trucking and the financial system of our country," which he called "the greatest change in the relationship between Government and business since the New Deal." He ignored the steel and auto industries.[75]

Eizenstat pressed on, but neither Carter nor his top economic advisers paid any heed. The OMB concluded that it was better to rely on "market forces to encourage the mobility of labor and capital to their more productive uses." Schultze told the president in August 1980 that "with two exceptions [steel and auto] individual American industries had not suddenly turned into problem children."[76] Minimizing the significance of two of America's leading industries and ignoring many others was a triumph of ideology over common sense. Seeking to downplay the problem by renaming it, Schultze now concluded that steel suffered from world overcapacity. "Up until the [current] recession this problem in Europe was worse than in the U.S."[77] Only the president could have overcome this opposition. But Carter's interest, even understanding, was minimal.[78]

The Europeans had approached the matter differently. In 1977, they had maintained capacity. In 1980, however, they planned to eliminate 27 million tons of capacity (23 percent) by 1985. To gain acceptance, the EC provided and permitted subsidies for investment, closure costs, and operating deficits and import quotas. Both Europe and Japan, and eventually key Third World nations, had made steel a priority. Most nations considered steel vital to national security. Forty-five percent of world capacity (more than 50 percent of European tonnage) had been nationalized by 1980. In countries like Japan, where the industry was in private hands, government credit, licensing, and trade policies nurtured the steel industry from the 1950s. Although the interventions were diverse, reflecting national traditions, most concluded that government assistance was necessary to effect the transition to the new global steel market and fund new steel technologies. Some echo of such a program could be heard from the Congress. A Government Accounting Office report in 1980 urged a national policy on steel that would set goals, provide technological assistance, and offer tax incentives for advanced, pollution-free equipment. In its last days, the Carter administration rejected the report. Schultze denied that the industry required government assistance.[79] The judgment ended the marriage of American Keynesianism and progressive politics.

Choosing the market over tripartite agreements had political consequences. The president apparently believed that the self-interest driving his market solutions should not infect politics. He regularly denounced special interests and hectored the nation to pursue the public interest. But words could not overcome the actions his policies unleashed.

U.S. TRADE AND INDUSTRIAL POLICIES

Although a priority everywhere, steel was only one example of the international response to the tariff reductions of the Kennedy Round completed in 1967. Europeans voted new aid, value-added taxes, quotas, and other industrial policies in manufacturing, the key affected sector. The United States did nothing. Its industrial policies in agriculture, defense, housing, real estate, and energy were products of earlier American history but unrelated to the new global trade. Dominated by strategic purposes, U.S. foreign economic policies supported the multinationalization of American manufacturing. Beginning in the Eisenhower years, corporations unable to enter closed foreign markets had invested instead of exporting. Government policies privileged direct foreign investment and facilitated offshore production. For most of the postwar years, the overvalued U.S. dollar discouraged industries producing tradable goods and overdeveloped those producing services.[80] The beneficiaries of these actions—transnationals and banks—now added weight to the imperatives of cold war politics.

Older liberal policies made things worse. U.S. antitrust law, established when the home market was relatively secure, discouraged positive responses to the new global trade. Representative Emanuel Celler acknowledged that his strict new antitrust law of 1950, by prohibiting most horizontal and vertical mergers, fostered conglomerates, which responded to the new international competition by abandoning pressed industries. Until the middle of the 1980s, the antitrust division of the Justice Department ignored imports when measuring markets."[81]

Facilitating inaction, the U.S. government possessed a domestic kit containing only macroeconomic tools. Postwar Keynesianism emerged at a time when U.S. industry seemed invulnerable. The emphasis on aggregate demand was an understandable conclusion in the 1930s and 1940s. But it was an incomplete diagnosis. American Keynesians concluded that markets may not work in the aggregate, but they accepted their role in the microeconomy. Competition would allocate resources to their optimal uses. They never considered that markets might fail to reliably price innovation, that competition could be ruinous, that government promoted technological advance, that financial markets structure incentives, and that the industrial policies of other states affect U.S. investors. In short, their economic models ignored the ways institutions, culture, and states shape markets.

In the economic environment of the late 1970s, Keynesianism became a doctrine of passivity. The Democrats lacked the intellectual muscle to power their historic promises. Their 1980 convention theme, "fairness," was appropriate to a growing economy but became sentimental in the current one. Put another way, Democrats were neither modernizers nor social reformers.[82]

By stepping aside in auto and steel, Carter prepared the way for his successor's radical shift of resources away from manufacturing. Ronald Reagan's supply-side tax cuts, combined with his free trade, strong dollar, and foreign policies, channeled investment to the nontrading service, real estate, insurance, and defense industries and away from the manufacturing sector. Similarly, Carter's approval of increased imports paved the way for his successor's celebration of rising imports. In 1984, Reagan said, "If the demand can be met more cheaply by producers abroad, then it makes good economic sense for the firms that use the input to buy it abroad."[83] The trade deficit rose from $25.5 billion in 1980 to a record $159.49 billion in 1987. Caused by manufacturing shortfalls, the deficit became structural.[84]

Carter's memoir omitted discussions of trade and industrial policies because he failed to reconcile the conflicts between American strategic and domestic goals. That failure had severe political repercussions. Wedded to free trade and macro-economic demand management, he and his Keynesian advisers did not devise supply-side policies that strengthened U.S. industries, whose workers and unions constituted the political base of the Democratic party. During the 1970s and especially in 1980, increasing numbers simply stopped voting.[85] On the other hand, Reagan's actions in manufacturing cost him little, as he gained voters working in favored sectors.

Although Carter's personality and experiences as governor made him peculiarly unsuited to the kind of tripartite bargaining necessary to formulate new policies, his advisers, like Schultze and Solomon, had been active in Democratic policy making during the Johnson years. The problem was as much the party as the president. The inadequacies of social policy during the Carter years resulted from failures of economic policy. Formulated as adjuncts to the growing economy of the 1960s, these social policies failed to meet the needs of the U.S. economy in the late 1970s. The public jobs programs advocated by liberal Democrats, while appropriate for a healthy economy, provided no solution for an economy whose core industries required investment. The Humphrey-Hawkins bill to require full employment, originally formulated in 1974, the last year of the postwar boom, became utopian during the Carter years without a companion economic strategy, which its proponents failed to offer. In the end, the Achilles' heel of the Democratic party was its economic, not its social, policy.[86]

NOTES

1. Jimmy Carter, *Keeping Faith: Memoirs of a President* (New York: Bantam Books, 1982). Scholars of Carter's presidency have followed suit. Discussions of Carter's trade policy, as well as those of other postwar presidents, rarely leave the pages of specialized monographs. Otis L. Graham, Jr.'s *Losing Time: The Industrial Policy Debate* (Cambridge, Mass.: Harvard University Press, 1992) includes a brief discussion of Carter's industrial policy. Unlike most analysts of the Carter presidency, Graham recognized that the economy required supply-side solutions, that departed from recent Democratic policy making.

2. Cited in Steve Dryden, *Trade Warriors: STR and the American Crusade for Free Trade* (New York: Oxford University Press, 1995), 220.

3. Daniel Verdier, *Democracy and International Trade: Britain, France, and the United States, 1860–1990* (Princeton, N.J.: Princeton University Press, 1994), 203.

4. Cited in Melvyn P. Leffler, *A Preponderance of Power: National Security, the Truman Administration, and the Cold War* (Stanford, Calif.: Stanford University Press, 1992), 317.

5. Cited in Paul A. Tiffany, *The Decline of American Steel: How Management, Labor, and Government Went Wrong* (New York: Oxford University Press, 1988), 77.

6. Stephen D. Krasner, "The Tokyo Round: Particularistic Interests and Prospects for Stability in the Global Trading System," *International Studies Quarterly* 23 (December 1979): 494; George Curzon and Victoria Curzon, "The Management of Trade Relations in the GATT," in *International Economic Relations of the Western World, 1959–1971*, ed. Andrew Shonfield (London: Oxford University Press, 1976), 200.

7. Dryden, *Trade Warriors*, 38; Alfred Eckes, "Trading American Interests," *Foreign Affairs* 71 (Fall 1992): 133–54.

8. Notes taken at residence of Prime Minister Erland of Sweden, July 13–15, 1963, 4, Trip files, Senatorial files, 1949–64, Hubert H. Humphrey papers, Minnesota Historical Society, St. Paul, Minn.

9. Joint Economic Committee, Hearings, *Steel Prices, Unit Costs Profits, and Foreign Competition*, 88th Cong., 1st sess. (Washington, D.C.: Government Printing Office, 1963), 572–77.

10. The criticism of U.S. trade policy practiced by the State Department forced Kennedy to create the position of the Special Trade Representative in 1962. However, the policy remained the same (Dryden, *Trade Warriors*, 53).

11. The legislation, first introduced by Senator Vance Hartkey (D-Ind.) and Representative James Burke (D-Mass.) in September 1971, would have ended the tax advantages multinationals enjoyed and empowered the president to regulate international capital transactions if he determined that they reduced domestic employment. The bill also would have created a tripartite commission with strong power to regulate imports and capital flows. See Robert A. Pastor, *Congress and the Politics of Foreign Economic Policies, 1929–1976* (Berkeley: University of California Press, 1980), 132–34.

12. Judith Goldstein, *Ideas, Interests, and American Trade Policy* (Ithaca, N.Y.: Cornell University Press, 1993), 163–68; Dryden, *Trade Warriors*, 146; Pastor, *Congress and the Politics of Foreign Economic Policies*, 128–29.

13. Lloyd Cutler Interview, October 23, 1982, William Burkett Miller Center of Public Affairs, University of Virginia, Project on the Carter Presidency, Transcripts (hereafter cited as Miller Center), 34–35, located in the Jimmy Carter Library (JCL).

14. I. M. Destler and Hisao Mitsuyo, "Locomotives on Different Tracks: Macroeconomic Diplomacy, 1977–1979," in *Coping with U.S.-Japanese Economic Conflicts*, ed. I. M. Destler and Hideo Sato (Lexington, Mass.: Heath, 1982), 246–47; Frederick B. Dent to Carter, January 18, 1977, Box 208, White House Central Files (WHCF); Stu Eizenstat and Bob Ginsburg to Carter, August 12, 1977, Box 227, DPS-Eizenstat, JCL. Japan's surplus rose from $2.5 billion in 1976 to $9.7 billion in 1977; Germany's from $13.8 to $16.6 billion (Richard C. Thornton, *The Carter Years: Toward a New Global Order* [New York: Paragon House, 1991], 47–50).

15. Zbigniew Brzezinski, *Power and Principle: Memoirs of the National Security Adviser, 1977–1981* (New York: Farrar, Straus and Giroux, 1981), 314–15.

16. Diane B. Kunz, *Butter and Guns: America's Cold War Economic Diplomacy* (New York: Free Press, 1997), 309.

17. I. M. Destler, *American Trade Politics,* 2d rev. ed. (Washington, D.C.: Institute for International Economics, 1992), 45; Bob Ginsburg to White House Staff, April 22, 1977, Box 226; Alan Wm. Wolff, "U.S. International Trade Policy," March 21, 1977, Box 227; Eizenstat and Richard Cooper to Brzezinski, n.d., Box TA-1, WHCF, JCL.

18. C. Fred Bergsten, "U.S. Trade Policy and the World Economy," *Atlantic Community Quarterly* 15 (1977–78): 442–49.

19. Dryden, *Trade Warriors,* 238; Charlie Schultze to Carter, July 11, 1978, Box 94, Staff Secretary File, JCL.

20. See Carter's interview with editors and news directors, November 18, 1978, *Public Papers of Jimmy Carter, 1978,* 2065–66.

21. "Interview with the President," July 11, 1978, in ibid., 1254–55.

22. Paul A. Volcker and Toyoo Ghohten, *Changing Fortunes: The World's Money and the Threat to American Leadership* (New York: Times Books, 1992), 368.

23. *Wall Street Journal,* May 3, 1977, 8.

24. Nevertheless, in 1979 the Senate Finance Committee estimated that the just-completed Tokyo Round would reduce the U.S. price index by a modest .05 percent (Krasner, "The Tokyo Round," 500–501).

25. Anthony S. Campagna, *Economic Policy in the Carter Administration* (Westport, Conn.: Greenwood Press, 1995), 112.

26. Strauss told the president that there was little he could do in the short run, but he could review a quota for specialty steel, imposed by the Ford administration after a surge of dumped imports. Specialty steel composed only 4 percent of the industry, but it was a high-value product. Ford acted under the 1974 trade legislation, which permitted remedies to those who could establish that imports were "a substantial cause of serious injury or the threat thereof." The EC had asked for the end of the restriction. Instead of evaluating the health of the industry, Carter announced the review in order to signal the basic steel industry to keep prices low, as well as improve relations with the EC (STR, "Specialty Steel Options: Background Paper," February 10, 1977; Eizenstat and Ginsburg to Carter, May 17, 1977, Box 284, DPS-Eizenstat; W. Michael Blumenthal to Carter, May 11, 1977, Box TA-19, WHCF, JCL).

27. Schultze to Carter, May 12, 1977; Strauss to Carter, May 13, 1977, attached to letter, Henry Owen to Zbigniew Brzezinski, November 21, 1977, Box CM-6, WHCF, JCL; Press Release, August 5, 1977; Schultze to Carter, July 27, 1977; Bert Lance to Carter, July 30, 1977; Eizenstat and Ginsburg to Carter, July 30, 1977, Box 284, DPS-Eizenstat, JCL.

28. Despite the conventional opinion, steel prices and wages followed, not led, the others. See, for instance, E. Robert Livernash, *Collective Bargaining in the Basic Steel Industry: A Study of the Public Interest and the Role of Government* (Washington, D.C.: U.S. Department of Labor, 1961).

29. *Wall Street Journal,* April 28, August 8, 1977; Eizenstat to Carter, May 14, 1977, Box CM-6, WHCF, JCL.

30. Yves Meny and Vincent Wright, "State and Steel in Western Europe," in *The Politics of Steel: Western Europe and the Steel Industry in the Crisis Years, 1974–1984,* ed. Yves Meny and Vincent Wright (Berlin: Walter de Gruyter, 1987), 30–31; Ray Hudson

and David Sadler, *The International Steel Industry: Restructuring, State Policies, and Localities* (London: Routledge, 1989), 83–94.

31. Hudson and Sadler, *The International Steel Industry,* 32–33; Peter F. Marcus and Karlis M. Kirsis, *World Steel Dynamics,* "Steel Strategist #11" (September 1985); *Wall Street Journal,* January 24, September 18, 19, 1978.

32. Jeffrey A. Hart, *Rival Capitalists: International Competitiveness in the United States, Japan, and Western Europe* (Ithaca, N.Y.: Cornell University Press, 1992), 54–55; Clyde V. Prestowitz, Jr., *Trading Places: How We Are Giving Our Future to Japan and How to Reclaim It* (New York: Basic Books, 1989), 273–74.

33. Leon Hollerman, "Locomotive Strategy and United States Protectionism: A Japanese View," *Pacific Affairs* 52 (1979): 196.

34. *Wall Street Journal,* August 11, 1977; Eizenstat, "Memorandum of Conversation," August 8, 1977, Box 286, DPS-Eizenstat, JCL; *Japan Metal Bulletin,* September 20, 1975; *Nihon Keizai,* November 23, 1975, cited in Thomas R. Howell, William A. Noellert, Jesse G. Kreier, and Alan Wm. Wolff, *Steel and the State: Government Intervention and Steel's Structural Crisis* (Boulder, Colo.: Westview Press, 1988), 227–29.

35. Eizenstat, "Memorandum of Conversation."

36. Ibid.

37. *Wall Street Journal,* October 14, 1977, 2.

38. *Wall Street Journal,* August 16, 1977; Wolff to Economic Policy Group, February 11, 1977, Box 284, DPS-Eizenstat, JCL.

39. *Wall Street Journal,* May 13, August 16, 1977; Curt Hessler to EPG Steering Committee, n.d. [late August 1977], Box 284, DPS-Eizenstat, JCL.

40. *Wall Street Journal,* July 27, 1977; Lee Smith, "Hard Times Come to Steeltown," *Fortune,* December 1977, 87–93.

41. Smith, "Hard Times, 92; Ted Sorensen to Eizenstat and Strauss, October 12, 1977, Box 284, DPS-Eizenstat, JCL.

42. *Wall Street Journal,* October 12, 1977, 1; *Youngstown Vindicator,* September 11, 22, 25, 1977; President's News Conference, September 29, 1977, 1690; "Session with . . . Editors and News Directors," October 14, 1977, *Public Papers of Jimmy Carter, 1977,* 1801.

43. Blumenthal to Carter, September 29, 1977, Box 284, DPS-Eizenstat, JCL.

44. Strauss to Carter, December 27, 1977, Box 67, Staff Secretary File, JCL.

45. Richard Rivers, Strauss's general counsel, said, "President Carter would have never stood for it" (Dryden, *Trade Warriors,* 249).

46. Jack Sheehan to Lloyd McBride, October 28, December 29, 1977, Box 75, Legislation Department, United Steelworkers of America, Labor Archives, Pennsylvania State University (USWA Files); Press Conference, October 13, 1977, *Public Papers of Jimmy Carter, 1977,* 1789; Hideo Sato and Michael Hodin, "The U.S.-Japanese Steel Issue of 1977," in Destler and Sato, *Coping with U.S.-Japanese Economic Conflicts,* 47; Charles Vanick to Jimmy Carter, October 11, 1977, Box CF TA4–8, WHCF, JCL; Blumenthal to Carter, November 23, 1977, Box 61, Staff Secretary File, JCL; Hugh Patrick and Hideo Sato, "The Political Economy of United States Japan Trade in Steel," in *Policy and Trade Issues of the Japanese Economy: American and Japanese Perspectives,* ed. Kozo Yamamura (Seattle: University of Washington Press, 1982), 222–23; David P. Calleo, *The Imperious Economy* (Cambridge, Mass.: Harvard University Press, 1982), 14.

47. American Embassy, Brussels, to Secretary of State, October 31, 1977, Box CF TA4–8, WHCF, JCL.

48. Author's interview with Jack Sheehan, May 18, 1993.

49. Eizenstat and Ginsburg to Carter, November 30, 1977, Box C-284, DPS-Eizenstat JCL; Congressional Budget Office, *How Federal Policies Affect the Steel Industry* (Washington, D.C.: Government Printing Office, 1987), 34.

50. Anthony Solomon to Carter, November 23, 1977, 2, Box CM8, WHCF; Alfred E. Kahn to Interested Parties, December 4, 1979, Box 283, DPS-Eizenstat JCL; Michael Burrus, "The Politics of Competitive Erosion in the Steel Industry," in *American Industry in International Competition: Government Policies and Corporate Strategies,* ed. John Zysman and Laura Tyson (Ithaca, N.Y.: Cornell University Press, 1983), 95.

51. Marshall to Anthony Solomon, November 14, 1977, Box 286, DPS-Eizenstat, JCL; Vanik to Carter, September 30, 1977, Box TA-19, WHCF, JCL; *Congressional Quarterly Almanac* 34 (1979): 223.

52. Ronald F. King, *Time, Money, and Politics: Investment Tax Subsidies and American Democracy* (New Haven, Conn.: Yale University Press, 1993), 408.

53. Solomon, "Report to the President: A Comprehensive Program for the Steel Industry," December 1977, Jim Smith to Sheehan, June 2, 1980, Box 79, Legislation Department, USWA Files.

54. Ginsburg to Eizenstat, November 8, 1977; Carter's comments on Eizenstat to Carter, December 1, 1977; Strauss to Carter, November 29, 1977, Box 284, DPS-Eizenstat, JCL.

55. Strauss to Carter, November 29, 1977, Box 284, DPS-Eizenstat, JCL.

56. *Wall Street Journal,* July 19, 1978; *Fortune,* February 13, 1978, 130.

57. Press Release, March 10, 1978, attached to James W. Smith to Charles J. Carney, April 4, 1978, Box 77, Legislation Department, USWA Files; Robert M. Immerman to Strauss, March 6, 1978, Box CO-33, WHCF, JCL.

58. Ginsburg to Eizenstat, July 31, 1980, Box 283, DPS-Eizenstat, JCL; Etienne Davignon to Reubin D. Askew, September 30, 1980, Box TA-22, WHCF, JCL.

59. Carter accepted the Chrysler plan only after he was convinced that it would pass the Congress (Robert B. Reich and John D. Donahue, *New Deals: The Chrysler Revival and the American System* [New York: Times Books, 1985], 105, 129).

60. Graham, *Losing Time,* 46–51; *Wall Street Journal,* July 10, 1980, 18.

61. Graham, *Losing Time,* 17–18; Organisation for Economic Cooperation and Development, *Economic Outlook Historical Statistics, 1960–1980* (Paris: Organization for Economic Cooperation and Development, 1982), Table 3.7.

62. Raymond Vernon, "International Investment and International Trade in the Product Cycle," *Quarterly Journal of Economics* 80 (May 1966): 190–207. Even if the theory was valid for industries like textiles, where cheap labor is often decisive, steel requires capital and cheap labor is not decisive. Despite higher labor costs, U.S. steel was produced more efficiently than Japanese steel in the 1960s, unlike the 1970s, when capital became decisive.

63. Howell et al., *Steel and the State,* 394–419.

64. Daniel Bell, *The Coming of Post-Industrial Society: A Century in Social Forecasting* (New York: Basic Books, 1973).

65. Organisation for Economic Cooperation and Development, *Economic Outlook Historical Statistics,* Table 3.7.

66. Graham, *Losing Time,* 16.

67. Steve Merrill to Chairman Cannon, 24 May 1978, p. 2, Box 32, DPS-Stern, JCL.

68. See John Zysman and Laura Tyson, eds., *American Industry and International Competition: Government Policies and Corporate Strategies* (Ithaca, N.Y.: Cornell University Press, 1983). But this was published later, after the deep recession in 1982. It was followed by a full-scale assault on the notion of the postindustrial society: Stephen S. Cohen and John Zysman, *Manufacturing Matters: The Myth of the Post-Industrial Economy* (New York: Basic Books, 1987).

69. Andrew Levison, *The Working-Class Majority* (New York: Coward, McCann and Geoghegan, 1974), 238–39.

70. David Vogel, *Fluctuating Fortunes: The Political Power of Business in America* (New York: Basic Books, 1989), 231–33; Barry Bluestone and Bennett Harrison's *The Deindustrialization of America: Plant Closings, Community Abandonment and the Dismantling of Basic Industry* (New York: Basic Books, 1982) was the first statement from the generation of the 1960s.

71. Arnie Packer to Stuart Eizenstat, October 12, 1979, Box LA2, JCL; Graham, *Losing Time,* 39; Margaret Weir, *Politics and Jobs: The Boundaries of Employment Policy in the United States* (Princeton, N.J.: Princeton University Press, 1992), 126.

72. Eizenstat to Carter, May 24, 1980, Box BE-13, WHCF, JCL; OMB Review, attached to Josh Gotbaum to Eizenstat, June 2, 1980, Box 224, Eizenstat-DPS, JCL; Herbert Stein, *Presidential Economics: The Making of Economic Policy from Roosevelt to Reagan and Beyond,* 2d rev. ed. (Washington, D.C.: American Enterprise Institute, 1988), 229–31.

73. "Statement by the AFL-CIO Executive Council on Reindustrialization," August 1980, Box BE-13, WHCF, JCL; Press Release, "Economic Program for the Eighties," August 28, 1980, Box 201, Staff Secretary File, JCL.

74. *Public Papers of Jimmy Carter, 1980–1981,* 1585–91; Landon Butler to Carter, August 24, 1980, Box 201, Staff Secretary File, JCL.

75. Cited in Elizabeth Drew, *Portrait of an Election: The 1980 Presidential Campaign* (New York: Simon and Schuster, 1981), 250.

76. Between 1978 and 1980, auto imports rose from 17.7 to 26.7 percent of the U.S. market, as sales of American-made cars plunged from 9.3 to 6.6 million.

77. Schultze, "Memorandum for the President," August 24, 1980, Box 202, Staff Secretary File, JCL.

78. OMB, "Review of Industrial Policy," attached to memo Gotbaum to Eizenstat, June 2, 1980, Box 224, DPS-Eizenstat, JCL.

79. Schultze to Peace, October 15, 1980, Box 176, Staff Secretary File, JCL.

80. Calleo, *Imperious Economy,* 69.

81. James R. Williamson, *Federal Antitrust Policy during the Kennedy-Johnson Years* (Westport, Conn.: Greenwood Press, 1995), 17, 36; Alfred Chandler, Jr., "The Competitive Performance of U.S. Industrial Enterprises since the Second World War," *Business History Review* 68 (Spring 1994): 10, 17.

82. See David Coates, "New Labour, or Old?" *New Left Review* 219 (1996): 62–88, for a parallel formulation of the British Labour party.

83. Burton I. Kaufman, *The Presidency of James Earl Carter, Jr.* (Lawrence: University Press of Kansas, 1993), 194–95; *Public Papers of Jimmy Carter, 1980–81,* 1537.

84. The United States is the only major steel producer that possesses less steel capacity now than it had in 1960. The bulk of the reduced capacity, which continues today,

occurred during the first Reagan administration. Although it is today the most efficient in the world, by taking the adjustment for global overcapacity in the 1980s, it can no longer supply its own market. In 1994, imports were 25 percent of U.S. consumption (*American Metal Market,* May 19, 1995; July 9, 1996). The structural problems of the industry are analyzed in Economic Strategy Institute, *Can the Phoenix Survive? The Fall and Rise of the American Steel Industry* (Washington, D.C.: ESI, 1994). They are ignored in the latest celebratory book, Robert S. Ahlbrandt, Richard J. Fruehan, and Frank Giarratani, *The Renaissance of American Steel: Lessons for Managers in Competitive Industries* (New York: Oxford University Press, 1996).

85. Thomas Byrne Edsall, *The New Politics of Inequality,* (New York: Norton, 1984), 184, 187.

86. For examples of social policy failures during the Carter administration, see the chapters by James Patterson, Thomas Sugrue, Bruce Schulman, and Melvyn Dubofsky in this volume.

5

Jimmy Carter and the
End of the Politics of Productivity

Melvyn Dubofsky

Little of the published scholarly literature concerning the administration of Jimmy Carter treats labor policy or the relationship between the president and the twentieth century's most important Democratic party constituency, organized labor. That fact is easily explicable. Carter's rural south Georgia origins and his subsequent experiences offered him little familiarity with issues vital to working people or contact with labor leaders. Thus, in seeking the Democratic nomination for the presidency and in his subsequent presidential campaign, Carter rarely discussed labor issues. Indeed, the themes Carter stressed—smaller, cheaper, more efficient government—troubled labor leaders committed to expensive job programs and an expansive welfare state. Labor preferred other candidates during the Democratic primary, and only the threat from George Wallace prompted Leonard Woodcock of the United Automobile Workers (UAW) to throw his support to Carter in the Florida primary. Organized labor supported Carter as the lesser evil during the general election. Once elected, however, Carter had no choice other than to develop a labor policy and to deal with what remained the largest, best-organized constituency in his party, organized labor.[1]

Carter's labor policies also must be set into a historical and structural context, which is lacking even in the best published analyses of Carter and labor. Nearly all the scholarship stresses the personal antipathy between Carter and George Meany, the substantive public policy issues that divided the Carter administration and organized labor, and the extent to which Carter's relations with labor were worse than in any previous twentieth-century Democratic administration. One gets the impression from the existing literature that something odd, perhaps even alien, occurred in the encounters between Carter Democrats and labor, something at war with the Democratic party's twentieth-century tradition.

In this chapter, I argue instead that the relationship between the Carter administration and organized labor fit neatly into the customary pattern of Democratic party coalition politics. But Carter assumed the presidency at a moment unlike that faced by any other twentieth-century Democratic president. His predecessors held power when organized labor grew increasingly influential. They had successfully practiced the "politics of productivity." Ever since World War II had created a full-employment economy, the Democratic party had committed itself to public policies that stimulated economic growth, expanded the labor market, and pushed wages and earnings higher. Truman's Fair Deal, Kennedy's New Frontier, and Johnson's Great Society all aimed to foster social harmony and mend the nation's ills by using the surplus created by rising productivity rather than by redistributing wealth and income. Even Dwight Eisenhower practiced a "modern" Republican version of the politics of productivity, which Richard Nixon adopted in his own singular way.[2]

Carter, unfortunately, became president precisely when trade unionism declined and the politics of productivity no longer worked. Indeed, as Bruce Schulman's chapter on the economics of the Carter administration suggests, Carter served as a parenthetical president, the pregnant pause between the halcyon years of postwar prosperity and the Reagan-Bush years of supply-side economics, neoliberal politics, and unregulated markets. Carter was the first Democratic president forced to come to grips with the forces of economic globalization, capital hypermobility, and the new information/communications economy. That fateful encounter spelled disaster for Carter, the Democratic party, and organized labor (see pp. 51–71).

By the time Carter entered the White House in January 1977, the politics of productivity was in disarray. The Nixon-Ford years already had suggested the limits to a political strategy based on unlimited economic growth. As the United States' global economic hegemony declined in the late 1960s and early 1970s, Nixon discarded the foundation stone of the postwar international economy, the Bretton Woods financial system; he devalued the dollar, allowing it to float in relation to other currencies. Ford proved less adept at managing the nation's relative economic decline, failing to restrain inflation and bequeathing to Carter a high federal budget deficit.[3]

In January 1977, the new president faced an economic conjuncture that offered him few opportunities to practice the politics of productivity. Carter inherited inflation, rising unemployment, a weakening dollar, worsening international terms of trade, and the looming presence of what soon came to be characterized as *stagflation*, a pernicious combination of rising prices and falling employment. As foreign competitors captured markets from U.S. manufacturers at home and abroad and U.S. capital chased cheap labor around the globe, the core mass-production industries, home to some of the largest unions, shriveled, turning much of the old industrial heartland into a Rust Belt. As the sectors of the economy in which trade unions had their greatest strength faltered, jobs grew in newer service, retail, and white-collar sectors in which unionism's power was weakest. As a result of the changed global economic environment, everywhere in the advanced industrial world social democracy, welfare statism, and Keynesian economics based on public spending retreated.[4]

Carter recognized early on that the character of national and global politics had changed. In a postpresidential interview, Carter recalled his differences with the leaders of the Democratic party in the House who still practiced the politics of productivity. He described the reaction of congressional leaders when he stressed the need to balance the federal budget and restrain public spending. "You should have seen the stricken expression on the faces of those Democratic leaders when I was talking about balancing the budget," Carter recalled. "John Brademas and Shirley Chisholm and Tip O'Neil, even Jim Wright. I mean it was anathema to them to be talking about balancing the budget. That wasn't something that a Democratic president was supposed to do. . . . All they knew about was stimulus and Great Society programs, new social opportunities."[5]

Carter entered the White house equally estranged from most spokespersons for the labor movement. During the Democratic primary campaign in 1976, Carter was the most conservative of the candidates. A key union leader observed, "I don't know who he is, where he's going or where he's been." Carter rejected the role of special interests in politics and the practice of "interest group liberalism" in which labor served as the Democratic party's primary liberal interest group.[6] Yet to win the general election and gain labor's financial support, Carter had to promise jobs programs and national health insurance, policies that conflicted with his more fundamental commitment to fiscal restraint and a balanced budget.[7] Hamilton Jordan caught the gap in thought and perception between Carter and the old Democratic political order. As he recalled, party chieftains complained, "We've got this Democrat who's not doing what Hubert Humphrey or Lyndon Johnson would have done." To Jordan, Carter was more in harmony with the sentiments of ordinary citizens than labor leaders or nonsouthern Democratic leaders, precipitating "a basic cleavage . . . as to what the party was all about and what the mood of the country was."[8]

Not only did Carter and most labor leaders differ about policy and the role of organized labor in the Democratic party, but Carter and many labor leaders, most especially George Meany, seemed personally and emotionally alien to each other. Indeed, unlike the man who became Carter's secretary of labor, Ray Marshall, who said that the president chose him because he was bilingual ("I also speak Baptist"), Meany and his closest allies spoke a tongue foreign to Carter. Stuart Eizenstat recalled an incident early in Carter's presidency when the president invited AFL-CIO leaders to the White House for a lunch at which the president grew upset at the labor leaders' coarse language. "It was painfully obvious at that point," remembered Eizenstat, "that regardless of what he might do or say neither was going to feel terribly comfortable with the other." Or, as Marshall recalled, "George Meany and Jimmy Carter were just not a good chemical mix. If you got them together it was just clear that these fellows didn't communicate."[9]

The first substantive decision the president had to make on labor policy, the appointment of a new secretary of labor, graphically exposed the chasm that separated the two men. When Carter asked Meany for his first three choices for the position, the AFL-CIO leader responded, "Dunlop, Dunlop, Dunlop."[10]

Meany, however, was not displeased with Carter's choice of Ray Marshall. Indeed, Marshall was probably a better appointment than John Dunlop. Marshall had good relations both with organized labor and with women's and African American constituencies. He also appeared as a relative outsider in the circumscribed universe of Washington politics yet knew the rules of the game. He shared Dunlop's commitment to "industrial pluralism" and collective bargaining, but he was a southerner by birth, education, speech, and career, having served as an academic economist in southern institutions of higher education. Marshall believed that his primary purpose as secretary was to serve the interests of workers and their organizations. As he stressed, the Department of Labor had to represent the interests of workers and act as a lobbying force inside the administration for them. Nearly all other domestic cabinet departments speak for business. Most economists, moreover, favor neoclassical, marginal economics in which competitive markets set wages. "When Adam Smith's invisible hand moves in the labor market," Marshall asserted, "it's all thumbs. . . . My own experience is that the one who's likely to get neglected in a market-oriented society like ours is the worker."[11]

Marshall fought for policies that benefited union members and unorganized workers. He endorsed reforms in federal labor law that others condemned as special interest legislation, yet he worked equally hard to obtain legislation that would benefit all workers, especially those clustered at the bottom of the wage and occupational ladder who tended to be nonunion and overwhelmingly female or minority. In fact, he believed that nothing was more important than to create jobs for all those willing and able to work, and particularly to move minority youths and welfare recipients into the labor market. Market forces by themselves, he asserted, will never produce desired results, but evidence exists "that we can change the direction of unemployment and put people to work. We need to do that."[12] His commitment to creating jobs for the underemployed and unemployed, sponsoring training programs to improve human capital, and raising wage levels caused Marshall to combat persistently the advice that Carter received from his economic advisers to fight inflation through reduced expenditures and tight money. Nothing stimulated excess public spending and unbalanced the budget more, responded Marshall, than high unemployment.[13]

Marshall, however, was not an unreconstructed New Dealer who believed that federal spending could solve all problems or that the politics of productivity still functioned effectively. "It was very clear," he later recalled, "that we were in a period of economic ferment, and that many of the traditional approaches to economic policy-making were inappropriate." The primary problem, he suggested, was "that the American economy had become internationalized and that fundamentally changed the way we had to make economic policy. We were also undergoing substantial technological changes and significant demographic changes. All those things tended to change the fundamentals of economic policy.

We can no longer make economic policy in the United States in isolation from other countries."[14]

Marshall clashed persistently with the president's leading economic advisers, men who preferred to fight inflation before stimulating job growth and who considered unions too influential in the economy and the Democratic party. Charles Schultze, the chair of the Council of Economic Advisers (CEA) and Alfred Kahn, who served as Carter's czar in the war against inflation, spoke the language of neoliberalism, deregulation, and freer markets. Kahn said: "I'd love the Teamsters to be worse off. I'd love the automobile workers to be worse off." He actually believed that powerful trade unionists exercised monopoly power, interfered with the proper working of a free market, and exploited less fortunately situated workers. "I'm helping the unemployed, who have been exploited by the UAW," Kahn asserted, "those unemployed automobile workers are being screwed by the employed automobile workers."[15] Schultze shared Kahn's antipathy toward the unions. "Whenever big management and big labor get together," Schultze remarked, "they normally . . . screw the public," with labor doing most of the damage because "management has always been a patsy for large wage increases," always wanting to give labor all that it asks for.[16] Kahn and Schultze advised the president that it might be in his best interest to break openly with labor, even if doing so threatened his chances for renomination in 1980.[17] Kahn insisted that in a time of diminishing resources and possibilities, Carter had to put labor in its place, and the economic adviser believed that the president understood that the Democratic party must no longer "simply kiss Doug Frazier's [sic] ass," because "it cannot simply accept the bankrupt."[18] Kahn also believed that Meany and Lane Kirkland, soon to succeed an ailing Meany as AFL-CIO president, "represented a bankrupt labor movement." He thought that Eizenstat, Marshall, and Mondale were always assuaging labor, especially the automobile workers, defending social security, and advocating reduction of unemployment. "The country's never going to solve its problems," Kahn maintained, if it listens to such liberals.[19]

THE CARTER ADMINISTRATION AND LABOR: FIRST STEPS

In describing and analyzing how the Carter administration grappled with public policy matters vital to labor, it is important to distinguish between those issues of first-order importance to organized labor and those of secondary concern. The AFL-CIO fought hardest for two reforms in federal labor law: a common situs picketing bill that would free building and construction trades unions from judicial rulings that denied them the right to tie up construction sites in disputes between only one union and a single contractor; and amendments to the National Labor Relations Act that accelerated the holding of union representation elections, simplified the process of union certification, and punished employers expeditiously and stringently for violations of federal labor law. The two largest unaffiliated unions, the UAW and the Brotherhood of Teamsters, also lobbied hard for the latter measure.

On many other issues labor assumed that it shared a common agenda with the Carter administration. From programs intended to widen job training opportunities, promote job growth, increase the minimum wage, reform welfare by expanding employment opportunities, and initiate a program of national health insurance, labor and the Carter administration pursued shared goals. On all these issues, moreover, Secretary Marshall endorsed labor's priorities and its programs. And, on these issues, national health insurance excepted, labor won a measure of victory, yet not without conflict with the president and other influential members of his administration.

On policy issues of secondary importance to the AFL-CIO, Carter and his domestic policy advisers agreed at first that no issue was more important than reducing the level of unemployment estimated to have reached 9 percent. In an address to Congress on January 31, 1977, Carter presented an economic recovery program that would reduce unemployment without worsening the federal budget deficit. He proposed over the two fiscal years 1977 and 1978 to spend more than $4 billion on public works; add 415,000 more public service jobs; expand training and youth programs under the Comprehensive Employment and Training Act (CETA); and provide other jobs through economic stimulus aimed at disadvantaged youths, minorities, and Vietnam veterans. Six weeks later, Carter presented Congress a second jobs program specifically geared to the needs of unemployed youths and implemented through extension and expansion of CETA. The president described this proposal as reminiscent of Franklin D. Roosevelt's Civilian Conservation Corps.[20] These proposals reflected the concerns of the secretary of labor, who was committed to jobs programs that focused on the most disadvantaged sectors of the labor force. Marshall also believed that public funding of jobs was less costly and less inflationary than subsidizing unemployment through insurance or welfare. He insisted that federal programs that aimed to elevate the human capital of their beneficiaries be directed toward the areas and people with the highest need. In Marshall's estimation, it required an antidiscrimination program as well as a jobs program to break down labor market segmentation and move people from the secondary to the primary labor market.[21]

Carter's job training and public service employment proposals failed to satisfy labor leaders and caused disagreement inside the administration. For labor, Carter's desire to stimulate the economy without unbalancing the budget suggested that the stimulus would be too small to have a significant impact on unemployment. Its focus on disadvantaged youths and minorities also promised too small a payoff to unionists. Even more important were the warning signals that went off inside the administration when Carter appeared to act on Marshall's preferences for combating unemployment. Although high unemployment troubled most of the president's economic advisers, they, especially Schultze, worried more about potential inflation and unbalanced budgets. Schultze opposed nearly all Marshall's job programs as being too ambitious and too costly. In his estimation, Carter faced a different world than his Democratic predecessors in the White House: "No longer can you go to the American people and say if you just get rid of your economic myths and let us expand the economy you can have everything all at the same time . . . it was no longer the situation. How does a Democratic president cope with this problem given the constituencies that elected him?" Schultze later remembered how difficult it was to educate Carter about the limitations and liabilities of Marshall's approach. The differences between Marshall and Schultze exemplified the frictions over labor policy in the administration that made it nearly impossible for the president ever to satisfy his labor constituency. Schultze insisted that Carter knew his economic advisers were right and that the party constituencies were wrong, but that the president was damned if he didn't and also if he did. In Schultze's words, Carter had to say, "By God, I know that I'm on this side and can't go there [the CEA], and I know I'm too far on that side [the constituencies but not far enough for labor]."[22]

The same dilemma trapped the administration in its attempt to reform the welfare system by linking support payments more tightly to an expanded public service employment program (see James Patterson's discussion of welfare reform in the Carter administration, pp. 117–36). As a consequence, welfare policy impinged directly on labor policy, affected relations with the AFL-CIO, and foreshadowed other basic divisions over economic policy inside the administration.[23]

Like most presidents who preceded him and those who would follow him, Carter believed that the national welfare system had failed. Like them, he considered paid employment for the able-bodied vastly superior to direct cash grants or payments in kind. And like them, he also maintained that welfare could be reformed without adding substantially to federal expenditures. Within the administration, however, no consensus could ever be reached concerning how to reform welfare, provide jobs for those in need, and contain costs. The Labor Department preferred to focus on the creation of jobs. In the words of Arnold Packer, the Department of Labor's liaison on welfare reform, "We rejected what I would call the reservation theory . . . that there is a large group of people, mostly black and poor, who are too goddamn ignorant to be of any use, so we simply pay them a humane amount of money to keep them out of our hair. [We] emphasize . . . a responsibility on the part of society to provide an opportunity to work, but then an equal responsibility on the part of families that could work to send somebody out to do jobs."[24]

Even had the administration not been split over the Labor Department's jobs program, Carter's antipathy toward increasing federal expenditures would have rendered it largely ineffective. Nearly everyone in the administration agreed that the costs of moving welfare recipients into the labor market exceeded the cost of the existing system.[25] When Carter finally unveiled his welfare reform proposals, he conceded that his intention to "make a complete and clean break with the past," to revise a welfare system "too hopeless to be cured by minor modifications," necessitated additional expenditures in the amount of $2.8 billion, which prompted Congress to reject it.[26]

Two years later, when the president's domestic policy advisers again tried to reform the welfare system, believing they could build a "broad, centrist coalition, tapping liberals who favor raising the lowest welfare benefits and providing greater work opportunities, conservatives who favor . . . making work requirements meaningful, and state and local governments that . . . most of all want relief from welfare costs," the same forces doomed their efforts. Those party to the proposal knew that moving welfare recipients into decent jobs would substantially increase the number of such beneficiaries and hence the costs of the proposal. To a specific cost proposal from his advisers that recommended a $5.7-billion reform package, the president added at the bottom of the memorandum in his own handwriting, "Do not ask me to approve a higher figure in the future."[27]

A similar clash of interests played itself out with comparable results on the issue of increasing the federal minimum wage, which inflation had driven well below its customary relationship to average manufacturing wages. On one side stood the AFL-CIO and the Department of Labor, eager to raise the minimum and provide increased protection to the most vulnerable workers. On the other side stood the Treasury Department, the Commerce Department, and the CEA, all of whom feared that an excessive increase would stimulate inflation and aggravate unemployment. Somewhere in between stood the president's own Domestic Policy Staff, eager to satisfy the party's primary constituencies, aware of the party's long-standing commitment to aid the less fortunate, yet swayed by economic advice that linked wages, inflation, and employment.

Marshall disputed the CEA's estimates concerning the inflationary impact of a higher minimum wage, and he reminded Carter of the link between higher wages and welfare reform. "The primary beneficiaries of the minimum wage," the secretary cautioned the president, "are the unorganized minority and female adult wage earners."[28] "Not to increase the minimum wage—on the ground of either inflation or unemployment—would be to transfer too much of the cost of the policy to the people who can least afford it, the people at the bottom of the economic ladder."[29]

Marshall's position ultimately prevailed. Carter obtained precisely the compromise that Eizenstat favored and Marshall could tolerate.[30] Congress increased the minimum wage immediately to $2.65 an hour with future yearly increases to $3.35 in 1981. In signing the bill, Carter asserted that it would increase low- and middle-income family earnings by $2 billion, stimulate the economy, and increase the wealth of the nation without intensifying inflation or worsening youth unemployment.[31] As Marshall later remembered, the president finally realized that the minimum wage was a moral, not an economic, issue and that 5 million people, without unions and without power, would not obtain a raise unless government mandated one. Employers unable to pay a livable minimum wage should go out of business, declared the labor secretary, for the sorts of

jobs that they offered not only exploited workers but also failed to train or educate them for better employment.[32]

The struggle over the Humphrey-Hawkins employment bill, however, most
graphically laid bare the limits of the Carter administration's ability to satisfy the
party's labor constituency and its allies. No legislative battle of the Carter years
exposed more vividly how the politics of productivity had reached its limit. When
Carter entered the White House, the nation was experiencing its first serious
encounter with chronic unemployment since the Great Depression. Northern
Democrats in Congress whose experience linked the New Deal to the Great Society
refused to surrender the "politics of productivity." Instead, they proposed legislation reminiscent of the Employment Act of 1946 but with specific implementing
clauses that would require the federal government to spend money and to create
jobs sufficient to guarantee all able-bodied workers employment, whether in the
private sector or on public works. The resulting Humphrey-Hawkins Act, named
after the senator from Minnesota and an African American representative from
southern California, not only united what remained of the New Deal–Fair Deal–
Great Society Democrats in Congress but also pulled together organized labor and
African American interest groups inside the party.[33]

Few members of the administration endorsed Humphrey-Hawkins as drafted
by its sponsors. Charles Schultze, chair of the CEA, the advisory committee created by the Employment Act of 1946, led the resistance to Humphrey-Hawkins.
For Schultze, combating inflation took precedence over creating jobs. He demanded that all the specific targets for reducing unemployment be eliminated from
the bill, as well as precise requirements to create public service jobs. Otherwise,
Schultze reasoned, the bill might accelerate inflation when, instead, "the goal of
achieving reasonable price stability should . . . be given more prominence." He
preferred a law more comparable to the 1946 act, one that proclaimed a commitment to a full employment economy yet defined such a goal broadly and required
no particular actions that might boost federal spending.[34]

Eizenstat and presidential adviser Mark Siegel saw immediately that Schultze's
position threatened fundamental Democratic party constituency relations. In
Eizenstat's estimation, Schultze's disagreements went to "the heart of the Humphrey-
Hawkins Bill" and "crystallize[d] the distance between the Administration's economic views and those of the Black Caucus and other Congressional liberals." To
publicize such views would subject the administration to maximum criticism and
embarrassment. Instead, Eizenstat proposed additional discussion by the Economic
Policy Group and a more muted response.[35] Siegel reported to the president that
to act on Schultze's proposal meant the administration had decided "to change
everything about Humphrey-Hawkins except the name of the bill." Conceding that
liberals, blacks, and labor would be angry anyway, Siegel recommended that
Schultze's tone be softened because "we do not need to throw down the gauntlet
so explicitly."[36] As Carter's domestic policy advisers labored to arrange a compromise that would keep peace in the party, additional objections to Humphrey-

Hawkins emerged from the Office of Management and Budget. Bert Lance, like Schultze, argued that no version of the bill could be written that would recognize economic realities and also satisfy the real objectives of its sponsors. He wondered how the administration could get that message through without "exacerbating already strained relations with the most liberal wing of the party."[37]

Yet, because the administration refused to alienate the party's liberal wing any further, Eizenstat, Schultze, and Marshall strained to negotiate a compromise. By October, the negotiators had made some progress, although disagreements remained over a precise date to achieve the target of 4 percent unemployment and sufficient flexibility for the president to combat inflation. "We cannot afford to support a bill," Eizenstat and Schultze advised Carter, "that appears to set economic objectives so ambitious that efforts to achieve them would be very likely to generate much stronger inflationary pressures." The president agreed with his advisers.[38]

At a news conference on November 11, 1977, Carter made it clear that he would tolerate only a final bill that included a strong anti-inflation component and protection against unwarranted costly public programs.[39] Even after the bill's sponsors agreed to substantial compromises with the administration, the bill died in the first session of Congress.[40] Increasingly, Carter's advisers recognized, as Eizenstat recalled some years later, that "the labor constituency . . . had just waned in power unbeknownst to us, and so the receptivity for these programs simply wasn't there."[41] But because Humphrey-Hawkins was, in Eizenstat's words, "one of the few bills in which we are clearly aligned with our major constituencies— labor and the minority community—to disappoint them . . . on a bill on which we have already taken whatever heat we will take would be a dramatic mistake."[42] Thus the administration continued to work with its constituency allies to fashion a bill that could pass congressional scrutiny. Preparatory to a meeting at the White House with the bill's supporters on August 18, 1978, Eizenstat suggested to the president a strategy to get the bill already passed by the House and acceptable to the administration through the Senate, where more conservative influences sought to link it to a zero-inflation goal. That was no easy matter because the labor-minority coalition itself quarreled over the relation between jobs and inflation, with some members willing to compromise and others adamantly rejecting any link between job creation and inflation. Eizenstat advised Carter to inform the coalition that the president would urge the Senate to pass a bill that aimed at reducing unemployment by 1983 to a maximum of 4 percent but left the inflation target more ambiguous.[43] At the end of September, as the bill made its way through the Senate, Carter told an audience of African American journalists, "We can never stop moving toward full employment until every man and every woman in the United States who's able and willing to have a job has a job. And I'm determined to see this bill [Humphrey-Hawkins] passed this year, because I don't want to hear the unemployed child or man with a dependent family cry out this verse, 'Inasmuch as ye did it not to one of the least of these, ye did it not to me.'" The bill ultimately passed Congress as a final gesture to the New Deal–Great Society heritage, in deference to the residual influence of the liberal-black-labor bloc in the party, and as homage to the recently deceased Humphrey.[44]

The struggle over the administration's effort to shepherd a compromise full employment bill through Congress, one aggressively lobbied for by a relatively united coalition of labor, African American, and women's interest groups, hinted at why organized labor's attempts to enact legislation specifically addressing the needs of trade unions failed.

THE FAILURE OF LABOR LAW REFORM

The two issues dearest to the heart of organized labor were legislative reforms, first, to liberate building trades unions from restraints that federal courts had placed on their right to picket construction sites and, second, to add clauses to the National Labor Relations Act (NLRA) to expedite union representation elections and to punish more stringently employers who violated the law. Labor lobbyists pushed for a common situs picketing bill almost as soon as Carter took office, assuming that its passage would be quick and easy. In a series of White House meetings and memorandums in February 1977, the president's advisers discussed how to deal with organized labor's political agenda. The administration much preferred to approach labor's demands as a whole and as part of a coordinated political strategy, but it saw no alternative to supporting labor immediately on common situs picketing. As Jody Powell scribbled on a memorandum to the president, "Sounds like a lot of work to arrive at the position we'll need to take anyway, i.e., support and sign something similar to the 1975 bill. Let's make sure we're asked before we commit, but not wait so long that it looks like we were pressed."[45] On the substantive issue, moreover, no one in the administration disagreed. Schultze, Marshall, and Carter's domestic policy and constituency advisers all agreed that the common situs bill should be supported and steered through Congress.[46] Without realizing it, however, Landon Butler, the White House liaison to the labor movement, presciently prophesied the outcome when he observed in a strategy memorandum that if "we take the piecemeal approach, we run the risk of making an isolated issue a litmus test of our commitment to Labor."[47] Which is precisely what happened. The House rejected the bill, labor found much to blame on the Carter administration, and labor exposed its growing political weakness.[48]

The loss of political influence by organized labor became even clearer in the aftermath of the tumultuous struggle over labor law reform. By the middle of the 1970s, trade union leaders had become convinced that, as a consequence of the ease with which employers violated the NLRA, workers had lost the right to act collectively. In order to restore workers' legal right to unionize and to enable organizers to enroll employees in independent unions, labor leaders asserted that federal labor law had to simplify the process of union certification and protect workers against employers who violated federal law with impunity. Carter himself knew little about the intricacies of labor law or the specifics of labor's proposals for reform, but his closest advisers, especially Ray Marshall, perceived both justice and political gains in supporting labor law reform.[49]

Carter's staff urged him to support labor law reform. Eizenstat explained precisely why the president should make it a priority administration measure. He reminded Carter: "It is difficult to overestimate the importance of this matter in terms of our future relationship with organized labor. Because of budget constraints and fiscal considerations, we will be unable to satisfy their desires in many areas requiring expenditure of government funds. This is an issue without adverse budget considerations, which the unions want very much. I think it can help cement our relations for a good while."[50] Hamilton Jordan, Marshall, Vice President Mondale, and even Bert Lance recommended that Carter follow Eizenstat's advice. Like Eizenstat, Jordan noted that *"by supporting labor on this issue, we can encourage a reasonable approach on future issues. In short, a labor law reform bill as proposed by Stu and Ray is consistent with our approach to government, and also holds the promise of improving substantially our relations with labor on terms which we can accept"* (emphasis in original).[51] Although Carter remained loath to get involved in details, he went along with his advisers' recommendations to send a bill to Congress as formulated by the administration in consultation with organized labor.[52]

Carter sent the bill to Congress on July 18, 1977.[53] By the first week of October, it had passed the House by a substantial majority (257–163) only to bog down in the Senate, where a minority, cognizant of labor's defeat on common situs picketing, stalled. While Senate opponents tied up the bill through arcane procedures and filibusters, the business community unleashed a highly effective propaganda campaign against it that allied labor's traditional enemies and its former "friends." The bill became one of the most heavily lobbied in history, what one high AFL-CIO official called a "holy war," and what both Meany and Douglas Fraser of the UAW referred to as "part of class warfare" by business and the right wing. Meany called it "the right wing's biggest assault on labor since big business fought Roosevelt's New Deal."[54]

Prodded by Marshall and Eizenstat, Carter did all he could to break the Senate filibuster against labor law reform. He consulted closely with Meany and Lane Kirkland on the bill's progress. In speeches to business and citizen groups in May and June 1978, Carter insisted that reform represented modest and moderate legislation that only gives "workers the right that was guaranteed them in the Wagner Act of 1935."[55] Working the telephones and pressuring senators, Carter labored to get the votes needed to invoke cloture and bring the bill to the floor for a vote. On June 19, Carter learned from his advisers precisely how slender the chances were for positive action, how the most likely result would be to fall one vote short of cloture, in a struggle against "the most expensive and powerful lobby ever mounted against a bill in the nation's history." Aware that the administration would lose, Eizenstat and Bill Johnston advised the president to go down fighting. "The present circumstances," they declared, "present us with an unusual opportunity to show the depth of our commitment to labor. . . . we think your own standing with the AFL-CIO . . . would be greatly enhanced if . . . you publicly became more involved in the effort to get cloture. . . . I do not think that there is much political downside to a more visible presence in this effort by you; the business groups already know of your position on the bill."[56]

When the bill died in the Senate, Carter, as advised, made his disappointment quite public. "That was the one bill," he told an audience of international journalists, "that I sat down and . . . wrote, with the help of my advisers, myself, every paragraph of it." But it failed because of "an unwarranted outpouring of distortion and political pressure from some business organizations and some right-wing organizations, highly effective, that caused the defeat of good legislation." Later, speaking to an audience at a convention of the steelworkers' union, Carter promised to make labor law reform his top legislative priority in 1979.[57] But labor law reform was a dead issue. Business and its allies in Congress had carried the day, in the process burying the much-praised postwar accord between labor and capital. As one businessman later recalled, "The defeat of labor law reform during the Carter years was a watershed for organized labor from which they have never fully recovered. . . . it was not the Carter administration that lost that bill; organized labor lost it."[58] As the postwar accord collapsed, Marshall commented acidly about labor's business opponents, "Here we've got the only labor movement in the world that embraces capitalism and . . . [they were] trying to destroy it."[59]

What business sensed and administration insiders also realized was organized labor's declining influence in national affairs and as a power bloc within the Democratic party. Jordan and Eizenstat later remembered that unions represented a declining percentage of the labor force, especially in the rapidly growing South and West, and that they scarcely spoke for a united membership. Many unionists, according to Eizenstat, had become middle-class consumers more worried about taxes than government benefits. According to party pollsters, such union members wanted government off their backs and out of their pockets, hence they opposed the creation of new public programs to benefit low-income people. Members of Congress also realized the impotence of labor lobbyists and practiced a new brand of constituent politics attuned to pleas for lower taxes and reduced federal expenditures. Jordan added that the AFL-CIO was a stale operation, "barely functioning as an institution," led by a declining old man no longer in control of his officers and troops.[60]

Marshall still harbored hopes that wise job-creation programs and necessary reforms in labor law could revitalize unionism and link minorities to organized labor as a decisive bloc in a rebuilt Democratic party, but other advisers in the administration saw this as a Sisyphean task. Eizenstat and the Domestic Policy Group acted primarily to propitiate labor and minorities for the least possible cost yet believed that the future of the party lay in building its strength among southern, western, and suburban voters antipathetic to unions, welfare programs, and interest groups. For new Democrats and their economist allies, such as Schultze and Kahn, who had rejected Keynesian politics of productivity in favor of neo-liberal free markets, the old New Deal–Great Society Democratic party built on cities, blue-collar industrial workers, and ethnic and racial minorities had seen its best days. The future lay with those Democrats who had rejected labor law reform, full employment legislation, and deficit financing in obeisance to their suburban middle-class, professional/managerial constituents.[61]

THE POLITICS OF INFLATION AND LABOR

These new political realities guaranteed that Carter would clash with labor leaders over the most insoluble economic problem of the day. Persistent inflation, particularly during the administration's last two years, caused Carter to combat rising prices rather than reduce unemployment. On the one hand, the administration offered its allies in the labor and minority communities job-creation programs; on the other, it combated inflation by cutting federal expenditures, restraining wage increases, and raising interest rates. Carter, moreover, never hid his belief that government had limited resources and hence "cannot eliminate poverty or provide a bountiful economy or reduce inflation or save our cities or cure illiteracy or provide energy."[62]

As one economist later wrote, the Carter administration faced "total chaos . . . the end of consensus economics. . . . The president was forced not only to deal with stagflation, but to do so at a time when the experts could not agree on a solution."[63] How true! The president's leading economic advisers in the struggle against inflation, Schultze and Alfred Kahn, were suspicious of unions. Carter held these two men responsible for setting the anti-inflationary policies that required labor as well as management to cooperate in a voluntary administration program to restrain wage and price rises.

By contrast, Marshall and Eizenstat understood that a successful fight against inflation required cooperation from union leaders. That is not to say that Marshall and Eizenstat saw a labor movement without blemishes. Marshall thought that Meany, by resisting moderate wage increases, worked against the best interests of the labor movement, undermined his own people, and evinced a gross ignorance of the economic forces at work in the 1970s. Eizenstat, on occasion, considered labor and its allies "insatiably greedy liberal interest groups."[64] Nevertheless, both men believed that labor had to be induced to cooperate with the administration on inflation policy, and Marshall, in particular, opposed fighting inflation by sacrificing workers' jobs. He told the president that the Democratic party would pay the price in 1980 if it fought inflation with unemployment, a policy choice that would be bad economics as well as poor politics. Schultze's and Kahn's advice reminded Marshall of his favorite *New Yorker* cartoon, in which surgeons gather around the operating table and one says, "Thank God we operated just in time. Another week and he wouldn't have needed it."[65]

Only a year into his administration, Carter seemed to share the anti-inflationary proclivities of his economists. At the end of January 1978, the president urged business and labor to negotiate noninflationary wage settlements, inviting Meany to a luncheon where Carter urged the labor leader to accept voluntary compliance. In a public address several months later, the president asked American workers "to accept a lower rate of wage increase . . . in return . . . [for] a comparable restraint in price increases for the goods and services they buy."[66] By the fall of 1978, Carter heated up his anti-inflationary rhetoric. "We *must* control inflation," the president urged a convention of union steelworkers. Finally, in a televised speech to the nation on October 24, Carter informed viewers, "We must face a time of national austerity. Hard choices are necessary if we want to avoid consequences even worse." The president asked citizens to join in accepting voluntary price-wage guidelines under which workers would agree to limit total wage increases to a maximum of 7 percent annually, except for the lowest-paid employees (those earning four dollars an hour or less), and promising workers "real-wage insurance" through a tax rebate provision that would kick in when the inflation rate exceeded 7 percent.[67] The last was a program pushed by Schultze and Kahn, with some input from Marshall and Eizenstat. The influence of the latter could be seen in the exemption for low-wage workers. The counsel of the former was apparent in Carter's failure to consult labor, particularly Meany, before announcing the initiative and the president's appointment of Kahn as head of the Council on Wage and Price Stability (COWPS), the agency that would implement the policy.[68] As Marshall later remembered, the administration's failure to consult with Meany in advance and to build consensus guaranteed a breach with labor.[69]

Had the administration followed Marshall's advice and built consensus first, a public dispute with labor over wage restraint might have been averted. Instead, Meany precipitated a rhetorical and successful legal battle against the administration's voluntary wage-price restraint program, although other union leaders sought to be more accommodating. After the fact, Kahn and Schultze accepted Marshall's approach, agreeing to try to seek Meany's cooperation with a voluntary anti-inflation policy. In a December 8 memorandum to the president, the two economists and Eizenstat advised Carter to invite Meany to the White House in order to mollify the labor leader by obtaining his consent to an anti-inflation policy but without capitulating on any substantive issues. They agreed that the exempt wage level might be raised above four dollars without damaging the initiative and that it was more important to buy Meany's cooperation than simply to hold the line. Carter accepted the proposal on the assumption that the administration would get something out of it, because Meany "looks like shit and we look good and he knows it. He is looking for a way to get off the hook." Yet Carter made it clear that his primary aim remained to restrain inflation.[70]

As suggested in the memorandum of December 8, Marshall brokered the agreement with the AFL-CIO. On January 22, 1979, Marshall reported to the White House that he had arranged a consultation process with the AFL-CIO that would ensure regular exchanges between the administration and labor on all major issues. Under the terms of the agreement, the labor secretary and the vice president promised to meet monthly with top officials of the AFL-CIO and other participants; Marshall and Eizenstat, not Kahn or Schultze, would be the administration's primary policy contacts with the AFL-CIO; and the administration would notify the AFL-CIO before acting on issues of major importance.[71] Three days later, in his annual message to Congress, Carter enunciated an anti-inflation policy that merged the approaches of Kahn-Schultze and Marshall-Eizenstat. The president made reducing inflation his administration's economic priority, stressing that the battle necessitated budgetary austerity and reduced economic growth. Yet he promised not to fight inflation on the backs of those least able to support the war. Carter also informed Congress that organized labor had consented to participate in voluntary wage and price standards with a 7 percent maximum wage increase and a real-wage insurance program to protect workers' earnings.[72]

Carter's announcement of the AFL-CIO's enlistment in his anti-inflation war proved premature. On February 19, 1979, the AFL-CIO Executive Council denounced real-wage insurance as "a tool to enforce wage controls, not an incentive to encourage voluntary compliance."[73] The continuing influence of Kahn and Schultze in setting economic policy fed labor's suspicion. And for good reason. As head of COWPS, Kahn intended to fight inflation hard.[74]

It took Marshall and Eizenstat much of the remainder of the year to patch up administration relations with organized labor. Their cause was advanced by a number of labor leaders who dealt with the administration without Meany's knowledge, by Meany's retirement from office, and by his replacement with the more malleable and accommodating Lane Kirkland. At the end of September, Carter could announce that the AFL-CIO had entered a national accord to fight inflation by agreeing, among other conditions, to serve on a tripartite pay advisory committee chaired by John Dunlop.[75]

However much the national accord may have healed relations between organized labor and the Carter administration, it failed to promote consensus on national economic policy. With prices surging and interest rates climbing ever higher, the administration saw no choice but to intensify the war against inflation. To win that war the administration had to reduce public expenditures, maintain high interest rates, and restrain wages and prices. The war's casualties would be those least able to pay the cost. Thus, no matter how much administration insiders conferred with union leaders in the winter and spring of 1980, they could not dissuade labor leaders from seeking a Democratic alternative to Carter in the election of 1980, preferably Edward Kennedy. As Marshall had warned, to fight inflation with budgetary restraints would carry a heavy political cost. Although Carter defeated Kennedy and rallied organized labor to his cause when the alternative was Ronald Reagan and the Republicans, both Democrats and trade unionists paid dearly for the war against inflation. The politics of productivity had imploded, and with its obliteration the coalition between organized labor and the Democrats that stretched from Woodrow Wilson into the early Carter years reached its limits. No longer could Democrats support the policies labor most wanted; no longer could a labor-led coalition guarantee Democrats control of Congress, if not the White House.

CONCLUSION

Carter's dilemma was caught best by the two advisers, Marshall and Schultze, who offered the president conflicting counsel on labor policy. Labor's advocate, Marshall, claimed Carter had the best record on labor issues of any president since Franklin D. Roosevelt. In the labor secretary's estimation, the Carter administration had successfully defended all protective labor laws; strengthened the Occupational Safety and Health Administration; bolstered collective bargaining through appointments to the involved federal agencies; created job growth in the private sector; doubled the job corps and expanded public service employment with a special focus on training programs for youths and minorities; and, finally, fought hard in a losing cause to reform basic labor law.[76] Schultze proved equally proud of the administration's economic record. He gloated that employment in the United States had increased by 10 percent in the Carter years and that U.S. unemployment remained far lower than that of any of our major European competitors, especially Germany. If we could have exported our unemployment to Mexico (as the Germans and Swiss did with their Turkish guest workers) or been less generous in raising the minimum wage, Schultze maintained, the economy would have created even more jobs. Overall, however, Schultze bragged, "Our incomes policy protected profits better than almost any other country, including our major European competitor, Germany."[77]

Schultze's evaluation of the administration's economic policies illustrated precisely how the politics of productivity had collapsed. Instead of stressing workers' claim to a larger share of rising economic productivity, the chair of the CEA emphasized wage restraint, incomes policy, and protection for profits. It took a Reagan administration to set firmly in place the neoliberal economic policies already endorsed by Schultze and Kahn and foreshadowed in several of Carter's own initiatives. The succeeding Republican administrations only hastened labor's economic and political decline, adjusting national politics to the dominant influence of southern, western, suburban, and corporate constituents.

NOTES

The author would like to thank David Brody, Gary Fink, and Robert Zieger for their careful reading and astute criticism of an early draft of this chapter. Martin Elzy and the staff of the Carter Library provided me with copies of many of the documents cited in the essay, as did Gary Fink. Judson MacLaury, historian of the Department of Labor, generously shared with me a transcript of the department's interview with Ray Marshall.

1. For the relationship between Carter and labor, see the two unpublished papers that Gary Fink has generously shared with me: "Jimmy Carter, George Meany, and the Failure of Democratic Party Constituent Politics" and "Labor Law Revision and the End of the Postwar Labor Accord" in *Organized Labor and American Politics, 1894–1996*, ed. Kevin Boyle (Albany: State University of New York Press, 1998). Also see Fink's "F. Ray Marshall: Jimmy Carter's Ambassador to Organized Labor," *Labor History* 37 (Fall 1996): 463–79. Other worthwhile treatments of Carter and labor include the interview by Ray Marshall in Kenneth W. Thompson, ed., *The Carter Presidency: Fourteen Intimate Perspectives of Jimmy Carter* (Lanham, Md.: University Press of America, 1990); the essays by Taylor Dark ("Organized Labor and the Carter Administration") and Gary Fink ("Fragile Alliance: Jimmy Carter and the American Labor Movement") with comments by Ray Marshall and others in *The Presidency and Domestic Policies of Jimmy Carter*, ed. Herbert D. Rosenbaum and Alexej Ugrinsky (Westport, Conn.: Greenwood Press, 1994); and Numan V. Bartley, *Jimmy Carter and the Politics of the New South* (St. Louis, Mo.: Forum Press, 1979), for a sensitive treatment of how Carter's southern Populist and Progressive roots put him at odds with organized labor, especially George Meany. For the rare books that include some substantial material on the administration and labor, see Erwin C. Hargrove, *Jimmy Carter as President: Leadership and the Politics of the Public Good* (Baton Rouge: Louisiana State University Press, 1988); and Burton I. Kaufman, *The Presidency of James Earl Carter, Jr.* (Lawrence: University Press of Kansas, 1993).

2. David Plotke's *Building a Democratic Political Order: Reshaping American Liberalism in the 1930s and 1940s* (New York: Cambridge University Press, 1996), esp. chaps. 4–8, is now the finest scholarly study of the centrality of labor to what Plotke defines as a "Democratic political order." For a similar perspective, see Karen Orren, "Liberalism, Money, and the Situation of Organized Labor," in *Public Values and Private Power in American Politics*, ed. J. David Greenstone (Chicago: University of Chicago Press, 1982), 173–206; "Organized Labor and the Invention of Modern Liberalism in the United States," *Studies in American Political Development* 2 (1987): 317–36; and "Union Politics and Postwar Liberalism in the United States," *Studies in American Political Development* 1 (1986): 215–52. For the best general analysis of the meaning and implications of the "politics of productivity," see Charles Maier, "The Politics of Productivity: Foundations of American Economic Policy after World War II, *International Organization* 31 (Autumn 1977): 607–34; and "The Two Postwar Eras and the Conditions for Stability in Twentieth-Century Western Europe," *American Historical Review* 86 (April 1981): 327–52. For the view that no radical alternative existed to the "politics of productivity," see Plotke, *Building a Democratic Order*.

3. See Bruce Schulman's chapter in this volume, pp. 51–71.

4. Again, see ibid., and Judith Stein's chapter in this volume, pp. 72–94, for the plight of the steel industry as an example of the changes affecting core mass-production enterprises.

5. Jimmy Carter Interview, William Burkett Miller Center of Public Affairs, University of Virginia Project on the Carter Presidency, Transcripts (hereafter cited as Miller Center), November 29, 1982, 68–69, located in the Jimmy Carter Library (JCL).

6. Hargrove, *Jimmy Carter as President,* 34.

7. Stuart Eizenstat Interview, Miller Center, January 29–30, 1982, 10, JCL.

8. Hamilton Jordan (including Landon Butler) Interview, Miller Center, November 6, 1981, 8, JCL. See also Fink, "Jimmy Carter, George Meany."

9. Ray Marshall Interview, Miller Center, May 4, 1988, 13, 24–26, JCL; Eizenstat Interview, Miller Center, 113. Also see Fink, "Jimmy Carter, George Meany."

10. John Dunlop, the secretary of labor in Gerald Ford's administration, the organizer of the Labor Management Advisory Group, creator of the building trades industry management-union council, Harvard University economist, and leading exponent of "industrial pluralism," was unacceptable to Carter because he antagonized the other two basic party constituencies, African Americans and women.

11. Marshall Interview, Miller Center, 27–29; see also Marshall Interview, Oral History Project No. 135, February 26, 1981, Department of Labor, 3–4; *A Conversation with Ray Marshall, Inflation, Unemployment, and the Minimum Wage* (Washington, D.C.: American Enterprise Institute for Policy Research, 1978); Ray Marshall and Brian Rungeling, *The Role of Unions in the American Economy* (Joint Council on Economic Education, 1976); cf. Fink, "F. Ray Marshall."

12. *Conversation with Ray Marshall,* 27.

13. For Marshall's views on all these subjects as well as others, see *Conversation with Ray Marshall;* Marshall Interview, Miller Center, Marshall Interview, Department of Labor, 28–30; Thompson, *Carter Presidency,* 41; and Fink, "F. Ray Marshall."

14. Thompson, *Carter Presidency,* 41. On this theme see especially the chapters by Bruce Schulman and Judith Stein.

15. Alfred Kahn Interview, Miller Center, December 10, 11, 1981, 41–42, JCL.

16. George Schultze Interview, Miller Center, 40–43.

17. Archie Robinson, *George Meany and His Times: A Biography* (New York: Simon and Schuster, 1981), 366–67.

18. Kahn Interview, Miller Center, 96–97, 121, 136; Schultze Interview, Miller Center, 40–43.

19. Kahn Interview, Miller Center, 121.

20. *Public Papers of the Presidents of the United States: Jimmy Carter, 1977* (Washington, D.C.: Government Printing Office, 1978), book 1, 47–55, 349–50.

21. *Conversation with Ray Marshall,* 5–6; Marshall Interview, Miller Center, 2–3.

22. Schultze Interview, Miller Center, 2–3, 26–27, 71, 80.

23. See James T. Patterson's "Jimmy Carter and Welfare Reform" in this volume. For other treatments of welfare policy see, among other sources, Laurence E. Lynn, Jr., and David Whitman, *The President as Policymaker: Jimmy Carter and Welfare Reform* (Philadelphia: Temple University Press, 1981); Lester M. Salamon, ed., *Welfare: The Elusive Consensus* (New York: Praeger, 1978), especially the essay and its appendix A by Harvey D. Shapiro, "Welfare Reform Revisited—President Jimmy Carter's Program for Better Jobs and Income," 175–218.

24. For Packer's proposals and his defense of them, see Lynn and Whitman, *President as Policymaker,* 70–71, 80–84.

25. On this point see especially appendix 5 in Lynn and Whitman, *President as Policymaker,* 292–94.

26. For Carter's news conference see, *Public Papers of Jimmy Carter, 1977,* book 2, 1443–44; see also his message to Congress outlining his proposals for welfare reform in ibid., 1451–58.

27. Eizenstat et al. to Carter, May 15, 1979, Box 132, Staff Secretary File, JCL.

28. Marshall to Carter, March 22, 1977, Box 17, Staff Secretary File, JCL. See also Marshall Interview, Department of Labor, 30–31.

29. *Conversation with Ray Marshall,* 19.

30. Marshall to Carter, April 14, 1977; Jack Watson to Carter, April 15, 1977; Eizenstat to Carter, April 15, 1977, Box 17, Staff Secretary File, JCL. See also Hargrove, *Jimmy Carter as President,* 77; Dark, "Organized Labor and the Carter Administration," 764–65; Fink, "Fragile Alliance," 786–88; Marshall Interview, Miller Center, 38–41.

31. *Public Papers of Jimmy Carter, 1977,* book 2, 1947–48.

32. Marshall Interview, Miller Center, 38–41; *Conversation with Ray Marshall,* 18.

33. For the complex history of the administration and Humphrey-Hawkins, see, among other sources, John Dumbrell, *The Carter Presidency: A Re-Evaluation* (Manchester, England: University of Manchester Press, 1993), 100–102; Kaufman, *Presidency of James Earl Carter,* 100–111; Fink, "Fragile Alliance," 790–94. See also especially the paper presented by Timothy N. Thurber at the Carter Conference: "Liberalism and the Economic Crisis in Black America: Hubert Humphrey, Jimmy Carter, and the Battle for Full Employment" (in author's possession).

34. Schultze to Carter, May 23, 1977, Box 26, Staff Secretary File, JCL. Schultze attached to his memorandum a draft he had prepared for the EPG laying out his objections to the bill.

35. Eizenstat to Carter, May 24, 1977, Box 26, Staff Secretary File, JCL.

36. Siegel Comments on Schultze Letter, May 24, 1977, Box 26, Staff Secretary File, JCL. For comparable advice about the language to use in rejecting the bill as drafted, see Jack Watson to President, May 24, 1977, Staff Secretary File, JCL.

37. Bert Lance to Carter, May 31, 1977, Staff Secretary File, JCL.

38. Memo, Eizenstat and Schultze to Carter, October 6, 1977, Staff Secretary File, JCL.

39. *Public Papers of Jimmy Carter, 1977,* book 2, 1994–95.

40. For Carter's support of the compromise bill, see ibid., 2023.

41. Eizenstat Interview, Miller Center, 35.

42. Fink, "Fragile Alliance," 790–94.

43. Eizenstat to Carter, August 17, 1978, Box 100, Staff Secretary File, JCL.

44. Dumbrell, *The Carter Presidency,* 100–102; Fink, "Fragile Alliance," 790–94. Cf. Thurber, "Liberalism and the Economic Crisis."

45. Rick Hutcheson from Landon Butler with attachments, February, 21, 1977, Box 9, Staff Secretary File, JCL.

46. Ibid. See also Eizenstat and Butler to Carter, February 21, 1977; Jack Watson to Carter, February 22, 1977; Marshall to Carter, February 14, 1977, Staff Secretary File, JCL.

47. Butler to Hutcheson, February 21, 1977, Staff Secretary File, JCL.

48. See Fink, "Jimmy Carter, George Meany," 12.

49. See Fink, "Labor Law Revision."

50. Eizenstat to Carter, June 30, 1977, Box 35, Staff Secretary File, JCL.

51. Jordan to Carter, June 29, 1977; Mondale to Carter, June 30, 1977, Staff Secretary File, JCL.

52. Eizenstat to Carter, June 30, 1977, as in note 50. The president noted in his own handwriting on Eizenstat's original memo: "I prefer a message endorsing concepts and principles. We can deal with specifics later. I'll have to learn more."

53. *Public Papers of Jimmy Carter, 1977,* book 2, 1277–79.

54. James A. Gross, *Broken Promise: The Subversion of U.S. Labor Relations Policy, 1947–1994* (Philadelphia: Temple University Press, 1995), 238–40; Robinson, *George Meany and His Times,* 373, 378–79; Fink, "Fragile Alliance," 788–90, and "Labor Law Revision," passim.

55. *Public Papers of Jimmy Carter, 1978,* book 2, 994, 1079–80.

56. Frank Moore and Bob Thomson to Carter, June 9, 1978; Moore to Carter, June 19, 1978; Moore and Thomson to Carter, June 19, 1978; Moore to Carter, September 23, 1978, Box 111, Landon Butler Papers, JCL.

57. *Public Papers of Jimmy Carter, 1978,* book 2, 1496, 1547.

58. Rosenbaum and Ugrinsky, *The Presidency and Domestic Politics,* 810–11.

59. Thompson, *Carter Presidency,* 52–54; Gross, *Broken Promise,* 237.

60. Eizenstat Interview, Miller Center, 62, 104–5; Jordan-Butler Interview, Miller Center, 10, 35.

61. On this theme see the chapter by Thomas J. Sugrue in this volume.

62. For the quotation see Kaufman, *Presidency of James Earl Carter,* 74; see also W. Carl Biven, "Economic Advice in the Carter Administration," in Rosenbaum and Ugrinsky, *Presidency and Domestic Policies,* 611, 616–17; Dark, "Organized Labor and Carter," 769–72; Schultze Interview, Miller Center, 2–3, 26–27.

63. Biven, "Economic Advice in the Carter Administration," 611.

64. Stuart Eizenstat, "President Carter, the Democratic Party, and the Making of Domestic Policy," in Rosenbaum and Ugrinsky, *The Presidency and Domestic Politics,* 11; Marshall Interview, Miller Center, 34.

65. Marshall Interview, Miller Center, 42–43.

66. *Public Papers of Jimmy Carter, 1978,* book 1, 316, 725.

67. Ibid., book 2, 1550, 1839–48.

68. Dark, "Organized Labor and Carter," 769–72; Fink, "Jimmy Carter, George Meany," 20–23. On the real-wage insurance program, see Landon Butler to Hamilton Jordan, December 20, 1978, Marshall to Carter, December 22, 1978, Box 113, Staff Secretary File, JCL.

69. Marshall Interview, Miller Center, 20–21; Marshall Interview, Department of Labor, 31–32.

70. Eizenstat, Schultze, Kahn to Carter, December 6, 1978, Box 143, Domestic Policy Staff (DPS)-Eizenstat, JCL.

71. Marshall to Eizenstat and Butler, January 22, 1979, Box LA3–LA7, White House Central Files (WHCF), JCL.

72. *Public Papers of Jimmy Carter, 1979,* book 1, 110–15.

73. Statement by AFL-CIO Executive Council, Box 107, Landon Butler Papers, JCL. See also, Dark, "Organized Labor," 769–72; Fink, "Fragile Alliance."

74. Kahn Interview, Miller Center, 121.

75. *Public Papers of Jimmy Carter, 1979,* book 2, 1777–79, 1953–54; Fink, "Jimmy Carter, George Meany," 23–26; Dark, "Organized Labor," 769–72. For a negative evaluation of the National Accord, see Robert J. Flanagan, "The National Accord as a Social Contract," *Industrial and Labor Relations Review* 34 (October 1980): 35–50.

76. Marshall in response to the papers of Taylor Dark and Gary Fink as published in Rosenbaum and Ugrinsky, *Presidency and Domestic Policies,* 812–14.

77. Schultze Interview, Miller Center, 97–98.

6

Jimmy Carter and Welfare Reform

James T. Patterson

President Jimmy Carter's top adviser for domestic policy, Stuart Eizenstat, insisted in 1982 that his boss "felt deeply about problems of poverty. He'd come from the rural south. He knew what *poverty* was all about. He felt deeply about his commitment to try to help people."[1] James Fallows, while ambivalent about Carter, seconded Eizenstat's opinion. Recalling a meeting on welfare reform, Fallows wrote in 1979 that the president "dressed down a team of experts from HEW who were lecturing him about the unemployability of the underclass. These were people he had lived with, Carter said; they may not have been educated, some may have been lazy and drunk, but most of them understood the meaning of dignity, self-sufficiency, and work. No one could miss Carter's real message: unlike anyone else in the room, he was talking about people he had seen."[2]

Advisers close to Carter also recognized that reform of welfare held fairly high priority in his plans for domestic change. As Joseph Califano, Carter's secretary of Health, Education, and Welfare (HEW), emphasized later, "'Cleaning up the welfare mess' [had been] the best ear-of-the-listener issue in Carter's campaign" the year before.[3] Early in 1977, moreover, Carter had some reason to expect legislative action on the issue, for students of poverty and social policy thought that reform was possible. These experts emphasized that the "rediscovery" of poverty in America since the 1960s had significantly enhanced comprehension of complicated issues. The creation of Medicaid and Medicare in 1965, of the Supplemental Security Income program in 1972, and the indexing of Social Security, also in 1972, seemed to represent great steps forward, indicating that government had answers to social problems. Liberal students of such policies, understanding that most poor people stayed on welfare for relatively short periods of time, believed that poverty was not so deep as had been imagined, and that dramatic improvements could be achieved at manageable cost.

Researchers, pursuing such objectives, had already conjured up a range of promising proposals for change, including varieties of "negative income tax" plans that promised to guarantee minimum incomes for Americans. Laurence Lynn, who later coauthored a detailed study of welfare policy in the Carter years, was one of a number of experts who hoped for real reform in the near future. He wrote in 1975, "The sum total of experience with the existing system, and the results of research on poverty have irrevocably altered the context of the welfare reform debate in a manner that should be favorable to welfare reform." He added, "Although cost is not an insurmountable obstacle to significant reform, the momentum to overcome it is likely to be more easily generated during a change of Administration by a new President personally concerned about the issue."[4]

By mid-1977 it became clear that welfare reform faced formidable obstacles. Still, when the president at last outlined his plan in August 1977, some influential politicians reacted enthusiastically. A Harris survey taken shortly after the release of Carter's program found "unprecedented" backing for it; 70 percent of those polled approved of the proposal (versus 13 percent opposed). Califano, who earlier had confessed that "welfare is the Middle East of U.S. politics," was obviously elated when he appeared on CBS's *Face the Nation* on the day after Carter announced the plan. "This is the day," he said, "in which we're finally going to reform the welfare system. . . . This program is going to go through Congress."[5]

Califano's prediction, like many optimistic pronouncements of the Carter administration, proved to be wildly off base. Indeed, welfare reform soon ran into a storm of criticism from Congress, which in mid-1978 formally abandoned efforts to bring the measure to the floor of either chamber. The president, chastened by his experience, recognized that "simplifying" welfare was extraordinarily complicated, and he endorsed a much more modest welfare reform in 1979. This passed the House but stalled in Senate committee. By 1980, with budget-cutting fever rampant on Capitol Hill, chances for liberalization or simplification of the American welfare system had disappeared.

These efforts were not the only initiatives that the administration endorsed in its struggles against poverty in the United States. Some of these were enacted into law. Parts of the president's "economic stimulus package," unveiled early in 1977, made it through Congress, thereby doubling (to 742,000 people) the number of Americans at work in public service employment (PSE) by March 1978. Most of these workers were engaged in projects authorized by expansion of the Comprehensive Employment and Training Act (CETA), which had initially passed in 1973.[6] A watered-down version of the so-called Humphrey-Hawkins bill, which endorsed countercyclical spending on public jobs, was enacted in 1978.[7] Most significant, in 1977 Congress approved a plan to liberalize the Food Stamps program, which grew rapidly in the next three years.[8] But these and other lesser modifications of existing social policies fell far short of what Carter had hoped to enact.

Meanwhile, economic problems that beset the country after 1977 pushed even more people below the poverty line. The number of Americans living in poverty, which had declined slightly between 1975 and 1977, began to rise in 1978—from 24,497,000 in that year to 29,272,000 in 1980 and to 34,398,000 in 1982. The poverty rate, as measured by the government, increased by 32 percent between 1978 and 1982—from 11.4 percent to 15 percent of the population. This was by far the sharpest increase in post–World War II American history.[9] By then, moreover, anguished commentators were bewailing the rise of an inner-city "underclass," whose behavioral deficiencies, conservatives maintained, stemmed directly from the flaws of America's welfare system.[10]

By these and other criteria, it is obvious that the federal government failed to "reform" welfare or to reduce poverty during the Carter years. Popular perceptions of such failure, indeed, contributed to the administration's mounting political difficulties and to the triumph of Ronald Reagan and the Republican party in 1980. Reagan then abolished a number of social programs, notably CETA, and chased the guaranteed income idea from the national agenda. The goals of Humphrey-Hawkins were ignored. Political support for government "jobs" programs, never sturdy in the United States, disintegrated and failed to regain strength thereafter. So did agitation for "guaranteed minimum income" proposals, a form of which—the Program for Better Jobs and Income (PBJI)—Carter had endorsed in 1977.

With the benefit of twenty years of hindsight, we can see that the collapse of Carter's efforts for welfare reform represented a dying gasp of enthusiasm for guaranteed income plans in the United States. The nearly twenty years since 1978, culminating in 1996 with passage of the revealingly named Personal Responsibility and Work Opportunity Reconciliation Act, were in many ways an era of growing reaction and rollback against the perceived excesses of liberal thinking about social policy developed during the Great Society years.[11] Could this rollback have been otherwise?

The welfare "system" that Carter and his advisers hoped to simplify was indeed complex in 1977. Politicians, social scientists, and journalists raged that it was a "mess," a "patchwork quilt," a monument to the power of special interests and to the prevalence of hostile stereotypes of poor people. In addition to "insurance" programs such as Social Security and Medicare, the system featured a number of means-tested benefits targeted to various groups of needy Americans. These means-tested plans, paid for by income tax dollars, were what Americans normally thought of when they talked about the pros and cons of "welfare."

One important welfare plan was Supplemental Security Income (SSI), which aided the needy aged, blind, and disabled. In fiscal year 1977, it paid an estimated $6.3 billion ($4.7 billion of it from federal funds) to around 4.4 million beneficiaries. A second plan was Food Stamps, a purely federal program that assisted many low-income people in their purchase of food. Offering some $5.4 billion in benefits in fiscal year 1977, stamps went to 17.4 million people per month when Carter took office. A third set of programs, those featuring housing assistance, cost some $3 billion in fiscal 1977, a sum that included various subsidies to approximately 3 million families. A fourth was the Earned Income Tax Credit (EITC), established in 1975, which extended tax credits to low-income working families with children. In 1977, EITC was to cost $1.3 billion in benefits going to 6.3 million households. By far the most expensive of American welfare programs was Medicaid, a federal-state plan that offered medical assistance mainly to welfare recipients, notably people on the rolls of SSI or Aid to Families with Dependent Children (AFDC). It was anticipated in early 1977 that Medicaid costs would total $17.2 billion ($9.7 billion of it in federal money), and that its "in-kind" services would go to 24.7 million Americans.[12]

What Americans *really* considered "welfare" was AFDC. Enacted as part of the Social Security law of 1935, it was a federal-state program that provided grants to needy families—most of them headed by single mothers.[13] The majority of the adult recipients until the early 1960s had been "deserving" women, such as destitute widows with young children. Thereafter, however, the rolls of AFDC swelled rapidly, from 3.1 million people in 1960 to 10.8 million by 1974. By then, some 90 percent of eligible women, many of them divorced, separated, or never married, were taking advantage of the program. The size of AFDC rolls leveled off in the mid-1970s but remained much larger than it had been twenty years earlier. In 1977, there were around 11.4 million recipients per month. Total cost of the program at the time was around $10.3 billion a year, of which the federal share was slightly more than 50 percent ($5.7 billion).[14]

Criticisms of this complicated apparatus of welfare were many and varied. Conservatives protested against the costs. These were in fact considerable, though far lower than many Americans imagined: all the means-tested programs cost around $50 billion in federal and state money in 1977. This was much less than the $130 billion spent at the time for social "insurance" programs.[15] The federal share of means-tested welfare costs, $34.7 billion, was a small percentage of overall federal outlays of $409 billion.[16] Still, conservatives looked with alarm at the mounting costs of welfare, which seemed destined to advance over time unless stopped in their tracks. Adult recipients of AFDC, many of these critics added, must be required to work as a condition of aid.

Conservatives made special targets of AFDC recipients. Disabled adults and the elderly receiving Disability Insurance or Social Security had paid payroll taxes for their benefits; they (and family members) had "earned" their support. Most of the recipients of SSI—the needy blind, aged, and disabled—could not reasonably be expected to work. They, too, were thought to be "deserving." The Food Stamps and Medicaid programs were expensive, to be sure, but they offered aid that was in-kind and specifically directed at basic needs.[17] But cash for AFDC, opponents alleged, was flowing to millions of "undeserving" women, some of whom were using it to raise children born out of wedlock. Other recipients, it was thought, took the money to subsidize boyfriends or to nurture a range of bad habits such as alcohol abuse and drug addiction. Newspapers ran exposés under banner headlines about "welfare fraud." Other critics noted that more than 40 percent of AFDC recipients were black, even though blacks made up only 12 percent of the national population.

Many of these critics complained above all that welfare—especially AFDC—damaged incentives to work. In states with relatively generous welfare payments, a few AFDC families received nearly as much as low-income families with a full-time worker, and sometimes even more. Liberals responded to anomalies such as these by demanding hikes in minimum wages (set at $2.30 per hour for federally covered jobs in early 1977). But although Congress increased the federal minimum in November 1977 (it rose in steps to $3.35 per hour by 1981), the value of this wage in real dollars was compromised by the galloping inflation of the late 1970s and early 1980s. The arithmetic of angry conservative arguments about disincentives, moreover, was hard to ignore. An AFDC family of four in New York State, which offered relatively high benefits, received $430 per month in 1977, plus coverage under Medicaid. No one in the family worked in the market. By contrast, a full-time worker, toiling hard at $2.30 per hour for 160 hours in a month, earned only $368 and probably did not qualify for coverage under Medicaid.

Complaints such as these had long stymied liberals who sought to expand means-tested social policies, especially AFDC. They were to bedevil Carter and his aides as well. But Califano and others who crafted PBJI in 1977 tried not to be cowed by them. Instead, they embarked on developing a fairly generous guaranteed annual income program. This goal, too, had a history. Advocates of such a guarantee emphasized first that the American social safety net had large holes in it. Millions of the nonelderly poor, notably able-bodied single people and married adults without young children, did not qualify for programs such as AFDC or SSI. While some of them received modest aid from Food Stamps or state and locally funded general assistance, others had to make do without public support of any sort. Liberals also complained that benefits varied dramatically by state (an AFDC family of four received $60 per month in Mississippi compared with $430 per month in New York; the national average was $320 per month).[18] For years these liberal critics had demanded that AFDC be transformed (as SSI had been transformed in 1972) from a federal-state matching grant program to one that was wholly supported by national funds—and therefore (with cost-of-living variables figured in) uniform for all.[19]

Liberals insisted, finally, that benefit levels be increased. These levels were indeed low. As Califano emphasized at the time, AFDC families received grants (including the value of Food Stamps) that in nearly half of the states amounted to less than three-fourths of the poverty line. Moreover, adult AFDC recipients who found work had benefits reduced at the rate of sixty-seven cents for each dollar earned after the first $720 per year. This "marginal tax rate" did nothing to promote work incentives among people on welfare. As Carter prepared to take office, liberal students of welfare called on the new president to jettison the old "patchwork" of programs and replace it with a system that would attain at least one central goal: a guaranteed national minimum income for all who qualified.

Perhaps five things can be said about Carter's attitudes toward welfare reform in early 1977. First, he had long been interested in the subject, offering support between 1970 and 1972 for President Nixon's Family Assistance Plan (FAP), which had sought—unsuccessfully—to provide a guaranteed minimum income for many Americans. Second, Carter seemed receptive to liberal positions. Identifying welfare reform as an important priority for 1977, he set Califano and Labor Secretary Ray Marshall to work on developing remedial legislation. Third, an engineer in politics, he hoped to achieve some sort of "comprehensive" reform that would simplify the complexity and clean up the "mess." His ardent quest for greater simplicity led him in 1977 to favor legislation that would consolidate existing programs—such as AFDC, Food Stamps, and SSI—and establish guaranteed minimum incomes.[20] Fourth, he proved amenable to the creation of government jobs for low-income people with children—like most Americans, he yearned to move as many welfare recipients as possible into work. Last, he soon made it clear to advisers that he opposed plans that would result in greater welfare costs to the federal government.[21]

Presidential aides who set to work on welfare reform in early 1977 operated in a political climate that in many ways boded poorly for substantial innovations in domestic policies. This was after all the post–Great Society, post-Watergate era, in which neoconservative dirges about the state echoed loudly. Washington bashing—much of it fine-tuned by Carter himself during the presidential campaign of 1976—resounded in political rhetoric.[22] Congress, invigorated by its clash with Nixon over Watergate, remained aggressively suspicious of executive leadership. "We got such fun out of popping Nixon and Ford," one Democratic Senator observed, "we didn't want to give it up and be good guys any more."[23] The Democratic party, though in control of Congress, was badly fragmented, and liberal pressure groups—labor unions, blacks, advocates for the poor, women's organizations—were reeling under conservative backlash.[24]

Powerful cultural and demographic trends erected further barriers to liberal reformers of welfare in 1977. The most significant of these trends was the substantial increase in the percentage of women who were joining the workforce. By the late 1970s this was approaching 50 percent of all adult women, up from around 30 percent in 1950. Feminist leaders were hailing work in the market as a good thing for women, thereby assailing older notions that mothers should stay in the home. In this rapidly changing world of gender relations, it was becoming problematic indeed for welfare reformers to oppose work requirements for recipients of public aid. On the contrary, conservatives—and others—loudly denounced "guaranteed annual income" programs. "I find it difficult," Senator Russell Long of Louisiana said in August 1977, "in saying a mother with children is not expected to work when most women with children are working."[25] Any comprehensive welfare system, Long and others declared, must require all but the most deserving of recipients to work for their aid.

One other serious obstacle blocked Carter's welfare reformers: the very complexity of the existing system.[26] Gordon Weil, an expert who looked carefully at America's welfare state in 1977, counted 182 federal programs (as well as others on the state and local levels) "relating to income maintenance." These programs, he added, cost an estimated $248 billion and consumed 69 percent of federal tax receipts.[27] Many of the programs would not be much affected by targeted, incremental reforms. But "comprehensive" changes of the sort that Carter seemed to envision might create all sorts of unanticipated consequences.

Weil and others pointed to central questions concerning the impact of guaranteed benefits on incentives to work. If a guaranteed income program were to be approved, how high should the minimums be set? If these were to be modest, they would presumably help recipients only in the poorer states, where existing welfare benefits were low. Such guarantees, however, would be lower than welfare benefits in the more generous states. What kind of "reform" was that? The answer to such concerns, liberals concluded, was to establish generous minimums. But achievement of such a goal not only would cost more money but it also might harm work incentives among the working poor, unless they received supplements to their wages. This assistance, too, would cost money. How high up the income ladder, indeed, should the government promise to help people? Difficult questions such as these had helped to kill Nixon's FAP a few years earlier. They had not gone away by 1977.

As if these obstacles were not formidable enough, Carter's political style brought him few allies in a fight for reform. Having antagonized many congressmen with his anti-Washington campaign rhetoric, he worsened his relations with Capitol Hill by taking what many legislators thought was a self-righteous approach to congressional relations. Thomas "Tip" O'Neill, the Democratic Speaker of the House, once asked Carter how he would deal with Congress, to which the president replied that he would manage it the way he had handled Georgia legislators when he was governor—"by going over their heads directly to the people." O'Neill retorted, "Hey, wait a minute, you have 289 guys [House Democrats] who know their districts pretty well. They ran against the [Ford] administration and they wouldn't hesitate to run against you." Carter answered, "Oh, really?"[28] In his memoirs O'Neill observed that Carter's congressional liaison people "didn't know beans about Congress," that Hamilton Jordan, Carter's top aide, should have been named "Hamilton Jerkin," and that Ronald Reagan later proved more sensitive to the needs of congressional Democrats than Carter ever was.[29]

The president's administrative procedures may also have harmed his efforts at welfare reform. In dealing with this issue in 1977—as in many of his activities—Carter worked hard to try to understand the formidable complexities of the existing system. But it was too much to expect that a new president could handle welfare reform on his own. He therefore dropped the issue on the capacious laps of HEW, headed by Califano, and of labor, headed by Marshall. These two cabinet officials, however, differed in their analysis of the welfare problem. Their conflicts were to delay creation and presentation of his "reform," which did not reach Capitol Hill until September. By that time, Congress was struggling with a host of other proposals—Carter had overloaded the legislative agenda—and presidential popularity, as revealed in polls, was sagging badly.

Some students of Carter's style, then and later, have speculated that his welfare plan—and other proposals—might have done better in Congress if he had set up a better administrative system. In particular, they regret his refusal to name a powerful "chief of staff." Instead, he made Eizenstat a top aide in domestic affairs, but at the same time encouraged Califano, Marshall, and others to report directly to the Oval Office. These criticisms have some merit. It probably would have been better if Carter had demanded that a chief of staff settle interagency and cabinet disagreements before they reached him. Eizenstat himself, an able, loyal aide, later lamented Carter's tendency to micromanage, perceiving it as "fatal in those early days" of 1977.[30]

These difficulties frustrated Califano, Marshall, Eizenstat, and their many aides (a great deal of bureaucratic battling ensued), who labored between January and May to reach agreement even on basic principles. From the beginning, Carter involved himself personally in the deliberations. It was obvious, however, that two internal debates would delay announcement of principles. The first pitted Marshall and his advisers in the Labor Department, who demanded that welfare reform include a large-scale program of government jobs, against Califano's aides in HEW, who were focusing on creation of a guaranteed minimum income program. This debate—like much in the struggle for welfare reform in 1977—replicated disputes that had divided experts in the late 1960s and early 1970s. HEW experts expressed great skepticism about jobs programs. They wondered if government could really create the 1 million or so jobs that labor wanted, and they doubted that very many welfare recipients could do much in the way of work. Most of the people on AFDC, after all, were women and small children. Would Labor saddle taxpayers with the costs of make-work, dead-end jobs?[31] Marshall and his aides retorted by accusing HEW staffers of being patronizing. Many welfare recipients, they said, were eager and able to work, and government jobs could train them for advances into the private market. Carter tried to resolve the impasse between his advisers by bringing in Charles Schultze, chairman of the Council of Economic Advisers, to act as "honest broker." Schultze, who harbored serious doubts about jobs programs, tried hard to resolve the matter, but without success.

"I threw up my hands," he said later, because they had "two fundamentally opposed ideas."[32]

The second internal debate revolved around costs and pitted the president against Califano in a clash of wills. Califano, a self-assured lawyer and insider dating to his days as a close aide to LBJ, entered upon the task of developing a new welfare system with the belief that comprehensive reform would necessarily cost more money. His advisers crafted proposals accordingly. When Califano presented these to Carter on March 25, however, he learned that the president opposed any additional spending on welfare. Taking over the meeting, Carter asked Califano, "Joe, if you had to start over from scratch, is this the kind of system you would create?" Califano shook his head. "In that case," Carter said, "I want you to take all the money that is now being spent on welfare programs and redesign the whole system using the same amount of money."[33] He told his secretary to report back with such a plan within two weeks.

Califano, shaken, began looking about for funds from other departments. Writing to James Schlesinger, who was developing energy programs, he lamented, "Our real problem is to find some money to put into the welfare package. . . . We are just beginning to get cost data, but, frankly, it appears that every penny we can lay our hands on will be needed for fiscal relief and benefit extensions to uncovered groups. Can you help on this, perhaps by routing some energy tax monies into the transfer pot?"[34] Neither Schlesinger nor others in the administration had cash to spare, leaving Califano to shift for himself.

When Califano returned to the White House on April 11, he sketched out three different proposals but concluded, "Mr. President, I don't think that any of these plans is really adequate unless we increase present spending." Carter then exploded, "Are you telling me that there is no way to improve the present welfare system except by spending billions of dollars? In that case, to hell with it! We're wasting our time."[35] The meeting meandered on, settling little.

Carter's stand against added spending for welfare made sense if the primary goal was to hold the line on government expenditures. But it was foolish if he hoped for comprehensive reform of the welfare system. It is clear in retrospect, as it was to Califano and others at the time, that the president did not fully understand the complexity of the issues. As Jordan warned him immediately before this meeting, "You don't have a clear idea yet of what kind of program you want."[36] It is equally clear that the president should never have entered into the process of welfare reform, thereby arousing expectations, without conveying clear objectives to his aides and without appreciating a basic fact: there was no spending-neutral way to overhaul the welfare system so that it would be more generous for recipients.

These internal disagreements made it impossible for Carter and Califano to present anything remotely similar to a final plan. Under fire from New York's Senator Daniel Patrick Moynihan and others for dawdling, they temporized by

offering statements of principles.[37] These attempted to paper over the still significant differences between HEW and Labor by promising something for both
camps.[38] But these statements, which conceded that welfare policy was complicated, made it even more obvious that the administration was still groping for
answers. A characteristic reaction from editorialists came from the *Los Angeles
Times*, which called the statement of principles "about as controversial as the Boy
Scout oath."[39] The *Washington Post* observed, "Nobody should be under the
impression that the President has indicated how he intends to fulfill these ambitious goals."[40] The conservative columnist George Will cracked that Carter's
confession about the complexity of welfare reform "was the most enchanting
understatement since Admiral John Rushworth Jellicoe, watching his battleships
being blown to smithereens at Jutland, observed, 'There seems to be something
the matter with our bloody ships today.'"[41]

Reactions from Congress were negative, to say the least. Senate Majority
Leader Robert Byrd of West Virginia spoke for many on the Hill when he declared,
"welfare reform will simply have to wait. We can't do welfare reform in this session
of Congress."[42] When Califano and Marshall went to the Hill in order to sketch
out their thinking, they received a rough reception, especially from Moynihan, a
loose cannon who seemed to revel in making them feel uncomfortable. After
observing that the financing for welfare reform was inadequate, the senator told
Califano, "I would like you to go back to the Director of Management and Budget
when you next see him. He has sent you up here to make bricks without straw,
and it is not easy to do."[43]

Chastened, Carter officials labored hard in the next three months trying to
devise a practical plan. Staffers from HEW, Labor, and the White House held long
and often bitterly contested arguments. Documentary evidence at the Carter Library
indicates that the president remained personally engaged in this process—mainly
by attending to a flurry of memorandums. Relying on the advice of Schultze, who
was worried about inflation, he continued to demand cost controls. At one point
he rejected Marshall's appeal for prevailing wage rates on government jobs. He
scrawled, "Seems very high" on a memo in which Califano suggested a fairly
generous income support plan.[44]

The flurry of memorandums grew to blizzard proportions in late July and early
August, the deadline for completion of a plan. By July 25, Califano was able to
forward to the president a "detailed proposal" that advocated minimums of guaranteed cash assistance, from the federal government, for needy Americans. The
proposal set up two tiers of recipients. One tier was composed of poor people who
were not expected to work or for whom no job was available. These were the needy
aged, blind, and disabled, single parents with children under the age of seven, and
single parents with children aged seven to thirteen if a job and day care could not
be found. It was hoped that the parents of such families could find part-time jobs
while the children were in school. The second tier was for low-income people
expected to work full-time: two-parent families with children, single parents whose

youngest child was over thirteen, and single people and childless couples. The plan proposed to consolidate AFDC, Food Stamps, and SSI into one program that would give eligible people flat cash payments, the size of which depended on which tier they were in, the size of their family, and their income.

Spelling out specifics, Califano's plan indicated that in the tier of those not expected to work, a single-parent family with three young children and no other income would receive a minimum in federal money of $4,200 per year in 1978 dollars. This was more, Califano emphasized, than the value of AFDC plus Food Stamps in all but seven states. (The poverty line for such families was then $6,191.) In the other tier—composed of families in which one person was expected to work—a two-parent family with two young children and no income would receive $2,300. Wages from work were expected to supplement this guarantee. The plan also called for funding of 1.4 million public service jobs and training slots, 300,000 of them part-time, and for government help in placement of numerous participants in private sector jobs. The public service jobs, which would offer the federal minimum wage, were expected to provide work for some low-income families with children, not just persons receiving welfare under existing programs.

A major complexity in designing a guaranteed income plan—as Nixon had discovered a few years earlier—centered on balancing a decent minimum of support with work incentives. In coping with this complicated matter, Carter and Califano emphasized a critically important point: monetary incentives would encourage work. The new plan called for relatively low "marginal tax" rates—reductions in benefits given to people who earned income. It proposed to disregard the first $317 per month (or $3,800 a year) of the earnings of many of those who worked—that is, they could keep that amount without losing basic benefits—and thereafter to reduce the benefit at the rate of fifty cents for each dollar of earnings up to $4,600. This meant that the plan would help working people whose income from work was $8,400 a year or less. The plan also recommended expansion of the earned income tax credit. Califano estimated that his proposal would initially cost perhaps $2.8 billion more than was then being spent on the programs to be consolidated. Much of this extra money was aimed primarily at providing fiscal relief ($2.1 billion in the first year) for states.

In transmitting the plan, Califano assured the president that it "places a heavy emphasis on work and establishes an incentive structure that favors private over public employment. It consolidates and simplifies the nation's cash assistance programs."[45] His proposal, however, was bewilderingly complex. Consisting of sixty-two single-spaced pages (with an additional seventy-five pages of tables), it was known by insiders as the "monster memo." Schultze later observed that it outlined a program "so complicated that nobody could understand it. There were probably three people in the world who understood it, and no one of these fully."[46]

As the proposal circulated among top officials it generated a bundle of memorandums. Carter arose at 5:30 A.M. on July 28 to read these, a process that took him three hours. The memos revealed that the planners still had not settled their internal conflicts or anticipated the manifold consequences of comprehensive reform. The harshest reaction came from Tom Joe, an expert on welfare who had served as a consultant. The plan, Joe wrote, was "divisive, punitive, administratively complex, and conceptually confusing." He concluded, "To present the plan as is, as the first major domestic initiative could potentially embarrass the administration, make a mockery of the expectations of both Congress and the public and probably put off any constructive action on the subject for another eight years."[47]

While contending with reactions such as this, Califano and others made last-minute efforts to consult key congressional Democrats, notably Long of Louisiana, chairman of the Senate Finance Committee, and Al Ullman of Oregon, chairman of the House Ways and Means Committee. Their committees would have to approve welfare legislation before it could get to the floor. Both men were conservative on the subject of welfare spending. Long was an advocate of workfare, which would require single parents with children over six years of age to work off their grants. Ullman had no stomach for guaranteed income proposals and, like Long, shrank from giving government money to people able to work. He also opposed basing the amount of benefits on the size of families.[48] Califano's overtures to congressional leaders, in any event, were too little too late.

Carter, Califano, and staffers worried about the critiques of Joe and others, and they agreed to some last-minute changes. These alarmed other advisers, including Ben Heineman, an aide to Califano, who quipped, "I have this vision of Joe Califano and Jimmy Carter flying over Washington in a B-1 bomber. They open the bomb bays and drop out one of the biggest turkeys Washington ever saw."[49] In general, however, the final version did not differ significantly from earlier drafts. On August 6, Carter announced his plan, christening it the Program for Better Jobs and Income (PBJI). At last, the administration had bitten the bullet on welfare reform.[50]

"The liberals and the conservatives will get together and kill it," one observer predicted of the PBJI. "There's little chance we'll ever get welfare reform enacted."[51]

To some this opinion seemed unduly pessimistic. A few influential voices could be heard in support of the president's efforts. Moynihan, ever unpredictable, lauded the president. The New York Times endorsed the PBJI with reservations. So did Vernon Jordan, head of the National Urban League, and the National Governors Conference (by a vote of thirty-one to four).[52] Supporters especially liked four features of the plan: it would mandate uniform, nationwide eligibility standards and minimum levels of income; in the twelve lowest benefit states it would establish higher federally financed levels than currently existed; for the first time the government would give cash to families of the working poor, thereby helping such families to remain together; and provision of government jobs, among other features, would give substance to talk about the promotion of work incentives. Many observers anticipated that the plan's financial incentives to states would encourage state spending, thus raising benefit levels well above the federally supported minimums.

In general, however, pessimistic predictions proved both easy to make and accurate, for the PBJI—like Nixon's FAP—got whipsawed from both the left and the right. A number of liberals, including Moynihan, soon came out with sharp critiques of aspects of the plan. Also skeptical about the proposal were such liberal organizations as the American Public Welfare Association, the National Association of Social Workers, the AFL-CIO, and the United States Catholic Conference. Their arguments were familiar: the proposed minimum benefits, at around two-thirds of the poverty line, were too low; thirty-eight states would have to supplement Carter's minimums if their recipients were to be better off; the PBJI offered far too little fiscal relief to hard-pressed northern states and cities; there were not enough proposed public service jobs—6.9 million people were then unemployed; the public jobs would pay only minimum wages and entail no training; and day care costs would punish people who went to work.[53]

Conservatives proved to be equally vociferous—and as predictable. As in the past, they insisted that guaranteed income plans encouraged greater welfare dependence. Why work if you could get a government check? They further argued that public service jobs would be wasteful and expensive. Many demanded that able-bodied welfare recipients (except mothers of very young children) work for whatever benefits they received. Senator Long introduced such a workfare proposal in his committee, which approved it in November. These critics advanced negative stereotypes of idle welfare clients and expressed hostile attitudes toward "welfare" that were older than the Republic. As Senator Carl Curtis, a Republican from Nebraska, put it, "Working men and women across America want fewer people on welfare, not millions more."[54] Conservatives grew especially hostile when the Congressional Budget Office calculated in late November that the additional expense involved in the PBJI would total $14 billion, not $2.8 billion as HEW and Carter had predicted.[55] By mid-December, Ullman dropped all pretense of support for the reform. "I oppose it strongly now," he announced. "It's totally unworkable and it would put a burden on the American taxpayer that's totally intolerable."[56]

Carter's supporters, hoping for the best, persevered. A welfare subcommittee in the House, which had been formed especially to consider the bill, approved a slightly modified version of the plan in February. But Carter had already indicated in his State of the Union Address in January that he had higher priorities. None of the parent House committees that would ultimately have to consider plans for "simplification"—Ways and Means, Education and Labor, and Agriculture—took action on the subcommittee bill. The administration, deaf to compromise, refused to consider more incrementalist approaches. In March 1978, Carter's congressional liaison, Frank Moore, warned that welfare reform might be "dead for the year."[57]

Amid such gloomy prospects, reports on income maintenance experiments conducted by HEW lent further ammunition to conservatives. As described by the *New York Times* in May (under the headline "Experiment Finds Cash Grants Tend to Split Families"), the experiments appeared to show that poor families receiving cash grants—that is, guaranteed incomes—were more likely to break up than were families that did not receive grants. The experiments further suggested that publicly generated income support caused the work effort of family heads to diminish. These findings, given greater publicity later in the year, cast doubt on the whole idea of guaranteed income maintenance.[58]

As time passed, some House leaders seemed ready to work with Carter to develop a politically acceptable version of the PBJI. By June, however, congressmen were worrying about rising inflation and about defiant popular feelings against taxes—feelings dramatically expressed in California, where voters approved Proposition Thirteen against higher property taxes. Later that month, on June 22, O'Neill pronounced the PBJI dead for the Ninety-fifth Congress of 1977–78.[59]

One could embark on a fairly lengthy narrative about Carter's subsequent efforts for changes in the nation's welfare system. In May 1979, he asked for passage of a measure that would have increased federal welfare spending so as to establish a national minimum for AFDC benefits at 65 percent of the poverty line. Such a law would have created the first statutory relationship between official government poverty lines and actual relief spending. The bill would also have mandated that all states provide benefits for low-income two-parent families in which the primary earner was unemployed or earning very low pay. These changes, estimated to cost the federal government $5.7 billion a year, would have affected thirteen and twenty-four states, respectively, rescuing an estimated eight hundred thousand families from poverty. In November 1979, the House actually passed a modified version of these proposals, 222 to 184.[60]

To describe this effort in detail, however, would be to suggest wrongly that Carter cared much about it. He did not, for it fell far short of his larger dreams of 1977. Gone were grander hopes for consolidation and simplification, and for establishment of a national uniform minimum benefit for all low-income Americans. Moreover, the president continued to seek economy in welfare spending. Reluctantly approving the proposal, he scribbled on a memo, "Do not ask me to approve a higher figure in the future."[61] In 1979–80, Carter had many things on his mind other than welfare reform, notably securing renomination and reelection. He recognized, finally, that Russell Long would never approve his new proposal and that it therefore had no chance in the Senate. This was an obvious and correct analysis of the political prospects for welfare reform, which virtually disappeared from the agenda of American policy in 1980.

Why did comprehensive welfare reform fail to pass—or even to get to a vote in Congress—during the Carter years? The number of answers to this question is large indeed. Some observers assign at least part of the blame to Carter. One authoritative account emphasizes the flawed planning process, which "as a whole seemed feckless and fumbling, wasteful of the time and energies of the officials involved. The President appears to have lost control of it altogether."[62] This is a valid conclusion. Carter imposed a series of unrealistic deadlines; he did not fully understand the problems of the system; he did not resolve serious interagency disputes; he did not communicate well with advisers; and he was cavalier in his approach to Congress. Demanding major "reform" without understanding that this would cost a good deal of money was his worst failing of all, a failing compounded by the inaccurate cost estimates of his staffers.

Carter also can be faulted for his engineering zeal on behalf of "comprehensive" reform. Given the "mess" that was welfare, this zeal was understandable. But the staggering complexity of the existing system should have lowered the president's sights. He would have done better to fold up his computerized charts and graphs and settle for more modest designs, such as those he finally drew up in 1979.[63]

The argument against seeking "comprehensive" reform can also be stated in a slightly different manner: "interests" were to blame for the failure of the PBJI. This way of explaining the outcome in 1977–78 is also valid. Some liberal organizations, such as labor unions and civil rights groups, did not work hard for the plan, which seemed to offer little for their most influential members.[64] Union leaders, indeed, could hardly be expected to rejoice about government sponsorship of a large class of low-wage public service workers. Other players who were ordinarily labeled "liberal," such as urban governors and mayors (and Moynihan), harped on the administration's failure to offer large-scale fiscal relief to their states and cities. Conflicts involving regional interests—notably those pitting officeholders in the urban North against those in the South—exposed an especially discordant theme in the long-running drama of efforts for welfare reform in the United States: already established welfare policies in a huge, pluralistic nation are surely hard to simplify.

The most fundamental cause of Carter's failure, however, lay in the enduring strength of long-standing popular feelings about poverty. These feelings, reflected in Congress, were complicated, for polls regularly indicated that Americans believed in helping the deserving poor. But most people did not care deeply about the subject. And popular attitudes toward "welfare" were volatile, contradictory, and in many ways profoundly conservative, rooted in negative stereotypes about lazy, "undeserving" people who fattened at the public trough. Califano understood the strength of these feelings and tried repeatedly to demolish popularly held "myths," as he termed them, about recipients of welfare.[65] In his heart, however, he knew that these myths possessed extraordinary resilience. Indeed, neither he nor Carter could shake widespread public perceptions that the PBJI would undermine work effort and that it was essentially a scheme to redistribute income.[66]

These popular feelings, however, also expressed values that resist the simple label of "conservative." The PBJI, many people thought, offered costly, overly generous entitlements; it promoted greater equality of condition instead of equality of opportunity; it departed from the Great Society liberalism of Lyndon Johnson, whose War on Poverty had offered a hand up. Instead, these people thought, the PBJI promised a handout.[67] This is another way of saying that Carter's welfare reform, though fiscally conservative, ventured beyond widely held American notions of the proper role of government social policy. The PBJI failed for many reasons, to be sure. But among these reasons was that it seemed to threaten a range of historically powerful ideas about the central value to the Good Society of work, individual effort, and local approaches to need. The political power of these notions—and of the interest groups that profited from them—had frustrated liberals in earlier eras, and they would have defeated the deftest of presidents in the late 1970s, which were in any event unconducive to major domestic reforms.[68]

NOTES

Thanks go to the following people who helped me with this chapter: Sarah Phillips, Alice O'Connor, and Edward Berkowitz.

1. Stuart Eizenstat Interview, January 29–30, 1982, 102, William Burkett Miller Center of Public Affairs, University of Virginia Project on the Carter Presidency, Transcripts (hereafter cited as Miller Center), Jimmy Carter Library (JCL).

2. James Fallows, "The Passionless Presidency: The Trouble with Jimmy Carter's Administration," *Atlantic Monthly,* May 1979, 45.

3. Joseph A. Califano, *Governing America: An Insider's Report from the White House and the Cabinet* (New York: Simon and Schuster, 1981), 320.

4. Laurence Lynn, Jr., "A Decade of Policy Developments in the Income Maintenance System," in *A Decade of Federal Anti-Poverty Programs: Achievements, Failures, and Lessons,* ed. Robert Haveman (New York: Academic Press, 1977), 55–117. The book mentioned above is Laurence Lynn, Jr., and David Whitman, *The President as Policymaker: Jimmy Carter and Welfare Reform* (Philadelphia: Temple University Press, 1981). Lynn had served the Ford administration as an assistant secretary of the Department of Health Education, and Welfare.

5. Lynn and Whitman, *The President as Policymaker,* 230–31.

6. Nancy Rose, *Workfare or Fair Work: Women, Welfare, and Government Work Programs* (New Brunswick, N.J.: Rutgers University Press, 1995), 97–117; Margaret Weir, *Politics and Jobs: The Boundaries of Employment Policy in the United States* (Princeton, N.J.: Princeton University Press, 1992), 117–25.

7. Rose, *Workfare or Fair Work*, 121–22.

8. In late 1977, Food Stamps went to approximately 16.7 million people. By 1980, the rolls had mounted to around 21 million. See Gordon Weil, *The Welfare Debate of 1978* (White Plains, N.Y.: Institute for Socioeconomic Studies, 1978), 82–86.

9. Committee on Ways and Means, U.S. House of Representatives, "Overview of Entitlement Programs" ("1992 Green Book"), 102d Cong., 2d sess. (Washington, D.C.: Government Printing Office, 1992), 1274–75. The poverty line in 1982 was $6,281 for a family of two persons and $9,862 for a family of four.

10. See Martin Anderson, "Welfare Reform on 'The Same Old Rocks,'" *New York Times*, November 29, 1978; Tom Bethell, "Treating Poverty," *Harper's*, February 1980, 16–24; and George Gilder, "The Coming Welfare Crisis," *Policy Review* 11 (Winter 1980): 25–36.

11. Theda Skocpol, "The Limits of the New Deal System and the Roots of Contemporary Welfare Dilemmas," in *Social Policy in the United States: Future Possibilities in Historical Perspective*, ed. Theda Skocpol (Princeton, N.J.: Princeton University Press, 1995), 208–9.

12. Other welfare programs included General Assistance, administered by state and local governments ($1.3 billion to 900,000 recipients in fiscal year 1977); veterans' pensions, for the permanently and totally disabled, survivors, and dependents ($3.1 billion to 2.6 million recipients); and Basic Educational Opportunity Grants ($1.8 billion to 1.9 million students at postsecondary schools).

13. From 1935 until 1950, the program was entitled Aid to Dependent Children (ADC). Addition in 1950 of a grant to the parent (usually the mother) of the dependent children led to a change in name to AFDC.

14. See James T. Patterson, *America's Struggle against Poverty, 1900–1994* (Cambridge, Mass.: Harvard University Press, 1995), 171–81, for explanation of the growth. The percentage of the total grant from the federal Treasury depended on the per capita income of the state: the poorer the state, the higher the federal contribution (which ranged from 50 to 83 percent).

15. The most important of these were Social Security and Medicare. Other such programs included Railroad Retirement, Workmen's Compensation, Black Lung, Unemployment Insurance, and Veterans' Compensation. Social Security, by far the biggest of these programs, went to 29.2 million recipients in 1977, at a cost of $84.6 billion ("Green Book," 121–25). Social Security was indexed for inflation; AFDC was not.

16. Nick Kotz, "The Politics of Welfare Reform," *New Republic*, May 14, 1977, 16–21.

17. These programs also benefited interest groups, such as doctors and farmers.

18. Benefit levels were merely the most glaring inequities in the system. In 1977, roughly half the states did not authorize payment of AFDC benefits to needy two-parent families in which the primary wage earner was unemployed and unable to work.

19. Political leaders from "high benefit" states and cities called especially loudly for a national system that would offer them budget relief. In 1977, some 25 percent of the national caseload was borne by two states, California and New York.

20. A third track of low-income people, the working poor, were to be aided by other programs, such as Food Stamps and Earned Income Tax Credits.

21. Lynn and Whitman, *The President as Policymaker*, 35, 46–49; Stuart Eizenstat, "President Carter, the Democratic Party, and the Making of Domestic Policy," in *The*

Presidency and Domestic Policies of Jimmy Carter, ed. Herbert Rosenbaum and Alexej Ugrinsky (Westport, Conn.: Greenwood Press, 1994), 2–16.

22. A bashing much resented by many congressmen. William Cable, a liaison with Congress, recalled, "You don't spend a year and a half running against Washington, then come to Washington, and not have to pay for some of that rhetoric" (Frank Moore Interview, Miller Center, September 18–19, 1981, 14, JCL).

23. Cited in Michael Riccards, *The Ferocious Engine of Democracy,* vol. 2 (Lanham, Md.: Rowman and Littlefield, 1995), 371.

24. For the weakness of liberal interest groups, see comments by Carter aide Landon Butler in Hamilton Jordan Interview, September 6, 1981, Miller Center, 10, JCL. He noted the "almost total paralysis that existed in the labor movement, in the black institutions, in the civil rights institutions, in the women's groups, and to a lesser extent in the environmental groups."

25. *Time,* August 15, 1977, 7.

26. A complexity reflected in Congress, where many committees and subcommittees were likely to involve themselves in welfare reform.

27. Weil, *The Welfare Debate of 1978,* 4–6. These included Social Security and other insurance programs.

28. Cited in Lynn and Whitman, *The President as Policymaker,* 277.

29. Thomas O'Neill, with William Novak, *Man of the House: The Life and Political Memoirs of Speaker Tip O'Neill* (New York: Random House, 1987), 297, 308–11.

30. Eizenstat Interview, Miller Center, January 29–30, 1982, 33–34, JCL; Charles Schultze Interview, Miller Center, January 8–9, 1982, 68–69, 76, JCL.

31. There was also considerable debate over wage rates on the government jobs. If these were set at the "prevailing rate" (of jobs in the area), as Marshall and his aides wished, the new public service employees would be relatively well compensated, and local labor markets would not be demoralized. Others retorted that such wages—or even rates at the level of minimum wages—would draw many low-paid workers out of their jobs, incite inflationary pressures, and give rise to unacceptable budgetary stresses.

32. Charles Schultze Interview, Miller Center Interview, January 8, 9, 1982, 70, JCL.

33. Kotz, "The Politics of Welfare Reform," 18–19; Lynn and Whitman, *The President as Policymaker,* 89, 98; Califano, *Governing America,* 333–36.

34. Califano to Schlesinger, March 31, 1977, Box 19, Schlesinger Files, JCL.

35. Kotz, "The Politics of Welfare Reform," 19. For Califano's plans see Califano to Carter, April 11, 1977, Box 317, Domestic Policy Staff (DPS)-Eizenstat, JCL.

36. Jordan to Carter, April 11, 1977, Box 37, Chief of Staff/Jordan Files, JCL.

37. For Moynihan's restiveness, see *New York Times,* April 26, 1977. "You can draft that bill in a morning," he declared with characteristic immodesty.

38. Lynn and Whitman, *The President as Policymaker,* 136–38; *New York Times,* May 3, 1977. For Califano's remarks, see April 27, 1977, Box 5, Speechwriters/Chronological File, JCL.

39. Cited in Lynn and Whitman, *The President as Policymaker,* 137.

40. Cited in Robert Shogan, *Promises to Keep: Carter's First Hundred Days* (New York: Thomas Y. Crowell, 1977), 241.

41. Cited in Lynn and Whitman, *The President as Policymaker,* 140.

42. Cited in Shogan, *Promises to Keep,* 241.

43. Cited in Lynn and Whitman, *The President as Policymaker,* 141; Califano, *Governing America,* 342.

44. These documents are all in Box 317, DPS-Eizenstat, JCL.

45. Califano to Carter, July 25, 1977, Box 40, Staff Secretary File, JCL.

46. Schultze Interview, Miller Center, 89, JCL.

47. Joe to Eizenstat, July 27, 1977, Box 318, DPS-Eizenstat, JCL.

48. Eizenstat, Bert Carp, and Frank Raines to Carter, August 2, 1977, Box 319, DPS-Eizenstat, JCL; Califano to Carter, August 1, 1977, DPS-Eizenstat, JCL. See also Lynn and Whitman, *The President as Policymaker,* 221–26, which summarizes these and other memos. On Ullman, see *New York Times,* August 3, 1977.

49. Cited in Lynn and Whitman, *The President as Policymaker,* 221.

50. See Carter, "Announcement of Welfare Reform Package," Box 319, DPS-Eizenstat, JCL.

51. *New York Times,* August 2, 1977, 14.

52. *New York Times,* August 2, 7, 22, and September 10, 1977.

53. "The 'Welfare Reform' Charade," *Progressive,* August 1977, 6–7; "A Very Modest Proposal," *Nation,* August 20, 1977, 131–32; Elliot Currie, "A Piece of Complicated Gimmickry," *Nation,* September 17, 1977, 230–33. For Moynihan's objections, sent to Carter along with his hostile testimony on the Hill, see Moynihan to Carter, September 30, 1977, Box 318, DPS-Eizenstat, JCL. Eizenstat complained to Carter of Moynihan's "disturbing pattern of first endorsing Administration programs and then backing-off in order to obtain further concessions. We should not put ourselves in the position of encouraging this" (Eizenstat to Carter, October 11, 1977, DPS-Eizenstat, JCL).

54. *New York Times,* August 7, 1977.

55. Lynn and Whitman, *The President as Policymaker,* 234–37. The CBO issued a still higher estimate, of $17.4 billion, in January 1978.

56. *New York Times,* December 11, 1977, 1.

57. Moore to Carter, March 9, 1978, Box 318, DPS-Eizenstat, JCL.

58. *New York Times,* May 21, 1978. The results of these experiments were subject to varying interpretations by experts and remain debated years later. Liberals countered conservative claims by noting that the declines in work effort and the increases in family breakup were modest and to be expected. They added that job opportunities had to be increased. But some liberals, Moynihan included, were shaken by the results. See *New York Times,* November 16, 1978.

59. *New York Times,* June 23, 1978; Weil, *The Welfare Debate of 1978,* 102–3; Califano, *Governing America,* 357–63, labeled Proposition Thirteen the "final nail in the coffin of welfare reform for 1978."

60. *New York Times,* November 8, 1979; Weil, *The Welfare Debate of 1978,* 249–55.

61. Carter comments on memo, Christopher Edley and Bill Spring to Eizenstat, May 23, 1979, Box 317, DPS-Eizenstat, JCL.

62. Lynn and Whitman, *The President as Policymaker,* 264.

63. Weil, *The Welfare Debate of 1978,* 13. Eizenstat later tended to agree. "If we had come up with the '79 proposal in '77," he said in 1982, "I think it would have passed. . . . It wouldn't have solved the welfare problem but it would have been a significant step forward" (Eizenstat Interview, Miller Center, January 29–30, 1982, 129, JCL).

64. David Whitman, "Liberal Rhetoric and the Welfare Underclass," *Society* 21 (1983): 63–69.

65. Califano, *Governing America,* 364–67.

66. Leslie Lenkowsky, "Welfare Reform and the Liberals," *Commentary* 67 (March 1979): 56–61.

67. For the transition in liberal thinking during the 1960s, see Gareth Davies, *From Opportunity to Entitlement: The Transformation and Decline of Great Society Liberalism* (Lawrence: University Press of Kansas, 1996), 5, 421.

68. These same forces overcame liberal ideas for "reform" in 1996. See Jason DeParle, "Mugged by Reality," *New York Times Magazine,* December 8, 1996, 64–67, 99–100.

7

Carter's Urban Policy Crisis

Thomas J. Sugrue

If American cities ever had a golden age, it was certainly not the 1970s. Deep pessimism prevailed about the future of urban life in the United States. In 1971, the journal *Public Interest* asked, "Is the Inner City Doomed?" By 1976, the widespread answer was yes. Cities had become "dumping grounds for poor people" and "cemeteries" for the American dream. Many agreed with *U.S. News and World Report*'s pessimistic prognosis that urban problems were "terminal." Indeed, the bleak cityscapes of the Northeast and Midwest offered observers little ground for hope. Almost every major industrial center in the Rust Belt had lost population and jobs since the mid-1950s. Blue-collar workers bore the disproportionate burden of economic restructuring, a process that left city centers increasingly bereft of the well-paying, unionized jobs that had been the bulwark of the postwar economy. At the same time, city governments lumbered through financial crises of a magnitude not seen since the Great Depression. New York was bankrupt; Cleveland, Philadelphia, Boston, Newark, and Detroit teetered on the brink of insolvency. Urban race relations, never particularly amicable, remained tense, as frustrated blacks and "unmeltable" white ethnics faced off on city streets. Black youth unemployment rates skyrocketed; crime rates rose by nearly a third in the early 1970s. Working-class whites, many Catholics among them, rebelled against civil rights and welfare legislation. During the nation's bicentennial year, white opponents of school integration in Boston pelted school buses carrying black children into their neighborhoods. Above all, millions of white Americans continued their massive exodus to sprawling suburbs, looking with increasing alienation and hostility toward the cities they had abandoned.[1]

Jimmy Carter stepped reluctantly into the arena of urban policy. During the 1976 campaign, he offered a handful of statements on urban problems pitched to the Democrats' traditional northeastern and midwestern constituencies. To big-city mayors, Carter vaguely promised, if elected president, to be "a friend, an ally, and a partner in the White House." He failed, however, to propose any large-scale urban initiatives. Instead, the Democratic candidate challenged city governments to "root out inefficiency and waste"; called for a "partnership" between business, cities, states, and the federal government; and suggested that he would "orient" government expenditures "toward the more deprived areas, instead of to the suburbs where most of the political influence lies." After the election, the administration assigned a low priority to fashioning a coherent urban policy from sentiments about "partnership" and efficiency.[2]

But Carter could not avoid urban problems for long. A week after the election, one hundred urban mayors held an emergency meeting to demand that Carter "set a national tone of concern for America's cities." At first, Carter largely ignored the mayors. Civil rights leaders demanded an "urban Marshall Plan" as a reward for their loyalty at the ballot box. Carter's aides sent out mixed signals about what direction the new administration's urban policy would take. Stuart Eizenstat, director of the Domestic Policy Staff (DPS) promised that "this will be an administration with a commitment to urban America." But other officials dampened the enthusiasm. Joe Califano, secretary of Health, Education, and Welfare (HEW), bluntly told the mayors to expect little: "It takes money to deal with these problems—it does not come out of the sky." By the summer, pressure on Carter mounted. Rioting erupted on the streets of New York City during a power blackout, a grim reminder of the long hot summers of the 1960s. In addition, federal statistics painted a bleak portrait of rising urban unemployment, declining center-city population, and worsening poverty. National civil rights leaders joined prominent mayors in expressing impatience with the new administration. In June, Newark's mayor Kenneth A. Gibson accused Carter of attempting to balance the budget "at the expense of the cities, the unemployed, and the poor." In July, Carter attended the National Urban League's annual convention and heard its president, Vernon Jordan, accuse him of ignoring black America. Other Civil rights leaders joined Jordan, charging the administration with "callous neglect" and "falling short on programs, policies, and people." The Southern Christian Leadership Conference threatened a new "March on Washington" to force Carter to confront urban issues. As the political costs of inaction mounted, Carter promised to develop a "comprehensive" urban policy.[3]

Throughout 1977 and early 1978, Carter and his aides debated the shape that a new urban policy should take. As with most of Carter's domestic policy initiatives, his advisers offered a welter of complicated, often inconsistent recommendations, the result of unsettled debates and interagency conflicts that the president did little to resolve. But, however muddled, Carter's urban policy reflected his belief about the proper role and responsibility of the federal government in the wake of the 1960s. Carter came to believe that a successful urban policy required undoing what he considered the excesses of Great Society liberalism, while maintaining the traditional liberal commitment to social justice for the dispossessed. Carter never wholly repudiated liberalism, as many of his detractors charged, but by directing attention to what he viewed as the deficiencies of federal urban policy, Carter served as a bridge between the expansive liberalism of the 1960s and the antistatism of the 1980s. He accelerated the process of the devolution of federal social policy to the states and localities that continued unabated through succeeding administrations. Finally, through his naive belief that urban problems could best be solved by the private sector, both profit and nonprofit, he provided a model for the privatization of urban reform that has prevailed through the remainder of the century.

THE URBAN POLICY CRISIS

The legacies of the 1960s loomed like dark clouds over the Carter administration. During the Great Society, cities had been the proving ground for liberal social reforms devised by government officials, foundations, and academics. By the mid-1970s, critics on both the right and the left agreed that those experiments had failed miserably. Conservatives looked at urban renewal and public housing and saw a "federal bulldozer" that had rolled over neighborhoods. They argued that urban job training programs had become a bureaucratic boondoggle and that welfare had sapped poor peoples' work ethic and fostered family breakup. Left-leaning skeptics argued that the federal government had uncritically embraced the private sector, channeling funds that should have gone to the poor themselves to the construction and real estate industries, banks, building trades unions, and corrupt urban mayors. Urban renewal had destroyed viable ethnic and African American communities, while lining the pockets of corporate elites who were the true beneficiaries of government largesse. Activists at both ends of the political spectrum, then, blamed federal policy for many of America's most pressing urban problems.[4]

Carter became one of the most prominent voices to call into question some of the fundamental verities of liberalism. Liberal social programs, he maintained, emanated from big, unresponsive government too far removed from its constituents. During his campaign, Carter had emphasized the need for "limits," criticized the "Washington mess," and endorsed the argument that "selfish special interests," who were a "menace to our system of government," had shaped federal policy. Social programs had failed because policy makers had lost touch with "the American people." The marriage of bureaucracy and expertise that had been central to reform politics since the Progressive Era came under siege as elitist and undemocratic. Carter's aides regularly reinforced this sentiment in memos, referring pejoratively to past liberal reform efforts. Reflecting the administration's mentality, Legislative Projects director Les Francis repudiated "the New Deal/Great Society approach of creating dozens of new programs and spending billions of additional tax dollars."[5] Two currents, often in tension with each other, whirled around the critique of past liberal policy: a call for greater individual liberty, particularly in the economic realm, and the desire for community control, which, it was argued, would provide a democratic alternative to technocratic statism.[6]

Carter and his advisers also drew strategic lessons from the Great Society. The "excesses" of 1960s liberalism, political strategists and pundits argued, unglued the New Deal coalition. By targeting African Americans, Johnson's domestic policy had alienated white Democrats, winnowed support for the supposedly universalistic promises of the New Deal, and rewarded extremist advocates of black power and urban violence. In this view, the party of FDR collapsed because it capitulated to the demands of angry urban minorities, thereby disregarding the white majority and dividing the electorate into hopelessly polarized factions. Carter's advisers warned about the "Balkanization of politics that has made it harder to muster a majority for important causes" and urged the president to "speak clearly for the common good."[7] By the mid-1970s, conventional wisdom held that the antidote to balkanization (and the key to electoral success) would be policies that appealed to one crucial segment of voters—the disaffected white middle class. Throughout the early 1970s, commentators identified an upswell of "middle-class rage," led by angry working-class and middle-class whites who felt marginalized by the Democratic party, treated with contempt by cultural elites, and unfairly barraged by accusations of parochialism and racism. Particularly sensitive to the ethnic rebellion—but unwilling to resort to the polarizing rhetoric of Nixon and Agnew—Carter fashioned an appeal to the vital center of the electorate who were "fair," "honest," and believed in "work" and "self-reliance." They included the "average, hardworking American" who toiled in the nation's "homes, factory shift lines, beauty parlors, barber shops, livestock sale barns, and shopping centers." Part of that appeal was a rejection of the supposedly particularistic programs of the War on Poverty.[8]

Carter's suspicion of liberalism, his distrust of special interests, and his concern for the forgotten white middle class bred deep suspicion of 1960s-style social policies. Carter drew several lessons from his understanding of the Great Society. First, he inherently distrusted large-scale government programs. Big government, he believed, inevitably failed. Second, Carter generally opposed increasing federal urban expenditures—a decision rooted in his disapproval of "special interest" politics and in his fiscal conservatism. Third, and most important, Carter believed in the capacity of the private sector (profit and nonprofit) to solve urban problems.

GOVERNMENT RESTRUCTURING

Government reorganization, Carter's first priority as president, was the very essence of his vision of reform. He lamented the apparent inefficiency, bureaucratic complexity, and jurisdictional overlap that plagued the federal government. Drawing from the experience of his most celebrated prepresidential achievement—the reorganization of the Georgia state government—Carter set out to impose order and efficiency on the federal government. Three interlocking goals made up the heart of Carter's domestic policy: to reduce the size and complexity of the federal government; to eliminate costly federal programs, particularly those that existed solely for the benefit of "special interests"; and to take power from the federal government and redirect it toward states and localities.[9]

Urban policy provided a case study, in Carter's view, of the deficiencies of disorganized government. In the 1960s, urban issues had fallen under the purview of a number of federal agencies with "jurisdictional uncertainty, duplication of effort, and lack of coordination."[10] By reducing overlap and preventing interagency conflict, Carter hoped to reduce expenditures while maintaining or improving service delivery. In March 1977, Carter created the interagency Urban Policy Research Group (URPG) to be the primary vehicle for the reorganization and coordination of federal urban reform efforts. But difficulties plagued URPG from the outset. Its meetings brought together a large, unwieldy group of officials from the president's Domestic Policy Staff (DPS), the Departments of Housing and Urban Development (HUD), HEW, Labor, and numerous other government agencies. Bridging the political differences and jurisdictional controversies that divided government agencies proved a far more difficult task than Carter had imagined.[11]

The URPG exhibited little sense of urgency. But that changed in the summer of 1977, in the aftermath of widely publicized criticism of Carter's seeming inaction on urban issues. Black denunciations of Carter, on the front pages of newspapers around the country, spurred the administration to action. Facing outside pressure, fearful of alienating his black supporters, Carter jump-started the URPG and charged it with developing a comprehensive urban policy by December.[12] Stung by the criticism of his erstwhile black allies, the president urged his advisers to solicit "written suggestions re urban policy from black leaders & other groups so as to derive good ideas & to minimize the inevitable criticisms later on." URPG officials stepped up "outreach" efforts to consult minority groups and community organizations.[13]

Under the gun in the fall of 1977, URPG officials met with a sense of urgency, indeed desperation, as they tried to formulate a coherent urban policy. They presented complex memorandums and reports, consisting of pages of largely undigested information. The first draft of their urban policy memorandum, produced in December, was a "laundry list" of programs, reflecting unresolved disputes between different cabinet departments. Immediately suspicious of the plan's incoherence and expense, Carter reportedly told his advisers: "Don't tell me we'll spend more money all around, then we'll call it an urban policy. Give me something worth funding if you want more money." After the press obtained a copy of the lengthy draft, the administration came under a new barrage of criticism. Civil rights groups, mayors, and urban reformers intensified their lobbying efforts. Between January and March 1978, Carter administration officials struggled under heightened public scrutiny to revise the URPG memorandum.[14]

URPG members differed widely on their diagnosis of urban problems and their suggested remedies. But, attentive to the president's overarching concern for governmental restructuring, they pressed forward with reorganization plans. Members of the DPS advocated "measures to improve and streamline planning and delivery of existing programs," including the creation of an urban policy "coordinating mechanism" and the establishment of local "economic development units" to link government initiatives in housing, employment training, community development, and public transportation. Such interagency and federal-local coordination, argued aide Jack Watson, would "produce enormously increased benefits for the cities with dollars we already have."[15]

Carter and his aides believed that urban policy was best left in the hands of state and local officials. When one memorandum argued that states should provide greater assistance to cities, President Carter responded with an enthusiastic "Jack and Stu—Push this." Local control had a wide base of support in the administration for a variety of reasons. Al Stern of the DPS asserted that a reliance on federal programs and expenditures "leads to a weakening of resources and resourcefulness" on the local level "where the problems must be solved."[16] Stuart Eizenstat called for "modest" local initiatives "designed to improve the functioning of base programs."[17] But the most vocal support for local control came from the administration's advocates of grassroots neighborhood organization, who appealed to the ethic of voluntarism and self-help that Carter himself found so captivating.

EMPOWER THE PEOPLE

To view Carter merely as a technocrat, dedicated to reengineering government, is to miss his most distinctive contribution to urban policy. In Carter's view, government restructuring, although necessary, could not solve urban problems. Carter dipped into a deep well of American urban reform that looked to neighborhood-based initiatives to eradicate poverty. He drew from 1960s-era notions of community control, refracted through the lens of a distinctive Christian communitarianism that emphasized small-scale, self-help efforts that would be accomplished through the empowering work of voluntary community organizations.

One of the most important strands of American urban policy from the Progressive Era forward has been neighborhood self-help. Beginning with the settlement house movement, an influential group of urban reformers who believed that the causes of poverty were environmental rather than innate looked to uplift the poor by improving their physical surroundings. In addition, they hoped that community organizations would become incubators of citizenship, providing opportunity for disenfranchised and alienated urban residents to take control of seemingly impersonal forces that governed their lives. And, more important, given the deep-rooted American belief that poverty was essentially an individual problem, they hoped that neighborhood-based reform efforts would provide poor people with the tools to escape the debilitating behaviors of defeatism, present-mindedness, idleness, and dependence. The idea of community control took on renewed significance during the War on Poverty. Local control would provide opportunities for the poor and renew a sense of grassroots democracy that, activists contended, had been trammeled by the increasingly impersonal, bureaucratic forms of American government.[18]

The mid-1970s witnessed a resurgence of communitarian ideals, particularly among religious intellectuals, urban planners, and academics. On the right, cleric Richard John Neuhaus and sociologist Peter Berger lamented the decline of "mediating institutions" such as churches and voluntary associations and called for a revitalization of civil society and family life. On the left, many veterans of the community action programs of the Johnson administration called for renewed efforts to empower the urban poor. Notions of local control and empowerment found fertile soil in the Carter administration. The most influential advocate of neighborhood-based voluntarism was DPS member Marcia (Marcy) Kaptur. Born to a Polish-American family in Toledo, Kaptur had worked as an urban planner and community organizer in her hometown and in Chicago, and had joined the Catholic Church–sponsored Campaign for Human Development. A vocal advocate of community self-determination, Kaptur argued in an early memorandum that an urban policy must "recognize families and neighborhoods as the basic units of our democratic society." Carter's urban policy, she concluded, "should be aimed at unleashing local forces of self-help." In addition, she promoted "voluntary incentive programs" to support "mediating institutions" such as churches and community organizations "to minimize psychological dependence on government and build self-confidence in a group's ability to accomplish an objective." Kaptur viewed urban policy through a Tocquevillian lens, calling for revitalizing cities through the actions of nongovernment voluntary associations.[19]

Monsignor Geno Baroni, an assistant secretary of HUD, joined Kaptur in calling for neighborhood revitalization. Baroni came to the administration as a longtime community activist, a Catholic supporter of civil rights, and one of the nation's most outspoken advocates for urban ethnics. Kaptur and Baroni both framed their policy prescriptions in terms of ethnic identity politics. The son of an Italian immigrant miner, Baroni had worked in the 1960s as a civil rights organizer. By 1970, influenced by the Black Power movement, he argued that the "black community should do its own thing," and moved into parallel organizing among whites. Described as "the Catholic Church's chief ethnic strategist," he founded the National Center for Urban Ethnic Affairs and drafted the 1970 U.S. Catholic Bishops' Labor Day statement, which lamented the nation's "continued neglect of the white ethnic working class."[20] Like Kaptur, Baroni made a vigorous argument that "neighborhood and voluntary associations" and "indigenous neighborhood redevelopment programs" should be at the center of urban reform, for they alone could "alleviate the alienating effects of big government, big industry, and big institutions." An ethnic populist who was concerned with the "ethnic workers' crisis with America," he contended that the problems of racial conflict and urban decline would persist unless the Democratic party embraced the working-class whites whom it supposedly had abandoned in the 1960s.[21]

Sensitive to the concerns of ethnic whites and rooted in a grassroots Catholic communitarianism, Kaptur and Baroni repudiated what they saw as the failures of Great Society–style urban policy. Kaptur believed that the War on Poverty had failed because it falsely presumed a "rich-poor, black-white dichotomy." Kaptur blamed liberal intellectuals and black activists for white backlash politics. The War on Poverty, she argued, "gave us . . . not only Richard Nixon but Philadelphia's Rizzo, both products of liberal neglect." The key to a successful urban policy was to broaden its constituency. "The framework we establish must be inclusive, not exclusive." A "stress only on the 'poor'" would inevitably fail, for "which middle-class family wants to feel they're paying for the 'poor'?"[22]

In addition, Kaptur expressed deep suspicion about an urban policy that focused on job creation and industrial redevelopment. "I would disagree that the heart of the problem is jobs and restoring the economic base of the cities," wrote Kaptur in a 1977 memorandum. At root, the cities suffered from problems of psychology and perception. To her, the goals of urban policy should be redemptive. Cities would be revitalized only if policies encouraged "human development and opportunity." In addition, Kaptur pushed hard for a rethinking of urban policy as one of "conservation" rather than redevelopment. The city, she contended, had rich resources in its neighborhoods, especially endangered white working-class communities, that ought to be treasured rather than jettisoned. Kaptur and Baroni hoped that neighborhood development would become a vehicle for the mobilization of white, working-class urban ethnics, the stabilization of their communities, and the revitalization of the Democratic party.[23]

Not all Carter administration officials agreed with the idea of community conservation. Despite Kaptur's repudiation of the Great Society, her plan for neighborhood mobilization bore a striking resemblance to the War on Poverty's Community Action Program. Kaptur reported that many DPS members were suspicious of the neighborhood-centered approach. And many Democratic mayors, especially veterans of the 1960s-era turf wars between radical community groups and urban machines, doubted the wisdom of government programs that put funds directly in the hands of nongovernment neighborhood groups and community development corporations. Kaptur recalled mayors' fears that "you're going to give money to political power bases out there in cities that are going to work against us."[24]

But despite political objections to federally subsidized voluntary programs, they stayed alive in part because of strong presidential support. In Carter's view, community control and government restructuring went hand in hand. Putting power in the hands of neighborhood organizations could be the first step in the return of power to the "people." Indeed, both President Carter and First Lady Rosalynn Carter shared a "special interest in non-governmental, self-help efforts" and hoped that urban policy would play a role in "encouraging voluntary action." In their view, the federal government would help people help themselves by providing seed money for programs for what Kaptur argued would become "self-sustaining local ventures."[25]

Thus when Carter visited the rubble-strewn South Bronx in the fall of 1977, he viewed it through the lens of government reform and neighborhood control. The South Bronx was, for the president, a symbol of the failure of federal urban policy and a sign of hope that voluntary, community efforts could solve urban problems. During his visit, Carter focused on the twin questions of federal service delivery and the self-help efforts of local community organizations. In October and November 1977, he sent a parade of officials from the Small Business Administration and the Departments of Commerce, Labor, Transportation, HEW, HUD, Interior, and Treasury to the South Bronx to meet with local politicians and community activists. Advisers Jack Watson and Bruce Kirschenbaum came back with a clear message: big government did not work. A "massive multi-billion dollar infusion of federal funds into the area" would not solve the problems of the South Bronx. Indeed, local activists seemingly endorsed Carter's vision of small government: "The community people themselves do not want such federal intrusions of money, but rather the tools to help themselves and reliable, longer-term commitments of incremental assistance." Voluntary efforts by community groups in the neighborhood especially interested Carter. Watson and Kirschenbaum drew special attention in their report to the sort of project that Carter found so appealing—the "sweat equity" rehabilitation of a deteriorating building that Carter had viewed in October.[26]

The South Bronx experience confirmed Carter's faith in small government and hardened his commitment to voluntarism. But it also raised vexing questions about the scale and approach of urban policy initiatives. Many administration officials doubted that the problems afflicting American cities could be solved by community organizations alone. Sam Brown, the head of ACTION (the federal agency that oversaw volunteer programs like VISTA and the Peace Corps), worried that "most of the problems with current policy are perpetuated and no structural changes which reflect alternative views of urban development are discussed." In late 1977, ACTION brought together a group of left-leaning political economists, including Ann Markusen, Barry Bluestone, Richard Child Hill, and John Mollenkopf, to discuss more radical urban policy options.[27] Another skeptic, domestic policy staffer Al Stern, noted the benefits of the "good media coverage" that the South Bronx project had generated but argued that the focus on single neighborhoods "would consume large amounts of funding" and leave "the bulk of urban problems untouched."[28] And a number of influential administration officials, particularly in HUD and the Department of Labor, argued that economic conditions lay at the root of urban problems; without attention to the intertwined problems of joblessness and poverty, the urban crisis would continue unabated.

THE URBAN ECONOMY: PLACE OR PEOPLE?

Whether federal policies should be targeted to depressed places or to impoverished people, regardless of their location, remained a central, unresolved question in twentieth-century American urban policy. From the 1940s through the 1960s, reformers fluctuated back and forth on the merits of "place-based" versus "people-based" federal spending. In the flush years of economic growth after World War II, federal urban renewal and public housing money, meager as it was, went disproportionately to cities. But the federal government intervened only reluctantly in urban labor markets. By the late 1950s, however, observers began to worry about "islands" of poverty in the midst of plenty and urged federal intervention to stem industrial and agricultural decline. In 1961, President Kennedy signed the Area Redevelopment Act (ARA), a proposal to channel federal funds to "depressed areas," including old industrial cities, dying mining towns, and impoverished farm communities. The Great Society also channeled federal money to poor urban neighborhoods through its Model Cities program. But such programs were never popular. Economists derided the ARA for intervening in the natural course of the economy. Politicians often justifiably derided programs targeted to "depressed areas" as pork-barrel programs. But place-based policies were a small part of the federal budget. Far more consequential was the expansion of non-place-specific antipoverty policies in the 1960s. The majority of Great Society initiatives, from Aid to Families with Dependent Children (AFDC) to Medicare to the Elementary and Secondary Education Act, targeted poor and middle-class people, not poor places.[29]

Carter administration officials engaged in an intense debate about place-based versus people-based policies. The administration's more hardheaded urban analysts offered a sobering picture of the structural causes of urban decline. URPG officials amassed voluminous data about "distressed areas" and their largely African American populations. Particularly influential in shaping the administration's analysis of urban problems was a Brookings Institution study that identified 123 cities in a "condition of distress," characterized by population decline, high concentrations of poverty, job loss, and fiscal instability. The Brookings researchers clearly sympathized with the plight of the cities. But Carter administration officials read the study's findings two ways. DPS and HUD officials generally argued for place-based policies that targeted federal funds to "distressed areas" with the hopes of stemming urban decline. Department of Labor officials, on the other hand, held out little hope for cities and argued for people-based initiatives that encouraged the mobility of poor people away from cities toward areas, largely suburban and rural, that were attracting jobs.[30]

Secretary of Labor Ray Marshall and Secretary of HEW Joe Califano became the strongest proponents of a people-based urban policy. Marshall argued vehemently that "tax incentives, whether in the form of investment or employment credits, should not be tied to location." Marshall's suspicion of place-based programs grew out of his sense of the inevitability of continued urban economic decline. "No feasible amount of Federal urban aid," he wrote, "will provide sufficient incentive for business to return to those places besieged by a critical mass of problems." In his view, government needed to retrain unemployed urban workers, improve transportation to outlying areas, and, above all, provide incentives to help poor people move from cities to outlying suburban and rural areas that had attracted new industry. "Our focus on location," he argued, "should be placed on helping people to achieve sufficient mobility to locate where the jobs are."[31] Califano made an even more pointed case against place-based strategies, which he believed "fly in the face of economic and political facts of life and human experience." The federal government "cannot and should not presume to change" decisions of firms to relocate "for economic gain." Trotting out the hoary cliché about America as a nation of immigrants, Califano argued that the United States was "built by people who migrated to America for a better life. Why shouldn't they migrate within America?"[32]

Those favoring government incentives to increase mobility looked to a celebrated 1976 federal court case, *Hills v. Gautreaux,* which required the Chicago Housing Authority to offer low-income, African American families vouchers to move from public housing to predominantly white, suburban communities. Though the evidence on the effects of *Gautreaux* was still mixed, advocates of mobility programs cited the increased economic opportunity available to suburban migrants. Skeptics like Marcy Kaptur worried that by encouraging poor people to move out of cities, *Gautreaux* would benefit "the suburbs at the expense of the central city communities."[33] In the end, most Carter officials shared Kaptur's suspicion about such "people-based" strategies. When Department of Labor officials proposed an amendment to the Comprehensive Employment and Training Act (CETA) to provide "relocation assistance" to the unemployed, some administration officials considered it "anti-urban."[34]

Ultimately, the most influential Carter administration officials supported an urban policy that targeted "distressed areas." But they also worried about the political liabilities of urban programs that would benefit northeastern and midwestern cities at the expense of small towns, rural areas, and the South. Many northern liberals believed it a matter of justice that the federal government target aid to troubled Rust Belt cities. New York's Daniel Patrick Moynihan, for example, argued the necessity of a targeted urban policy to counterbalance forty years of federal subsidies to the Sunbelt. Others pointed out that federal policies had encouraged suburban sprawl. HUD official Bob Embry gave a nod to this argument, pointing out that government office location and procurement policies had disadvantaged center cities. Still, policies targeted to the northern center cities took political heat, as suburban elected officials and Sunbelt legislators saw few obvious benefits from a targeted urban policy. How could a southern president, who hoped to make inroads among white suburbanites and win back the Solid South, expect to gain politically from a Rust Belt–dominated urban policy?[35]

The way out of the dilemma, Carter officials believed, was an emphasis on programs that offered "incentives," "leverage," and "catalysts" to the private sector. Government efforts to assist businesses were far less politically assailable than direct federal expenditures in cities. The federal government, argued Carter advisers Stu Eizenstat and Bert Carp, should have as its major focus "developing (and/or retaining) a viable base of *private sector* activity." The government had a twofold role: to fund programs that enhanced "positive perceptions" of cities as good places to live and invest, and to assist investors who needed loans and subsidies to relocate in cities. Thus administration officials supported tax incentives for urban investments and called for an Urban Development Bank to make credit available for inner-city redevelopment projects. Public incentives for private initiatives would stem the flow of capital away from inner cities. Incentives alone, however, failed to satisfy HUD officials: they supported more aggressive federal funding of public housing and low- and middle-income housing subsidies. But such proposals had little support among the president's economic and domestic policy advisers. Carter aides found an emphasis on public-private ventures politically salable, relatively cheap, and compatible with the administration's goals of restructuring government.[36]

THE NEW PARTNERSHIP TO CONSERVE AMERICA'S COMMUNITIES

In March 1978, Carter announced a "comprehensive" urban policy initiative, "The New Partnership to Conserve America's Communities." In preparation for a major speech outlining the plan, Secretary of HUD Patricia Harris, Domestic Policy Adviser Stu Eizenstat, and OMB director James T. McIntyre, Jr., presented the president with a decision memorandum and detailed summary of the proposals that had grown out of URPG and DPS meetings. Remarkable in its turgidity and length, the 178-page memorandum offered forty-three urban policy initiatives, culled from more than seventy proposals considered by the URPG. A separate 13-page introductory memo and 18 pages of letters from administration officials elaborating their conflicting positions on such programs as an Urban Development Bank and proposed public works programs accompanied the document.[37]

The memorandum served up a strange combination of hubris and resignation. On one hand, the very length of the memorandum and its pretentiousness in offering a "comprehensive" set of proposals suggested the administration's optimism that urban problems could be solved. It reflected Carter's firm belief, as adviser Stuart Eizenstat recalled, "that there are comprehensive answers to problems. The most frequently used word in [Carter's] first year in office was 'comprehensive.'" On the other hand, a tone of pessimism about the intractability of urban problems and the limitations of federal policy laced the document. Clearly, many administration officials worried about the possibility of urban change. Urban decline, the memo stated, resulted from "economic forces over which the government has little control." The document offered a catalog of the problems besetting cities, ranging from job and population loss, to physical deterioration, to political fragmentation. Downplaying the consequences of the federal government's long-standing policies like highway subsidies, tax laws, and housing policy, the memorandum argued that "technological changes, residential preferences, disparities in business costs, and automobile ownership" had irreversibly restructured American cities. Administration officials resigned themselves to the cacophony of diagnoses and proposals: "There is clearly no monolithic urban problem which can be addressed easily."[38]

The central theme of the proposal—a self-conscious reprise of Carter's campaign promise to urban mayors—was a "partnership" between federal, state, and local governments, the private sector, and community groups. Reiterating a theme that had come up again and again in Carter's speeches and in URPG deliberations, the memorandum argued that the problems of the city "cannot be solved by Washington alone." Right from the outset, the assumptions behind the administration's urban policy led in one direction: toward small-scale, gradualist, locally administered programs.

The urban memorandum started with fiscally conservative premises, but even those proved to be insufficient for the budget-conscious president. OMB officials vetted each proposal to ensure that it met the administration's budgetary objectives. And Carter's aides reassured the president that the proposed urban initiatives would uphold his desire to cap spending and reduce the size of government. A highlighted passage at the beginning of the memorandum insisted that the urban policy initiatives, however sweeping they appeared, would support Carter's promise of a leaner, more efficient government: *"None of these changes will have any effect on the budget. The effect of these changes, however, will be a government which is more responsive, more streamlined, more coordinated and more supportive of your urban policy."* Again and again throughout the document, Carter's aides promised the president that proposed urban initiatives could be enacted at little or no new cost to the federal government.[39]

By and large, Carter rejected large-scale job-creation programs, urban medical and welfare initiatives, and increased federal housing subsidies. He had little patience for HUD recommendations for urban housing subsidies and endorsed virtually none of them.[40] On the other hand, he supported relatively cheap programs, with significant symbolic benefits, that channeled more money into neighborhoods and community organizations. Hence, the president approved a

$35-million outlay for the National Endowment for the Arts "Liveable Cities" program, which would fund local arts programs and public mural projects. He also authorized a relatively inexpensive challenge grant program for the rehabilitation of city parks and recreation centers and supported a voluntary "community anti-crime initiative," which he hoped to promote through "an adequately financed PR program" and "max free radio/tv time."[41]

The "New Partnership" emphasized place-based strategies. Calling for a federal effort to "conserve America's communities," the urban policy memorandum offered both a cultural and an economic rationale for programs targeted to "existing cities and communities." To that end, Carter approved a proposal to give preference to cities in the location of federal facilities, one that promised significant symbolic benefits because it was "a virtually *no cost* way to provide" new jobs in center cities and "dramatizes the Federal government's leadership role in remaining in or relocating to cities." In addition, Carter supported a federal procurement program that targeted cities with high unemployment rates, despite opposition from his defense secretary, Harold Brown. These two programs represented an important symbolic shift away from forty years of federal support for urban decentralization. But large-scale federal subsidies that encouraged suburbanization—like home mortgage loan guarantees, tax deductions, and highway subsidies—remained intact. Finally, Carter supported initiatives to promote private sector investment in cities, most notably an Urban Development Bank under the joint control of HUD and the Department of Commerce.[42]

The president's sympathy for place-based policies led him to be more skeptical of "mobility-based programs." His advisers offered a watered-down version of the Department of Labor's relocation assistance plan, calling for a "modest" demonstration program to help workers move to areas "in which bona fide jobs can be found." Although the Council of Economic Advisers (CEA) concurred that programs to encourage mobility were a "very useful endeavor," Harris, Eizenstat, and McIntyre gave the idea little support. The decision memorandum counterpoised three terse "pros" against three detailed "cons," including arguments that a relocation program would be "politically controversial" because it would "encourage depopulation in existing poverty areas" and "encourage movement of minorities and low income persons into more affluent communities and labor markets." Clearly skeptical about the plan, Carter checked the approve option but indicated that he supported a "small, demonstration [program] only." Meanwhile, the White House opposed a "soft public works" program that would set aside jobs on government contracts for "disadvantaged workers." The CEA had warned that the program might be plagued by "abuses and wasteful expenditures." Worried about both costs and the impact on his anti-inflation policy, Carter squashed even small-scale job-creation programs by early 1978.[43]

In the end, only largely symbolic initiatives survived, programs that cost little and shifted the burden of urban policy from the federal government to local organizations. Fifteen million dollars would be targeted to neighborhood groups, but

in a nod to mayoral fears about community autonomy, the projects would be selected on a case-by-case basis in collaboration with city governments. Carter read
this section of the memorandum especially closely; indeed, the section on assistance to community organizations elicited an unusually lengthy and pointed presidential comment. "The more federal financing," wrote Carter, "the less volunteer/
neighborhood/private responsibility." Rather than large-scale expenditures, the
president wanted the administration to "use $ in tiny grants, etc." While pre-
paring his urban policy speech, Carter insisted on an emphasis on "volunteer,
private, neighborhood responsibility," encouraging Stu Eizenstat to develop the
theme of self-help. Whatever skepticism many administration officials had about
neighborhood-based initiatives, Carter's heart obviously lay with the proposals
that had been most fervently pitched by Kaptur and Baroni.[44]

THE LEGACY OF CARTER'S URBAN POLICY

Carter's urban policy died a quiet death, mourned by few and quickly forgotten.
On March 27, 1978, the president made his major address on urban policy. It got
a mixed reception. The U.S. Conference of Mayors lamented that Carter failed to
increase funding for housing and transportation needs. African Americans were
especially critical. New York's *Amsterdam News* lambasted "Carter's feeble urban
policy." Vernon Jordan labeled it "disheartening." In a postmortem, the *New York
Times* argued that Carter's "New Partnership" proposals had been limited by
"lengthy debate, quarrelling, lobbying, and finally uneasy compromise," all the
fault of a "distracted" chief executive. When a leaked memo outlining disputes
between HUD and DPS officials appeared in mid-April, the *Times* further documented the confusion and conflict surrounding Carter's reform initiative.[45]
     Urban policy fell off the list of the administration's priorities nearly as
abruptly as it had risen in prominence. Aid to cities fell victim to the administration's growing concern about inflation. In May 1978, the DPS considered a
proposed presidential trip to major northeastern cities and opposed the visit on
the grounds that an emphasis on urban redevelopment would "run somewhat
counter to our overall anti-inflation theme."[46] By the winter of 1978–79, Carter
began the process of trimming urban expenditures in his austerity budget. The
administration's anti-inflation adviser, Alfred E. Kahn, bluntly told urban officials that the government could ill afford to rebuild troubled cities, stating that
"the prescribed medicine is restraint." Only small-scale efforts in government
restructuring remained. In August 1978, Carter signed four executive orders that
represented the heart of what remained in his urban policy: he established an
interagency body to coordinate urban initiatives; required government agencies
to prepare "urban impact analyses" of federal programs; stated the government's
commitment to locate federal offices in cities; and called for procurement set-
asides for "labor surplus areas."[47]

At the end of Carter's term in office, the situation of American cities remained grim. Whatever optimism had animated Carter administration officials in 1977 and 1978 had evaporated, and most of the administration's initiatives, tepid as they were, had not been implemented. Poverty rates had risen, and urban unemployment rates remained high. The flight of people and jobs to suburban areas continued unabated. The President's Commission for a National Agenda for the Eighties reflected the increasing pessimism about urban reform: "Industrial cities such as Boston, Cleveland, and Detroit stand as brick-and-mortar snapshots of a bygone era." Writing off the possibility of urban revitalization, the commission gave a ringing endorsement to the relocation policies that had been greeted with skepticism only a few years earlier. The country would be better off if poor, urban residents migrated to the booming towns of the Sunbelt rather than remaining behind. However stark its findings were, the commission reaffirmed the administration's resignation to the seemingly irreversible forces that had reshaped American cities. Government could not—and indeed should not—attempt to interfere with the workings of the market. In the 1980s, Republicans celebrated the "free" market and urged an even more complete withdrawal of the federal government from urban affairs.[48]

In early 1979, a prominent urban activist, questioned about Carter's urban policy, stated that "we are heading into a complete new era and we don't know what to make of it." That complete new era witnessed a steady attack on urban funding that continued largely unabated for the next twenty years. But the most important aspect of Carter's new path was that he pointed the way to a complete reorientation of government's role toward cities. Carter's urban initiatives redefined the civic sphere in ways that provided a theoretical justification for government cutbacks. He shifted the burden of urban problems to the private sector and to community groups. By diminishing government's role, Carter ensured that urban problems would remain unsolved. The market had the capacity but lacked the will to stem the forces that eroded urban life. Neighborhood organizations had the will but lacked the capacity to turn back urban decline.

In his postpresidential career Carter has remained deeply sympathetic to notions of community control and worked closely with self-help and community-based urban initiatives. In his speeches and memoirs, the former president has referred glowingly to community self-help initiatives. Indeed, in the years after his presidency, Carter directed more and more of his energies to community redevelopment initiatives like the Atlanta Project and to local volunteer programs like Habitat for Humanity. Such small-scale projects have had great successes in rebuilding low-income housing in ravaged neighborhoods like the South Bronx. But this emphasis on community self-reliance ignores the root causes of the urban crisis, which are not local but regional and national in scope. Community efforts, however well organized they might be, simply cannot address larger problems such as economic restructuring, the city-suburban divide, and entrenched racial discrimination.

The legacy of Carter's urban policy is fraught with irony. Carter's fiscal conservatism and his critique of "interest group" domination paved the way for harsh Republican critiques of urban policy. His emphasis on state and local responsibility for urban problems became a justification for federal withdrawal from the urban arena. And in states where antiurban hostilities run deep in state legislatures, cities have battled with decreasing success for their share of stingy state funding. Carter's urban policy initiatives are certainly not all to blame for what followed. But he unwittingly legitimated his successors' neglect of urban problems. His emphasis on community organization and self-help became a surrogate for necessary government investment in inner cities. Twenty years after Carter announced a "comprehensive" urban policy, the problems of the cities have worsened. Even if Carter's programs themselves failed, his successors followed on a path that he began in 1977.

NOTES

Thanks to Dana Barron, Gary Fink, and Hugh Davis Graham for their comments on earlier drafts of this chapter and to Katie Rode for her outstanding research assistance.

1. "Cities in Peril," *U.S. News and World Report,* April 7, 1975, 29; William Baer, "On the Death of Cities," *Public Interest* 45 (Fall 1976): 3–19; on the sense of crisis in the 1970s, see Robert A. Beauregard, *Voices of Decline: The Postwar Fate of U.S. Cities* (Oxford: Blackwell, 1993), 219–45; Jon Teaford, *The Rough Road to Renaissance: Urban Revitalization in America, 1940–1985* (Baltimore, Md.: Johns Hopkins University Press, 1990), 200–231; Thomas J. Sugrue, "The Structures of Urban Poverty: The Reorganization of Space and Work in Three Periods of American History," in *The "Underclass" Debate: Views from History,* ed. Michael B. Katz (Princeton, N.J.: Princeton University Press, 1993), 85–117. For a statistical overview, see John Kasarda, "Urban Change and Minority Opportunities," in *The New Urban Reality,* ed. Paul Peterson (Washington, D.C.: Brookings Institution, 1986), 43–47, esp. Tables 1 and 2.

2. *New York Times,* March 31, 1976, 1, 20; June 30, 1976, 1, 20; October 28, 1976, 1.

3. *New York Times,* November 9, 1976, 19; January 19, 1977, 17; February 13, 1977, 1, IV5; June 14, 1977, 27; July 27, 1977, 18, II8.

4. Raymond A. Mohl, "Shifting Patterns of American Urban Policy since 1900," in *Urban Policy in Twentieth-Century America,* eds. Arnold R. Hirsch and Raymond A. Mohl (New Brunswick, N.J.: Rutgers University Press, 1993), 14–21; Michael B. Katz, *The Undeserving Poor: From the War on Poverty to the War on Welfare* (New York: Pantheon, 1989); James T. Patterson, *America's Struggle against Poverty, 1900–1994* (Cambridge, Mass.: Harvard University Press, 1995), esp. 126–209; Martin Anderson, *The Federal Bulldozer: A Critical Analysis of Urban Renewal, 1949–1962* (Cambridge, Mass.: MIT Press, 1964); Lawrence M. Friedman, *The Government and Slum Housing: A Century of Frustration* (Chicago: Rand McNally, 1968); Chester Hartman, "The Limitations of Public Housing," *Journal of the American Institute of Planners* 29 (November 1963):

283–96; Daniel Patrick Moynihan, *Maximum Feasible Misunderstanding* (New York: Free Press, 1969); Frances Fox Piven and Richard Cloward, *Regulating the Poor: The Functions of Public Welfare* (New York: Random House, 1971).

5. Erwin C. Hargrove, *Jimmy Carter as President: Leadership and the Politics of the Public Good* (Baton Rouge: Louisiana State University Press, 1988), 33–36; *New York Times,* March 25, 1976; June 4, 1976; *The Presidential Campaign 1976,* vol. 1, pt. 2 (Washington, D.C.: Government Printing Office, 1977), 701–5; Jimmy Carter, *Keeping Faith: Memoirs of a President* (New York: Bantam Books, 1982), 20; Les Francis to Stu Eizenstat, Bert Carp, Bo Cutter, Harrison Wellford, January 5, 1978, Box 304, Domestic Policy Staff (DPS)-Eizenstat, Jimmy Carter Library (JCL).

6. My thinking on these issues has been shaped by Brian Balogh, "Introduction" to *Integrating the Sixties: The Origins, Structures, and Legitimacy of Public Policy in a Turbulent Decade* (University Park: Pennsylvania State University Press, 1996), 20–28. The best discussion of the tensions between libertarian and communitarian ideals in the politics of the 1960s, 1970s, and 1980s remains E. J. Dionne, *Why Americans Hate Politics* (New York: Simon and Schuster, 1992).

7. Jim Fallows to Carter, May 17, 1978, Box 222, DPS-Eizenstat, JCL.

8. James Q. Wilson, "The Urban Unease," *Public Interest* 12 (Summer 1968): 25–39; Kevin Phillips, *The Emerging Republican Majority* (New Rochelle, N.Y.: Arlington House, 1969); Murray Friedman, ed., *Overcoming Middle Class Rage* (Philadelphia: Westminster Press, 1971); Michael Novak, *The Rise of the Unmeltable Ethnics: Politics and Culture in the 1970s* (New York: Macmillan, 1971); Richard Krickus, *Pursuing the American Dream: White Ethnics and the New Populism* (Garden City, N.Y.: Anchor Press, 1976). For a historical overview, see David R. Colburn and George E. Pozzetta, "Race, Ethnicity, and the Evolution of Political Legitimacy," in *The Sixties from Memory to History,* ed. David Farber (Chapel Hill: University of North Carolina Press, 1994), 119–48; Jonathan Rieder, "The Rise of the Silent Majority," in *The Rise and Fall of the New Deal Order,* ed. Steve Fraser and Gary Gerstle (Princeton, N.J.: Princeton University Press, 1989), 243–68.

9. On Carter's efforts to reorganize the Georgia state government, see Gary M. Fink, *Prelude to the Presidency: The Political Character and Legislative Leadership Style of Governor Jimmy Carter* (Westport, Conn.: Greenwood Press, 1980). On his efforts in the White House generally, see Donald A. Marchand, "Carter and the Bureaucracy," in *The Carter Years: The President and Policy Making,* ed. M. Glenn Abernathy, Dilys M. Hill, and Phil Williams (New York: St. Martin's Press, 1984), 192–207.

10. See President's Reorganization Project, Office of Management and Budget, "Work Program, Local Development Study," August 1977, Box 397, DPS-Eizenstat, JCL.

11. On the creation of the URPG, see Carter to Blumenthal et al., March 21, 1977, Box 307, DPS-Eizenstat, JCL. See also Kaptur to Eizenstat, April 25, 1977, Box 307, DPS-Eizenstat, JCL; and Harold L. Wolman and Astrid E. Merget, "The Presidency and Policy Formulation: President Carter and the Urban Policy," *Presidential Studies Quarterly* 10 (1980): 402–15.

12. On the importance of the Jordan speech, see Marcy Kaptur, Exit Interview, October 17, 1979, JCL; Wolman and Merget, "The Presidency and Policy Formulation," 402.

13. On URPG outreach programs, see Kaptur to Eizenstat and Bert Carp, September 29, 1977, Box 307, DPS-Eizenstat; see also materials in Box 311, DPS-Eizenstat, JCL.

See also Carter to Pat Harris and Stuart Eizenstat, February 16, 1978, Box 310, DPS-Eizenstat, JCL.

14. *New York Times,* December 18, 1977, 14; December 25, 1977, 1; February 1, 1978, 1.

15. Eizenstat and Bert Carp to Carter, December 12, 1977, Box 309, DPS-Eizenstat; Les Francis to Eizenstat, Bert Carp, Bo Cutter, Harrison Wellford, January 5, 1978, Box 304, DPS-Eizenstat, JCL; Meg Armstrong to Marcy Kaptur, October 27, 1977, Box 308, DPS-Eizenstat, JCL; Kaptur to Eizenstat and Carp, October 29, 1977, Box 308, DPS-Eizenstat, JCL.

16. Jack and Stu were Jack Watson and Stuart Eizenstat. See Rick Hutcheson to Watson and Eizenstat, December 21, 1977, and Carter's marginal notes on the attached memorandum from Intergovernmental Relations Subcommittee Staff to Edmund Muskie, December 16, 1977, Box 309, DPS-Eizenstat; Al Stern to Eizenstat, December 14, 1977, Box 309, DPS-Eizenstat, JCL.

17. Eizenstat to Carter, December 14, 1977, Box 309, DPS-Eizenstat, JCL.

18. The best overview of community-based politics is Robert Halpern, *Rebuilding the Inner City: A History of Neighborhood Initiatives to Address Poverty in the United States* (New York: Columbia University Press, 1995). For the link between environmental reform and citizenship, see Robert B. Fairbanks, *Making Better Citizens: Housing Reform and Strategy in Cincinnati, 1890–1960* (Urbana: University of Illinois Press, 1988). On the War on Poverty, see Alan Matusow, *The Unraveling of America: A History of Liberalism in the 1960s* (New York: Harper and Row, 1984); Thomas F. Jackson, "The State, the Movement, and the Urban Poor: The War on Poverty and Political Mobilization in the 1960s," in *The "Underclass" Debate: Views from History,* ed. Michael B. Katz (Princeton, N.J.: Princeton University Press, 1993), 403–39; Alice O'Connor, "Evaluating Comprehensive Community Initiatives: A View from History," in *New Approaches to Evaluating Community Initiatives,* ed. James P. Connell, Anne C. Kubisch, Lisbeth Schorr, and Carol H. Weiss (Washington, D.C.: Aspen Institute, 1995), 23–63. On the neighborhood movement in the 1970s, see Teaford, *Rough Road to Renaissance,* 240–52.

19. Kaptur, Exit Interview, October 17, 1979, JCL; Eizenstat and Kaptur to Carter, October 17, 1977, Box 308, DPS-Eizenstat. On Kaptur's efforts in Chicago, see Ed Marciniak, *Reviving an Inner-City Community* (Chicago: Department of Political Science, Loyola University, 1977); Marcia C. Kaptur, "East Humboldt Park Copes with the Chicago 21 Plan," *Planning* 43 (August 1977): 14–16; Richard John Neuhaus and Peter Berger, *To Empower the People* (Washington, D.C.: American Enterprise Institute, 1977).

20. Kaptur, Exit Interview, October 17, 1979, JCL. On Baroni, see also Murray Friedman, "Middle America and the New Pluralism," in Friedman, *Overcoming Middle Class Rage,* 36; John T. McGreevy, *Parish Boundaries: The Catholic Encounter with Race in the Twentieth-Century Urban North* (Chicago: University of Chicago Press, 1996), 230.

21. Baroni to Robert C. Embry, September 13, 1977, Box 311, DPS-Eizenstat, JCL. For a statement of Baroni's ethnic populism, see Michael Wenk, S. M. Tomasi, and Geno Baroni, eds., *Pieces of a Dream: The Ethnic Worker's Crisis with America* (New York: Center for Migration Studies, 1972). For his discussion of community organizing, see Geno Baroni, "The Neighborhood Movement in the United States from the 1960s to the Present," in *Neighborhood Policy and Planning,* ed. Phillip L. Clay and Robert M. Hollister (Lexington, Mass.: Heath, 1983).

22. Kaptur to Orin Kramer, July 29, 1977, Box 307, DPS-Eizenstat, JCL; Kaptur to Kramer, n.d. [August 1977], Box 307, DPS-Eizenstat, JCL.

23. Kaptur to Kramer, July 29, 1977, Box 307, DPS-Eizenstat, JCL.

24. Kaptur, Exit Interview, October 17, 1979, JCL.

25. Ibid.; "Proposed Language for the Neighborhoods and Communities Section of the State of the Union Address," Box 302, DPS-Eizenstat, JCL; Eizenstat to Rosalynn Carter, February 14, 1978, Box 303, DPS-Eizenstat, JCL; Kaptur to Ralph Schlosstein and Eizenstat, March 7, 1978, Box 304, DPS-Eizenstat, JCL.

26. *New York Times,* October 6, 1977; October 13, 1977; Jack Watson and Bruce Kirschenbaum to Carter, November 20, 1977, Box 308, DPS-Eizenstat, JCL. See also Jill Jones, *We're Still Here: The Rise, Fall, and Resurrection of the South Bronx* (Boston: Atlantic Monthly Press, 1986), 311–23.

27. Sam Brown to Eizenstat, January 17, 1978, Box 309, DPS-Eizenstat, JCL. On the ACTION conference, see program material in ibid.

28. Al Stern to Eizenstat, December 14, 1977, Box 309, DPS-Eizenstat, JCL.

29. James L. Sundquist, *Politics and Policy: The Eisenhower, Kennedy, and Johnson Years* (Washington, D.C.: Brookings Institution, 1968), 57–83; Irving Bernstein, *Promises Kept: John F. Kennedy's New Frontier* (New York: Oxford University Press, 1991), 160–91; Gary Mucciaroni, *The Political Failure of Employment Policy, 1945–1982* (Pittsburgh: University of Pittsburgh Press, 1990), 17–53; Margaret Weir, *Politics and Jobs: The Boundaries of Employment Policy in the United States* (Princeton, N.J.: Princeton University Press, 1992), 54–58, 63–67.

30. "Meeting Emergency Needs of Communities and People in Distress," Box 309, DPS-Eizenstat, JCL.

31. Ray Marshall to Carter, March 10, 1978, Box 310, DPS-Eizenstat, JCL; Marshall to Eizenstat and Patricia Harris, March 15, 1978, Box 302, DPS-Eizenstat, JCL.

32. Califano to Eizenstat, January 11, 1978, Box 303, DPS-Eizenstat, JCL.

33. *Hills v. Gautreaux,* 425 U.S. 284 (1976); U.S. Department of Housing and Urban Development, *Gautreaux Housing Demonstration* (Washington, D.C.: Government Printing Office, 1979); Kaptur to Eizenstat and Ralph Schlosstein, February 23, 1978, Box 304, DPS-Eizenstat, JCL.

34. Eizenstat to Bob Hall et al., [Date?], Box 305, DPS-Eizenstat, JCL.

35. On Moynihan's concern about the regional inequities in tax burdens and government spending, see material in Box 301, DPS-Eizenstat, JCL, especially Schultze and Eizenstat to Daniel Patrick Moynihan, September 22, 1977, and Carter to Moynihan, October 22, 1977; Robert C. Embry, Jr., to Eizenstat, October 20, 1977, Box 308, DPS-Eizenstat, JCL. For the most influential statement of the Sunbelt-Snowbelt divide, see Kirkpatrick Sale, *Power Shift: The Rise of the Sunbelt Rim and Its Challenge to the Eastern Establishment* (New York: Vintage Books, 1975); Bruce Schulman, *From Cotton Belt to Sun Belt: Federal Policy, Economic Development, and the Transformation of the South, 1938–1980* (New York: Oxford University Press, 1991), 203–5. For suburban elected officials' critiques of place-based initiatives, see "Major Urban Initiatives of the Carter Administration, January 1977 to Date and NACO's Position Thereon," and Jack Watson to William Beach, April 6, 1978, both in Box 304, DPS-Eizenstat, JCL.

36. "Some Assumptions Underlying a National Urban Policy," Box 311, DPS-Eizenstat, JCL. Emphasis in the original. See also *New York Times,* September 19, 1977.

37. Urban Policy Memorandum, 11.

38. Harris, Eizenstat, and McIntyre to Carter, March 10, 1978, Box 305, DPS-Eizenstat, JCL; Stuart Eizenstat, "President Carter, the Democratic Party, and the Making of Domestic Policy," in *The Presidency and Domestic Policies of Jimmy Carter,* ed. Herbert Rosenbaum and Alexej Ugrinsky (Westport, Conn.: Greenwood Press, 1994), 5.

39. Urban Policy Memorandum, 9–10. For examples of proposals earmarked as "no cost," see Urban Policy Memorandum, 25, 29. Carter's aides reinforced their budgetary conservatism in the introductory memo as well. See Eizenstat and McIntyre to Carter, March 21, 1978, 2, DPS-Eizenstat, JCL.

40. Urban Policy Memorandum, 118–20.

41. Ibid., Carter's marginal notes on page 177.

42. Harold Brown to Carter, Box 309, DPS-Eizenstat, JCL; Urban Policy Memorandum, 25–29.

43. Arnold Packer to Eizenstat and Embry, February 17, 1978, Box 306, DPS-Eizenstat, JCL; Lyle E. Gramley to Carter, March 21, 1978, Box 306, DPS-Eizenstat, JCL; Urban Policy Memorandum, 55.

44. Carter to Eizenstat, March 23, 1978, Box 306, DPS-Eizenstat, JCL; Urban Policy Memorandum, 2–3, 8, Carter's notes on page 166.

45. *Amsterdam News,* April 1, 1978; *New York Times,* March 28, 1976; April 2, 1978; April 16, 1978; Dilys M. Hill, "Domestic Policy," in Abernathy, Hill, and Williams, *The Carter Years,* 25.

46. Schlosstein to Eizenstat, May 3, 1978, Box 310, DPS-Eizenstat, JCL; Carp to Eizenstat, May 26, 1978; attached to Watson and Kirschenbaum to Hamilton Jordan et al., Box 309, DPS-Eizenstat, JCL; *New York Times,* December 5, 1978; January 11, 1979; January 21, 1979; January 27, 1979.

47. Robert Lipschutz to Carter, August 9, 1978, Box 308, DPS-Eizenstat, JCL.

48. President's Commission for a National Agenda for the Eighties, *Urban America in the Eighties: Perspectives and Prospects* (Washington, D.C.: Government Printing Office, 1980).

8

An Age of Limits: Jimmy Carter and the Quest for a National Energy Policy

John C. Barrow

As Jimmy Carter took the oath of office on January 20, 1977, the nation was gripped by both a record cold wave and the most severe natural gas shortage in its history. Snow fell in Miami, and eight-inch-thick ice on the Mississippi River brought barge traffic to a halt. The concurrent shortage of natural gas forced schools and factories throughout the nation to shut down, leaving hundreds of thousands of workers temporarily unemployed and thousands of students stranded at home. Even in Carter's normally temperate home state of Georgia, more than 80 percent of the state's schools were closed, and all of the state's industrial consumers were without natural gas. Given this context, it was perhaps not surprising that one of Carter's first legislative accomplishments would be the enactment of an emergency natural gas pricing bill. The natural gas legislation, however, would be only the first of many attempts by Carter to deal with growing energy problems in the United States. In fact, energy issues would dominate the president's domestic and international policy-making efforts during the next four years. As Walter A. Rosenbaum would later note, "The Carter administration began with a natural gas crisis and ended with the Iranian hostage crisis. . . . From start to finish, energy issues crowded its agenda." While Carter considered his work on energy matters to be "equal in importance to any other goal" of his administration, he also admitted that his efforts on the issue were "like chewing on a rock that lasted the whole four years" of his presidency.[1]

In many ways Carter's somewhat quixotic quest for a national energy policy defined his presidency. On no other issue did Carter risk so much of his political capital, and on no other issue did Carter experience his greatest triumphs and most humiliating defeats. In energy policy, one could see the strengths of Carter's leadership—his willingness to tackle inherently difficult national problems without regard to the political costs and his conception of the presidency as leadership for the public good. Conversely, energy policy also revealed the weaknesses of the president's leadership—his difficulty in building political coalitions, his inability to marshal his party, and his failure to inspire confidence in his ability to lead the nation. Despite Carter's unwavering commitment to reorienting the nation's energy policy, energy issues haunted the Carter administration, particularly in his last two years in office, and greatly contributed to his defeat at the polls in 1980.

Two weeks after his inauguration, as the nation continued to suffer from the unusually cold winter and the natural gas shortage, President Carter delivered his first nationally televised policy address to the American public. Attired in an unbuttoned cardigan sweater and casually seated in an armchair in the White House library, the president told the nation that on April 20, 1977, he would present to Congress a "comprehensive long-range energy policy." Calls to action on energy policy such as Carter's televised statement were not novel in the 1970s. Since the 1973 Arab oil embargo and subsequent energy crisis, policy makers had repeatedly attempted to find ways to either increase energy production or curb energy consumption. As Presidents Nixon and Ford had discovered, however, finding consensus on energy matters proved to be an elusive task. Republicans and oil-state Democrats tended to favor policy that relaxed the labyrinth of federal rules and regulations in order to increase domestic production, while most Democrats preferred policy that would encourage conservation, thereby preserving the environment from new resource extraction hazards and protecting consumers from rising energy prices. The most contentious and central debate on energy policy had centered on the issue of energy pricing. Federal regulation of domestic oil and natural gas prices kept energy costs at artificially low levels, encouraging waste and discouraging expensive new exploration and extraction efforts. Any successful energy policy, therefore, would need to find a way to bolster energy prices. Not surprisingly, neither Democrats nor Republicans welcomed the opportunity to raise the costs of energy to American consumers.

Efforts to find other ways of increasing domestic energy production and conservation encountered controversy as well. Congressmen with environmentalist-friendly constituents viewed any attempts to increase the use of coal resources or relax environmental rules with great suspicion, regardless of any increased energy production that might result. Expansion of nuclear power, once widely regarded as the cure-all for the nation's energy woes, continued to attract growing opposition. Conservatives, on the other hand, saw government involvement and funding in new energy production efforts as contrary to the free market and a wasteful use of public funds. They also argued that additional layers of government bureaucracy would hinder rather than encourage the development of new energy technologies. Added to these policy disagreements was an array of interest groups ranging from consumer activists to the major oil companies that supported often conflicting policy options. The intensity of interest group lobbying and the inability of Congress to achieve consensus during the Nixon and Ford administrations caused then House majority leader Thomas P. "Tip" O'Neill, Jr., to remark that energy policy was "perhaps . . . the most parochial issue that could have ever hit the floor."[2]

Because of the economic chaos created by fuel shortages and skyrocketing energy prices, the period 1973–76 should have been a propitious moment for the formulation of new energy policy. Virtually all economists, energy experts, politicians, and business leaders agreed that the nation must change its energy consumption habits and reduce its dependence on petroleum. The Arab embargo had demonstrated the economic dislocation and upheaval that could be caused by the nation's production and consumption habits. Even so, as time elapsed after the embargo, consumption levels began to rise again, and the federal government appeared paralyzed and incapable of dealing with the problem. Three years of intense and often rancorous policy debate under Nixon and Ford had resulted in little significant change in federal energy policy. In fact, the energy policies that Carter inherited in 1977 differed little from those that existed in the months before the oil embargo.

Given the unsuccessful efforts of the two previous administrations and the fading public memory of the oil embargo, Carter's decision to make energy the first major policy initiative of his administration surprised both Washington insiders and the American public. The most talked about issues of the 1976 presidential campaign had been the 1975 recession, tax reform, and welfare reform, not energy policy. To be sure, Carter had mentioned energy matters and had harshly criticized President Ford's energy initiatives, but he never hinted that he would pursue such a massive effort to redefine the manner in which the nation used its energy resources. Throughout the campaign Carter spoke only in general terms, calling for measures that would increase conservation, create a Department of Energy, strengthen automobile and appliance efficiency standards, and provide for more uses of coal. His most specific and controversial proposal on energy— to deregulate natural gas prices over a five-year period—illustrated the candidate's apparent lack of intense interest in energy issues. With virtually no discussion or study of the problem, Carter took a stand on the matter late in October 1976, primarily as the result of a letter sent to him by Domestic Policy Adviser Stuart Eizenstat, who advocated deregulation as a means of obtaining political support in gas-producing states. As Eizenstat later recalled, the episode demonstrated the limited extent of Carter's interest in energy policy during the campaign and the degree to which energy was a nonissue.[3]

As president-elect, however, Carter's disinterest in energy issues would prove short-lived. The natural gas crisis of late 1976 and early 1977 forced renewed attention to the nation's heavy dependence on limited fossil fuels. Furthermore, a number of people with whom Carter consulted during the transition period, such as Senator Henry Jackson (chair of the Energy and Natural Resources Committee), S. David Freeman (director of the energy policy project at the Ford Foundation), Omi Walden (director of the Georgia Office of Energy Resources), and Ralph

Nader (well-known consumer advocate and political gadfly), urged Carter to make the development of a comprehensive energy policy one of the foremost priorities of his administration. Probably the most persuasive argument affecting Carter's thinking came from his old mentor from the navy, Admiral Hyman Rickover. The admiral, "father" of the nuclear navy and Carter's commanding officer in the early 1950s, had lectured Carter on what he saw as the nation's almost suicidal dependence on fossil fuels. Arguing that the growth of energy consumption soon would exhaust the world's oil fields, Rickover's lecture had an immense effect on the policy decisions the newly elected president soon would make.[4]

Carter also saw the question of energy policy as one having vital implications for both domestic and international policy. On the domestic front, Carter believed that sporadic energy shortages and price increases would wreak havoc on the U.S. economy by creating spiraling inflation and increased unemployment. He expressed even greater fear about the effect that the lack of a new energy policy would have on international policy, particularly in the area of national security. Because of the nation's rapidly increasing dependence on oil imported from politically unstable foreign regions (U.S. oil imports had risen from 35 percent of domestic consumption in 1973 to almost 50 percent by the time he took office in 1977), the president-elect believed that the country risked being brought to its knees by foreign powers. Taken together, these factors led Carter to make the creation of a national energy policy the top priority of his administration.[5]

Yet the story of Carter's postelection decision to embark on his energy crusade cannot be explained completely without noting certain characteristics of his personality and his sense of presidential responsibilities that compelled him to enter the energy frontier. As a moralist, Carter believed that the nation's lack of an energy policy led to the irresponsible waste of precious natural resources. The present generation had an obligation to provide future generations with energy alternatives. In short, he had an unyielding moral conviction that the nation should act with greater prudence as stewards of the earth's resources. Trained as an engineer, Carter also looked on the energy situation as a problem that could be solved through careful, analytical study and deliberate action. Because of his convictions and training, it is not surprising that Carter decided to make energy policy a priority in his administration.[6]

The effort to formulate a national energy policy also meshed well with Carter's conception of his role as president. As political scientist Erwin Hargrove has noted, Carter believed it the duty of the president to overcome the needs and wants of special interest groups and represent the "public good." Only the president, Carter believed, could formulate a policy that would benefit the nation as a whole. In Carter's mind, "good" public policy focused not on politically safe, short-term fixes but on comprehensive, long-range solutions. In the case of energy policy, previous attempts to alter the nation's energy use had failed, partly because various interest groups obstructed any meaningful reform and partly because many politicians typically shied away from any type of reform that could be disruptive to either energy-producer or energy-consumer constituents. Unlike many others in Washington, Carter did not conceptualize energy policy primarily as a matter of market freedom versus government control. Rather, he saw the creation of a new energy policy as a moral responsibility to develop an energy program that would increase conservation, fuel production, and alternative energy development, yet also protect the environment, provide economic equity between producing and consuming regions of the country, and balance the interests of energy producers and consumers. As president, Carter viewed himself as the national trustee, whose moral obligations included stewardship for future generations with no voice or vote in the American policy-making process. Looking at the past attempts at energy reform, Carter undoubtedly saw the supreme test for his beliefs concerning presidential leadership. By the time of his inauguration, he had become convinced that tackling the energy problem head-on with a sweeping comprehensive new policy could lead the nation to a promising new energy future.[7]

To develop the specific details of this new energy future, Carter turned to James R. Schlesinger, a former defense secretary who now served as Carter's adviser for energy matters. Carter insisted that Schlesinger adhere to three basic guidelines in the development of energy policy. First, he placed a ninety-day deadline on the creation of the plan. Carter insisted on this three-month deadline because he believed that the energy problem required immediate resolution, and he wanted Congress to act on the plan before the end of 1977. Apparently subscribing to the belief that presidents lose popularity over time, Carter also thought the ninety-day time frame would allow him to maximize his personal approval ratings. Second, Carter pursued a comprehensive plan rather than a piecemeal approach because he thought it would provide the most rational, effective way to deal with the problem. A comprehensive plan, he believed, also would make it more difficult for interest groups to pick apart the proposal. By making the policy an all-or-nothing proposition, Carter hoped to force Congress to enact the policy even if it contained certain provisions that might be detrimental to certain local and state constituencies. Finally, Carter insisted that the plan be developed in secrecy. Involvement of existing government agencies would be kept to a minimum, and the planners of the policy were to keep a safe distance from the vast array of constituents who had a vested interest in the program. With the exception of members of the energy task force, White House advisers would be excluded from the process in order to maintain its confidentiality. Carter hoped that formulating the plan in this manner would keep press leaks to a minimum and also thwart efforts by interest groups to influence its development. To meet these general guidelines, Schlesinger handpicked a small group of policy specialists to form the energy policy task force and immediately set to work on creating what would later become the National Energy Plan.

Together Carter and Schlesinger agreed on the general principles that would undergird the energy plan. The central rationale for the proposed plan was to provide an orderly transition from energy policy predicated on "cheap and abundant energy used wastefully and without regard to international and environmental imperatives to an era of more expensive energy with concomitant regard for efficiency, conservation, international and environmental concerns." The plan would redirect current policies in order to facilitate this transition and reduce the possibility of future economic and political crises caused by sharp price increases, shortages, and supply disruptions. To achieve this goal, Carter and Schlesinger identified four general components the plan would embody. Conservation and the more efficient use of energy resources would be the cornerstone of the policy. Reduction of oil imports also would receive priority in the Carter energy program, although the Ford and Nixon goals for total energy independence from imported oil were discarded as unfeasible. Reflecting Carter's interest in environmental issues, Schlesinger and the president agreed that energy needs would be balanced with environmental stewardship, even if this added to energy costs or limited the program's options. The final component of the plan, and potentially the most controversial, embraced the proposition that "society must begin to value energy now at its true value"; in other words, the energy program must find a way to raise the prices of nonrenewable resources (Schlesinger and Carter understood "true value" to be the world price of oil).[8]

Within three months of the inauguration, Schlesinger and his task force had taken these general guidelines and transformed them into the National Energy Plan (NEP), a comprehensive energy plan, massive in both its breadth and its complexity. Whereas previous energy proposals under Nixon and Ford had favored increased exploitation of existing energy sources, the NEP stressed conservation through the centralization of federal energy planning, higher prices for oil and natural gas, incentives for energy conservation, major expansion of federal regulatory authority over energy producers, suppliers, and consumers, and an increase in federal expenditures for alternative energy research and development. Policy proposals ranged from a "gas guzzler" tax, levied on the purchase price of low-gas-mileage cars to encourage the purchase of more fuel-efficient vehicles, to tax credits for home insulation and the use of solar energy. A host of new federal regulations would be implemented to strengthen the energy efficiency standards for new buildings, automobiles, and even kitchen appliances. New federal taxes would be placed on utilities and industries that burned oil or natural gas rather than coal.

The two most important components of the plan—and potentially the most politically explosive—centered on the issue of oil and natural gas pricing. Rather than embracing outright deregulation as a means of raising natural gas prices (and thereby increasing production and discouraging consumption), the Schlesinger proposal created a complex formula that continued the labyrinth of interstate price controls on existing gas wells. New natural gas well prices would be subject to federal control on both interstate and intrastate sales, but prices would be allowed to rise to the energy equivalent cost of oil. Although the decision to continue natural gas pricing regulation would satisfy many congressional Democrats, it clearly violated Carter's campaign promise to deregulate natural gas prices and would not satisfy the demands of those close to the industry who expected the plan to embrace deregulation.[9]

Schlesinger proposed an even more intricate procedure for raising oil prices. The government would adopt a new three-tiered pricing system for domestically produced oil. A price ceiling reflecting current prices for wells in production before 1975 (first-tier oil) would continue indefinitely. Oil from "new" or "second-tier" wells (wells in production after 1975) would have a price ceiling of approximately twice that of old oil, and oil from "stripper" wells (wells producing ten barrels or less per day) would be allowed to sell at the world price. As with natural gas pricing, the price ceilings of oil would be adjusted to rise at the rate of inflation. Taking the final step to bring domestic prices up to world oil prices, Schlesinger proposed a crude oil equalization tax on oil sales to be applied in three stages beginning in 1978. All proceeds from this tax would be passed back to the public in the form of tax credits.

The complex pricing schemes of the NEP reflected an attempt by Schlesinger and Carter to raise energy prices and yet avoid the politically explosive issue of price decontrol. In doing so, however, these provisions aroused opposition from both Carter's top advisers and congressional leaders. Shortly before the plan was unveiled, Eizenstat, Secretary of the Treasury Michael Blumenthal, and Vice President Walter Mondale had expressed serious reservations about the political and practical wisdom of these proposals. Eizenstat, whom Carter unofficially designated as the keeper of campaign promises, expressed amazement that Schlesinger had discarded Carter's campaign pledge to decontrol natural gas prices and suggested that Schlesinger's multitiered system of oil and gas prices "might pose severe administrative problems." Blumenthal worried that the Rube Goldberg machinery of Schlesinger's price control system unnecessarily delayed getting U.S. prices to world levels. Mondale feared that the higher fuel prices embraced by the plan would invite the enmity of organized labor, an essential constituency for the administration. As a group, the president's senior economic and domestic policy advisers took a wary view of a plan that they believed not only continued regulation but increased the cumbersome administrative rules governing energy resources and use. They also cited the plan's lack of substantive economic analysis and expressed reservations about its cumulative inflationary impact. All urged Carter to delay the plan's announcement to allow further consideration of the pricing apparatus, even suggesting that the failure to do so would doom the policy's chances of enactment. Carter, eager to move forward on energy matters, ignored this advice. Ninety-one days after his inauguration, he appeared before a joint session of Congress to unveil the NEP. Calling on the nation and its legislators "to act now—together—to devise and to implement a comprehensive national energy plan to cope with a crisis that could otherwise overwhelm us," Carter outlined the most sweeping energy policy proposal in U.S. history. In all, the NEP featured 113 proposals to alter American's energy consumption habits. Although the NEP would result in higher energy costs in the short term, Carter conceded, its implementation would reduce sharply the domestic energy growth rate, drastically curtail oil imports, and achieve a 10 percent reduction in gasoline consumption by 1985. Unlike past attempts at energy policy reform that emphasized increased domestic fuel supplies through market deregulation, the Carter program promoted conservation as the primary vehicle for energy stability. His plan would create the higher prices sought by Nixon and Ford but would make the increases more politically palatable by diverting a portion of the new revenue away from oil companies and back to the consumer via the federal Treasury. The pricing schemes, though complex, eased the burden of price increases on consumers but also allowed producers additional revenues. Like the president who advocated it, the plan sought a rational means to increase conservation through higher costs but also to ensure equity by distributing the costs broadly to consumers and producers alike. As Carter had noted in his Oval Office address two nights earlier, the quest for a new national energy policy would be "the moral equivalent of war," and the sacrifices required by the plan would "be fair." "No one will gain an unfair advantage through this plan," he pledged. "No one will be asked to bear an unfair burden."[10]

Reaction to the NEP was decidedly mixed. Many Republicans charged that Carter's program represented yet another ill-fated attempt to use big government to solve problems best left to private industry. Oil interests fumed, claiming that the NEP would "aggravate rather than alleviate domestic petroleum shortages." Texas Governor Dolph Briscoe charged that the NEP "is like a cocked gun" aimed at energy-producing states, while General Motors chairman Thomas Murphy concluded that the policy was "rash, ill-conceived and ill-prepared." The GM boss also added that the gas guzzler tax was "the most simplistic, irresponsible proposal ever made" (a comment to which Carter's energy adviser James Schlesinger responded: "I guess what's good for General Motors is still not necessarily good for the United States"). Even labor unions, traditional supporters of Democratic party policies, expressed dismay over the plan. Construction union leader Robert Georgine, for instance, claimed the plan contained "serious shortcomings" and would lead to the loss of thousands of jobs.[11]

Others, however, responded positively to Carter's proposal. Governor James Thompson of Illinois, a Republican, praised Carter's courage in addressing the energy issue, while even an automobile executive, American Motors corporate chairman Roy Chapin, declared the program "a sensible approach" to the energy problem (not coincidentally, Chapin's company specialized in the manufacture of compact, fuel-efficient cars). Environmental and consumer groups also expressed their support for the plan. Perhaps most encouraging to the president, an ABC News/Louis Harris poll taken after his address revealed that Carter's approval rating had increased three points rather than dropping, as the president and his advisers had feared. Read carefully, however, the poll raised serious concerns about some of the more crucial aspects of the program. In particular, a majority of those polled expressed opposition to the standby gasoline tax—a central provision of the bill—and 62 percent felt that the plan did not provide for "equality of sacrifice."[12]

As Carter's advisers predicted, the pricing mechanisms for oil and natural gas aroused the most opposition in Congress and would eventually create the most obstacles to the enactment of the NEP. Structural changes in Congress and the scope of the NEP arguably posed more serious threats to the legislation's enactment. As Carter recognized, the NEP was one of the most complicated legislative packages ever presented to the Congress. The plan's reliance on higher energy prices through continued regulation was likely to arouse opposition from three groups: conservatives in both parties opposed to any form of government regulation, Democrats from oil- and gas-producing states whose constituencies favored deregulation, and liberal Democrats from consuming regions who abhorred the prospect of supporting higher energy prices. Giving opponents to the plan additional strength, organizational reforms in Congress in the early and mid-1970s had weakened the power of senior committee chairs, decentralized the decision-making process, and given new power and authority to subcommittee chairs. As a result of the reforms, subcommittees with overlapping jurisdictions proliferated—a situation that inevitably slowed the progress of legislation through both the House and the Senate. Because of these reforms and the breadth of the NEP, the bill faced the prospect of hearings in as many as seventeen committees and subcommittees in the House alone—a ripe feeding ground for interest groups seeking to alter specific portions of the plan. Speaker Tip O'Neill eliminated many of these obstacles in the House of Representatives by creating a special ad hoc committee on energy issues to consider the plan as a single legislative package. Largely as a result of this decision, almost all of the provisions of the NEP would be approved by the House before the summer recess.[13]

In the Senate, however, majority leader Robert Byrd refused to alter the traditional committee system and advised Carter to "let the Senate work its will." Unlike O'Neill, Byrd refused to create a single "super committee" to coordinate the legislation and instead broke the NEP down into six individual bills that would be reported separately to the Senate floor following committee action. Further complicating the chances of passage in the Senate, the energy committee lacked a pro-consumer majority, and the finance committee was widely regarded as a bastion of oil industry supporters. As congressional analyst Charles O. Jones later noted, "It did not take lobbyists long to identify the merits of this more disjointed method of acting on the President's energy package." The decentralized committee structure of the Senate allowed for more intense lobbying against various components of the plan and made swift consideration of the plan all but impossible. Not until the end of October 1977, after a total of 73 roll-call votes on five different bills (not including the 109 votes that occurred during a filibuster on natural gas pricing), did the Senate finally approve a program—one that resembled Carter's original proposal in name only. The Senate voted down the natural gas pricing provisions of the NEP, opting instead for decontrol of prices. Both the crude oil equalization tax and the gas-guzzler tax were soundly rejected. Reflecting on the Senate's action, Senator Abraham Ribicoff (D-Conn.) suggested, "I'm just wondering . . . if the President shouldn't admit that his energy program is a shambles."[14]

Carter, however, continued to push the NEP. Despite the intense lobbying efforts of the administration, reconciling the House and Senate versions of the bill would prove exceedingly difficult, particularly over the issue of natural gas pricing decontrol. Not until October 1978 would the House and Senate finally reach an agreement on the NEP. Following an eighteen-month battle, Carter finally achieved a partial victory in his quest for a national energy plan. The issue of natural gas pricing—the subject of heated debate for the previous thirty years—had achieved resolution as both the House and Senate approved the deregulation of prices. Although many of Carter's less controversial conservation programs remained intact (tax credits for energy conservation measure, appliance efficiency standards), the victory was far from complete. The Senate's unwillingness to approve taxes to discourage consumption deprived the NEP of its most significant mechanism for increasing conservation. The plan as enacted eliminated the proposed gasoline tax, reduced the gas-guzzler tax, and rejected Carter's proposal to tax industrial users of oil and natural gas. The centerpiece of Carter's conservation plan—the crude oil equalization tax—was also not included in the final version of the plan. Carter signed the legislation into law on November 10, 1978, but because of these omissions, his quest to redirect the nation's energy policy remained far from complete and in some ways had been compromised almost beyond recognition.

The fight over the NEP had exacted a heavy toll on the Carter administration. The president (and a number of House and Senate leaders) originally envisioned a legislative effort that would be concluded by the end of his first year in office, but discussion and debate over the policy had dragged on for almost two years. During that time, Carter's approval ratings began and continued a steady decline. Many in the press and Congress placed the blame for the long and only moderately successful fight over energy policy squarely on the shoulders of the president. According to the critics, Carter erred by rushing into the program, by drafting it in virtual secrecy, and by failing to lobby Congress effectively. Regardless of where fault lay for the failure of the NEP to address fully the energy problems facing the United States, however, Carter would soon be forced to deal once again with the contentious issue of oil pricing.

Events in Iran in late 1978 would reopen the need for further energy policy development. Isolated protests against the regime of Mohammed Reza Pahlavi had grown into a full-scale revolution, leading to a virtual shutdown of Iranian oil fields and causing wholesale crude prices to skyrocket. Creating further turmoil in world energy markets, on December 17 representatives of the Organization of Petroleum Exporting Countries (OPEC) announced their decision to raise export prices by 14.5 percent during the coming year. From the vantage point of late 1978, it became increasingly apparent that the energy policy victory the administration claimed in October might amount to little more than a cease-fire, and an unstable one at that. To deal with the worsening energy situation, Carter directed Eizenstat to convene a multiagency task force to develop new energy policy proposals. Perhaps as a result of criticism leveled against the secretive nature of the NEP task force, the new planning group's decision-making process was characterized by a high degree of collegiality and collaboration between the politically attuned White House staff and the technical expertise of department officials. Although the process used by the group could not match the speed of policy development exhibited by Schlesinger's task force, Eizenstat hoped that a more consultative process that also included members of Congress and affected interest groups would reduce any proposed policy's political liabilities.

As the energy situation continued to worsen in 1979, the need for action became even more urgent. On March 19, 1979, Carter called his closest advisers together in a daylong meeting at Camp David, Maryland. For eight hours his advisers sought to reconcile energy policy options with the administration's commitment to reduce inflation. In particular they discussed the many energy policy options developed by Eizenstat's task force and the effect these options would have on the inflation rate. This proved to be a particularly vexing dilemma. Efforts to lessen dependence on foreign oil, encourage the development of alternative sources of energy, and compel conservation could not occur without higher oil prices that, in turn, would lead to higher inflation. Yet without higher oil prices and given the current shortage of world oil supplies, inflation as well as severe economic hardship were likely to occur. In short, it appeared likely that every policy option would exact a tremendous political cost. As one aide gloomily noted, "We've got to do what is in the best interests of the country—but it's damn hard to see how anything we do will be in the best interests of Jimmy Carter."[15]

Mirroring the debate that had taken place on oil deregulation during the past five years, the administration was divided on which specific policy option to pursue. Mondale initially expressed reservations about the political repercussions of decontrol, arguing that such a move would lead to much higher prices and alienate the administration's supporters in organized labor and consumer groups—two vital Democratic constituencies. Inflation adviser Alfred Kahn feared the economic consequences of decontrol and urged the president to maintain some level of price ceilings on oil to prevent skyrocketing inflation. Schlesinger and Blumenthal advocated a complete phasing out of price controls beginning on June 1, 1979, and culminating in September 1981. To make this option more palatable politically, they suggested that the administration concurrently send Congress a tax program to capture any excess profits resulting from the lifting of price ceilings. They emphasized, however, that decontrol should occur regardless of congressional action on the administration's tax proposals. Budget director James McIntyre sought a compromise position that would phase out price controls more gradually than Schlesinger and Blumenthal favored and make the decision on decontrol contingent on the Congress's enactment of tax provisions on windfall profits. The revenue from these taxes would be used to provide tax credits for lower-income groups and fund an alternative energy development program. The debate within the administration on the direction new energy policy should take would continue until mid-April before Carter made the final decision on the issue of oil prices.[16]

"Our nation's energy problem is serious—and it's getting worse." So began Jimmy Carter's April 1979 address introducing a second round of energy policy initiatives, almost two years to the day after he first declared the "moral equivalent of war" on the United States' energy woes. In what *Newsweek* termed his "prime-time TV summons to the Age of Limits," Carter outlined to the nation his plan to free the country from its addiction to foreign oil. The plan Carter proposed resembled his rhetoric in its simplicity and bluntness. The president said he would phase in the gradual decontrol of oil prices beginning on June 1, with all controls to be lifted by September 30, 1981. In conjunction with decontrol, Carter called on Congress to enact a windfall profits tax that would appropriate 50 percent of the extra revenue oil companies would receive as a result of decontrol. Proceeds from the tax would be used to fund mass transit, offset increased fuel expenses for low-income families, and finance a proposed Energy Security Fund that would develop alternative sources of energy. Other provisions of Carter's plan included expedited federal approval of pipelines and other energy projects, increased energy production from federal lands, and restrictions on thermostats of nonresidential buildings. Throughout the address, the president readily acknowledged that several of these measures, particularly decontrol, would require immediate sacrifice by most Americans. Only through such sacrifice, Carter emphasized, could the United States achieve a secure energy future.[17]

The decontrol decision had not been an easy one for a man who expressed almost conspiratorial suspicions about the "greed" of the oil industry, who pledged during the 1976 campaign to continue controls on oil prices, and who ran on a party platform that reiterated the pledge to continue controls. In 1977, he had attempted to avoid decontrol by proposing a complicated pricing scheme that would raise prices to world levels but maintain government regulation. The attempt failed. Because of his unyielding belief that oil prices must rise in order to encourage conservation and production, Carter decided he could not risk another futile legislative battle over the issue and instead chose to act under the authority given him by the 1975 Energy Policy and Conservation Act, which empowered the president to remove controls after June 1, 1979. To soften the financial (and political) impact of decontrol and to satisfy his own reservations, Carter proposed the windfall profits tax on oil companies, with part of the proceeds to be redistributed to consumers through tax credits. Windfall profits revenues would also be used to finance an energy security fund to develop alternative sources of energy. Carter saw these measures as the most efficient, balanced, and expedient way of dealing with the nation's energy woes, even if this meant reversing both his and his party's long-standing stance on the politically treacherous issue of oil pricing.[18]

Initial reaction to the April 1979 proposals seemed encouraging for the president. An ABC News/Louis Harris poll taken immediately following the speech indicated that 73 percent of those polled approved of the president's proposals. House Speaker O'Neill supported the president's actions, pledged to work for swift passage of the legislative components of the package, and said he would fight legislative attempts to stop decontrol. Louisiana Senator Bennett Johnston, who had opposed the crude oil equalization tax, expressed tentative approval for the windfall profits tax as a reasonable trade-off for decontrol. Even opponents of Carter's NEP offered support. Shell Oil president John F. Bookout called Carter's decision "courageous," and House minority leader John J. Rhodes said he generally endorsed the plan.[19]

Opponents of the administration's plan greatly outnumbered its supporters, however, with the harshest criticism coming from members of the president's own party. On the issue of decontrol, liberal Democrats from consuming areas condemned Carter's decision. Senator Ted Kennedy of Massachusetts called the move an "unnecessary self-inflicted wound," and Representative Pete Stark of California charged that Carter "sold out to the oil companies." Representative Toby Moffet of Connecticut said that decontrol amounted "to a declaration of war on the Northeast" and added that Carter's standby conservation measures would be defeated in retaliation. A coalition of New England Democrats, citing the already escalating cost of home heating oil, feared that decontrol would wreak havoc on New Englanders trying to heat their homes in the coming winter. While liberal Democrats voiced disapproval of decontrol, more conservative Democrats from producing regions questioned the wisdom of the windfall profits tax. Senator Long said he would seek to table the windfall profits tax in the finance committee unless the proceeds were plowed back to the industry rather than to consumers and the energy security fund, and fellow finance committee member Lloyd Bentsen of Texas refused to support the tax in any form. Even Democrats who supported the plan disagreed on whether the tax was too harsh or too lenient and on whether decontrol would proceed too quickly or too slowly.[20]

Of course, congressional Democrats were not alone in their opposition to the plan. A number of Republicans in both the House and the Senate expressed reservations about imposing a new tax of any type. Also, in an odd alliance that recalled some of the battles over the NEP, several consumer and business groups expressed opposition to the Carter program, albeit for different reasons. Ellen Berman, executive director of the Consumer Energy Council, charged that "it is the height of hypocrisy to remove price controls from the oil industry." Her counterpart at the Business Roundtable said that the president's tax proposal was unacceptable and vowed to fight it. Despite charges that Carter "sold out" to the oil industry, the majority of producers objected to the plan as well. Charles DiBona, president of the American Petroleum Institute, charged that windfall profits taxes were "unnecessary," and the president of Mobil Oil complained that Carter was unfairly singling out the oil industry for punishment.[21]

Making matters even more difficult for Carter, energy prices and inflation continued to rise in May and June, contributing to a rapid decline in the president's approval rating. The consumer price index in May and June 1979 disclosed a 12.5 percent annual inflation rate. Energy prices rose even faster, as average gasoline prices had increased by 55 percent since January. The gasoline shortages that initially had appeared only in California began spreading to the East Coast as well, and in many areas oil companies provided stations with only 80 to 90 percent of their normal gasoline allotment. As gas lines grew, so did consumer frustration. Sporadic instances of violence by irate customers stuck in blocks-long gas lines began to be reported on the evening television news. By the end of June, an energy crisis gripped the nation and rivaled the 1973 crisis in its severity. In just over half a year, the price of OPEC oil had doubled. By June 23, the American Automobile Association reported that 58 percent of the nation's gas stations were closed because of low inventories. Compounding the situation, economic growth had stalled, and experts predicted a zero rate of growth in GNP for the month of June.[22]

Responding to the growing crisis, Carter delivered yet another national address on energy and unveiled additional energy policy proposals. On July 15, 1979, in what later would be derisively referred to as his "malaise" speech, Carter outlined additional steps to be taken to alleviate the growing shortages of fuel. His most ambitious proposal called for the creation of an independent, congressionally chartered Energy Security Corporation (ESC) to develop synthetic fuels. Modeled after the Reconstruction Finance Committee, the ESC would receive $88 billion in revenue from the windfall profits tax over a ten-year period, with a total energy savings target of 1 to 1.5 million barrels of oil per day by 1990. Carter also proposed the creation of an Energy Mobilization Board (EMB) empowered to speed construction of energy projects such as pipelines and refineries and expedite local, state, and national permit policies if necessary. The president wanted to use another portion of the windfall profits tax revenue to fund a solar energy program. Additionally, he would seek to direct $16.5 billion in windfall tax revenue to fund mass transit systems over the next decade. The president pledged to pursue another standby gasoline-rationing gas plan and declared that he would limit oil imports to 1977 levels of 8.6 million barrels per day, using the powers granted him by the Trade Expansion Act of 1953.[23]

Perhaps due to the urgent need for action created by gasoline shortages, Congress and the public reacted more favorably to Carter's initiatives than they had to any of his previous proposals. Senate minority leader Howard Baker said the program warranted bipartisan support, and Texas Democrat Lloyd Bentsen, a frequent critic of the administration's energy policies, pledged his support. Senator Byrd and House Majority Leader Wright both predicted most of the legislation would receive congressional approval no later than early fall, and Wright forecast that the House would act on the synfuels and EMB provisions by the August recess. Speaker O'Neill called it the best speech Carter had ever made, and Republican Senator Jacob Javits praised Carter's broad approach to the problem. Irving S. Shapiro, chairman of DuPont and a board member of the Business Roundtable, called the president's plan "sensible," and AFL-CIO leader George Meany, who opposed most of Carter's economic policies, endorsed the plan. A CBS News/*New York Times* poll taken the night following the speech found that Carter's approval rating had jumped 11 points (37 percent) from the previous week.[24]

Despite this initial optimism, however, congressional action on energy issues was agonizingly slow. The windfall profits tax won final congressional approval in March 1980, almost a full year after Carter first proposed it. Similarly, the House and Senate did not approve the Energy Security Corporation and solar energy program until June 1980, and the EMB was abandoned altogether. The bill creating the Energy Security Corporation was the last major energy legislation bearing Carter's signature. By the fall of 1980, the deteriorating economy and the uncertain energy situation had all but doomed Carter's chances for reelection. In November, the American people overwhelmingly rejected Carter's stern stewardship in favor of the more optimistic alternative offered by Ronald Reagan. Ironically, Carter's conservation policies would contribute to an energy glut in the mid-1980s. With the specter of gas lines and energy crises largely forgotten, Reagan and Congress began the systematic dismantling of Carter's energy programs. By 1986, the energy conundrum that had consumed the Carter presidency ceased to exist.

The story of Jimmy Carter's quest for a national energy policy reveals much about both the Carter presidency and the challenges of governing in the late 1970s. Perhaps no other policy initiative of the Carter administration better demonstrates

Carter's approach to governing than does energy. The decision to make energy policy his first domestic policy priority resulted not from an electoral mandate, an immediate crisis, or calls for action from either Congress or the public. Rather, Carter based his decision largely on the belief that, as president, he bore the moral responsibility to identify national problems that could be dealt with through the exercise of presidential power and initiative. Carter's conception of presidential leadership as practicing the politics of the public good meant that he would pursue policies regardless of their immediate political benefits. This was clearly the case with energy policy, as demonstrated by the lukewarm response of both the public and Congress to Carter's energy proposals.

In energy policy, one also sees Carter's basic approach to policy making. Once he identified energy as an area requiring urgent attention, Carter sought rational, comprehensive solutions to alter the nation's energy consumption habits. Fearful of the influence of interest groups and disdainful of political horse-trading, Carter attempted to circumvent traditional policy-making processes by using a confidential task force that could evaluate policy options on the basis of merit rather than political considerations. By employing this process, Carter sought to achieve the most rational and effective policy possible. He would seek compromise only if his initial legislative efforts failed to secure enactment of the policy. Further demonstrating his commitment to governing in the "national interest," Carter sought to mobilize grassroots support of his proposals as a means of blunting the influence of interest groups on Capitol Hill. His decision to pursue policy in this manner, however, entailed substantial political costs. Carter alienated members of Congress and interest groups by failing to consult extensively with them, and he expended much of his political capital in pursuing public policy that had no highly organized constituency.

Many critics have cited this approach to energy policy as an example of the incompetence of Carter's presidential leadership. Emphasizing his failure to consult adequately with Congress and his insistence on sweeping energy policy changes, these critics charge that Carter brought upon himself four years of unnecessary conflict over energy policy. While there is some validity to these assessments, Carter's critics fail to consider fully the political environment of the late 1970s and the effect it had on Carter's presidency. In *The Politics Presidents Make: Leadership from John Adams to George Bush* (1993), Stephen Skowronek argues that Carter served during a period of political "disjunction." According to Skowronek, Carter—a "late regime" president like Herbert Hoover and John Quincy Adams—took office at a time when established commitments were beginning to be called into question by the public as failed or irrelevant responses to the problems of the nation. As a result, Carter faced a daunting leadership situation. To affirm and continue the party's established commitments would identify the president with failure, yet repudiating the establishment legacy (in Carter's case the FDR-LBJ legacy of liberal regulation) would isolate the president from his natural political allies and lead to political impotence. As a result, presidents during periods of disjunction lack a degree of legitimacy and frequently stress their comprehension of and desire to solve the nation's problems as a means of justifying their leadership. This can create even more hazards for the president because he risks becoming "submerged in the problems he is addressing and finds himself an easy caricature of all that has gone wrong."[25]

In regard to energy policy, Carter's presidency fits the disjunctive model outlined by Skowronek. Although Carter repeatedly warned of impending economic crisis if the nation failed to address the energy problem, he nonetheless was blamed for the gas lines and high inflation caused by energy dislocations in 1979 and 1980. Ironically, many of the same political leaders who faulted Carter for moving too fast on energy in 1977 chided him in 1979 for not moving fast enough. Compounding matters, changes in energy policy threatened some of the more sacred precepts of the Democratic party's ideological commitments. In seeking to raise prices of oil and gas, through either increased taxation or deregulation, Carter outraged his party's liberal wing, which charged that the president was unfairly burdening the poor and the middle class with higher energy costs. Impatience with further delay in changing the price structure of oil led Carter to abolish oil price controls in 1979—a decision that represented a clear break from the Democratic legacy of regulation. Although some recent appraisals of Carter's presidency see the decontrol decision as yet another sign of Carter's Reaganesque supply-side policies, assessments such as these are not valid—at least in terms of energy policy. At no time did Carter assert that the energy problems could best be solved by the private sector. Carter reluctantly and begrudgingly opted for decontrol because he saw it as the only means of raising prices to discourage consumption and increase conservation measures. Furthermore, the decontrol decision was but a single component of an overall energy program that increased direct government involvement in energy issues to an unprecedented level. The solar energy program and, more significantly, the Energy Security Corporation represented a commitment of billions of dollars in federal funds to redirect the nation's energy habits. The Carter energy program, like Carter himself, attempted to straddle the competing forces of regulation and the free market. By no means did it signal Carter's conversion to Republican economic policies. In spite of, and perhaps because of, Carter's novel, dual approach to energy policy, Ronald Reagan succeeded in linking Carter to the failed regulatory policies of the Democratic party. By the time of the election, the man who had done more to reorient the nation's energy policy than any other president in history was seen by many as the living embodiment of past energy policy failures.

Carter's difficulty in obtaining new energy policy, however, had causes that extended beyond the disjunctive political environment described by Skowronek. The rapacious growth of congressional oversight committees in the early 1970s, coupled with the decentralization of power in both houses of Congress and the growing power of interest groups, created numerous avenues for obstruction on energy policy. In the absence of either immediate tangible crisis or strong congressional leadership, Carter's energy proposals floundered in committee hearings. Comparing the deliberations over the NEP in the House and Senate is particularly instructive in this regard. In an extraordinary move, Speaker Tip O'Neill briefly reasserted the powers of the leadership and created an Ad Hoc Committee on Energy to protect the NEP from obstructionist tactics at the committee level. Largely because of the more centralized structure used by O'Neill, the bill emerged largely intact from the House in less than three months of deliberations. In the Senate, however, where centralized authority was weak, the bill was broken into six parts and largely emasculated by interest groups and their representatives. The crucial issue of oil pricing failed even to clear committee hearings for a floor vote. As a result, prices remained artificially low on domestically produced oil, and the plan's most important conservation measure (higher oil prices) was abandoned. This failure to reach consensus on oil pricing served to make more severe the oil shock of 1979.

In addition to the problems posed by congressional obstructionism, Carter also had to contend with the scarcity of consensus on the form energy policy should take. While few at the time doubted the need to reduce the nation's dependence on imported oil, agreement on the proper path to pursue proved elusive. In his attempt to create a new energy policy, Carter found himself in a whirlwind of competing forces that frustrated his policy goals. Regional interests frequently superseded party and ideological commitments as producer-state Democrats battled with consumer-state Democrats over the issues of decontrol and higher energy prices. Antigovernment Democrats and Republicans from the South and West argued against the expansion of the energy bureaucracy, while the left wing of the Democratic party pushed for greater government control over the energy industry. Labor and consumer groups favored new taxes on the oil industry but resisted conservation taxes on retail sales of gasoline and automobiles. Environmentalists supported the president's solar energy initiatives and conservation proposals but opposed his coal conversion program and his continued support of nuclear power. The oil industry welcomed Carter's decontrol decision, but it lobbied against many of his energy tax plans. The issue of equity frequently emerged during policy debates. Liberals believed that the government should protect low-income consumers from escalating energy prices, while conservatives and producer-state Democrats argued that many policy proposals unfairly penalized the energy industry. As inflation began to rise in late 1978 and 1979, the issue of equity became more contentious, and liberal Democrats argued that higher energy prices would further penalize low- and middle-income groups. While few of these groups disagreed on the need for a new energy policy, fewer still agreed on the form that policy should take.

Since he first directed Schlesinger to develop the national energy plan, Carter had feared that the scope of energy policy would invite the aforementioned controversy among the scores of affected interest groups. In order to overcome the power of "organized interests," Carter had hoped to mobilize public support behind his energy initiatives and pressure Congress to adopt the plan as presented. Yet here Carter faced the most difficult obstacle in promulgating a new energy policy. In his attempt to fashion an equitable policy, Carter sought to distribute the costs of energy conservation on all segments of the population. Producers and consumers, industry and labor, rural dwellers and urbanites, all would bear a portion of the costs of the Carter energy proposals. In exchange for these widely distributed costs, the program would yield widely distributed benefits in the form of future economic stability and a more secure energy supply. As Carter soon discovered, however, the task of convincing the American public of the possible severity of energy dislocations proved almost impossible. Nor could he convince Americans that the costs of his programs would be offset by the future benefits. In essence, Carter sought to mobilize public support for a program that had no constituency. Future, not present, generations would receive the most benefits from his energy policy.

Not until the United States experienced the economic dislocations that Carter had predicted could he finally mobilize the public and Congress to pursue significant change in energy policy. Carter's greatest legislative successes on energy did not occur until late 1979 and 1980, when gasoline shortages and the turmoil in Iran and other Middle Eastern nations created a sense of panic and fear that legitimized Carter's earlier "sky is falling" pronouncements on energy policy. The price for delay, however, was great. The 1979–80 energy dislocations contributed to unprecedented levels of inflation and unemployment that crippled the U.S. economy. Arguably, the delay also cost Carter his political future. Since he had taken office, Carter had exerted the energies and powers of his position to create a new national energy policy. When disagreement among legislators and interest groups delayed that policy, however, Carter received the blame. Ironically, although Carter's energy policies contributed substantially to curbing domestic consumption and increasing production that led to an oil surplus by the mid-1980s, only "future" politicians received the political benefits of his policy. Nevertheless, Carter's persistent and at times ill-fated quest for energy policy has become an enduring symbol of both his presidency and his personality.

NOTES

1. Walter A. Rosenbaum, *Energy, Politics, and Public Policy,* 2d ed. (Washington, D.C.: Congressional Quarterly Press, 1987), 6; Jimmy Carter, *Keeping Faith: Memoirs of a President* (New York: Bantam Books, 1982); Charles O. Jones, *The Trusteeship Presidency: Jimmy Carter and the United States Congress* (Baton Rouge: Louisiana State University Press, 1988), 137.

2. *Energy Policy,* 2d ed. (Washington, D.C.: Congressional Quarterly, 1981), 2.

3. U.S. Congress, House, Committee on House Administration, *The Presidential Campaign, 1976* (Washington, D.C.: Government Printing Office, 1978); Linda Charlton,

"Carter Watches the Convention and Confers on Energy Policy," *New York Times,* August 18, 1976, 20; Richard H. K. Vietor, *Energy Policy in America since 1945: A Study of Business-Government Relations* (Cambridge: Cambridge University Press, 1984), 306; Stuart Eizenstat Interview, January 29–30, 1982, William Burkett Miller Center of Public Affairs, University of Virginia, Project on the Carter Presidency, Transcripts, 1982 (hereafter cited as Miller Center), Jimmy Carter Library (JCL).

4. It is unclear exactly when Carter decided to make energy policy one of his administration's top priorities. Neither Katherine "Kitty" Schirmer Cochrane (who worked on the energy issues cluster group during the transition and later served as the energy specialist on the domestic policy staff) nor James R. Schlesinger (who served as Carter's first energy adviser and energy secretary) could recall when Carter made clear his decision, but both agreed that it was clear by December 1976 that Carter intended to pursue energy policy as a major domestic initiative. They also suggested that the natural gas shortages in December and January influenced the urgency that characterized Carter's pursuit of energy policy (James R. Schlesinger Interview, [Date?], Miller Center, 15–16, JCL; author's interviews with Schlesinger, October 1995, and Katherine Schirmer Cochrane, March 1996).

5. Carter, *Keeping Faith,* 91–93.

6. James Schlesinger Interview, [Date?], Miller Center, 15–16, JCL.

7. Erwin Hargrove, *Jimmy Carter as President: Leadership and the Politics of the Public Good* (Baton Rouge: Louisiana State University Press, 1988); Jones, *Trusteeship Presidency.*

8. Schlesinger to Carter, March 9, Box 2, Schlesinger Files, JCL.

9. I have yet to find a full explanation for Schlesinger's and Carter's decision to continue price controls on natural gas. The proposal clearly violated Carter's campaign pledge to deregulate gas. Although Carter never explained this reversal, Schlesinger indicates in his Miller Center interview that political pressure from Senator Jackson and Representative Dingell caused him to abandon natural gas deregulation. Likewise, Eizenstat identifies the influence of Dingell and Jackson, but also speculates that members of Schlesinger's planning staff influenced him to continue controls (Schlesinger Interview, Miller Center; Stuart Eizenstat Interview, Miller Center, January 29–30, 1982, JCL.

10. *Public Papers of the Presidents: Jimmy Carter, 1977* (Washington, D.C.: Government Printing Office, 1978), 656, 661, 663.

11. "The Energy War," *Time,* May 2, 1977, 10–14; Allan J. Mayer, "The Battle Begins," *Newsweek,* May 9, 1977, 22–24; Bob Rankin, "Carter's Energy Plan: A Test of Leadership," *Congressional Quarterly,* April 23, 1977, 732.

12. Chapin quoted in Rankin, "Carter's Energy Plan," 732; Thompson quoted in "The Energy War," 10; polling data cited in "The Energy War," 14.

13. For an overview of congressional reforms, see Samuel C. Patterson, "The Semi-Sovereign Congress," in *The New American Political System,* 3d ed., ed. Anthony King (Washington, D.C.: American Enterprise Institute for Public Policy Research, 1978), 125–77; Nelson W. Polsby, "Political Change and the Character of the Contemporary Congress," in *The New American Political System,* 2d ed., ed. Anthony King (Washington, D.C.: American Enterprise Press, 1990), 29–46; Bruce I. Oppenheimer, "Congress and the New Obstructionism: Developing an Energy Program," in *Congress Reconsidered,* 2d ed., ed. Lawrence C. Dodd and Bruce I. Oppenheimer (Washington, D.C.: Congressional Quarterly Press, 1981), 275–95.

14. Charles O. Jones, "Congress and the Making of Energy Policy," in *New Dimensions to Energy Policy,* ed. Robert Lawrence (Lexington, Mass.: Lexington Books, 1979), 173; Bob Rankin, "Senate Continues Dismantling Energy Plan," *Congressional Quarterly,* October 8, 1977, 174.

15. For information about the meeting at Camp David, see "Agenda for Monday's Camp David Meetings," March 19, 1979, Box 123, Staff Secretary Files, JCL; "DOE Energy Briefing Book, Camp David Meeting," March 19, 1979, Box 123, Staff Secretary File, JCL; Carter aide quoted in "Next: Challenges at Home," *Time,* April 2, 1979, 14.

16. Eizenstat to Carter, March 26, 29, 1979, Box 124, Staff Secretary File, JCL; James T. McIntyre to Carter, March 26, 1979, Box 124, Staff Secretary File, JCL; Mondale to Carter, March 26, 1979, Box 124, Staff Secretary File, JCL.

17. *Public Papers of Jimmy Carter, 1979;* "The Energy Tangle," *Newsweek,* April 16, 1979, 21.

18. Carter had not attempted decontrol in the NEP for two reasons. First, the 1975 Energy Policy and Conservation Act gave the president discretionary power on oil control only after June 1, 1979. (The act also stipulated that price control authority would expire on September 30, 1981.) Second, even had he had the power to do so, Carter most likely would not have exercised this option. The president viewed the oil industry as a monopoly that required government regulation. Because of the fight waged over natural gas decontrol and the crude oil equalization tax in 1977 and 1978, however, Carter believed that another attempt to find an alternate means of raising prices would not receive congressional approval in the near future. His commitment to U.S. allies and his own belief about the need to raise prices to encourage conservation required swift action, so he reluctantly decided to authorize phased-in decontrol of prices. See Carter's Handwritten Notes for News Conference, October 13, 1977, Box 54, Staff Secretary File, JCL.

19. J. P. Smith and Mary Russell, "Gas Prices Seen Rising," *Washington Post,* April 7, 1979, 1; Merrill Sheiks, "What Decontrol Will Mean," *Newsweek,* April 16, 1979, 24–26; "Carter's Energy Plan," *U.S. News and World Report,* April 16, 1979, 19–20.

20. "Carter's Energy Plan," 19–20.

21. Ann Pelharn, "Carter Pledges Oil Decontrol, Wants Windfall Profits Tax," *Congressional Quarterly,* April 7, 1979, 619–20; "Carter's Energy Plan," 19–20.

22. Economic data cited in Eizenstat to Carter, June 28, 1979, Staff Secretary File, JCL; Daniel Yergin, *The Prize: The Epic Quest for Oil, Money and Power* (New York: Touchstone, 1992), 694.

23. *Public Papers of Jimmy Carter, 1979,* 1239–41.

24. Thomas C. Hayes, "Business Praises Carter Concept," *New York Times,* July 17, 1979, A1; Ann Pelham, "Congress Ahead of the Game on Energy," *Congressional Quarterly,* July 21, 1979, 1436; "Meany Backs Energy Program," *New York Times,* July 2, 17, 1979, A12; Adain Clymer, "Speech Lifts Carter to 37%; Public Agrees on Crisis of Confidence," *New York Times,* July 18, 1979, A1.

25. For a description of the politics of disjunction, see Stephen Skowronek, *The Politics Presidents Make: Leadership from John Adams to George Bush* (Cambridge, Mass.: Belknap Press of Harvard University Press, 1993), 39–41. For Skowronek's overview of the Carter presidency, see pp. 361–406.

9

Environmental Policy during the Carter Presidency

Jeffrey K. Stine

Many people concerned about environmental quality in the United States rank Jimmy Carter with Theodore and Franklin Roosevelt as the nation's most conservation-minded presidents. In many ways, Carter benefited from a political climate that made such a stand more popular. As the environmental movement gained broader appeal during the 1960s and 1970s, its values began to infuse politics at all levels, including presidential. Lyndon B. Johnson, for example, had been an active conservation advocate early in his administration, before the Vietnam War redirected his priorities; and Richard M. Nixon, while tepid in his personal sympathy toward ecological objectives, saw political advantages in tapping the growing popularity of environmentalism, and he followed Congress's lead by signing into law some of the nation's most significant environmental legislation. Carter, however, recognized the real political potential of the environmental movement and became the first U.S. presidential candidate to campaign successfully on environmental issues, and his administration openly pursued a broad environmental policy agenda.[1]

As a presidential candidate, Carter generated unprecedented enthusiasm among environmentalists, and he carried this hopefulness into the White House, where he made conservation a priority item early in his administration, appointing seasoned specialists into second-tier administrative posts, attempting a major reform of water resources development policy, and outlining a bold and sweeping environmental agenda in his May 1977 message to Congress. Intense resistance, however, often greeted Carter's environmental policy package. Frustrated in his efforts to reorient federal water policy, forced into numerous compromises because of internal contradictions among his own domestic policies, especially his energy and economic policies, as well as his campaign for regulatory reform, and unable to solve the tenacious problems of runaway inflation and a stagnant economy, Carter inevitably fell well short of meeting the environmental community's unrealistically high expectations.

Despite these shortcomings, the Carter administration left a substantial record of action on environmental issues. Carter signed clean air and water acts and strip-mining legislation that had been rebuffed by previous administrations; he revitalized the Environmental Protection Agency (EPA) by sharpening its focus on the protection of human health; he used his presidential authority to issue executive orders to protect wetlands, floodplains, and desert environments; and he lobbied successfully for the passage of two monumental pieces of legislation—the Comprehensive Environmental Response, Compensation, and Liability Act that created "Superfund" and the Alaska National Interest Lands Conservation Act that set aside nearly 105 million acres of Alaskan wilderness under federal protection.

In their discussion of the spectrum of concerns confronted by the Carter administration, some authors in this volume argue that Carter reacted more in the tradition of liberal, Democratic New Dealers, while others contend that he represented the first wave of a conservative period in American politics. Environmental policy fails to fit neatly into either camp, however, for Carter pushed more forcefully in this area than any of his predecessors since World War II, while his successor, Ronald Reagan, tried—with only modest success—to unravel the environmental programs and regulations that Carter had put in place or strengthened. Since the 1970s, the environmental movement has helped to sustain federal regulatory apparatus in the face of persistent challenges, and that political strength explains in part the elevated status of environmental policy during the Carter presidency. The effort was aided by Carter's own predisposition toward the goals of environmentalism, despite countervailing forces within American society and even within the Executive Office of the President itself.[2]

COURTING THE ENVIRONMENTAL VOTE

As a presidential hopeful seeking to establish winning political coalitions, Carter looked for campaign issues that had broad, cross-cutting appeal. Environmentalism emerged as just such an issue in the 1970s, and Carter and his campaign staff pursued these concerns vigorously. Indeed, even Carter's campaign colors—green and white—suggested his environmental orientation.

Carter was no newcomer to the environmental movement in 1976, and his decision to target conservation-minded individuals and groups in his presidential campaign was spurred by two things: his recognition that environmental issues were drawing increasingly large and faithful voting blocks, especially in states such as California, Oregon, and Florida; and his personal experiences in Georgia, where the state's environmental community rallied behind his actions as governor from 1971 to 1975. The early 1970s were formative years in the United States with regard to environmental legislation, and Carter established himself as one of the country's leading governors in this movement, boosting the state's expenditures on natural resources, moving aggressively to enforce air, water, and surface mining regulations, advocating land-use planning, restoring the Chattahoochee River for recreation, and taking steps to protect the state's coastal zone, flood-plains, and cultural resources. Building on this reputation in his campaign autobi-ography, Carter claimed that, as governor, "with the exception of reorganization itself, I spent more time preserving our natural resources than on any other one issue."[3]

Unlike some other areas of domestic policy, the political pragmatism of Carter's environmental stance was matched by his deep personal concern for those issues. This was perhaps most widely apparent in his long-standing and passion-ate enthusiasm for outdoor activities. "On one-day or two-day weekend trips, Rosalynn and I visited the naturally beautiful areas of our state," he recalled of his governorship. "We rode the wild rivers in rafts, canoes and kayaks. . . . We studied the wildlife programs on our isolated game preserves, and inspected the virgin cypress groves on Lewis Island in the mouth of the Altamaha River."[4]

In Carter's most acclaimed conservationist accomplishment as governor, he stopped the U.S. Army Corps of Engineers' planned Spewrell Bluff dam on the Flint River, at a place where it snaked through the scenic hill country of Georgia's fall line about fifty miles southeast of Atlanta. Carter initially endorsed the project, as had his predecessor and most other elected state officials. However, environ-mental and conservation groups, led by the Georgia Conservancy and the Flint River Preservation Society, spoke out strongly against the dam because it would have flooded a twenty-eight-mile stretch of the river that was popular with anglers, canoeists, and hikers. The Georgia Department of Natural Resources and the U.S. Fish and Wildlife Service voiced reservations, and more than a thousand individual citizens sent letters opposing the dam to the governor's office. Carter took these criticisms seriously and conducted a lengthy personal study of the pro-posed $133-million project and its likely impact on the state. After traversing the Flint twice by canoe and twice by helicopter, consulting scores of interested par-ties, reading all the petitions, resolutions, and transcripts of oral testimony, and evaluating the corps's engineering and economic reports, Carter issued a state-ment in October 1973 blocking construction of the dam.[5]

By vetoing a corps dam project that had already been authorized, studied, and scheduled for construction, Carter had taken a highly unusual step as a governor, one that drew national media coverage and gained him near-celebrity status among environmentalists critical of large-scale federal water projects. With the aid of environmental lobbyists, he subsequently defeated the efforts of the Georgia state legislature to override his opposition. Because Carter believed the problem tran-scended his state, he challenged the U.S. Congress to reassess similar projects around the country, asserting that "the construction of unwarranted dams and other projects at public expense should be prevented."[6]

As a Washington, D.C., "outsider" and presidential candidate with modest nationwide name recognition, Carter knew he had to build on his strengths. Distinguishing himself as a conservationist-oriented reformer fitted squarely into this plan. Seeking to cultivate his relations with environmental organizations across the nation, Carter began in his home state, asking Georgia-based environmentalists just prior to announcing his candidacy in December 1974 if they would assist him in his bid for the White House. This request attracted several volunteers to the campaign, including two full-timers: Jane Hurt Yarn and Carlton F. Neville, who formed the group Conservationists for Carter (CFC). Yarn—who had wide experience serving with the Nature Conservancy, Georgia Conservancy, and U.S. Forest Service Advisory Council—chaired the CFC, working out of its Atlanta headquarters to develop a national Conservationists for Carter Committee, made up of leaders of major environmental organizations who were willing to lend their support to Carter. Neville served as the CFC's director, focusing on state-based and grassroots environmental organizations, and organizing CFC branch organizations in key primary and caucus states known to have active environmental movements.[7]

One segment of the environmental movement that Carter vigorously sought to attract were those favoring the protection and restoration of America's rivers, especially the scores of grassroots organizations throughout the country fighting the damming, channelization, or other structural alterations of their favorite rivers and streams. This branch of the environmental movement had gained considerable momentum during the 1970s, spurred in part by their numerous successes in stopping federal water projects, often in the federal courts using the provisions of the National Environmental Policy Act.[8] As early as July 1975, for example, Carter's campaign office issued a press release stating his position that "the Army Corps of Engineers ought to get out of the dam building business." Attempting to resonate with certain segments of the environmental movement and to reinforce his image as an anti-Washington, outsider candidate, Carter declared, "I personally believe that we have built enough dams in this country and will be extremely reluctant as president to build any more." Moreover, he emphasized his larger commitment to preserving the environment, asserting that "the federal government can and must play a significant role in the preservation of natural areas and resources."[9]

During the 1976 primary elections, Carter competed against two other Democratic candidates with strong environmental credentials—Representative Morris Udall of Arizona and Senator Henry Jackson of Washington. When Carter emerged as the most electable of the three candidates, most environmental organizations threw their support to the former Georgia governor. Carter was helped in this by the League of Conservation Voters, who gave Carter and vice presidential candidate Walter Mondale high ratings for their records on environmental issues, as well as their positions on current environmental problems. The league gave low ratings on both accounts to President Gerald Ford and his running mate, Senator Robert Dole. Carter's campaign staff, however, refused to take the support of environmentalists for granted. In the weeks leading up to the Democratic National

Convention in New York City, the CFC "contacted each of the Udall delegates and alternates in key states," as well as delegates for other environmentally oriented candidates, to convert them to their candidate by stressing Carter's environmental positions and record.[10] These efforts paid off, and with Carter's victory in November, environmental activists became extremely hopeful that their concerns would be faithfully represented in the White House.[11]

The Carter-Mondale transition team addressed environmental policy within several cluster groups, each of which fell under the larger policy analysis unit, headed by Stuart E. (Stu) Eizenstat. Carlton Neville, for example, directed the energy group. Katherine P. Schirmer—who had joined Carter's election campaign in July 1976 after accumulating five years of experience dealing with policies for pesticides, toxic substances, and water development as a special assistant at the EPA and a legislative assistant to Senator Philip A. Hart—led the natural resources cluster, which developed briefing materials for the soon-to-be-appointed agency heads and explored the array of environmental laws requiring reauthorization in 1977.[12] Rather than putting forward a single, high-priority program, Schirmer recommended that the incoming administration focus on six initiatives in the natural resources area: energy reorganization, water resources development reform, president's energy message, energy conservation, president's environmental message, and National Parks/Refuge/Civilian Conservation Corps programs.[13]

The transition team consulted frequently with environmental leaders, and the president-elect met personally with a select group of them in Plains, Georgia, in December.[14] The feeling of inclusion among members of the environmental community was heightened still further during the early weeks of the administration, when Carter and his agency heads appointed a number of environmental professionals to subcabinet positions. The White House tapped public interest environmental organizations for several of these appointments, an action that had mixed results for the environmental community: on the one hand, it brought environmental leaders into government, where they could help shape the agenda; on the other, it robbed the organizations of many of their finest leaders.[15]

ARTICULATING AN ENVIRONMENTAL POLICY AGENDA

Carter's domestic policy advisers knew that the president-elect's "environmental leanings" had attracted significant political support and that much was now expected from the new administration. Toward that end, Schirmer urged Carter to deliver a high-profile environmental message soon after taking office to articulate the administration's environmental goals and assert his leadership. "There is a fear that while the new Administration will have better environmental policies than the previous Administration," she said, "a low priority would not provide the needed leadership to cope with the increasingly complex and controversial issues of energy development conflicts with environmental quality, harmful public works water development projects, toxic substances and growing delays in meeting our air and water quality goals." Moreover, a firm statement from the commander in chief would help counteract the "inertia and low morale in the agencies charged with environmental responsibilities," which had developed during the Ford presidency.[16]

Although energy and water resources development policy captured center stage during the first months of the administration, Carter sent Congress a major environmental message in May 1977. His agenda was breathtakingly broad and ambitious, advocating legislation and policies that would address pollution and public health, energy and the environment, the urban environment, natural resources, the "national heritage" (national parks, forests, wildlife refuges, cultural sites, wilderness, wild and scenic rivers), wildlife, the global environment, and the streamlining of government implementation of environmental laws. Carter praised Congress for its previous work on environmental legislation. He then positioned his presidency by stating that "the primary need today is not for new comprehensive statutes but for sensitive administration and energetic enforcement of the ones we have."[17] While granting a need for some new legislation, Carter would shift the action in the area of environmental protection to the executive branch, where he promised "firm and unsparing support."[18]

Speaking to fiscal conservatives within the House and Senate, Carter presented an economic framework for his environmental policy. "I believe environmental protection is consistent with a sound economy," he argued. "Previous pollution control laws have generated many more jobs than they have lost." Moreover, he concluded, "if we ignore the care of our environment, the day will eventually come when our economy suffers for that neglect."[19] In articulating the specifics of his environmental agenda, Carter began with the protection of human health, which he described as "our most important resource."[20] Consequently, because he viewed the widespread presence of toxic chemicals as "one of the grimmest discoveries of the industrial era," he called for government actions that would prevent those substances from entering the environment in the first place.[21] To accomplish this goal, he instructed the Council on Environmental Quality to generate a plan for eliminating duplication of efforts among federal agencies dealing with toxic wastes and for ensuring there were no gaps in the monitoring and collection of data on toxic chemicals. He also substantially increased the EPA's funding in his fiscal year 1978 budget for the implementation of the Toxic Substance Control Act.[22] Carter closed his message to Congress by saying that "the foregoing proposals, along with others which will follow in the coming years, constitute the most far-reaching environmental program ever put forward by any administration. My support for them is resolute, and it is personal."[23]

Carter's determination to back this ambitious environmental agenda was made tangible by his support of a trio of environmental bills that had been vetoed during previous congressional sessions: the reauthorization of the clean air and clean water acts, and the enactment of surface mining control legislation. Opposition to them by the Ford administration had proved extremely frustrating to environmental activists. Carter's aggressive support, and his subsequent signing of the acts later in 1977, gave credibility to his tough rhetoric.[24]

REFORMING WATER RESOURCES DEVELOPMENT POLICY

Within the broad constellation of environmental policy concerns, Carter began his presidency confidently by tackling what many considered to be one of the country's most ecologically damaging and economically wasteful federal programs, large-scale water resources development. These water projects, which were built, operated, and maintained by the Army Corps of Engineers, Bureau of Reclamation, and Tennessee Valley Authority, also happened to be among the most highly prized (and carefully protected) activities in the federal government, at least from the standpoint of those congressional members who used them to channel federal expenditures into their districts and states. Carter was not opposed to all water projects, just those whose environmental and economic costs far outweighed their benefits. His bold (some would say naive or reckless) effort to reform federal water resources development policy met stiff resistance from several key legislators, who resented both Carter's proposals and the unilateral manner in which he pursued them. The resulting confrontation quickly escalated and ended up costing Carter far more political capital and congressional goodwill than he and most of his senior staff had imagined. Upon reflection, Carter's director of the Office of Management and Budget (OMB), Bert Lance, called the president's decision to challenge federal water projects "the worst political mistake he made, and its effects lasted the rest of his term and doomed any hopes we ever had of developing a good, effective working relationship with Congress."[25]

Carter had repeatedly pledged to end pork-barrel water projects, and his transition team grappled with this campaign promise from the start. Katherine Schirmer was particularly concerned with how the president-elect approached the fiscal year 1978 budget, which he inherited from the Ford administration. As she told Eizenstat, by withholding funds from major water projects deemed to have "severe adverse environmental and social impacts," the new administration could save nearly $500 million out of the $2 billion allocated in fiscal year 1978 for some 320 water projects. Such an action would demonstrate the president's commitment to both sound fiscal policy and environmental quality. Schirmer stressed the need to act early to revise Ford's budget, otherwise "many major projects will progress close to or past the point where re-evaluation is impractical." "Congress may be more receptive to a reform package," she argued, "if it is clearly spelled out at the beginning of the Administration rather than after one or more years of continued funding of these projects." Acknowledging that there were several congressional members, including "some powerful committee chairmen," who were staunch defenders of public works, she agreed that "halting or slowing down controversial projects will enact a price and something must be given back in return."[26]

Following the lead of the transition team, the president's Council on Environmental Quality (CEQ) identified some twenty-two water projects unworthy of continued funding.[27] Carter's secretary of the interior, Cecil D. Andrus, agreed that the projects warranted careful review. "Many of these projects are of dubious merit and should be stopped or curtailed at this point—if political problems can be overcome," he told the president in February 1977. As a former governor of Idaho and as the current cabinet secretary responsible for the Bureau of Reclamation, Andrus was sensitive to the political pitfalls inherent in water policy reform. "An Administration strategy should not be confined to individual projects or groups of projects," he advised, "but to develop a more rational water development system involving improved planning, current discount rates, and more equitable cost-sharing responsibilities." He cautioned, however, that the congressional delegations from the seventeen western states covered by the bureau placed extreme importance on water projects. "If we attempt to alter any of these projects for whatever reason, our action will act as a catalyst to create political coalitions in the Congress," Andrus said. "I am not arguing against eliminating some of these projects—some definitely merit action—but, I want you to know that there will be political retaliation from the Congress when we do."[28]

Worried that Andrus had thrown cold water on the reform package the Domestic Policy Staff (DPS) had so carefully crafted, Eizenstat urged Carter to press ahead with the water projects review, primarily as a quick and effective means to institute "comprehensive water resources reforms." He urged the president to delete funds for all the projects then listed, rather than to pick and choose among them, which would leave the administration vulnerable to charges of political favoritism. He recommended that Carter "personally advise Congressional leaders prior to sending up the Budget" and, in line with Andrus's comments, "back up any decision to delete funds with a commitment to veto an appropriations bill which deviates significantly from your Budget."[29]

Despite the warnings of a congressional backlash, Carter remained confident in the correctness of his position. He believed he was elected to do what was right, not what was politically expedient, and this was a campaign promise he intended to keep. Nevertheless, on the practical side, he had every reason to believe that environmental organizations and fiscal conservatives would prove to be tireless and effective lobbyists on his behalf, as these two forces had found significant common ground in their opposition to controversial water projects. Moreover, seventy-four congressional members had already gone on record as supporting the president's "efforts to reform the water resources programs of the Army Corps and the Bureau of Reclamation."[30]

Carter announced his water resource projects review—which the media immediately dubbed the president's "hit list"—in late February. Acknowledging the earlier contributions of water projects to the U.S. economy, Carter cautioned that "many of the 320 current projects approved in the past under different economic circumstances and at times of lower interest rates are of doubtful necessity now, in light of new economic conditions and environmental policies." He recommended that funding for nineteen projects be rescinded for fiscal year 1978. He instructed the secretaries of the interior and the army to review each of these projects, in cooperation with the OMB and the CEQ, and to give him their findings by April 15. In addition to the detailed reevaluation of the nineteen targeted projects, Carter also directed the agencies to review "all other water resource projects," maintaining that final approval to proceed should occur only if the projects proved sound from an economic, environmental, and safety standpoint.[31]

As the DPS had hoped, Carter's hit list sent a message to the country that the president was serious about reforming the nation's federal water policy, that he was not going to waste any time getting started, and that he had the courage and commitment to challenge the most powerful and vested interests. Among environmentalists, expectations of the new president were practically soaring. And, as Carter had predicted, many environmental organizations pooled their resources to lobby Congress on behalf of the White House.[32] To reinforce his reform effort, Carter issued two executive orders in May 1977: one on floodplain management (No. 11988) and the other on protection of wetlands (No. 11990). With regard to floodplains, Carter's policy directed federal agencies to avoid subsidizing floodplain development; to site their own projects outside floodplains, unless there was no practicable alternative; and, whenever they must build in floodplains, to design their projects to minimize harm to those areas. Carter's executive order on wetlands was similar: federal agencies should not encourage or assist others to develop or harm wetlands, should themselves avoid actions that endanger wetlands unless absolutely necessary, and, if they must build in wetlands, should do so in a manner that minimizes harmful impacts.[33]

Just as Cecil Andrus and others had warned, however, Congress fought back furiously. Congressional leaders, determined to raise the stakes over the fate of water projects, threatened the administration's other, higher-priority domestic initiatives. When Congress presented the president with an appropriations bill stipulating that all previously funded dams continue to be built, his options boiled down to whether or not to veto the bill, which contained key elements of the White House's economic stimulus package. Knowing that Congress had the votes to override his veto, Carter reluctantly signed the water bill in August 1977. His capitulation caused many in the environmental community to feel betrayed. Environmentalists, elated by Carter's initial challenge to the water projects, were now disquieted by the realization that the administration's commitment to this cause was not as resolute as they had believed.[34]

OVERCOMING INTERNAL DIVISIONS

The controversy over the Tennessee Valley Authority's (TVA) Tellico Dam in eastern Tennessee proved a devilish problem for the Carter administration. The TVA's plan to dam the Little Tennessee River south of Knoxville had drawn heated opposition from many quarters since it was first seriously proposed in the early 1960s. Project proponents nevertheless succeeded in pushing the dam forward, gaining congressional authorization in 1966 and construction funds the following year. Landowners and conservationists sued the TVA in 1971, claiming the authority had not complied with the requirements of the recently enacted National Environmental Policy Act. The federal court agreed and enjoined the project for nearly two years, until the TVA submitted a satisfactory environmental impact statement. This episode proved to be a minor inconvenience to the TVA in comparison to what occurred two years later, when the battle over a small endangered fish—the snail darter—brought the agency's project to its knees.[35]

Ironically, the three-inch-long, snail-eating perch was discovered in 1973, the same year the Endangered Species Act was enacted. At that time, the Tellico Dam was roughly half complete. When the Department of Interior placed the snail darter on its endangered species list (the fish's only known habitat was the Little Tennessee River) in October 1975, the project had reached about the three-quarters mark. With the snail darter now protected by law, environmentalists filed suit to halt further construction of the Tellico Dam in February 1976. Three months later, the U.S. District Court for the Eastern District of Tennessee denied the request for a permanent injunction. In January 1977, the U.S. Court of Appeals for the Sixth Circuit reversed the lower court's decision, halting all construction work that harmed the snail darter's critical habitat. The news media could not resist this story (which they portrayed as the little fish versus the big dam), and the controversy over the snail darter became the most widely publicized enforcement of the Endangered Species Act.

The Tellico Dam controversy thus got passed on to the Carter administration, where it festered for several months at the subcabinet level. The contradictory positions already held by the Department of the Interior and the TVA were complicated in May 1977 when the Department of Justice accepted the TVA's request to appeal the case to the Supreme Court without first informing the White House. Under different circumstances, it would have been routine practice for the Department of Justice to follow such a course, given the fact that it had defended the TVA in both the district and circuit courts. But the Carter administration—as represented by the DPS, the CEQ, and the OMB—had adopted a distinct set of environmental priorities that placed it solidly behind the Department of the Interior. How this battle played out within the executive branch revealed much about how such crosscurrents of power influenced the style and development of Carter's environmental policy.[36]

Both sides of the debate vied for the president's ear. The Department of the Interior and the CEQ not only contended that petitioning the Supreme Court was wrong from a legal standpoint but also argued that it would undermine the Endangered Species Act, and therefore directly contradict the administration's position that the statute was a workable law. The CEQ also feared that a Supreme Court ruling in favor of the TVA would threaten other environmental laws, such as the National Environmental Policy Act. The DPS and OMB objected to the Justice Department's argument that Congress's continued (i.e., post–court injunction) appropriations for the project were an "implied exemption" from the Endangered Species Act and an explicit directive to TVA to complete the Tellico Dam. Such reasoning stood to undercut the power of the executive branch by allowing Congress to legislate via the appropriations process.[37]

It troubled the DPS that the "government's position," as officially represented by the Department of Justice before the Supreme Court, would be set forth as the TVA's position, when in fact the administration sided with the Department of the Interior. With the government's brief due to the Supreme Court by mid-January 1978, senior White House advisers debated the wisdom of asking the Justice Department to withdraw its representation of the TVA, or asking it to submit a "split" brief that would include both the TVA's and the Interior Department's interpretation of the law. "While we are reluctant to suggest intervention in this matter," they told the president, "unfortunately, the position of the TVA as articulated by the Associate Solicitor General is in serious conflict with the policies of this Administration." They presented him with "three realistic choices": "allow the Justice Department to proceed to represent TVA in this case on behalf of the U.S. Government"; "direct the Justice Department to withdraw representation from TVA, with the understanding that TVA would in all probability carry the case forward on its own"; and "direct the Justice Department to withdraw representation from TVA and to file the opposite position (the position of the Administration) in a brief to the Court." Carter agreed to pursue the last option, which was recommended by the majority of his advisers.[38]

Attorney General Griffin B. Bell recoiled at the White House's request that the Justice Department reverse its position. He asked for a meeting with Carter, in which he underlined the legal merits of the TVA's argument and explained that reversing the government's legal position in the middle of an appeal would erode the respect traditionally accorded the Justice Department and would cast a poor light on the president's leadership, making him appear inconsistent and indecisive. In asking Carter to reconsider his decision, Bell agreed that if the secretary of the Interior and director of the OMB remained strongly opposed to his legal conclusions after reviewing the Justice Department's brief, then "under the unique circumstances of this case I am prepared to include as an appendix to the brief the separate dissenting views of the Secretary and the Director."[39]

Carter's legal counselor, Robert J. Lipshutz, took the lead in working out a consensus position among the interested parties. With the Supreme Court filing deadline fast approaching, Lipshutz outlined a procedure to which the Justice and Interior departments agreed: all parties would work to protect the integrity of the Endangered Species Act; no argument would be made that appropriations should supersede established laws; nothing would be done to "encourage the Court to impede or stop the construction of the Tellico Dam because of the snail darter issue" (i.e., mitigation efforts would be pursued to transplant the fish to other streams); and the Justice Department would be allowed to represent the TVA, while at the same time presenting the Supreme Court with Interior's legal arguments and interpretations by way of a separate appendix to the brief. Despite the reservations voiced by the CEQ and the OMB to this procedure, Lipshutz and Eizenstat urged Carter to approve the plan, which he did.[40]

The Supreme Court heard the arguments in April 1978, and in June ruled six to three to uphold the appeals court's injunction. The extensive press coverage fueled a growing backlash against the Endangered Species Act, placing the act's citizen and government advocates on the defensive.[41] As a compromise to congressional members seeking to weaken the act, Congress created a seven-member, cabinet-level Endangered Species Committee (known popularly as the "God Committee") endowed with the power to exempt individual projects from the provisions of the Endangered Species Act. The committee, chaired by Secretary of the Interior Cecil D. Andrus, issued its first ruling in January 1979. Not coincidentally, its first case involved the Tellico Dam. To the dismay of the congressional critics of the Endangered Species Act, the committee voted unanimously against completion of the project, not because of threats to the snail darter but, ironically, because it deemed the dam to be economically unjustified, despite the fact that it was 90 percent complete.[42]

Congressional proponents of the dam, led by Tennessee Senator Howard Baker, were outraged by this ruling and sought a legislative remedy, attaching a rider to the energy and water development appropriations bill which mandated the completion of the Tellico Dam by exempting it from all federal regulations, including the Endangered Species Act.[43] Up to this point, Carter had remained firmly on the side of a strong Endangered Species Act and against the economically dubious dam. The Baker amendment forced his hand. If Carter made a stand in defense of the snail darter (which had become the butt of countless jokes and which had little popular appeal as a species worth saving), he would risk losing key elements of his energy package, which were also contained in the appropriations bill.

With an eye cast toward his reelection bid in 1980, Carter bowed to the political pressure and signed the appropriations bill in September 1979. Except for the congressional directive to flood the Little Tennessee River Valley, the president said he was pleased with the bill, which he described as "sound and responsible." Nevertheless, he knew that signing the bill would dishearten advocates of the Endangered Species Act and opponents of the TVA dam. He therefore emphasized his regret in accepting this aspect of the bill, which he said expressed "the will of Congress in the Tellico matter," and reaffirmed his personal belief "in the principles of the Endangered Species Act," which he promised to enforce vigorously. "As President I must balance many competing interests," he said, and by signing the bill he avoided a veto battle that would surely have threatened "many important national issues before Congress," such as energy legislation, the second Strategic Arms Limitation Treaty, the Panama Canal implementation legislation, and reauthorization of the Endangered Species Act itself.[44]

Environmentalists, however, found little comfort in Carter's words. They viewed the special Tellico Dam exemption as a serious setback to the Endangered Species Act, one that could have been remedied only by a presidential veto. Compromise was not something they accepted easily. In the subsequent months, many environmentalists began to distance themselves from the administration.

REAFFIRMING CARTER'S ENVIRONMENTAL AGENDA

Long before the Tellico Dam decision, Carter's advisers had worried about the administration's flagging support among environmentalists. In addition to the president's abandonment of his water projects hit list, his energy policy—which had initially stressed conservation, solar power, and rigorous air-quality standards—appeared increasingly to downplay environmental concerns. The administration's efforts to battle inflation by relaxing certain federal regulations also raised anxieties within the conservation community. As Phil Spector, associate director of the Office of Public Liaison, warned his colleagues in the Executive Office of the President in August 1978, "environmentalists feel 'seduced and abandoned,' with no friends and many enemies in the White House." This problem extended beyond broken campaign promises, he observed, and included the fear that the EPA, the CEQ, and the DPS lacked the clout to combat the president's senior energy and economic advisers, and that, in consequence, "environmental concerns are not being taken into consideration at all." As a result, Spector wrote, environmental organizations "are already beginning to talk about potential 1980 challengers to the President who might be better on environmental issues."[45]

When the energy crisis of 1979 hit, environmentalists found themselves even further dismayed by Carter's proposal to create an Energy Mobilization Board that would have the authority to accelerate the development of new power plants by exempting them from environmental regulations.[46] As these concerns mounted in 1979, the CEQ urged Carter to deliver a second major environmental message to Congress and the American people. Eizenstat was lukewarm about the suggestion, although he ultimately admitted that "the message could be a vehicle for reaffirming the Administration's environmental commitment" while at the same time allowing the president a high-visibility platform from which to launch new initiatives on hazardous wastes and coastal protection. Eizenstat told the president that such a message "would come reasonably close to the expectations of the environmental community and would be welcomed by them," but he warned that it would not "reconcile major differences with the environmental community over energy, timber and regulatory reform."[47]

Carter recognized the need to reassert his environmental leadership and agreed to deliver a second environmental message to Congress in August 1979. As he framed it, the White House was responding to problems that had emerged or intensified since January 1977. He therefore proposed to increase the percentage of federal transportation funds channeled into improving public transportation, to step up federal efforts to preserve coastal areas and public lands, to reduce losses of farmland, to dispose of toxic wastes in a safer manner, and to strengthen the enforcement of wildlife protection laws. "Certain basic ideas remain the foundation of American environmental policy," Carter asserted. "Our great natural heritage should be protected for the use and enjoyment of all citizens. The bounty of nature—our farmlands and forests, our water, wildlife and fisheries, our renewable energy sources—are the basis of our present and future material well-being. They must be carefully managed and conserved." Speaking to the growing international concerns of the environmental movement, he stressed that the United States has "a serious responsibility to help protect the long-term health of the global environment we share with all humanity."[48] Indeed, the most farsighted aspects dealt with his global environmental initiatives to curb the loss of the world's tropical forests (thereby addressing the accelerated extinction of species and averting potentially serious global climate change) and to arrest the growing problem of acid rain.[49]

Whereas Carter emphasized human health at the start of his 1977 environmental message, he began his 1979 message by defending the administration's energy policy. "Conservation and energy from the sun have been major thrusts of my energy program," he said, and they would continue to be so. He noted, however, that he was calling for the development of synthetic fuels to help reduce the nation's oil consumption. "I do not pretend that all new replacement sources of energy will be environmentally innocuous," he said. "Some of the new technologies we will need to develop pose environmental risks, not all of which are yet fully understood. I will work to ensure that environmental protections are built into the process of developing these technologies, and that when tradeoffs must be made, they will be made fairly, equitably, and in the light of informed public scrutiny."[50] Balance between energy needs and environmental considerations was the guiding light of his policy, he argued. "Solving the nation's energy problem is essential to our economy and our security. We will not lose sight of our other goals but we must not fail in ending the energy crisis. This Administration's basic commitment to clean air, clean water and the overall protection of the environment remains strong."[51]

ACTIONS AT THE END

Environmentalists may have been disappointed in several of Carter's actions, and their support of his reelection campaign may have been substantially less than it had been four years earlier, but this weakened support was not caused by Carter's dropping environmental policy from his list of priorities. Far from it. In his January 1980 State of the Union Address, for example, Carter went on at length about energy conservation and solar power remaining key elements of his administration's energy policy; nuclear safety forming the administration's "primary priority in the regulation and management of nuclear power"; and protection of Alaskan federal lands continuing as his "highest environmental priority." He affirmed his commitment to work with Congress to pass comprehensive legislation to deal with toxic, hazardous, and nuclear wastes; his efforts to expand the nation's wilderness preserves; his ongoing effort to reform water policy; and a host of initiatives aimed at fisheries and agricultural lands. Moreover, his resolve to pursue these initiatives in 1980 was magnified by the approaching tenth anniversary of the first Earth Day.[52]

The 1980 presidential primary elections were rough on Carter. Several of his Democratic party opponents (notably Edward Kennedy and Jerry Brown) had attracted substantial support from environmentalists, as did also the third-party candidates John Anderson and Barry Commoner. Robert W. Harris, appointed as one of three CEQ members earlier that year, was aware that the loosely knit environmental voting block that had rallied behind Carter four years earlier was unraveling, yet he remained optimistic that the majority of these voters would back the president in November. "Having been recently active in the environmental community, I can attest to the passion that environmentalists have for achieving *100* percent success on every issue," he wrote Carter in September 1980. "Although they are clearly disappointed at our having fallen short of this standard, the environmental community realizes full well that you have been the most environmentally minded President in history and . . . they are deeply and sincerely appreciative for your leadership and the accomplishments and policies of your Administration."[53]

Although the leaders of the major environmental organizations finally did go on record in support of Carter in early September, the president's advisers worried that this late endorsement indicated soft support among the environmentally inclined public. Gus Speth, who surveyed the environmental policy landscape at the behest of Jack Watson and Stu Eizenstat, found "a number of pending or imminent Congressional and Executive actions that provide significant opportunities for improving both the quality of our environment and our standing with grass roots environmentalists." "Similarly," Speth added, "there are several pending actions which pose pitfalls that should be avoided." Given California's large number of electoral college votes and the importance of environmental matters to many of its residents, Speth urged the administration to move forward quickly on such pending items as the California wilderness bill, designation of a Santa Barbara Channel Islands Marine Sanctuary, and Northern California Wild and Scenic River designations.[54] Carter's margin of victory had been slim in 1976, however, and his inability to command enthusiastic support within the environmental community in 1980 was mirrored among the other elements of his original political coalition, as he went down in defeat.

Ironically, nothing did more to enhance Carter's standing among environmentalists than his loss to Ronald Reagan, in part because it ushered in an era of stark comparison. The environmental backlash that took place during the Reagan administration was perhaps best symbolized by the appointments and actions of James G. Watt as secretary of the interior and Anne McGill Gorsuch as EPA administrator.[55]

Carter's lame-duck activities included two of his most enduring actions: signing into law the Comprehensive Environmental Response, Compensation, and Liability Act, which created a "Superfund" to be used to clean up toxic waste sites; and the Alaska National Interest Lands Conservation Act, which placed an expanse of Alaska wilderness the size of California under permanent federal protection. Both accomplishments were achieved only with significant postelection involvement by the president, and both testified to the depth of his personal commitment to environmental concerns.

The Superfund legislation had been developed in response to the discovery of a highly toxic abandoned chemical waste site in the Love Canal neighborhood of Niagara, New York. The extensive media coverage of the Love Canal crisis helped reorient the nation's environmental agenda, elevating concern over the nation's multitude of toxic dump sites, and the Carter administration lent its support to passage of a broad bill requiring the polluting industries to finance the cleanup of abandoned hazardous waste sites and future oil spills. After the election, Carter intensified his personal involvement in successfully overcoming industry-led opposition to the bill, although he compromised with Congress in accepting a restricted version of the law that excluded oil spills.[56]

While the Superfund legislation originated in response to environmental degradation, the Alaska lands act was intended to prevent it. The lands at stake were associated with the Alaska Native Claims Settlement Act of 1971, which gave the Congress until 1978 to allocate nearly one-third of Alaska's territory—land that was still controlled by the federal government. Perhaps predictably, every special interest group (oil and gas developers, mining concerns, loggers, wilderness and park advocates, and Alaska natives, among others) had a different proposal for how the land should be used, and political pressure was intense. With time running out in December 1978 and with no agreement in hand, Carter used his presidential authority to create seventeen national monuments in Alaska, setting aside an unprecedented 56 million acres under the auspices of the Antiquities Act until such time as the administration and Congress could resolve the issue. Two years later, following considerable lobbying by the interested parties, the House and Senate agreed on a bill, which the president signed on December 2.[57] As Carter reflected in his 1982 memoirs, "There have been few more pleasant occasions in my life than when I signed the Alaska National Interest Lands Conservation Act."[58]

CONCLUSION

In assessing the first years of his presidency, Carter said that "the actions my administration has taken to protect the environment here and abroad, and the successes we have had, are among the most gratifying achievements of my Presidency."[59] Indeed, throughout his term, Carter and his administration anticipated and grappled with many environmental issues—acid rain, global climate change, loss of stratospheric ozone, biodiversity, and environmental justice—that remain on the political agenda today.

The policy objective of "balance," while not explicitly touted, served as a rudder for the Carter presidency. He and his staff understood that appearing to sacrifice economic growth and development for the sake of environmental quality alone would be unpopular, if not downright unacceptable, to the majority of voters. To avoid such reaction, the Carter administration chose to balance three goals that together contributed to quality of life: environmental regulation, jobs, and economic development. In this respect, as in his attention to global, not just domestic, environmental problems, Carter was ahead of his time.

Despite Carter's own deeply held environmental sympathies, his forceful rhetoric, and his administration's wide-ranging environmental agenda, environmental policy was never the administration's top priority. Although the administration encouraged and at times directed environmental considerations to temper programs, projects, and regulations throughout the federal government, on those occasions where it unavoidably conflicted with domestic policy, environmental protection always took a back seat to such central objectives as economic recovery, inflation and deficit control, and energy initiatives. That said, one must still conclude that the environmentalists' criticisms of Carter were overstated, attributed perhaps to the movement's political immaturity and what was then an absolutist approach to deal making. In later reassessing the Carter presidency, Stuart Eizenstat observed that "the president's environmental record was unimpeachable, except, it seemed, to the organized environmentalists." He went on to criticize the leaders of environmental organizations "who failed to praise his accomplishments and took great pains to point out one supposedly endangered species that he had failed to add to the protected list, thus, ironically, helping to make the most environmentally conscious president in modern times an endangered political species."[60]

In fact, when Carter left the White House, the federal government's environmental regulatory apparatus was far stronger and more active than it had been when he took office. And while his Republican successor vowed to undermine these programs, widespread public sympathy—played out largely within the legislative and judicial branches of government but reinforced, no doubt, by approval of the Carter choices—ensured that environmental quality remained a concern of the federal government. Carter had embraced the general goals of the environmental movement, and while internal conflicts within his administration and intense legislative battles led to compromises unacceptable to the more dogmatic environmental leaders, Carter nevertheless advanced the cause of environmental policy as has no occupant of the White House since FDR.

NOTES

The author wishes to thank Lyn M. Lawrence, Hugo M. Rodriguez, and Quoc Vuong for their outstanding work as research assistants, and Daniel A. Cornford, Gary M. Fink, Jane Adams Finn, Hugh Davis Graham, Samuel P. Hays, and Marcel C. LaFollette for their helpful comments on earlier versions of this chapter.

1. See Samuel P. Hays, *Beauty, Health, and Permanence: Environmental Politics in the United States, 1955–1985* (Cambridge: Cambridge University Press, 1987); Martin V. Melosi, "Lyndon Johnson and Environmental Policy," in *The Johnson Years,* vol. 2, *Vietnam, the Environment, and Science,* ed. Robert A. Devine (Lawrence: University Press of Kansas, 1987), 113–49; John C. Whitaker, *Striking a Balance: Environmental and Natural Resources Policy in the Nixon-Ford Years* (Washington, D.C.: American Enterprise Institute for Public Policy Research, 1976); Russell E. Train, "The Environmental Record of the Nixon Administration," *Presidential Studies Quarterly* 26 (Winter 1996): 185–96; John Brooks Flippen, "The Nixon Administration, Politics, and the Environment" (Ph.D. diss., University of Maryland at College Park, 1994); and Robert A. Shanley, *Presidential Influence and Environmental Policy* (Westport, Conn.: Greenwood Press, 1992).

2. For assessments of the enduring political potency of environmentalism, see Hays, *Beauty, Health, and Permanence;* Michael J. Lacey, ed., *Government and Environmental Politics: Essays on Historical Developments since World War II* (Washington, D.C.: Wilson Center Press, 1989); Riley E. Dunlap and Angela G. Mertig, eds., *American Environmentalism: The U.S. Environmental Movement, 1970–1990* (Philadelphia: Taylor and Francis, 1992); Kirkpatrick Sale, *The Green Revolution: The American Environmental Movement, 1962–1992* (New York: Hill and Wang, 1993); Philip Shabecoff, *A Fierce Green Fire: The American Environmental Movement* (New York: Hill and Wang, 1993); and Mark Dowie, *Losing Ground: American Environmentalism at the Close of the Twentieth Century* (Cambridge, Mass.: MIT Press, 1995).

3. Jimmy Carter, *Why Not the Best?* (Nashville, Tenn.: Broadman Press, 1975), 117. For insights into Carter's environmental activities while governor, see Frank Daniel, comp., *Addresses of Jimmy Carter: Governor of Georgia, 1971–1975* (Atlanta: Georgia Department of History and Archives, 1975), passim; Furman Smith, Jr., "Environmental Law—The Carter Years," *Georgia State Bar Journal* 13 (February 1977): 110–11; Betty Glad,

Jimmy Carter: In Search of the Great White House (New York: Norton, 1980), 180–81; and Kenneth E. Morris, *Jimmy Carter, American Moralist* (Athens: University of Georgia Press, 1996), 198–99.

4. Carter, *Why Not the Best?* 120. For his recollections of leisure time spent in nature and his general attitudes on the subject, see Jimmy Carter, *An Outdoor Journal: Adventures and Reflections* (New York: Bantam Books, 1988).

5. See "Statement on Spewrell Bluff Dam, October 1, 1973," in *Addresses of Jimmy Carter,* 17; Glad, *Jimmy Carter,* 197–98; and Tim Palmer, *Endangered Rivers and the Conservation Movement* (Berkeley: University of California Press, 1986), 100–102.

6. "Statement on Spewrell Bluff Dam," 18. See also Carter, *Why Not the Best?* 120; Eugene H. Methvin, "The Fight to Save the Flint," *Reader's Digest,* August 1974, 17–22, 26; and Brent Blackwelder, "Successes and Failures in Dam Fighting in Washington and in the Field," in *In Defense of Rivers: A Citizens' Workbook on Impacts of Dam and Canal Projects,* ed. Barry Allen and Mina Hamilton Haefele (Stillwater, N.J.: Delaware Valley Conservation Association, 1976), 13–14.

7. For background on Conservationists for Carter, see memo, Jane Yarn and Carlton Neville to Jimmy Carter Presidential Campaign National Office Staff, n.d. [probably July 1976], Box 18, Carlton Neville Collection, Jimmy Carter Library (JCL).

8. See, for example, Palmer, *Endangered Rivers and the Conservation Movement;* Hays, *Beauty, Health, and Permanence;* Lettie M. Wenner, *The Environmental Decade in Court* (Bloomington: Indiana University Press, 1982); and Jeffrey K. Stine, *Mixing the Waters: Environment, Politics, and the Building of the Tennessee-Tombigbee Waterway* (Akron, Ohio: University of Akron Press, 1993).

9. Jimmy Carter Presidential Campaign, News Release, July 25, 1975, Box 18, Carlton Neville Collection, JCL. See also Jimmy Carter, *The Presidential Campaign, 1976,* vol. 1, pt. 1 (Washington, D.C.: Government Printing Office, 1978), 660–81.

10. Yarn and Neville to Jimmy Carter Presidential Campaign National Office Staff, n.d.

11. Lewis Regenstein, "The Candidates and the Environment: An Analysis," *Washington Post,* October 19, 1976; and Gladwin Hill, "Conservationists Expecting Carter to Open New Era for Environment," *New York Times,* November 5, 1976.

12. Within the EPA alone, five acts were up for reauthorization in 1977, giving the Carter administration multiple opportunities to shape the debate. They included the Environmental Research, Development, and Demonstration Authorization Act; the Noise Control Act; the Marine Protection, Research, and Sanctuaries Act; the Safe Drinking Water Act; and the Solid Waste Disposal Act.

13. Katherine Schirmer to Stuart Eizenstat, December 4, 1976, Box 5, Domestic Policy Staff (DPS)–Al Stern's Files, JCL.

14. For a summary of that meeting, see Margaret Costanza, Schedule Proposal, September 12, 1977, Box 103, Office of Public Liaison (OPL)-Costanza, JCL.

15. For a partial list (and a partisan critique) of the environmental appointees within the Carter administration, see Ron Arnold, *At the Eye of the Storm: James Watt and the Environmentalists* (Chicago: Regnery Gateway, 1982), 40–45. The Carter-appointed leadership within the EPA is discussed in Marc K. Landy, Marc J. Roberts, and Stephen R. Thomas, *The Environmental Protection Agency: Asking the Wrong Questions* (New York: Oxford University Press, 1990), 39–40.

16. Schirmer to Eizenstat, 4 December 1976, DPS–Al Stern's Files, JCL.

17. "The Environment: Message to the Congress, May 23, 1977," in *Public Papers of the Presidents of the United States: Jimmy Carter, 1977* (Washington, D.C.: Government Printing Office, 1978), 967.

18. Ibid., 968.

19. Ibid., 967. Carter's attempt to break down the belief that economic growth and environmental protection were mutually exclusive placed him ahead of his time, as this argument did not gain currency until the 1980s and 1990s, when it was largely couched as "sustainable development." Carter had been developing this position—which merged fiscal conservatism with environmental values—long before he entered the White House, as evidenced by similar statements he made early in his campaign. In July 1975, for example, he proclaimed that "there is no incompatibility between careful planning and economic progress on the one hand, and environmental quality on the other." Quoted in Jimmy Carter Presidential Campaign, news release, July 25, 1975, Box 18, Carlton Neville Collection, JCL. See also Jimmy Carter, *Keeping Faith: Memoirs of a President* (New York: Bantam Books, 1982), 74.

20. "The Environment: Message to the Congress, May 23, 1977," 969.

21. Ibid.

22. Ibid., 970. Carter's fiscal year 1978 budget tripled the EPA's allocation for gathering information on chemical substances to $29 million. By shifting the EPA's principal goal to the protection of public health, Carter and EPA administrator Douglas M. Costle succeeded in increasing the agency's budget during a general climate of fiscal austerity. See Daniel J. Fiorino, *Making Environmental Policy* (Berkeley: University of California Press, 1995), 39; Joel A. Mintz, *Enforcement at EPA: High Stakes and Hard Choices* (Austin: University of Texas Press, 1995), passim; and Edmund P. Russell III, "Lost among the Parts Per Billion: Ecological Protection at the United States Environmental Protection Agency, 1970–1993," *Environmental History* 2 (January 1997): 35–36.

23. "The Environment: Message to the Congress, May 23, 1977," 984.

24. The circumstances surrounding the Surface Mining Control and Reclamation Act of 1977 (Public Law 95–87), the Clean Air Act Amendments of 1977 (Public Law 95-95), and the Clean Water Act of 1977 (Public Law 95–217) are discussed in Hays, *Beauty, Health, and Permanence,* passim. See also Richard H. K. Vietor, *Environmental Politics and the Coal Coalition* (College Station: Texas A&M University Press, 1980), 123–24.

25. Bert Lance, *The Truth of the Matter: My Life In and Out of Politics* (New York: Summit Books, 1991), 114. For an early assessment of the administration's water policy reform effort, see Paul E. Scheele, "President Carter and the Water Projects: A Case Study in Presidential and Congressional Decision-Making," *Presidential Studies Quarterly* 8 (Fall 1978): 348–64. See also Carter, *Keeping Faith,* 78–79.

26. Schirmer to Eizenstat, December 4, 1976, Box 5, DPS–Al Stern's Files, JCL. See also Katherine Schirmer to Stu Eizenstat, December 3, 1976, in Box 5, DPS–A1 Stern's Files, JCL.

27. Steven D. Jellinek to Thomas B. Lance, February 2, 1977, Box NR-14, White House Central Files (WHCF)–Natural Resources, JCL; and Lance, *The Truth of the Matter,* 117.

28. Cecil D. Andrus to Carter, February 14, 1977, Box NR-14, WHCF–Natural Resources, JCL.

29. Eizenstat to Carter, February 15, 1977, Box 315, DPS-Eizenstat, JCL.

30. William Proxmire et al. to Carter, February 14, 1977, Box 315, DPS-Eizenstat, JCL. See also, Charles O. Jones, *The Trusteeship Presidency: Jimmy Carter and the United States Congress* (Baton Rouge: Louisiana State University Press, 1988), 129, 143–44; and Robert Shogan, *Promises to Keep: Carter's First Hundred Days* (New York: Thomas Y. Crowell, 1977), 212–15. For Carter's long-standing penchant for projecting moral leadership, see Morris, *Jimmy Carter, American Moralist,* passim; and Peter G. Bourne, *Jimmy Carter: A Comprehensive Biography from Plains to Postpresidency* (New York: Scribner, 1997), passim.

31. "Water Resource Projects: Message to the Congress, February 21, 1977," in *Public Papers of Jimmy Carter, 1977,* 207.

32. The Environmental Policy Center, National Audubon Society, National Wildlife Federation, and Natural Resources Defense Council were among the most vocal advocates for the president's hit list. See Jim Free, Presidential Scheduling Proposal, August 10, 1977, Box 103, OPL-Costanza, JCL.

33. For background discussions on Carter's wetlands policy, see Charles Warren to Carter, March 30, 1977; Eizenstat to Carter, April 2, 1977; Peter R. Taft to Eizenstat, April 15, 1977; and Gus Speth to Eizenstat, April 18, 1977, Box 203, DPS-Eizenstat, JCL.

34. See Martin Reuss, *Reshaping National Water Politics: The Emergence of the Water Resources Development Act of 1986* (Washington, D.C.: Government Printing Office, 1991), 48–52; and Eizenstat and Kathy Fletcher to Fran Voorde, August 2, 1977, Box 315, DPS-Eizenstat, JCL.

35. The most thorough history of this controversy is William Bruce Wheeler and Michael J. McDonald, *TVA and the Tellico Dam, 1936–1979: A Bureaucratic Crisis in Post-Industrial America* (Knoxville: University of Tennessee Press, 1986).

36. Kathy Fletcher to Eizenstat, June 17, 1977; and John M. Harmon to Eizenstat and Margaret McKenna, October 5, 1977, Box 144, White House Office of Counsel to the President–McKenna (hereafter Counsel to the President–McKenna), JCL. For the attorney general's views of the internal debate over Tellico Dam, see Griffin B. Bell, *Taking Care of the Law* (New York: William Morrow, 1982), 42–45.

37. Harmon to Eizenstat and McKenna, October 5, 1977; and Kathy Fletcher to Eizenstat, December 22, 1977, Box 144, Counsel to the President–McKenna, JCL.

38. Eizenstat, Lipshutz, McIntyre, Andrus, and Warren to Carter, January 9, 1978, Box 47, Counsel to the President–Lipshutz, JCL. Eizenstat had recommended the second option; all the rest favored option three.

39. Bell to Carter, January 13, 1978, Box 144, Counsel to the President–McKenna, JCL. Bell's earlier reactions and arguments are spelled out in memos, Bell to Carter, January 9, 1978, and January 10, 1978, Box 47, Counsel to the President–Lipshutz, JCL.

40. Lipshutz to Carter, January 18, 1978, Box 144, Counsel to the President–McKenna, JCL. The positions of the CEQ and the OMB are presented in McIntyre and Warren to Carter, January 18, 1978, Box 47, Counsel to the President–Lipshutz, JCL.

41. See, for example, "Endangered Species Act Is Endangered," *Los Angeles Times,* September 11, 1978; and Bill Vogt, "Now, the List-Makers Are Endangered," *National Wildlife* 18 (December–January 1980): 17.

42. See Robert Cahn, "The God Committee," *Audubon* 81 (May 1979): 10, 13.

43. For editorial reactions to this legislative ploy, see "Pork-Barrel Victory," *Atlanta Journal,* September 12, 1979; and "Snail Darter on the Stump," *Washington Star,* September 12, 1979.

44. "Energy and Water Development Appropriation Act, 1980: Statement on Signing H.R. 4388 into Law, September 25, 1979," in *Public Papers of Jimmy Carter, 1979,* book 2, 1760. See also Marc Mowrey and Tim Redmond, *Not in Our Backyard: The People and Events That Shaped America's Modern Environmental Movement* (New York: William Morrow, 1993), 237–43.

45. Phil Spector to Anne Wexler and Mike Chanin, August 17, 1978, Box WE-2, WHCF-Welfare, JCL. For a discussion of the bitterness many environmentalists felt toward President Carter, see Lewis Regenstein, "The Carter Administration and the Environment," *USA Today* 107 (November 1978): 31–36; and Michael Frome, *Regreening the National Parks* (Tucson: University of Arizona Press, 1992), 34–39, 216–17.

46. See Burton I. Kaufman, *The Presidency of James Earl Carter, Jr.* (Lawrence: University Press of Kansas, 1993), 148; and Shanley, *Presidential Influence and Environmental Policy,* 20.

47. Eizenstat, Fletcher, and R. D. Folsom to Carter, May 2, 1979, Box 77, WHCF, Federal Government–Organizations, JCL.

48. "Environmental Priorities and Programs: Message to the Congress, August 2, 1979," in *Public Papers of Jimmy Carter, 1979,* 1353–54.

49. The global environmental initiatives flowed from the joint CEQ–Department of State work in progress, which was released the following year as Gerald O. Barney, ed., *The Global 2000 Report to the President: Entering the Twenty-First Century,* 3 vols. (Washington, D.C.: Government Printing Office, 1980).

50. "Environmental Priorities and Programs: Message to the Congress, August 2, 1979," 1355.

51. Ibid., 1356.

52. Jimmy Carter, "The State of the Union: Annual Message to the Congress, January 21, 1980," in *Public Papers of Jimmy Carter, 1980–1981,* 130–32, 157–60.

53. Robert H. Harris to Carter, September 10, 1980, Box 78, WHCF–Federal Government–Organizations, JCL. See also Philip Shabecoff, "Major Environment Leaders Back Carter Re-election Bid," *New York Times,* September 28, 1980; and Elizabeth Drew, *Portrait of an Election: The 1980 Presidential Campaign* (New York: Simon and Schuster, 1981).

54. Gus Speth to Watson, Eizenstat, Moore, and Wexler, September 19, 1980, Box NR-1, WHCF–Natural Resources, JCL.

55. For a discussion of the changes wrought by the Reagan administration, see Arnold, *At the Eye of the Storm;* Jonathan Lash, Katherine Gillman, and David Sheridan, *A Season of Spoils: The Reagan Administration's Attack on the Environment* (New York: Pantheon, 1984); Norman J. Vig and Michael E. Kraft, eds., *Environmental Policy in the 1980s: Reagan's New Agenda* (Washington, D.C.: CQ Press, 1984); and V. Kerry Smith, ed., *Environmental Policy under Reagan's Executive Order: The Role of Benefit-Cost Analysis* (Chapel Hill: University of North Carolina Press, 1984).

56. For a general discussion of the Superfund, see Daniel Mazmanian and David Morrell, *Beyond Superfailure: America's Toxics Policy for the 1990s* (Boulder, Colo.: Westview Press, 1989); and Harold C. Barnett, *Toxic Debts and the Superfund Dilemma* (Chapel Hill: University of North Carolina Press, 1994).

57. For a detailed history of the act, see G. Frank Williss, *"Do Things Right the First Time": The National Park Service and the Alaska National Interest Lands Conservation Act of 1980* (Washington, D.C.: Government Printing Office, 1985). The debate over protecting Alaska lands is discussed in Roderick Nash, *Wilderness and the American Mind,* 3d ed. (New Haven, Conn.: Yale University Press, 1982), 272–315; and Donald Worster, *Under Western Skies: Nature and History in the American West* (New York: Oxford University Press, 1992), 154–224.

58. Carter, *Keeping Faith,* 582. See also Kaufman, *Presidency of James Earl Carter,* 208–10.

59. Jimmy Carter, "The President's Message," in *Environmental Quality—1979,* Tenth Annual Report of the Council on Environmental Quality (Washington, D.C.: Government Printing Office, 1980), iv.

60. Stuart E. Eizenstat, "President Carter, the Democratic Party, and the Making of Domestic Policy," in *The Presidency and Domestic Policies of Jimmy Carter,* ed. Herbert Rosenbaum and Alexej Ugrinsky (Westport, Conn.: Greenwood Press, 1994), 10.

10

Civil Rights Policy in the Carter Presidency

Hugh Davis Graham

The literature on civil rights policy during the Carter presidency is disappointing. Carter, a "New South" governor with civil rights positions generally acceptable to national Democratic leaders, won 94 percent of the black vote in 1976. As president, he set a vigorous example of affirmative action in appointments, naming more minorities and women to executive and judicial posts than did any of his predecessors.[1] Yet civil rights issues ranked relatively low on Carter's agenda. As Gary Reichard observed in his survey of the Carter literature in 1990, on civil rights issues Carter "unquestionably followed the tradition of his liberal Democratic predecessors."[2] Still, Carter's presidency has drawn little attention from civil rights scholars, perhaps because he balanced mainstream Democratic orthodoxy on minority and women's rights with fiscal conservatism and an outsider's hostility toward Washington norms of interest group liberalism. The administration, quite simply, is not associated in the public mind with major civil rights legislation.[3]

Scholarly writers on civil rights policy generally have been too obsessed with passing and flunking presidents and praising or blaming their administrations largely on doctrinal grounds.[4] Rather than seeking to determine whether the Carter presidency did the right thing, whatever that was, the goal here is to understand why the administration's civil rights agenda took the shape it did, and with what consequences.

When Carter entered the White House in January 1977, he stepped into a policy stream that since the late 1960s had carried two conflicting currents. One was a conservative reaction, following the breakthrough civil rights legislation of 1964 and 1965, against ghetto rioting, black radicalism, government-funded antipoverty insurgency, and court-ordered busing for racial balance. The "backlash" politics associated with Nixon's "southern strategy" included conservative Supreme Court nominations and Nixon's call, in his reelection campaign of 1972, for a constitutional amendment banning racial school busing. In response to worsening racial conflict in such northern cities as Boston and Chicago, Congress in 1975 passed and President Ford signed a proviso known as the Byrd amendment, which prohibited the Department of Health, Education, and Welfare (HEW) from requiring school systems to transport children beyond their neighborhood schools for purposes of racial balance.[5]

Paralleling the backlash stream of the 1970s, but less widely publicized, was a contrary trend: the quiet mobilization of a comprehensive regime of civil rights regulation, wherein federal agencies extended affirmative-action requirements to virtually all business firms, educational institutions, and state and local governments receiving federal contracts or grants. The early benchmarks of the affirmative-action regime bear the stamp of executive agencies and the federal courts, not Congress. From the Office of Federal Contract Compliance (OFCC) in the Department of Labor came rules requiring rough proportional representation of minorities in construction employment (the Philadelphia Plan, 1969); extension of the proportional model to all federally assisted contracts and grants (Order No. 4, 1970); and equivalent employment requirements for women (Revised Order No. 4, 1971). From the Equal Employment Opportunity Commission (EEOC) during the same period came requirements for minority hiring and employee testing according to "disparate impact" standards of proportionally equal results. From the Office of Civil Rights (OCR) in HEW came bilingual education requirements (1970, 1975) for children whose first language was not English. Although challenged in court, these regulatory initiatives, based on the Civil Rights Act (Title VI for the OFCC and the OCR, Title VII for the EEOC), were upheld by the federal courts. In 1972, Congress began to extend the benefits of the new genre of cross-cutting civil rights regulation, originally designed to remedy past as well as current discrimination against African Americans, to other organized claimant groups— women in educational institutions (1972), the handicapped (1973), Hispanics and other nonnative speakers of English (1974, 1975), and the elderly (1975).[6]

By the mid-1970s, the expanded civil rights coalition, under the adept coordination of the Leadership Conference on Civil Rights, had won bipartisan respect in Congress for its ability to mobilize constituency group support. In the late 1960s, the civil rights coalition began to win regulatory benefits in complex areas little understood by the general public, such as employee testing and minority hiring tables.[7] Civil rights regulation typically concentrated benefits (preferences for minorities in hiring and promotion) and widely distributed costs because affirmative-action regulations were "unfunded mandates" paid for by regulated businesses and agencies. This was the "client" pattern in the politics of regulation, infamous in the annals of postwar liberal reform.[8] It featured strong incentives for organized interest groups to "capture" the regulatory machinery and maximize their benefits for constituent clienteles, while loosely organized consumers and taxpayers, poorly informed about the complexities of regulation, funded the benefits. In economic regulation, the abuses of client politics (high prices and low competition in air travel, surface transportation, lending institutions) had drawn the fire of economists and students of public administration. By the mid-1970s, a bipartisan reform movement in Congress pressed for the deregulation of airlines, trucking, banking, and communications. Carter, a champion of government reorganization to streamline the bureaucracy and increase market competition, took the lead in economic deregulation. But he generally defended the new social regulation of the 1960s and 1970s that shielded minorities, women, and the disabled from discrimination and protected citizens from environmental harm.[9]

In civil rights regulation, the Carter administration had a similarly mixed stance. By lobbying for Equal Rights Amendment (ERA) ratification, the Carter White House supported the vast, deregulatory sweep of nationwide sex nondiscrimination. A sex-blind Constitution would wipe out a century's accumulation of statutes and policies "protecting" women. But Carter, differing with feminist groups, favored some restrictions on abortion. On the civil rights of racial and national origin minorities, Carter criticized school busing for racial balance but otherwise generally supported his party's legacy and the goals of the Leadership Conference.[10] In a 1983 interview, Carter said of his administration's civil rights initiatives: "I looked on them as kind of a continuum of what had been initiated under Lyndon Johnson and talked about under President Kennedy. . . . And so I didn't look upon these achievements as notable in nature. I just felt as if they were my duty."[11] Looking back at the Carter presidency through the lens of the Reagan-Bush years and the sharp attacks on affirmative action of the 1990s, we may too easily underestimate the confidence of the new Carter government in January 1977, when Democrats once again controlled the elected branches of government, and the New Deal political order seemed restored.

In this chapter civil rights policy making in the Carter presidency will be explored through four case studies: government reorganization, especially of civil rights enforcement agencies; minority contract set-asides; fair housing enforcement; and bilingual education. The first of these, government reorganization, a Carter initiative, remains his most distinctive contribution to civil rights policy making. The second and third, minority contract set-asides and fair housing enforcement, were congressional initiatives developed by Democratic leaders in the civil rights coalition from subcommittee bases in the House. The final case study features policy entrepreneurs in executive agencies, in this case the efforts by ethnic partisans in the newly established Department of Education, using the Title VI authority of the Civil Rights Act, to set national standards governing bilingual education.

REORGANIZING THE CIVIL RIGHTS ENFORCEMENT AGENCIES

Civil rights issues neither played a major role in Carter's 1976 election campaign nor found a significant place on his legislative agenda. This posture reflected a broad consensus within the Democratic coalition that the chief civil rights challenge was to win office and more effectively enforce the existing statutes. Carter's domestic policy adviser, Stuart Eizenstat, winnowed the massive "Promises" book compiled in December 1976 by the transition staff from campaign commitments into a preinaugural agenda of comprehensive scope and unclear priorities.[12] Most domestic policy attention in Carter's legislative program centered on the economic stimulus package (especially public works jobs), energy policy, and regulatory reform (especially airlines). In its main strategy for improving the economic conditions of minorities, the administration targeted the disadvantaged, generally through such measures as new public housing, expanded rent subsidies, public works projects, and increasing the minimum wage.[13]

To improve civil rights enforcement, Carter won from Congress broad authority to reorganize executive agencies. Government reorganization was a favorite Carter theme, offering increased efficiency at minimal cost, catering to his self-image as a management expert, and evoking claims of reorganizational success in Georgia government.[14] Bert Carp, Eizenstat's deputy on the Domestic Policy Staff (DPS), referred to Carter as a "Common Cause monarch," anxious to fix the system through rational planning.[15]

In civil rights enforcement, as elsewhere, effectiveness was undercut by the uncoordinated sprawl of federal agencies with overlapping jurisdictions and conflicting roles. Private employers found dual policing by the EEOC and the OFCC most confusing. The EEOC protected minorities and women under Title VII from discrimination in private business employment, labor unions, and state and local governments by processing complaints, making findings of probable cause, conciliating disputes, and, after 1972, filing lawsuits through an independent counsel. In the process, the EEOC accumulated a complaint backlog that often delayed action for years.[16] The OFCC, authorized by President Johnson's Executive Order 11246 in 1965, policed discrimination in businesses and state and local government agencies receiving federal contracts and grants. It required contractors to report employment projections by protected-class category, conducted inspections, and ultimately (although rarely) debarred contractors.

Because most large private employers and government agencies received federal grants and contracts, most were subject to both EEOC and OFCC requirements.[17] Moreover, the OFCC shared contract compliance duties under Title VI and the executive order with eleven similar subagencies in a confusing sprawl of EEO machinery scattered throughout the executive departments. The result was interagency bickering, conflicting regulations, and growing dissatisfaction. Employers complained about multiple coverage, conflicting requirements, growing burdens of record keeping and reporting, and vulnerability to both government sanctions and reverse-discrimination lawsuits.

Carter's election followed a decade of ineffective efforts to coordinate federal civil rights enforcement. His ambitious reorganization project, headed by the deputy budget director, James T. McIntyre, Jr., concentrated in 1977 on streamlining the Executive Office of the President and in 1978 on restructuring civil rights enforcement.[18] Reorganization Plan No. 1 of 1978 made the EEOC the preeminent civil rights enforcement agency in the federal government.[19] It dismembered the Civil Service Commission and transferred its EEO responsibility for federal employees to the EEOC. Administration of the equal pay and age discrimination acts shifted from the Department of Labor to the EEOC. To strengthen the OFCC, Carter issued an executive order in 1979 consolidating in the Labor Department the functions of eleven contract compliance agencies in the executive departments and renaming the already awkwardly named agency the Office of Federal Contract Compliance Programs (OFCCP). As a consequence of the Carter consolidation, both the OFCCP and the EEOC experienced an extraordinary expansion. Between 1978 and 1980, the OFCCP expanded from 68 full-time staff members to 1,304; during the same period, the EEOC staff expanded from 267 to 3,433, and the EEOC budget increased from $74.2 million to $124 million.[20]

Far-reaching changes in regulatory strategy accompanied these changes in structure and authority. Eleanor Holmes Norton, appointed by Carter to chair the EEOC in 1977, emphasized class-action lawsuits against major employers. In the wake of the 1978 consolidation, the EEOC issued the Uniform Guidelines on Employee Selection Procedures, a set of rules grounded in disparate impact theory that sharply curtailed the use by employers of employee tests and other merit criteria, while offering cooperating employers a shield against reverse-discrimination lawsuits. As veteran EEOC lawyer Alfred Blumrosen observed, the agency's accelerated enforcement strategy under Norton, strengthened by the Carter reorganization, "precipitated an enormous pressure on employers."[21] The EEOC under the Uniform Guidelines denied businesses the use of traditional employee tests without expensive and vulnerable validation procedures. The OFCCP required government contractors to submit plans with their bids. American business leaders, fearing liability from suits filed by white males such as Allan Bakke and Brian Weber, shifted toward the proportional representation model for employing minorities and women as a necessary way of doing business.[22]

CONGRESS AND MINORITY CONTRACT SET-ASIDES

More important, in the long run, than Carter's reorganization of civil rights enforcement agencies was the enactment in May 1977 of the Public Works Employment Act, which established the minority contract set-aside program. Parren J. Mitchell, Democratic congressman and chairman of the Congressional Black Caucus, offered the set-aside provision as an amendment on the House floor on February 23, 1977. It required that at least 10 percent of the $4-billion appropriation for public works contracts should go to minority business enterprises (MBEs). Mitchell's amendment stipulated that "minority group members are citizens of the United States who are Negroes, Spanish-speaking, Orientals, Indians, Eskimos, and Aleuts."[23] At the time, Mitchell's amendment attracted little notice. In retrospect, it was one of the most significant turning points in modern civil rights history. Congress's creation of MBE set-asides in 1977 is striking in four ways.

First, the set-aside initiative represents a tour de force of policy entrepreneurship by leaders of the civil rights coalition in Congress. This group included a rising generation of urban black Democrats active in the Black Caucus, such as Mitchell, John R. Conyers of Detroit, and Augustus Hawkins of Los Angeles, working with white liberal allies such as Representative Don Edwards of California, a senior member of the House Judiciary Committee, and aided by the sympathetic House leadership, including Speaker Thomas P. "Tip" O'Neill. They took skillful advantage of changing institutional circumstances of the 1970s, including the huge Democratic majorities elected in 1974, the weakening grip of senior southern Democrats on committee leadership, the proliferation of subcommittees and congressional staff, and the resurgence of congressional initiative in policy making against an "imperial" presidency weakened by the Vietnam War and Watergate.

Mitchell and his colleagues carefully laid the groundwork. They created ad hoc and oversight committees and built a record of legislative findings demonstrating that past discrimination had left a legacy of institutional bias that crippled current efforts at minority participation. In 1972, the House Subcommittee on Minority Small Business Enterprise reported that minority businesses faced economic difficulties that "are the result of past social standards which linger as characteristic of minorities as a group."[24] By 1975, this effort had produced similar findings by the House Subcommittee on Small Business Administration (SBA) Oversight and Minority Enterprise, the General Accounting Office, and the U.S. Commission on Civil Rights.[25] In January 1977, in the last days of the Ford presidency, the House Committee on Small Business concluded that "over the years, there has developed a business system which has traditionally excluded measurable minority participation. . . . Currently, we more often encounter a business system which is racially neutral on its face, but because of past overt social and economic discrimination is presently operating, in effect, to perpetuate these past inequities."[26]

Second, in the field of government contracting, the civil rights coalition made a strong case for affirmative-action remedies. Minorities faced formidable structural barriers to entry, even though government procurement had stressed nondiscrimination at least since 1961. Large established firms held great advantages over new entrants in the form of experience in bidding, bonding, subcontracting, project performance, and reputation. Minorities, often excluded from lending or supplier networks, lacked familiarity with contracting agency protocols. In commercial enterprise generally in 1977, minorities accounted for 16 percent of the population but constituted only 3 percent of the nation's 13 million businesses and generated less than 1 percent of gross business receipts. The federal agency officials who designed the Philadelphia Plan in the late 1960s used similar historical arguments to justify minority hiring preference, citing Labor Department findings that skilled craft unions had long excluded minorities from the construction trades.[27]

Third, Mitchell's set-aside provision, by naming six groups as eligible for a 10 percent "share of the action," created a precedent that invited expansion accompanied by increasing political vulnerability. Set-aside payoffs became attractive objectives for other groups. If speakers of a particular language or persons claiming a certain ancestry could win such entitlements, why not include other groups? If an arbitrary 10 percent set-aside was permissible, why not more? In attempting to blunt criticism that a minority set-aside remedy for past discrimination would create a racial quota, Mitchell in 1977 emphasized continuity with the SBA's Section 8(a) program to assist "economically or culturally disadvantaged groups," begun under President Johnson's executive order in 1968 as a response to the urban riots and continued under his successor's executive orders. The SBA, pressed by applicants to define economically or culturally disadvantaged groups, had by 1977 developed a flexible, inclusive list: "Such persons include, but are not limited to, black Americans, American Indians, Spanish-Americans, Oriental Americans, Eskimos, and Aleuts."[28]

The MBE committee hearings and reports since 1972 had emphasized shared minority disadvantages and avoided distinguishing between particular groups. But the SBA 8(a) program, by aiding culturally *or* economically deprived groups, permitted inclusion of nonminority women and poor white men. Mitchell's original intention had been to name only "Negroes and Spanish-speakers," but in justifying his set-aside as a logical extension of the 8(a) program, he borrowed the SBA list of approved minority groups. In a 6–3 ruling in 1980, the U.S. Supreme Court upheld the set-aside provision in the *Fullilove* decision. Justice John Paul Stevens noted in his dissent, however, that Congress "for the first time in the Nation's history has created a broad legislative classification for entitlement to benefits based solely on racial characteristics."[29]

Fourth, despite the retrospective gravity of Mitchell's minority set-aside provision, Congress gave it overwhelming approval after only a perfunctory discussion, and the Carter administration then enthusiastically backed it. Congress held no hearings on the minority set-aside proposal, accepting Mitchell's House floor amendment by voice vote. It then passed the public works bill with routine majorities: 335–77 in the House and 71–14 in the Senate. The Carter White House, stung during its first year by attacks from black leaders for emphasizing budget balancing over full employment and by attacks from liberals for waffling on support for affirmative action in the *Bakke* case, seized the MBE set-aside as an opportunity to rally minority loyalty. Vernon Jordan, executive director of the National Urban League and a prominent supporter of his fellow Georgian in the 1976 election, told the Urban League annual conference in Washington in July 1977 that Jimmy Carter had forgotten the minority voters he had courted as a candidate.[30] Andrew Young warned at the August cabinet meeting that the phrase "balanced budget" was becoming a negative code word for "anti-black, anti-poor, anti-city." Jack Watson, in a memo to a half dozen senior presidential aides, including Eizenstat and Hamilton Jordan, warned that none of the administration's three main first-year themes—international human rights, government reorganization, and balancing the budget—addressed the concerns of minority leaders. Beth Abramowitz, on Eizenstat's staff, added that minorities shared a perception "that women and homosexual concerns are given greater attention than minority concerns."[31]

The Carter administration reacted decisively. At a "10% MBE Meeting" on August 26, Watson warned national leaders from banking, surety, and construction firms that "if a general contract bidder does not line up MBEs for at least 10% of the grant funds, its bid will be disqualified."[32] On September 12, Carter appointed an Interagency Council for Minority Business Enterprise to expand MBE programs in all federal agencies. He also directed the Office of Federal Procurement Policy to require evidence of MBE participation prior to awarding contracts and instructed all executive departments to double procurement purchases from minority firms within the next two fiscal years.[33] Secretary of Commerce Juanita Kreps, seeing the MBE set-aside requirement as an opportunity to win lead agency status in the burgeoning set-aside program—much as the Labor Department had used the new regulatory authority of the OFCC (1965) and OSHA (1970) to expand its domain—urged Carter in early 1978 to require set-asides not just in procurement but in all agency contracts, including construction.[34]

A review of the Carter White House files produced little evidence of second thoughts about difficulties that might flow from the set-aside principle, although some scattered cautions appeared. In 1978, when Kreps moved to seize the initiative in Carter's urban policy by capitalizing on the MBE programs within the Commerce Department, Eizenstat urged Carter to hold off, fearing that "a government-wide 10% set aside" could trigger an adverse reaction. "The Administration's efforts to promote minority business have sparked much controversy," Eizenstat wrote, including lawsuits by contractors and, "as [SBA director] Vernon Weaver recently explained to you, battle lines are being drawn up between women's groups and minority groups concerning eligibility criteria for participation in these business promotion activities."[35] Congress, however, passed a bill in 1978 that for the first time provided a statutory basis for the SBA 8(a) program. Approved by voice vote in both chambers, it required each federal agency to establish an Office on Small and Disadvantaged Business Utilization to implement MBE procurement requirements in the agency's contracts and grants.[36]

The emergence of minority set-asides in 1977–78 demonstrates the two-tiered nature of civil rights policy making in the 1970s. Policies like racial school busing, college admissions, or abortion rights, in which Washington authority directly impinged on such community institutions as schools, universities, and hospitals, engaged a broad public and brought elected officials under close scrutiny. Intense public disapproval of racial school busing, for example, led Congress in 1977 to pass and President Carter to sign an appropriations rider prohibiting HEW from requiring school districts to pair or cluster schools to facilitate racial integration. On the other hand, civil rights policies of a complex regulatory nature, such as the Philadelphia Plan, the SBA 8(a) MBE program, and contract set-asides in government procurement, escaped the notice of most voters. Regulatory politics was an inside-the-beltway game, where interest groups sought to join the game, not to break it up.

CONGRESS AND FAIR HOUSING ENFORCEMENT

Congress's second major civil rights initiative during the Carter presidency, the fair housing enforcement bill, shared many aspects of the set-aside initiative but differed in two important respects. The similarities included years of preparation by House Democrats using subcommittee hearings. Congressman Don Edwards of California, who chaired the House Judiciary Committee's Subcommittee on Civil Rights Oversight, led this effort. In 1971 Edwards began a series of hearings documenting the enforcement failures of the Fair Housing Act of 1968, which made nondiscrimination in housing a national policy. Or, more precisely, enforcement occurred only in a handful of cities, notably Chicago, Cincinnati, Cleveland, and Richmond, where well-organized fair housing organizations used nonminority testers to check discrimination complaints. The compromises necessary to pass the ban in 1968 left national policy essentially toothless.

Conservatives in Congress feared, not without reason, that an administrative subagency located in the Department of Housing and Urban Development (HUD) would be captured by the public housing coalition, much as the civil rights coalition from the beginning had controlled the OFCC in Labor and the OCR in HEW. In 1968, therefore, Congress limited HUD's enforcement powers in housing discrimination to receiving and conciliating complaints. The statute authorized the attorney general to file "pattern or practice" suits but not to sue on behalf of individuals. Conservatives knew that the Justice Department, a small agency whose litigators carefully selected test cases for their strategic policy importance, could offer little significant enforcement in the nation's massive, decentralized housing market. The 1968 law, like the failed voting rights laws of 1957 and 1960, made fair housing a private right, enforceable only through expensive, time-consuming lawsuits with little chance to succeed.[37]

The fair housing enforcement initiative in Congress differed from the set-aside initiative, first, by using committees not only to demonstrate the magnitude of the problem but also to explore alternative remedies. The Edwards subcommittee demonstrated increased racial segregation in housing.[38] The integration of American schools became virtually impossible if housing remained segregated. In the 1974 *Milliken* decision, the Supreme Court had protected most suburban school districts from inner-city busing, and in 1977, in *Village of Arlington Heights v.*

Metropolitan Housing Development Corporation, it found local zoning ordinances barring low-income housing constitutional unless *intentional* discrimination could be demonstrated. A broad acceptance of statutory remedies, however, paralleled the court's narrowing view of constitutional remedies. To provide more effective remedies for housing discrimination, by 1979 the Edwards subcommittee had developed a compromise to ease conservative fears of administrative enforcement by HUD bureaucrats. Congress would authorize HUD to investigate on its own or on behalf of individuals filing complaints. Enforcement authority, however, would be given to HUD-appointed administrative law judges (ALJs), who could order violators to cease discriminating, fine them up to ten thousand dollars and order compensation for the victims. Additionally, the Edwards bill would authorize the attorney general to bring housing discrimination lawsuits in federal court on behalf of individuals.

The second difference between the fair housing and MBE set-aside initiatives in Congress is that fair housing concentrated on nondiscrimination, whereas contract set-asides represented affirmative action through minority preference quotas. The Edwards bill protected individuals against housing discrimination on account of race, color, religion, national origin, or sex. Like many nondiscrimination provisions, the Edwards approach had the potential for expansion in affirmative-action directions. For example, because the Edwards bill covered discrimination in renting, selling, brokering, mortgages, insurance, and repair loans, fair housing enforcement officials could conceivably challenge lending and insurance portfolios for failing to meet the disparate impact standard of racial proportionality. As a practical matter, however, the widespread practice of racial "steering" by realtors (showing minority neighborhoods to minorities and white neighborhoods to whites) and of "redlining" by lenders (refusing mortgages and insurance to older, racially mixed neighborhoods) made enforced nondiscrimination in housing a potentially radical instrument of social policy in the Carter era.

Carter himself had ranked housing high in his legislative agenda. But his program concentrated on expanding construction, home ownership, public housing, and low-income rent subsidies. By the late summer of 1979, when the Edwards subcommittee reported its bill to the full Judiciary Committee, the Carter White House and the Justice Department joined HUD in supporting the bill. But the hour was late. Voters in 1978, worried by inflation and taxes, elected a more conservative Congress. In his January 1980 State of the Union Address, Carter called the fair housing bill "the most critical civil rights legislation before the Congress in years."[39] Yet the election-year legislative priorities recommended by Mondale and Eizenstat gave fair housing only a third-tier ranking. Not until April 1980, when the House Judiciary Committee reported the fair housing bill (HR 5200) to the floor, did senior presidential assistants begin a strong lobbying effort.[40]

To overcome opposition led by the 760,000-member National Association of Realtors and the Society of Real Estate Appraisers, the House leadership accepted numerous amendments to win support from Republicans and conservative Democrats. To insulate the ALJs from the urban-liberal coalition that dominated HUD, the House Judiciary Committee agreed that ALJs should be appointed by the Justice Department, not by HUD, that HUD investigators or prosecutors could not serve as ALJs, and that ALJ decisions could be appealed to federal district judges, who could collect additional evidence. By a one-vote margin (205– 204), the House on June 11 adopted the compromises; on June 12, by a deceptive vote of 310 to 95, the House sent the bill to the more conservative Senate.

Conservative suspicions of HUD were not misplaced. In late June, on the eve of crucial negotiations in the Senate Judiciary Committee, HUD secretary Patricia Roberts Harris sent the White House a proposed executive order of hubristic ambition. It would empower HUD to cancel all contracts with state and local governments upon their refusal to follow HUD's fair housing directives.[41] HUD wanted presidential authority to regulate fair housing even without the legislation pending so delicately in the Senate. The White House, recognizing that HUD's aggression would torpedo the bill in Congress, refused. In the Senate, majority leader Robert C. Byrd and floor manager Edward M. Kennedy offered further compromises, agreeing to drop the House ALJ approach in favor of hearings by federal magistrates. Senate conservatives led by Republicans Orrin G. Hatch of Utah and Strom Thurmond of South Carolina, however, demanded two further concessions: an intent rather than an effects standard for proving discrimination, and jury trials in bias cases.

When Ronald Reagan crushed Carter in the November 1980 elections and Republicans won control of the Senate in the Ninety-seventh Congress, prospects for the fair housing bill rapidly faded. Despite attempts by Attorney General Benjamin R. Civiletti and Drew Days, assistant attorney general for civil rights, to negotiate a bill-saving Senate compromise in December, fair housing proponents failed to break a filibuster led by Hatch and Thurmond.[42] Republicans were not about to allow a lame-duck Democratic Senate to pass a fair housing bill and a defeated Jimmy Carter to sign it.

By 1980, two of the nation's great postwar crusades in civil rights policy, the racial integration of America's schools and housing, had largely failed. Segregated neighborhoods lay at the heart of both failures, incurring staggering social and economic costs to African Americans in particular. Although by 1980 the black middle class as measured by income was rapidly expanding, partly as a result of affirmative-action requirements, the median household wealth of black families was only *one-eleventh* that of white families.[43] Business as usual in the American housing market isolated black Americans, including the burgeoning middle class, in neighborhoods where home values, the golden nest egg of wealth accumulation in postwar America, were least likely to appreciate and most likely to decline. The civil rights coalition, failing in 1980, would pass a fair housing enforcement bill in 1988, the last year of the Reagan presidency.

THE DEPARTMENT OF EDUCATION'S BILINGUAL REGULATIONS

The final case study centers on the attempt by the newly established U.S. Department of Education to impose controversial bilingual education requirements in the nation's schools. The first part of this story involves the politics of government reorganization. Political scientist Willis Hawley, who worked in the OMB with Carter's reorganization project, published a book-length study of the Education Department reorganization, and Charles Jones and Erwin Hargrove provide case studies in their books on the Carter presidency.[44] As a presidential candidate, Carter won endorsement from the 1.8-million-member National Education Association (NEA) by promising to create a cabinet-level department of education. Once elected, Carter sought to honor his pledge by proposing a broad department to consolidate uncoordinated and often competing education programs scattered throughout dozens of federal agencies.

For decades, blue-ribbon commissions and public administration experts had criticized the federal tradition of constituency-based mission agencies serving farmers, labor, small business, veterans, homeowners, and so forth. In this view, merely departmentalizing the U.S. Office of Education (USOE)—pulling the "E" out of HEW—would create yet another narrow, client-captured bureaucracy.[45] The issue divided Carter's advisers, and HEW secretary Joseph Califano actively opposed it.[46] Congress, protecting established agency-committee relationships, excluded from any new department most educational programs run by agencies other than the USOE. As a consequence, Carter's drive consumed eighteen months of uphill bargaining, passed the House by a narrow margin (215–201), and won congressional approval in September 1979 for an Education Department that consisted mainly of the existing USOE plus the Pentagon's 135,000-student school system for overseas military dependents.

The reorganization statute, by creating a narrow department, expanded within it the role of civil rights enforcement and bilingual education advocacy. Congress strengthened the OCR, elevating its head to assistant secretary status with authority to hold hearings, issue reports, make contracts, and appoint staff, including legal counsel independent of the secretary's control. This outcome produced intense pressure on the new secretary, especially from Hispanic political organizations and from the NEA, which had campaigned for bilingual education since the late 1960s, to use the OCR's regulatory authority under Title VI to expand bilingual education.[47]

On October 30, 1979, Carter appointed Shirley M. Hufstedler, a federal appeals court judge from California, as the nation's first secretary of education. She had no professional education experience, but her Ninth Circuit opinion in the *Lau* case, which the Supreme Court affirmed in its landmark 1974 decision, had pleased supporters of bilingual education. President Carter persuaded her to head the new department by agreeing to offer her his first Supreme Court appointment.[48]

Hufstedler's judicial background ill prepared her to control the direction of a new cabinet department with a staff of seventeen thousand and a budget of $14 billion. Far more experienced political executives than Judge Hufstedler had been "captured by the natives" running Washington agencies. Agreeing to make bilingual education regulations the new department's first priority, Hufstedler left her tenured judgeship to preside over a political disaster for her agency and, by association, for her president.

The chief decision facing Hufstedler was not *whether* to issue regulations governing education for students of limited English proficiency (LEP), but when and in what form. Since 1978, the OCR had been under federal court order, as part of a settlement in an Alaska lawsuit, *Northwest Arctic v. Califano,* to go through the formal rule-making process to codify the requirements of school districts receiving federal aid—meaning almost all of them—in identifying and teaching LEP students.[49] The controversy over the OCR's bilingual education requirements reached back to May 1970, when OCR director Stanley Pottinger sent school districts with large Spanish-surnamed student populations a three-page memorandum requiring unspecified "affirmative steps" to rectify language deficiencies.[50] When the U.S. Supreme Court in *Lau v. Nichols* (1974) affirmed this duty without specifying remedies, the OCR appointed a panel of consultants to draft compliance guidelines. The result was the "Lau Remedies," a twenty-three-page document the OCR and the Office of Education (OE) jointly sent to thousands of school districts.[51] Written in turgid, jargon-laden educationese, it signaled in two ways the intentions of the education and enforcement bureaucracy that Carter's departmentalization would empower.

First, the OCR's 1975 policy directive amounted to a preemptive strike against English-based teaching methods, such as English-as-a-second-language (ESL) and immersion techniques. The Lau Remedies required native-language instruction in math, science, and social studies for elementary and intermediate-level students with a primary language other than English. "Because an ESL program does not consider the affective nor cognitive development of students in this category," the statement directed, "an ESL program is *not* appropriate."[52] Instead, school districts must teach elementary and intermediate LEP children in their native language, using either transitional bilingual or bilingual/bicultural methods.

Second, the 1975 remedies telegraphed an intrusive future, reaching beyond teaching methods to include instructional personnel and course content. They urged school districts to use "paraprofessional persons with the necessary languages and cultural background." The OCR required a stream of reports from school districts detailing their bilingual curriculum. Didactic and condescending in tone, the Lau Remedies were often unclear and occasionally contradictory. For example, schools were instructed to develop a bilingual program but were warned, "There is a prima facie case of discrimination if courses are racially/ethnically identifiable."

Finally, the status of the Lau Remedies themselves was confusing. Until the reorganization of 1979, the OCR was a regulatory body within HEW, acting under

Title VI to police discrimination on account of race and national origin (1964) and under sequel statutes covering sex (1972), handicap (1973), and age (1975) discrimination. But the Lau Remedies were policy guidelines, not regulations. Under the *Lau* precedent, the OCR had the burden of proof to find individual noncomplying school districts. The blanket Lau Remedies, promulgated in the wake of *Lau,* were thus never published for comment in the *Federal Register* and therefore lacked regulatory authority. Nonetheless, between 1975 and 1980, the OCR used the Lau Remedies to negotiate bilingual education requirements with approximately four hundred school districts, concentrating on the major cities— Chicago, Houston, Los Angeles, New York, and Philadelphia. Many school districts resisted, however, some of them suing the OCR.

Because an estimated 80 percent of the nation's LEP students spoke Spanish in the home, the controversy over bilingual education centered on a single language and ethnic group. The 1970s coincided with soaring immigration from Latin America and the rise of Hispanic cultural nationalism, as reflected in the Chicano movement and such insurgent organizations as La Raza Unida and the GI Forum.[53] Hispanic rights organizations saw bilingual education requirements as affirmative action to improve the education and respect for the culture of Hispanic Americans, much as the Philadelphia Plan and MBE contract set-asides were seen as remedies for past discrimination against African Americans. The new Department of Education (DOE), uniting the OCR, the Office of Bilingual Education and Minority Language Affairs, and the NEA constituency in a single agency, agreed. Thus the bilingual regulations proposed by OCR officials in the fall of 1979 mandated native-language instruction in basic courses for an estimated 1,995,200 children. This would require school districts to hire 57,400 certified bilingual teachers—45,000 of them *new.* It offered an employment bonanza for native speakers of Spanish. Even Joe Califano, arguably the leading liberal in Carter's cabinet, complained about the demands of the bilingual education lobby. "HEW's bilingual program had become a captive of the professional Hispanic and other ethnic groups," Califano noted, with their "often exaggerated political rhetoric of biculturalism."[54]

Secretary Hufstedler's senior advisers worried about the contradictory goals in the bilingual regulations—"English proficiency versus maintenance of cultural identity," as one of her directors expressed it. But they emphasized the "political urgency" of publishing the proposed regulations in the *Federal Register* before the 1980 elections, or else face "extreme public resistance" from national Hispanic organizations.[55] The White House, anxious to appeal to Hispanic voters, urged Hufstedler to act before the elections.[56]

Hufstedler agreed to publish the proposed regulations on August 5, 1980, followed by sixty days of public comment, including regional hearings in six cities. This precipitated a major political brawl that badly damaged Carter's already crippled reelection campaign. National associations representing the state legislatures, state and local school boards, chief school officers, elementary and secondary school principals, and the American Federation of Teachers accused Education bureaucrats of violating the DOE's founding statute, which prohibited interference in local curricular decisions. Chicago school officials asked where they could find native-language teachers for ninety thousand students speaking 139 languages.[57] Even the *New York Times,* rarely at odds with the civil rights coalition, editorially attacked the proposed bilingual rules: "Deliberate abuses have combined with pedagogical ineptitude to turn much bilingual education into permanent detention for children, segregated and dependent, into a boondoggle for those who keep them there."[58] "Federal bilingual funds are intended to help Hispanic children," the *Times* lectured, "not to make Spanish an official language or to make jobs for Hispanic teachers unqualified to teach in English."

Carter's Regulatory Analysis Review Group (RARG), examining the proposed language minority rules as required by Carter's executive order of March 1978, sent Hufstedler a severe critique, couched in polite bureaucratese. The RARG found that by mandating native-language instruction while excluding without explanation other possible approaches, such as ESL or enrichment immersion, the proposed rules made no cost comparison of alternative methods. The department's reasoning for excluding all other approaches "may be impeccable, but it should make explicit the basis for its choice."[59] Moreover, by setting a low test threshold for entry into bilingual programs and a high one for exit while providing no rationale for either decision, the proposal seemed designed primarily to maximize the scope and duration of bilingual instruction.

By publishing the OCR's proposed regulations, Hufstedler had elevated a simmering dispute into a national controversy that linked President Carter and his new Education Department to an image of local schoolchildren forced by Washington bureaucrats to learn science, math, and social studies in Spanish. Unlike the Philadelphia Plan or MBE set-asides, bilingual education joined school busing and bans on father-daughter school banquets as high-profile symbols of social engineering from Washington. One month before the election, Congress passed a rider postponing any minority-language regulations until June 1981. On February 10, 1981, Ronald Reagan's new secretary of education, Terrell Bell, revoked the department's ham-handed first attempt at regulating the nation's schools.

CONCLUSION

Policy entrepreneurs in Congress and the subpresidency shaped the development of civil rights policy during the Carter administration much more than had the president. With two exceptions, Carter entered the White House without a significant new civil rights agenda. Carter's appointment of minorities and women to top administrative posts and federal judgeships in numbers far exceeding the tokenism of his predecessors constituted the first exception. In the flood tide of the feminist movement, this became especially important for women. For the first time, women, including Rosalynn Carter, entered the White House in significant numbers as senior policy advisers.

The second exception, Carter's reorganization project, while keyed to efficiency rather than to policy changes, included rationalizing the civil rights enforcement machinery. The Carter reorganizations, by strengthening the independent authority of the EEOC, the OFCCP, and the OCR, consolidated the federal government's shift from the equal treatment model of the 1960s to the equal results model that the Reagan administration would inherit.

Although driven primarily by nonpolicy considerations, Carter's reorganization of HEW had unintended civil rights consequences. Because Congress would approve only a narrowly focused Education Department, the new agency dangerously combined a client-captured agenda with sharpened regulatory teeth. The NEA constituency dominated an agency that now contained the rule-making OCR. Hufstedler's campaign to impose bilingual education regulations from Washington blew up in her face, damaging her president by reinforcing Republican charges that Democrats were incorrigible social engineers and Big Government centralizers. Carter, in his attempt to rally minority voters, helped hand the Republicans a potent election-year weapon.

Unfortunately for the civil rights coalition, the controversy over bilingual regulations coincided with the drive of the Democratic leadership in Congress for an enforceable fair housing law. Both drives were homestretch efforts, racing the clock in a presidential election year. Both identified the Democratic party and the Carter administration with expanding control from Washington, invading the traditional sanctuaries of community self-government in America, the school and the home. On the fair housing bill, Carter acted more decisively, but his largely ineffective support came too late. The Democrats' congressional leadership must share the blame for keeping the housing bill off the fast track until 1980.

From the perspective of the late 1990s, how should we assess Carter's record in civil rights policy? In other policy fields—international human rights, energy, economic deregulation, the environment—Carter's reputation, like that of other presidents denied reelection, has improved with historical perspective. Carter's record in appointing minorities and women to senior posts has always commanded wide respect. His belated drive to win effective enforcement against housing discrimination, though unsuccessful, was partially vindicated in 1988 when President Reagan signed a two-tracked fair housing law that provided both ALJ and jury trial enforcement.

On the whole, the Carter administration was effective in practicing "soft" affirmative action—antidiscrimination accompanied by vigorous outreach but not tied to numerical or proportional targets. On the other hand, the administration's identification with "hard" affirmative action—minority preference programs such as the admission set-asides in the *Bakke* medical school case, the MBE contract set-asides, the proportional minority employment standards of the EEOC and the

Labor Department—set the Democratic party at odds with public belief in equal individual rights. Carter's 1976 victory for the Democrats appears attributable to short-term, anomalous forces (Watergate, Vietnam). His 1980 defeat, however, fits the long-term, post-1968 pattern of a Democratic party rejected by most voters for being subservient to organized labor, leftist intellectuals, feminist groups, welfare rights organizations, and racial minorities.

The indictment, though effective for Republicans, was partly unfair, since Carter was also hammered by many of these same constituencies. In Carter's defense, his presidency coincided with a conservative shift in American political life that began in the late 1960s and that spelled trouble for the leader of the party of the left whatever his civil rights policies.[60] Also, in the international and economic turmoil of the late 1970s, the president faced crises far more demanding of his attention than the civil rights issues discussed here in artificial isolation. Nonetheless, by the end of his presidency, Carter's civil rights policies no longer fit the model of a centrist president struggling against the liberal constituencies of his party. By 1980, Carter's zigzag pattern, harkening first to one set of advisers and then to another, had settled in the civil rights arena into a firm reelection zag that rallied the rights-based core constituencies of his party.

Carter's distinctive model of a "trusteeship" presidency, shaped not by conventional interest group bargaining but by long-term solutions in the national interest, clashed with his party's traditions and strained his relations with Congress.[61] His commitment to budget balancing and inflation reduction produced tightening domestic budgets that his civil rights constituencies resented. But in expanding the role of the state through social regulation, where benefits were redistributed at small cost to the federal Treasury, Carter largely followed the lead of the civil rights coalition. Ironically, the president who instinctively resisted the pull of interest group government could not escape the demands of his party's base for group-based preferences in civil rights policy, even in defeat.

NOTES

1. Because Congress created 152 new federal judgeships in 1978, Carter appointed 258 new judges to federal district and appeals courts—more than any of his predecessors. His appointees included 29 women, 28 blacks, and 14 Hispanics. African Americans appointed by Carter to senior posts included Andrew Young and Donald McHenry as ambassador to the United Nations; Patricia Roberts Harris, secretary of Housing and Urban Development; Clifford Alexander, secretary of the army; Wade McCree, solicitor general; Chester Davenport, under secretary of transportation; Dennis Green, deputy secretary of the Treasury; Drew S. Days III, assistant attorney general for civil rights; Mary Frances Berry, assistant secretary of education; John E. Reinhardt, United States Information Agency director; and Barbara Watson, assistant secretary for administration, State Department.

2. Gary W. Reichard, "Early Returns: Assessing Jimmy Carter," *Presidential Studies Quarterly* 20 (Summer 1990): 603–20. John Dumbrell, in *The Carter Presidency: A*

Re-evaluation (Manchester, England: University of Manchester Press, 1993), offers a balanced and generally sympathetic interpretation emphasizing the dilemma of an instinctively centrist president caught between the rising expectations of liberal Democratic constituent groups and the constraints of tightening budgets and conservative voting trends.

3. See, for example, the disappointed assessments of President Carter's civil rights performance in Steven F. Lawson, *Running for Freedom* (Philadelphia: Temple University Press, 1991), 200–202; and Harvard Sitkoff, *The Struggle for Black Equality, 1954–1992* (New York: Hill and Wang, 1993), 214–15. For an early assessment, see M. Glenn Abernathy, "The Carter Administration and Domestic Civil Rights," in *The Carter Years: The President and Policy Making,* ed. M. Glenn Abernathy, Dilys M. Hill, and Phil Williams (New York: St. Martin's Press, 1984), 106–22.

4. Norman C. Amaker, a veteran plaintiff's lawyer for the NAACP Legal Defense Fund, offers such a partisan account in "The Faithfulness of the Carter Administration in Enforcing Civil Rights," in *The Presidency and Domestic Policies of Jimmy Carter,* ed. Herbert D. Rosenbaum and Alexej Ugrinsky (Westport, Conn.: Greenwood Press, 1994), 737–45.

5. Conservative trends mirrored in presidential elections, in the antibusing measures passed by Congress, and in rising public concern over "reverse discrimination" were less apparent in the federal judiciary, despite the five Supreme Court justices appointed by presidents Nixon (Burger, Blackmun, Powell, Rehnquist) and Ford (Stevens). The Burger Court protected suburban school districts from inclusion in court-ordered integration of city school systems (*Milliken v. Bradley,* 1974) and required evidence of discriminatory intent, not merely statistical evidence of "disparate impact," in claims of constitutional protection against discrimination (*Washington v. Davis,* 1976). On the whole, however, the Burger Court, under the effective leadership of Justice William Brennan, upheld the major provisions of affirmative-action regulation. See Paul Brest, "Racial Discrimination," in *The Burger Court: The Counter-revolution That Wasn't,* ed. Vincent Blasi (New Haven, Conn.: Yale University Press, 1983), 113–31.

6. U.S. Advisory Commission on Intergovernmental Relations, *Regulatory Federalism: Policy, Process, Impact, and Reform* (Washington, D.C.: ACIR, 1984), 70–91; Hugh Davis Graham, "Since 1964: The Paradox of American Civil Rights Regulation," in *Taking Stock: American Government in the Twentieth Century,* ed. Morton Keller and R. Shep Melnick (Cambridge: Cambridge University Press, 1998).

7. On the lobbying prowess of the LCCR, see Michael Pertschuk, *The Giant Killers* (New York: Norton, 1986), 148–80.

8. The opposite of the client pattern is found in environmental regulation, where benefits are widely distributed (clean air, water) and costs are concentrated (emission and effluent control technology). Fortunately, most government activity follows the "majoritarian" pattern, where both the benefits of policy (education, defense, criminal and civil justice, public health and sanitation) and their costs (tax dollars) are widely distributed. The opposite pattern, where both costs and benefits are concentrated and hence conflict is intense, is often found in business-labor regulation, for example, in collective bargaining (NLRB) and workplace safety (OSHA) regulation. For an explication of the standard four-cell model, see James Q. Wilson, ed., *The Politics of Regulation* (New York: Basic Books, 1980), 357–94; and James Q. Wilson, *Bureaucracy* (New York: Basic Books, 1989), 72–89.

9. Marc Allen Eisner, *Regulatory Politics in Transition* (Baltimore, Md.: Johns Hopkins University Press, 1993), 192–201; Martha Derthick and Paul J. Quirk, *The Politics of Deregulation* (Washington, D.C.: Brookings Institution, 1985), 29–35, 51–56.

10. Betty Glad, *Jimmy Carter: In Search of the Great White House* (New York: Norton, 1980), 306–8; Dumbrell, *The Carter Presidency,* 86–109.

11. Abernathy, "The Carter Administration," 106.

12. Stuart Eizenstat to Governor Carter and Senator Mondale, January 3, 1977; Eizenstat to Cabinet Secretaries-Designate, January 10, 1977, Box 232, White House Central File (WHCF), Domestic Policy Staff (DPS)–Eizenstat, Jimmy Carter Library (JCL).

13. Stuart Eizenstat Interview, January 29–30, 1982, William Burkett Miller Center of Public Affairs, University of Virginia, Project on the Carter Presidency, Transcripts (hereafter cited as Miller Center), 14–15, located in the JCL; "Carter Aide Lists Domestic Priorities," *Congressional Quarterly Weekly Report,* January 15, 1977, 85–86.

14. On Carter's record in government reorganization in Georgia, see Gary M. Fink, *Prelude to the Presidency: The Political Character and Legislative Leadership Style of Governor Jimmy Carter* (Westport, Conn.: Greenwood Press, 1980).

15. Bertram Carp and David Rubenstein Interview, March 6, 1982, Miller Center, 57.

16. Alfred W. Blumrosen, *Modern Law: The Law Transmission System and Equal Employment Opportunity* (Madison: University of Wisconsin Press, 1993), 161–63; Hanes Walton, Jr., *When the Marching Stopped: The Politics of Civil Rights Agencies* (Albany: State University of New York Press, 1988), 148–57.

17. John Battaile, "Businesses Resisting U.S. on Job-Bias Issue," *New York Times,* May 26, 1978.

18. Lipshutz and Eizenstat to Carter, June 27, 1978, Box 93, Staff Secretary File, JCL; Roger Wilkins, "New Legal Effort to End Job Discrimination," *New York Times,* January 9, 1978.

19. Eizenstat to Carter, February 6, 1978, Box 17, DPS–Civil Rights and Justice Cluster: Gutirrez file, JCL; Eleanor Holmes Norton to Eizenstat, August 24, 1978, Box 11, WHCF–Subject File, JCL; Martin Tolchin, "President Proposes Merger of Programs in Fight on Job Bias," *New York Times,* February 24, 1978.

20. U.S. Commission on Civil Rights, *The Federal Civil Rights Enforcement Budget: Fiscal Year 1983* (Washington, D.C.: Government Printing Office, 1982), 14–54.

21. Blumrosen, *Modern Law,* 167.

22. For a critical view of this transformation, see Herman Belz, *Equality Transformed: A Quarter-Century of Affirmative Action* (New Brunswick, N.J.: Transaction, 1991), esp. 111–33. For an approving view see Blumrosen, *Modern Law,* esp. 124–33, 161–81.

23. Section 103 (f) (2) of 91 Stat. 116, 42 U.S. 6705 (f); Mitchell quoted in 123 *Congressional Record,* pt. 4, February 23, 1977, 5098.

24. H.R. Rept. No. 92–1615, p. 3 (1972).

25. H.R. Rept. No. 94–466 (1975); General Accounting Office, "Questionable Effectiveness of the Sec. 8(a) Procurement Program," GGD-75–57 (1975); U.S. Commission on Civil Rights, *Minorities and Women as Government Contractors* (Washington, D.C.: Government Printing Office, 1975).

26. H.R. Rept. No. 94–1719, p. 182 (1977).

27. Hugh Davis Graham, *The Civil Rights Era* (New York: Oxford University Press, 1990), 278–97.

28. 13 CFR Sec. 124.8–1 (c) (1) (1977). On May 12, 1977, the Office of Management and Budget, following years of interagency discussions reaching back to 1964, promulgated Directive 15, which provided standard racial and ethnic classifications for data

collection and government record keeping. Directive 15 established four racial categories (American Indian or Alaskan Native, Asian or Pacific Islander, Black, and White) and one ethnic category (Hispanic), but it stipulated that the classifications should not be viewed as determinants of eligibility for participation in any federal program. See OMB, "Standards for Classification of Federal Data on Race and Ethnicity," 59 *Federal Register* 110, June 9, 1994, 29831–35.

29. *Fullilove v. Klutznick,* 448 U.S. 448 (1980), at 549. See George R. LaNoue and John C. Sullivan, "Presumptions for Preferences: The Small Business Administration's Decisions on Groups Entitled to Affirmative Action," *Journal of Policy History* 6 (1994): 439–67.

30. James T. Wooten, "President Suggests 'Demagogic' Remarks Are Harmful to Poor," *New York Times,* July 29, 1977; Louis E. Martin, "We Cannot Live by Spirit Alone," *Pittsburgh Courier,* August 6, 1977.

31. Watson to Costanza, Moe, Jordan, Eizenstat, Powell, Mitchell, and Aragon, August 23, 1977; Beth Abramowitz to Eizenstat, August 9, 1977, Box 237, DPS-Eizenstat, JCL.

32. "Talking Points for Jack H. Watson, Jr.," August 26, 1977, Box 237, DPS-Eizenstat, JCL.

33. "Minority Business Enterprise," September 12, 1977, *Public Papers of the Presidents of the United States: Jimmy Carter, 1977* (Washington, D.C.: Government Printing Office, 1978), book 2, 1579–80.

34. Eizenstat to Carter, February 13, 1978, Box 238, DPS-Eizenstat, JCL; Edward Cowan, "Agencies Reported Ready to Allot Building Contracts to Minorities," *New York Times,* February 20, 1978.

35. Draft, Eizenstat to Carter, February 10, 1978, Box 238, DPS-Eizenstat, JCL. In his signed memo of February 13, Eizenstat toned down his warning.

36. Office of Management and Budget to Carter, October 20, 1978; Eizenstat and Christopher Edley to Carter, October 24, 1978, Box 238, JCL.

37. Graham, *Civil Rights Era,* 258–65; Beth J. Lief and Susan Goering, "The Implementation of the Federal Mandate for Fair Housing," in *Divided Neighborhoods: Changing Patterns of Racial Segregation,* ed. Gary A. Tobin (Newbury Park, Calif.: Sage, 1987), 227–67.

38. *Fair Housing Act: Hearings before the Subcommittee on Civil and Constitutional Rights of the House Committee on the Judiciary,* 95th Cong., 2d sess. (Washington, D.C.: Government Printing Office, 1978); Douglas S. Massey and Nancy A. Denton, *American Apartheid: Segregation and the Making of the Underclass* (Cambridge, Mass.: Harvard University Press, 1993), 51–82.

39. "State of the Union Address," January 21, 1980, *Public Papers of Jimmy Carter, 1980,* book 1, 114.

40. Mondale to Carter, January 18, 1980; Eizenstat to Carter, January 21, 1980, Box 161, Staff Secretary File, JCL. Agenda, Fair Housing Legislative Meeting, from Anne Wexler and Louis Martin, April 16, 1980; Eizenstat to Carter, May 20, 1980, Box 205, DPS-Eizenstat, JCL.

41. Bob Malson to Eizenstat, June 20, 1980, Box 205, DPS-Eizenstat, JCL. On behalf of the congressional liaison staff, Malson's memo recommended against HUD's proposed executive order, and Carter noted, "I strongly agree."

42. *Congressional Quarterly Almanac 1980* (Washington, D.C.: Congressional Quarterly, 1981), 373–77; Martin Tolchin, "Battles in Congress over 2 Rights Issues Block Adjournment," *New York Times,* December 5, 1980. On December 9, the Senate voted 54–43 for cloture on HR 5200—six votes short of the sixty needed.

43. Gerald David Jaynes and Robin M. Williams, Jr., *A Common Destiny: Blacks and American Society* (Washington, D.C.: National Academy Press, 1989), 291–94.

44. Willis D. Hawley and Beryl A. Radin, *The Politics of Federal Reorganization: Creating the U.S. Department of Education* (New York: Pergamon Press, 1988); Erwin C. Hargrove, *Jimmy Carter as President: Leadership and the Politics of the Public Good* (Baton Rouge: Louisiana State University Press, 1988), 60–67; and Charles O. Jones, *The Trusteeship Presidency: Jimmy Carter and the United States Congress* (Baton Rouge: Louisiana State University Press, 1988), 184–88.

45. On the politics of federal education policy and government reorganization, see Hugh Davis Graham, *The Uncertain Triumph: Federal Education Policy in the Kennedy and Johnson Years* (Chapel Hill: University of North Carolina Press, 1984).

46. This was one reason Carter fired him in the cabinet shuffle of July 1979. Carp to Eizenstat, November 23, 26, 1977; Califano to Carter, November 26, 1977, Box 195, DPS-Eizenstat, JCL; McIntyre to Carter, November 28, 1977, Box 161, Staff Secretary File, JCL. Opposing the new department was an unusual left-right coalition including states-rights conservatives and traditional opponents of the NEA—the AFL-CIO, American Federation of Teachers, higher education interests, and the Catholic hierarchy.

47. Hawley and Radin, *Politics of Federal Reorganization,* 201–12; Coleman Brez Stein, Jr., *Sink or Swim: The Politics of Bilingual Education* (New York: Praeger, 1986), 29–70; Lawrence H. Fuchs, *The American Kaleidoscope: Race, Ethnicity, and the Civic Culture* (Hanover, N.H.: Wesleyan University Press, 1990), 458–73.

48. Marjorie Hunter, "Congress Approves Department of Education," *New York Times,* September 28, 1979; *Congressional Quarterly Almanac 1979* (Washington, D.C.: Congressional Quarterly, 1980), 465–74. Named to the Ninth Circuit Court of Appeals in 1969 by President Johnson, Judge Hufstedler was frequently mentioned in the press as a leading candidate to be the first woman appointed to the Supreme Court. According to the *Congressional Quarterly,* Hufstedler accepted the cabinet appointment on the condition that it would not exclude her from consideration for a Supreme Court nomination. See *Congress and the Nation, 1977–1980,* vol. 5 (Washington, D.C.: Congressional Quarterly, 1981), 668.

49. During the 1970s, the OCR in effect fell into court receivership, especially in the *Adams* case over school desegregation and the *Weal* case over sex discrimination. See Jeremy Rabkin, *Judicial Compulsions* (New York: Basic Books, 1989), 147–81; and Stephen C. Halpern, *On the Limits of Law* (Baltimore, Md.: Johns Hopkins University Press, 1995).

50. J. Stanley Pottinger to School Districts with More Than Five Percent National Origin–Minority Group Children, May 25, 1970, Box 15, Shirley M. Hufstedler Files, JCL.

51. Diane Ravitch, *The Troubled Crusade: American Education, 1945–1980* (New York: Basic Books, 1983), 274–80.

52. Office for Civil Rights, "Task Force Findings Specifying Remedies Available for Eliminating Past Educational Practices Ruled Unlawful under *Lau v. Nichols,*" Summer 1975, Box 15, Hufstedler Files, JCL.

53. Lewis H. Gann and Peter J. Duignan, *The Hispanics in the United States* (Boulder, Colo.: Westview Press, 1986), 232–39; David C. Gutierrez, *Walls and Mirrors: Mexican Americans, Mexican Immigrants, and the Politics of Ethnicity* (Berkeley: University of California Press, 1995), 183–87.

54. Joseph A. Califano, Jr., *Governing America: An Insider's Report from the White House and the Cabinet* (New York: Simon and Schuster, 1981), 312–14.

55. Glenn Kamber to Hufstedler, April 14, 1980, Box 12, Hufstedler Files, JCL. The coalition backing the minority-language regulations included the American G.I. Forum, Chicano Education Project, La Raza, Lawyers Committee for Civil Rights, League of United Latin American Citizens, Mexican American Legal Defense and Education Fund, NAACP, National Association for Asian and Pacific American Educators, National Association for Bilingual Education, and Native Americans for Bilingual Education ("Secretarial *Lau* Briefing: Key Advocate Groups Work Sheet," August 5, 1980, Box 12, Hufstedler Files, JCL).

56. Hawley and Radin, *Politics of Federal Reorganization,* 204.

57. Gene I. Maeroff, "U.S. Proposals Fuel Dispute over Bilingual Schooling," *New York Times,* August 19, 1980.

58. "Ending the Bilingual Double-Talk," *New York Times,* August 8, 1980, 28.

59. R. Robert Russell to Hufstedler, October 20, 1980, "Bilingual Education/RARG Review" folder, DPS–Bernick Files, JCL.

60. According to political scientist Stephen Skowronek's four-cell model of American presidencies, the Carter administration falls within a near-doomed category characterized by the politics of *disjunction,* wherein the president is affiliated with a regime facing public rejection (the Democratic tradition of New Deal–Great Society liberalism). See Stephen Skowronek, *The Politics Presidents Make: Leadership from John Adams to George Bush* (Cambridge, Mass.: Harvard University Press, 1993), 361–406.

61. See Jones, *Trusteeship Presidency.*

11

Feminism, Public Policy, and the Carter Administration

Susan M. Hartmann

As his presidential campaign entered its final month, Jimmy Carter outlined his positions on women's issues to representatives of women's organizations and to an additional crowd of three thousand people who had stood on a rain-soaked lawn for two hours to hear his words over a loudspeaker. Held just outside the nation's capital, the National Women's Agenda Conference attracted a broad spectrum of women, from Future Homemakers of America to members of the explicitly feminist National Organization for Women (NOW). President Gerald Ford had declined an invitation to the conference, and his challenger used the opportunity to stress differences between the two men. The Ford administration, Carter charged, had "only paid lip service to women's rights," offering women just "vetoes, indifference and empty rhetoric." Urging feminist leaders to "be as tough, as militant and as eloquent as you can be" in pushing demands, he outlined a nine-point program that included appointments of women to high government positions, a federal day care program, better enforcement of antidiscrimination policy, opportunities for women business owners, and support for ratification of the Equal Rights Amendment (ERA).[1]

The October speech highlighted Carter's recognition of the women's movement, then in its peak years, and his determination to seek women's votes by addressing gender-specific concerns. He negotiated directly with women's rights advocates at the Democratic National Convention, and he created the "51.3 percent committee" (named to reflect the percentage of women in the population) to advise his campaign on policy and strategy. Leading feminists responded warmly. Betty Friedan, who had contributed to the resurgence of feminism with her book *The Feminine Mystique*, commented, "This is so different from what it was eight years ago. I was moved to tears by Carter." Former Congresswoman Bella Abzug, one of the cofounders of the National Women's Political Caucus, echoed Friedan, calling Carter's pledge to involve women actively in his campaign and administration "a very important commitment we have never had from any President, candidate, or nominee." Carter, Abzug reported, wanted to eliminate legal barriers against women just as Lyndon Johnson had done with regard to blacks.[2]

Yet less than three years later, a deep rift divided the president from many politically active women. At the end of 1979, the NOW leadership voted to oppose his reelection, and prominent feminists lined up with other liberals behind Senator Edward Kennedy's campaign for the presidential nomination. Most feminist spokeswomen eventually came out for Carter, but only when confronted with the alternative of Ronald Reagan and a Republican platform opposing the ERA and calling for a constitutional amendment to ban abortions. Although the high levels of inflation and unemployment and the Iranian hostage crisis sealed Carter's defeat in 1980, his at best lukewarm support from key segments of the women's movement played into the hands of the antifeminist Ronald Reagan.

What caused this feminist fallout? Carter made good on his pledge to increase women's involvement in government; and the scant scholarship that has dealt with women's rights and the Carter administration has noted his unprecedented appointments of women to the executive branch and the federal judiciary. Scholars have attributed the breach between Carter and the women's movement to his stand on abortion, the failure of ERA ratification, and his dismissal of two very visible feminists, Midge Costanza in 1978 and Bella Abzug in 1979. Emily Walker Cook, in the most deeply researched and extensive study of the Carter administration and women's rights, charted this rocky relationship between the White House and the women's movement, analyzing the strategies of key White House advisers Costanza, Sarah Weddington, and Anne Wexler.[3]

This chapter expands on this existing scholarship by paying close attention to perceptions and expectations. First, there was a divergence between the Carter administration's perception of the women's movement and what that movement had actually become. In keeping with the president's emphasis on human rights worldwide, the administration fixed its attention on equal rights and opportunities; but the women's movement embraced a much wider range of issues that testified to the complexity of women's disadvantaged position and to the vast diversity of needs and interests among women. Second, just as Carter and his advisers misread the women's movement, so feminists—even while recognizing antifeminist forces that had been gathering momentum since 1971—tended to exaggerate both the power of their movement and the reach of the president's influence. As is true of social movements generally, activists' expectations in some regards exceeded the possible.

Finally, I will examine the considerable activity around feminist policy that did occur in the Carter administration but lay beyond the perceptions of his feminist critics and of later scholars. This action, taking place in such areas as education, employment, and domestic violence, is overshadowed by scholars' tendency to concentrate on the ERA and abortion. In fact, this activity often proceeded without presidential blessing, and the White House was slow to support or capitalize on such feminist policy initiatives. Yet they amounted to some significant advances for women, strengthening efforts against sex discrimination in higher education and employment, promoting women's ownership of business, and addressing such new issues as domestic violence and displaced homemakers.

THE ADMINISTRATION AND THE MOVEMENT

Any explanation of the breach between Carter and prominent feminists must begin with the recognition that social movements, by their very nature, are pitted against officials in power, setting goals far beyond the inclination or command of mainstream politicians to fulfill. To a certain extent, feminist leaders had become "insiders," able to capture the ear of Jimmy Carter during the 1976 campaign and appointed by him in relatively large numbers to his staff and the federal bureaucracy. Yet their very positions put constraints on them, as many found out when they tried to challenge Carter's opposition to federal funding of abortion.[4] They were often unable to satisfy the movement of "outsiders," fueled by the zeal of adherents who only recently had come to feminism.[5]

Feminists based their expectations of the Carter administration in part on the policy gains they had achieved in the past several years. Since 1970, Congress had passed the ERA, banned sex discrimination in education, strengthened enforcement of equal employment opportunity policy, outlawed discrimination in credit, opened the military academies to women, and authorized funding for a national women's conference to take place in 1977. All of these measures were approved by Republican presidents Richard Nixon and Gerald Ford. If the women's movement could accomplish all of this during Republican administrations, could they not achieve so much more with a Democrat in the White House?[6]

Carter encouraged such expectations during the campaign, wooing feminists as he did labor and civil rights leaders with liberal promises.[7] Yet his promise to do for women's rights what Johnson did for civil rights conflicted with his core principles of limited government and a balanced budget. Many feminist goals collided head-on with Carter's agenda because they would cost money and expand the size and reach of government. Moreover, the rapid rise of the New Right, with its emphasis on social issues that embraced traditional gender roles, only strengthened Carter's inclination to toe a centrist line. In the domestic policy realm, economic revival, deregulation, and a host of other projects claimed priority over women's issues even before stagflation and energy shortages took on crisis proportions. Both the quantity and the nature of the attention Carter paid to women's issues paled against feminist expectations.[8]

Not since Eleanor Roosevelt had a president's wife played such a strong role as Rosalynn Carter in her husband's political calculations. Yet, while Carter recognized his wife's intelligence and valued her advice, not all of his advisers respected the competence of women. Among the "good old boys" that Carter brought with him from Georgia, his key assistant, Hamilton Jordan, in particular did not appreciate powerful women and appeared particularly contemptuous of feminists. As one of Carter's closest advisers, Jordan displayed an overall indifference to women's issues and an open hostility to feminists who dared criticize the administration that fueled the strife between the president and the women's movement. A very moderate feminist and former federal employee urged Rosalynn Carter to get her husband "to consult with you, Judy [Carter] and Sarah Weddington on women's issues rather than Jody Powell or Ham Jordan, who manage to hurt the ERA and the women's movement with every move."[9]

Although the ERA was beyond Hamilton Jordan's ability to hurt or help, feminists criticized Carter for failing to deliver on that and abortion rights, the two issues of central importance to the women's movement. As Emily Walker Cook has shown, the Carters undertook "halfway efforts on behalf of the ERA" until 1980, when they went all out for ratification in Georgia during Carter's campaign for renomination. Yet the president had limited ability to influence the ERA, which after all required action by state legislatures. Long before he took office, a powerful STOP ERA campaign led by conservative Republican Phyllis Schlafly had stalled ratification. Having failed to organize ratification efforts at the state level until far too late, ERA supporters held Carter responsible for something largely beyond his control.[10]

Feminists came down even harder on the president's position on abortion. During the 1976 campaign, Carter had opposed a constitutional ban on abortion, but he also made clear his personal opposition to the procedure and to federal funding of it. Pro-choice advocates nonetheless hoped that his administration would liberally implement the Hyde amendment, a provision passed by Congress in 1976 that banned the use of federal Medicaid funds for abortion. But to many feminists Carter appeared insensitive when, confronted with the argument that the Hyde amendment was unfair to poor women, he replied that "many things in life . . . are not fair." Moreover, he promised strict enforcement of the amendment so that "women are not encouraged to lie and to use [the rape and incest exemption] as an excuse for abortions," and he encouraged Joseph Califano, his secretary of Health, Education, and Welfare (HEW), to issue stringent regulations to that effect.[11]

Differences over abortion led to another clash between feminists and the Carter administration. The first president to give a woman the title assistant to the president, Carter appointed Margaret (Midge) Costanza to head the White House Office for Public Liaison. A Democratic party activist and outspoken feminist who had campaigned for Carter, Costanza used her office to provide the women's movement and other groups access to the White House. But when she organized pro-choice advocates outside and within the administration and publicly challenged Carter on federal-funding-of-abortion policy, she lost her title and office in the summer of 1978. Relegated to the basement of the White House, deprived of most of her staff, and stripped of most of her duties, she resigned within a few weeks.[12]

Clearly Carter would not tolerate in his White House staff the militancy that he had urged upon feminists during the campaign.

Feminist displeasure with Carter's treatment of Costanza paled by comparison to the outrage expressed in January 1979 when he fired Bella Abzug as chair of the National Advisory Committee for Women (NACW), a body he had established to follow up on a broad policy agenda approved by the National Women's Conference that met in Houston, Texas, in 1977. Just as Costanza had considered her office to be a mouthpiece for disadvantaged groups, Abzug and other members of the NACW viewed that body more as a voice of the women's movement than as an instrument of the Carter administration. A founding member of Women Strike for Peace, Abzug saw the arms race as a factor contributing to poverty among women, who constituted 63 percent of the poor. Her committee took issue with the administration's economic and defense policies, in particular its plans to cut the domestic budget while increasing military spending. After the NACW issued a critical statement to the press and engaged in a heated discussion with the president, Hamilton Jordan told Abzug that she would be replaced. To protest the firing of a former congresswoman and one of the most prominent feminists in the country, a majority of the committee members resigned. Even feminists who disliked Abzug's aggressiveness considered her abrupt firing "stupid." Although Carter reconstituted the committee and a significant number of feminists remained loyal to him, what Gloria Steinem called "the Friday night massacre" further poisoned relations between the president and the women's movement.[13]

At the root of Carter's conflict with Abzug and the NACW was the administration's unresponsiveness to the changing nature of the women's movement. For a variety of reasons, both Carter and key movement organizations such as NOW, the Women's Equity Action League, and the National Women's Political Caucus placed ratification of the ERA at the top of their priorities. But by the mid-1970s the women's movement had so broadened and diversified that success on no single issue could begin to satisfy feminist aspirations.[14] For example, most of the organizations associated with the National Coalition for Women and Girls in Education supported the ERA, but they were equally concerned about enforcement of Title IX. And new organizations, such as the National Coalition Against Domestic Violence, sprang up as feminism encouraged exploration of every aspect of women's disadvantaged position.[15] As we shall see, the Carter administration moved slowly to embrace issues beyond the ERA, even when such support bore little cost.[16]

The controversy over Abzug and the NACW made clear that leaders of the women's movement understood sexism as much more than a simple denial of equal rights under the law. Contrary to popular—and even scholarly—assumptions about the women's movement, most feminists did not narrowly focus on providing equal opportunities, from which white, middle-class women could most easily benefit. Indeed, feminists and women's organizations expressed their concern for disadvantaged women to the administration from the beginning.

Just after Carter's election, his top campaign adviser on women's issues, Mary King, submitted a list of recommendations for the new president. Not even mentioning the ERA, her memo insisted that all policy decisions must include attention to women and specifically stressed the importance of reviewing "all government budgets as they pertain to women."[17] Early in 1977, representatives of more than fifty women's organizations protested that the president's economic stimulus plan lacked any mention of women or of their particular needs for employment and job training, noting that minority women faced "double discrimination."[18] Later that year, Gloria Steinem and others pressed White House staff to consider the availability of jobs for women in any strategy for welfare reform.[19] It should have come as no surprise in 1979 when Abzug and the NACW challenged the administration's budget, objecting to a proposed 10 percent hike in military spending and underlining the proposed cuts in social welfare programs that would hurt poor, working-class, and minority women.[20] In addressing women's deprivations that were rooted in the current resource-distribution structure and in claiming a role in setting national economic priorities, the women's movement issued a much more radical challenge than a call for equal rights.[21]

Left-liberals such as Bella Abzug and explicitly feminist organizations such as NOW exercised no monopoly over feminism's claim to place women's needs at the center of economic and defense planning. The NACW represented a broad range of women who belonged to traditional women's organizations as well as self-defined feminist groups. Abzug's temporary replacement, Marjorie Bell Chambers, headed a traditional organization, the American Association of University Women, yet within two months of Abzug's dismissal, Chambers was expressing some of the same concerns. Albeit with more diplomatic language and some recognition of administration efforts on behalf of women, Chambers insisted that Carter's anti-inflation program would hurt women because of their concentration in low-paying jobs and the wage gap between men and women, their low rate of union membership, and their relatively high presence in low-level federal jobs.[22]

Even after Carter reconstituted the committee as the President's Advisory Committee for Women, which emphasized its responsibility to the president, and after he appointed Lynda Johnson Robb as chair, he continued to hear from women about his economic priorities. In March 1980, Robb wrote Carter, expressing gratitude that representatives of women's organizations had for the first time taken part in budget consultations. Yet, as the administration continued to look for ways to trim the budget, Robb insisted that these not come at women's expense. Reducing expenditures in "vital programs," such as Food Stamps, assistance to poor women and their infants, job training for displaced homemakers, domestic violence prevention, and educational equity, she wrote, would be a "serious disappointment to the women of this country." Although even more conciliatory than Chambers, Robb continued to maintain women's stake not just in equal rights under the law but in the allocation of national resources. That position echoed in much stronger terms from a diverse group of women's professional, religious, welfare, and explicitly feminist organizations, which considered cutting only domestic programs "incredibly shortsighted and outrageous" and claimed that "one-sided slashes . . . strangle our most vulnerable citizens."[23]

FEMALE APPOINTMENTS AND "WOODWORK FEMINISTS"

The highly publicized discord between the Carter administration and the women's movement obscured significant feminist policy initiatives that did occur. Carter took particular pride in his appointments of women and minorities to federal agencies, the federal courts, and his White House staff. About 22 percent of his selections were women, and he named more than forty women to federal judgeships, quadrupling the number of women who had ever served on the federal bench. Although he could never satisfy movement advocates, he did make more diverse appointments than any president before Bill Clinton. And many of those whom he appointed played key roles in the development of feminist policy initiatives.

Not only did Carter set records in his appointment of women officials, he also was the first president to appoint visible feminists to important positions. (As a Democrat, he could hardly avoid selecting feminists, since so many prominent Democratic women had joined the women's movement.) When Midge Costanza left the White House staff, Carter pulled Sarah Weddington from the Department of Agriculture to concentrate on women's issues in the White House. A former Texas legislator, Weddington had established her feminist credentials when she took *Roe v. Wade* up to the Supreme Court. From mid-1978 until the end of the administration, Weddington cultivated women's organizations, represented their concerns to the president, and sought women's votes for Carter's reelection.[24] Another feminist, Margaret McKenna, served as deputy counsel to the president; and Elizabeth Abramowitz, a founder of the Lobby for the Black Women's Agenda, worked on women's issues in the domestic policy staff.[25]

Carter appointed feminists to high-level cabinet and agency posts as well, including Eleanor Holmes Norton as head of the Equal Employment Opportunity Commission (EEOC); Mary Frances Berry first as HEW assistant secretary and then as vice chair of the Commission on Civil Rights; Mary King as deputy director of ACTION (the agency that oversaw the Peace Corps, VISTA, and other volunteer programs); Juanita Kreps as secretary of commerce; and Patricia Roberts Harris initially as secretary of the Department of Housing and Urban Development (HUD) and subsequently as secretary of HEW. Each of these women had publicly supported feminist aspirations. For example, Patricia Roberts Harris wrote in 1972 that "women's liberation is the best thing that ever happened" to higher education, calling the university "one of the most sexist institutions in this country."[26] Juanita Kreps, an economics professor at Duke University, had also spoken out against sex discrimination. When Carter met with Commerce Department employees just three weeks after she became head, women thanked Carter for her appointment. According to one, "She has done more for our morale . . . than all former Secretaries put together," no doubt referring to Kreps's hiring of women into five of the top ten slots in the department.[27]

Mary King had spent the early 1960s working in the Student Nonviolent Coordinating Committee, and in 1965 she coauthored with Casey Hayden the memo that circulated around the New Left and sparked the rise of the women's liberation movement. She joined Carter's presidential campaign in 1974, headed his 51.3 percent campaign committee, and informally advised him on women's policy throughout his administration.[28] Her position as deputy director of ACTION enabled her to take certain initiatives without having to obtain congressional or presidential authorization. For example, within months of her appointment, King authorized ACTION to provide funds and support VISTA volunteers for women's centers that provided services to victims of domestic violence or displaced homemakers. In addition, King's personal ties to the Carters provided alternative opportunities to push feminist issues, as she did, for instance, in urging that the First Lady's project on aging include Tish Sommers, founder of the Alliance for Displaced Homemakers.[29]

Carter's appointment of these high-level women augmented the feminist presence in lower levels of the bureaucracy. For example, Connie Downey, in HEW's office of planning and evaluation, challenged her boss, Joseph Califano, on his antiabortion stand. When he promised to stress alternatives to abortion, she responded that "the literal alternatives to it are suicide, motherhood, and some would add, madness." More fruitfully, she worked with other feminists within and outside of HEW to obtain federal support for domestic violence programs.[30]

Feminist networks, both formal and informal, operated in the Carter administration. The oldest, Federally Employed Women (FEW), had formed in the 1960s and numbered more than three thousand in the late 1970s. FEW pressured the White House not just for policies that affected themselves and other government officials but also for legislation dealing with displaced homemakers, discrimination against pregnant women, and abortion rights.[31] Employees in the Women's Bureau of the Department of Labor organized a second network, the Feminist Connection. Composed of about forty individuals responsible for women's issues in various departments and agencies, the Feminist Connection met every three weeks to discuss "problems related to educational, occupational, health, financial, civil rights, and other needs of American women from all social classes, ethnic and racial groups."[32] In informal networks, feminists also enhanced their power and supported one another, as did Mary King when she wrote Sarah Weddington shortly after the Abzug debacle with advice about how to maintain her own position and also build support among women for Carter.[33]

FEMINIST INITIATIVES IN THE SUBPRESIDENCY AND CONGRESS

This feminist presence in the executive branch produced or assisted a variety of policy advances for women even in the absence of White House attention. Pushed by the women's movement, in some cases these measures originated in Congress and then won presidential approval; in others, the initiative developed in a particular department or agency. Most of them came in the last two years of the Carter administration, reflecting the effects of the National Women's Conference of August 1977, Sarah Weddington's arrival on the White House staff in 1978, damage control after the Abzug firing, the approaching election, and Senator Edward Kennedy's challenge to Carter's renomination.[34]

Widespread employment discrimination against pregnant women mobilized a diverse coalition of women's organizations and labor unions. In the 1970s, more than 25 percent of women workers had no right even to unpaid maternity leave or to reemployment; and a large majority of employers' benefits programs denied the use of sick leave for pregnancy-related disability or illness and excluded medical expenses related to pregnancy and delivery. On the basis of such practices, a group of women workers and their union charged General Electric with sex discrimination under Title VII of the Civil Rights Act of 1964. Although the plaintiffs won in the lower court, in 1976, the Supreme Court ruled against them. Making what appeared to many a ludicrous distinction, the Court explained that such denial of benefits did not constitute sex discrimination because it affected pregnant persons, not women. Consequently, feminists and labor unions turned to Congress for legislation.[35]

In April 1977, representatives from the Department of Labor, the Department of Justice, and the EEOC testified in favor of the bill, but Carter refused to put his own imprimatur on the legislation. On a recommendation from his top aides that he give it his personal support, he penned, "Leave me out of it for now." While, in this case, Stuart Eizenstat, head of Carter's Domestic Policy Staff, had recommended action, in general Carter's position reflected the tendency of his advisers to seal him off from matters that might be controversial. Leaving issues to be handled in the departments and agencies was, according to Beth Abramowitz, "an operating principle . . . you don't bring controversy in. You keep it out there."[36]

Carter remained silent on the pregnancy disability bill until September 1978, when he submitted a general report to Congress on policy concerning women. The report grew out of the National Women's Conference, which had included a ban on discrimination against pregnant women in its "National Plan of Action," a comprehensive agenda of policy demands for women. In outlining to Congress what the administration had done and would do in response to the National Plan of Action, Carter asked for passage of several measures, including the pregnancy disability act. The bill was already in conference, and Carter signed it one month later.[37]

Women's organizations and legislators similarly took the initiative in addressing the problem of displaced homemakers, forced by divorce or widowhood to support themselves after years of absence from the labor force. In 1974, a West Coast feminist and advocate for older women, Tish Sommers, coined the term and launched the Alliance for Displaced Homemakers the following year. During the 1976 campaign, Carter called displaced homemakers "among the most vulnerable members of our society," to whose needs "a compassionate government" would respond, but he avoided the issue once elected.[38] When Midge Costanza arranged a White House meeting for representatives of the Alliance for Displaced Homemakers in June 1977, she discovered that none of Carter's advisers knew how the administration should respond to pending legislation sponsored by Senator Birch Bayh and Representative Yvonne Braithwaite Burke. Eight months later, Beth Abramowitz reminded Eizenstat that the administration "has yet to fulfill its 'commitment' to displaced homemakers."[39]

Eventually the Department of Labor worked with congressional advocates to allocate funds for training and employment for displaced homemakers in a bill renewing the Comprehensive Employment and Training Act (CETA). As was the case with the pregnancy discrimination legislation, Carter weighed in near the end of the campaign, listing the CETA bill as another measure that Congress should pass in his report on the administration's response to the National Plan of Action. In the first year of funding, the administration budgeted just $5 million of CETA funds for displaced homemakers, but even these small grants made a difference to grassroots programs struggling for legitimacy and state support.

On a third feminist policy initiative, assistance to women business owners, the White House played a more active role, largely in response to feminists within the administration. While Mary King worked in Carter's 1976 campaign, she also served as president of the National Association of Women Business Owners (NAWBO), a group that began informally in 1974. King persuaded Carter to make a campaign pledge to support women's business enterprise, and Secretary of Commerce Juanita Kreps pushed him to establish an Interagency Task Force on Women Business Owners in August 1977.[40]

Carter accepted the task force report in July 1978, but it took more feminist prodding to produce action. Following a familiar pattern in which feminists capitalized on initiatives for minorities, Congress provided a precedent for them in 1978 when it passed legislation establishing a set-aside program, the so-called SBA 8(a) program, for minority businesses. Some feminists and business owners had sought to include white women in the legislation, but those associated with the task force did not want to undercut support for minorities. Upon signing the minority business measure, Carter promised new steps to aid women, but women in the administration had to remind him of that pledge. Thus, Patricia Cloherty, Kreps's deputy administrator and the key individual behind the women's business program, warned Carter that "we are . . . under some pressure to move quickly," so that women would not see the program for minority businesses "as a loss to women of resources which might have been made available to them." After Cloherty's successor threatened Eizenstat with a demonstration of women entrepreneurs at the White House, he met with her and forwarded a set of recommendations to the president. By executive order in May 1979, Carter established a women's business enterprise program, improving women's access to Small Business Administration loans and technical assistance, as well as to federal contracts.[41]

Although the abortion issue complicated passage of the Pregnancy Disability Act, for the most part these three issues evoked little controversy. The president could respond to initiatives coming from Congress or from his appointees in the executive branch at little cost, and he did so, however belatedly. Two other issues aroused much more contention and carried more political liabilities. A more detailed examination of policy development on domestic violence and on gender equity in intercollegiate athletics illuminates the forces promoting and constraining feminist policy and evinces the importance of the feminist presence in the executive branch.

Domestic Violence

Women in the radical branch of women's liberation first called attention to the problem of domestic violence in 1971. By the mid-1970s, feminists had established dozens of shelters for battered women throughout the country and had won some state and private support. Throughout the Carter years, advocates for battered women campaigned for a federal program of support for shelters. Although feminists could not persuade the president to get behind the issue until it was too late, activities in the subpresidency gave visibility to the problem, helped strengthen the movement, and provided material resources for domestic violence projects.

Feminists in the executive branch sponsored two events that spotlighted the issue and gave a shot in the arm to advocates for battered women, in effect helping grassroots activists to organize nationally so that they, in turn, could pressure the government. In July 1977, Midge Costanza and her associate Jan Peterson (who had helped found a Brooklyn battered women's shelter) organized a White House meeting that brought together battered women themselves, activists on the issue, and government officials.[42] Six months later, at the end of January 1978, the U.S. Commission on Civil Rights sponsored a consultation on policy issues relating to battered women. Both of these meetings enabled activists from around the country to build ties and exchange information. During the second meeting, they established a formal organization, the National Coalition Against Domestic Violence (NCADV). With offices in Washington, the NCADV represented about 150 community organizations that served battered women.[43] Several federal bodies had already initiated modest domestic violence projects, and these meetings gave shelter advocates information about programs from which they might obtain assistance. Betty Kaufman, an attorney at HUD, for example, explained that new HUD regulations being drafted (in response to recommendations of the Minnesota Women's Advocate Group) would specifically allow Community Development Block Grant funds to be used to purchase and rehabilitate property for battered women's shelters. Jeannie Niedermeyer announced a new program in the Law Enforcement Assistance Administration (LEAA) that would support three or four local demonstration projects. Deputy director of the Women's Bureau, Mary Hilton, explained how local battered women's programs could get CETA funds. And the Women's Bureau distributed a packet of information listing nine sources of federal funds for battered women's projects.[44]

The federally sponsored meetings also helped to spur policy development by bringing together officials from several departments and agencies. After the White House meeting, Costanza organized follow-up meetings, and an informal group drawn from federal bodies with domestic violence projects began to meet regularly.[45] Women staff members urged creation of a domestic violence program, and Democratic legislators, including Senators Edward Kennedy and Alan Cranston and Representatives Lindy Boggs and Barbara Mikulski, sponsored legislation in the Ninety-fifth Congress. But the president and HEW secretary Califano remained silent, satisfied to address the needs of battered women through projects already launched under existing authority. The domestic violence bill passed the Senate but failed in the House.[46]

Not until 1979 did Carter and Califano change their minds, after considerable pressure from the NCADV, other women's and feminist organizations, a group of women in HEW, and Sarah Weddington in the White House. In April 1979, Carter formalized the interagency network by creating an Interdepartmental Committee on Domestic Violence. On the same day Califano announced establishment of an Office on Domestic Violence within HEW. But despite pleas from the NCADV in February and March, Carter remained silent on legislation until December 1979, sending his endorsement just before a bill to fund community-based shelters and other services for battered women passed the House. By then the right had grasped its potential as a political issue. As the Senate considered the bill during 1979, Phyllis Schlafly, spokespersons for Jerry Falwell's Moral Majority, and others castigated shelters as feminist "indoctrination centers" and decried "federal intrusion into family matters." A bill squeaked by the Senate, but when a reconciled measure came back, the right prevailed. Activists laid the blame at the White House, charging that it "had to move earlier, but only its female staff cared about this legislation."[47]

June Zeitlin, head of the recently created Office of Domestic Violence (ODV), preferred to concentrate on how far the legislation had gotten. "It is very unusual that women's legislation is taken up so fast." The president could not take credit that it went so far, but many of the feminists appointed in his administration could because they had helped make visible the issue and assisted activists who organized around it. The legislation's failure meant that Zeitlin lost her job, because the ODV could not continue without authorization. It did not mean, however, the end of federal support for domestic violence programs, nor did it negate the important initiatives undertaken during the Carter years.[48]

Under Patricia Roberts Harris and urged on by its Office of Women's Policy and Program staff, HUD for the first time used Community Development Block Grant funds for domestic violence projects. By 1980, it had expended more than $3 million to assist fifty-three shelters. In addition, in 1978 the LEAA made violence in the home a priority. Even as the agency's discretionary funds were cut severely, it increased expenditures on domestic violence to $3 million by 1980, supporting projects providing counseling, shelter, hot lines, professional training, and data collection. Although these sums were minuscule in the context of the federal budget, small amounts of money could often mean survival to grassroots projects. And the visibility and credibility resulting from federal attention, however meager, leveraged advocates to seek assistance from state and local governments and the private sector.[49]

Title IX and Women's Sports

As HEW secretary Califano struggled with the issue of gender equity in intercollegiate athletics, he was reported to have moaned, "Why did I have to be Secretary when this mess came up?"[50] Unlike the issue of domestic violence, Title IX enforcement drew punishing attacks from the mainstream, specifically from higher education officials and the male sports establishment. In their claims to equity in athletics, women stood alone, abandoned by much of higher education's leadership. Consequently, action by the Carter administration on Title IX was all the more critical.

Congress passed Title IX in 1972 with little controversy. But when it became clear that Title IX meant that colleges and universities could no longer lavish funds on football without providing considerable sums for women's sports, hundreds of institutions and the National Collegiate Athletic Association, which represented more than seven hundred colleges and universities, entered a protracted campaign to exclude expenditures on football from counting in any equity plans. In 1974, an effort in Congress to exempt revenue-producing sports resulted in a compromise requiring colleges and universities to make "reasonable provisions" for women's teams that reflected the nature of particular sports. In 1975, HEW issued guidelines for implementing Title IX, but institutions were not required to be in compliance until 1978, and the intercollegiate sports establishment continued to seek to exempt football.

When Califano inherited the issue upon taking office in 1977, virtually nothing had been done about compliance. He soon recognized that it would be in some respect as difficult for women to get "a fair share of intercollegiate athletic programs at some of the big time football colleges as it had been to get James Meredith into the University of Mississippi in 1962." For his part, Califano could not grasp why equal opportunity in athletics was so important to women, especially when compared with "vicious racial discrimination and severe economic deprivation" that other groups suffered. Feminists on his staff made a difference. Califano's press officer, journalist Eileen Shanahan, had sued the *New York Times* for sex discrimination, and the chair of his Advisory Committee on the Rights and Responsibilities of Women, Aileen Hernandez, had been president of NOW. They and others instructed him about the symbolic and real significance of equity in college sports.[51]

In December 1978, nearly two years into the Carter administration and after the deadline for compliance had passed, Califano issued new guidelines for compliance with Title IX. They called for "substantially equal per capita expenditures" for women and men but also allowed for unequal spending if it resulted from "nondiscriminatory factors." Once they realized that football was still not excluded, the sports establishment stepped up its pressure. Presidents of fifty football giants, including Notre Dame, Ohio State, the University of Texas, and the University of Southern California, opposed the equal per capita provision and asked that institutions be allowed to develop their own nondiscrimination plans, which one feminist called "like asking the fox to come up with a plan for guarding the chickens."[52]

Texan Jim Wright, the House majority leader, communicated to Califano his surprise that football was not excluded and lofted a thinly veiled threat that Congress would act if the administration did not. Georgia Congressman Doug Barnard, Jr., wrote Stuart Eizenstat, repeating a warning made by Fred C. Davison, president of the University of Georgia. Compliance with Title IX would require the University of Georgia to spend an additional $1.1 million, "with the sole outcome being the destruction of the University's sole revenue producing sport."[53]

Although feminists were not entirely satisfied with Califano's interpretation, they mustered a strong defense against attempts to revise it to exclude revenue-producing sports. In April 1979, representatives from the Association for Intercollegiate Athletics for Women and the National Coalition for Women and Girls in Education met with Califano, and several hundred women rallied across from the White House and marched to the Capitol, chanting "Hold the line on Title IX." As the sports establishment stepped up its lobbying for Congress to rescue football, liberal legislators begged Califano to keep them out of it. Men whose districts included such schools as Michigan and Notre Dame sought rescue from the dilemma of angering either women's groups or football advocates. Consequently, Califano withdrew the guidelines and sent them back to the drawing board, where they stood when Califano left the administration in July 1979.[54]

Califano's successor, Patricia Roberts Harris, needed no persuasion about the gravity of sex discrimination in higher education, having spoken out against it before university presidents in 1972. She issued a new set of policy guidelines for enforcement of Title IX in December 1979. At the press conference announcing the interpretation, Harris held up a photograph of the 1885 Wellesley crew team to underscore the long history of women's interest in sports and by implication the long denial of their right to equity. Requiring that colleges and universities allocate financial aid in proportion to the numbers of men and women participating in athletics, the guidelines also exhorted institutions to improve opportunities for women coaches and athletic directors as well as students. Women's organizations were "delighted." Seven years after Congress enacted Title IX, the government put colleges and universities on notice that strict enforcement would begin.[55] Although Carter had spoken out for thorough enforcement of Title IX during his 1976 campaign, as president he managed to keep away from the issue of intercollegiate athletics. Unlike his practice regarding other gains for women, whether the administration had pushed for them or not, he did not even claim credit for the Harris guidelines on Title IX.[56]

CONCLUSION

Because the original New Deal policy order failed to embrace women's rights and the traditional New Deal political coalition never included feminists as feminists, the Carter administration's attention to the women's movement in terms of both policy and politics represented a break with the Roosevelt legacy. As one of the last movements to arise during the upheavals of the 1960s, the women's movement, like the environmental movement, continued on an upward trajectory and achieved small but significant policy goals during the Carter administration. Although most feminists were far from satisfied with Carter's record on women's issues, his record nonetheless represented striking discontinuity with that of his successor, Ronald Reagan. Notable, too, was the great difference in the two presidents' appointments: not only did Reagan appoint far fewer women, despite his naming of the first woman to the Supreme Court, but those he did appoint disdained the use of federal spending or regulatory power to enhance women's opportunities and welfare.

In contrast, new policies for women during the Carter administration modestly expanded the regulatory and welfare state. Those initiatives in turn reflected the evolution and diversification of a feminist agenda sensitive to the needs and interests of various groups of women. Although the women's business enterprise program and strict enforcement of Title IX would benefit relatively privileged women, Title IX also had the potential to create educational opportunities for minority women as intercollegiate athletics did for men of color. Banning discrimination against pregnant women was most critical for working-class women, as demonstrated by organized labor's strong role in the campaign. Domestic violence cut across all class, racial, and ethnic lines, but centers and services were even more essential to women with few material resources, as they were for displaced homemakers.

In addition, feminists' demands on the Carter administration reflected an understanding of women's subordinate status that required more than simply equal opportunity to remedy. Their attacks on Carter's budget proposals recognized that women suffered disproportionately from cuts in safety-net programs. In addition to claiming a voice in the setting of national economic and defense priorities, feminists also pushed entirely new issues into the spotlight. The concept of displaced homemaker did not exist before 1974, and when bills dealing with domestic violence first appeared in Congress, some legislators thought they were dealing with terrorism at airports.

Carter's equal rights approach to women's issues, along with his determination to hew to the center line and to harness inflation, made him a hesitant or reluctant partner to most of these initiatives. Indeed, as Hugh Davis Graham has concluded with respect to civil rights, Carter administration policy "was shaped less by the president than by policy entrepreneurs in Congress and the sub-presidency."[57] Of key importance were the feminists whom Carter himself had put on the White House staff and in the departments and agencies. They both initiated policy, as Mary King did when she enabled VISTA volunteers to work at centers for victims of domestic violence or for displaced homemakers, and pressured Carter to act, as Juanita Kreps did in the case of assistance to women's businesses. King, Kreps, Harris, Weddington, Shanahan, and others provided a voice for various elements of the feminist agenda throughout much of the executive branch. Thus, Carter's appointments may well have constituted his greatest contribution to the considerable range of feminist policy that ensued during his administration.

NOTES

The author is grateful for criticism and suggestions from Gary Fink, Hugh Davis Graham, Cynthia Harrison, Joan Hoff, and Leila Rupp.

1. *Washington Post,* October 3, 1976, A1, A3.

2. Peter G. Bourne, *Jimmy Carter: A Comprehensive Biography from Plains to Post-presidency* (New York: Scribner, 1997), 345; Irene Tinker, ed., *Women in Washington: Advocates for Public Policy* (Beverly Hills, Calif.: Sage, 1983), 46; Bella Abzug with Mim Kelber, *Gender Gap: Bella Abzug's Guide to Political Power for American Women* (Boston: Houghton Mifflin, 1984), 45–50. Abzug and Friedan quoted in Kandy Stroud, *How Jimmy Won: The Victory Campaign from Plains to the White House* (New York: William Morrow, 1977), 326–27.

3. Emily Walker Cook, "Women White House Advisors in the Carter Administration: Presidential Stalwarts or Feminist Advocates?" (Ph.D. diss., Vanderbilt University, 1995). See also John Dumbrell, *The Carter Presidency: A Re-evaluation,* 2d ed. (Manchester, England: Manchester University Press, 1995), 63–85; M. Glenn Abernathy, "The Carter Administration and Domestic Civil Rights," in *The Carter Years: The President and Policy Making,* ed. M. Glenn Abernathy, Dilys M. Hill, and Phil Williams (New York: St. Martin's

Press, 1984), 125–43; Anne N. Costain, *Inviting Women's Rebellion: A Political Process Interpretation of the Women's Movement* (Baltimore, Md.: Johns Hopkins University Press, 1992), 93–95; and Tinker, *Women in Washington,* passim.

4. The best account of the abortion controversy is provided by Cook, "Women White House Advisors in the Carter Administration." See also Joseph Califano, Jr., *Governing America: An Insider's Report from the White House and the Cabinet* (New York: Simon and Schuster, 1981), 54–67.

5. NOW, for example, grew from about 1,000 to 40,000 between 1967 and 1974, and then to 125,000 in 1978. The National Women's Political Caucus, founded in 1972, grew to 50,000 in 1978. See Jo Freeman, *The Politics of Women's Liberation* (New York: David McKay, 1975), 87; Joyce Gelb and Marion Lief Palley, *Women and Public Policies* (Princeton, N.J.: Princeton University Press, 1982), 28.

6. I am indebted to Cynthia Harrison for this insight.

7. Bourne, *Jimmy Carter,* 416–17.

8. Carter's memoirs, from which women are entirely absent, reflect this scale of priorities. Jimmy Carter, *Keeping Faith: Memoirs of a President* (New York: Bantam Books, 1982).

9. Bourne, *Jimmy Carter,* 314–15, 345, 363–64. Jordan played a key role in the firing of Bella Abzug. Jordan's memoir is almost gleeful when he notes that feminists' criticism of Carter gave them the antifeminist Reagan, whom they "so richly deserve." Letter, Catherine East to Rosalynn Carter, January 29, 1979, Box 13, Sarah Weddington Files, Jimmy Carter Library (JCL).

10. Cook, "Women White House Advisors in the Carter Administration," 196–210; Mary Frances Berry, *Why ERA Failed: Politics, Women's Rights, and the Amending Process of the Constitution* (Bloomington: Indiana University Press, 1986), 64–68. Just one state ratified in 1975 and another in 1977; after Congress extended the deadline in 1978, the window closed in 1982, three states short of the thirty-eight required for ratification.

11. Susan M. Hartmann, *From Margin to Mainstream: American Women and Politics since 1960* (Philadelphia: Temple University Press, 1989), 150–51; *Public Papers of the Presidents: Jimmy Carter, 1978* (Washington, D.C.: Government Printing Office, 1979), 356.

12. Cook, "Women White House Advisors in the Carter Administration," 20–25, 58–76.

13. Hartmann, *From Margin to Mainstream,* 151; Rhodri Jeffreys-Jones, *Changing Differences: Women and the Shaping of American Foreign Policy, 1917–1994* (New Brunswick, N.J.: Rutgers University Press), 131–54; Catherine East to Rosalynn Carter, January 29, 1979, Box 13, Weddington Files, JCL.

14. For an example of the breadth and diversity of the women's movement, see Ad Hoc Coalition for Women, Summary of Priority Requests Made by Coalition in Meeting with President Carter and Vice President Mondale at White House Meeting, March 10, 1977, Box 25, Martha Mitchell Files, JCL. For a survey of NOW's agendas in the 1970s, see Winifred D. Wandersee, *On the Move: American Women in the 1970s* (Boston: Twayne, 1988), 47–50.

15. For discussions of the changing nature of the women's movement, see Tinker, *Women in Washington;* Flora Davis, *Moving the Mountain: The Women's Movement in America since 1960* (New York: Simon and Schuster, 1991); Myra Marx Ferree and Beth

B. Hess, *Controversy and Coalition: The New Feminist Movement across Three Decades of Change* (New York: Twayne, 1994), 101–16; and Wandersee, *On the Move.*

16. Costain, *Inviting Women's Rebellion,* 94–95.

17. Mary E. King to Carter, November 2, 1976, Box 145, Margaret McKenna Files, JCL.

18. Ad Hoc Coalition for Women, Summary of Priority Requests Made by Coalition, March 10, 1977.

19. Beth Abramowitz to Eizenstat, September 12, 1977, Box 323, Domestic Policy Staff (DPS)-Eizenstat, JCL.

20. Bella S. Abzug and Carmen Delgado Votaw, Co-Chairs, National Advisory Committee for Women, Statement to President Carter, January 12, 1979, Box 14, Weddington Files, JCL.

21. Hartmann, *From Margin to Mainstream,* 151–52.

22. Marjorie Bell Chambers to Carter, March 30, 1979, Box FG-221, White House Central Files (WHCF), JCL.

23. Lynda Johnson Robb to Carter, March 5, 1980, and March 21, 1980, Box FI-11, WHCF, JCL; Statement on Women and the Federal Budget, March 12, 1980, Box 20, Weddington Files, JCL. Among the groups signing on to the sharp criticism of domestic budget cuts were the American Home Economics Association, the American Nurses Association, Federally Employed Women, the National Assembly of Women Religious, Rural American Women, the Mexican American Women's National Association, and the National Hook-Up of Black Women, as well as the explicitly feminist groups NOW, WEAL, and the National Women's Political Caucus.

24. Sarah Weddington, *A Question of Choice* (New York: Putnam, 1992), 186–99.

25. Beth Abramowitz, Exit Interview, August 23, 1979, 1, 4, 6, JCL.

26. Patricia Roberts Harris, "Problems and Solutions in Achieving Equality for Women," in *Women in Higher Education,* ed. W. Todd Furniss and Patricia Albjerg Graham (Washington, D.C.: American Council on Education, 1974), 12, 14.

27. Juanita M. Kreps, "The Woman Professional in Higher Education," in Furniss and Graham, *Women in Higher Eduction,* 75–94; *Public Papers of Jimmy Carter, 1977,* 113, 115.

28. Mary E. King, *Freedom Song: A Personal History of the 1960s Civil Rights Movement* (New York: William Morrow, 1987), 443–68, 541–42; King to Carter, November 2, 1976, Box 145, McKenna Files, JCL.

29. King to Costanza, August 23, 1977, Box FG-171, WHCF, JCL.; King to Mary Hoyt, May 16, 1977, WHCF, Name File: King, JCL.

30. *New York Times,* November 27, 1977, 1.

31. Jan Peterson to Costanza, July 1, 1977, Box HU-14, WHCF HU1-6, JCL.

32. Jean Lipman-Blumen to Costanza, February 9, 1977, Box 10, Costanza Files, JCL.

33. King to Weddington, February 26, 1979, Box 145, McKenna Files, JCL.

34. For the White House concern about Kennedy's challenge in the context of women's issues, see Weddington to Carter, December 3, 1979, Box 7, DPS Files, JCL.

35. Gelb and Palley, *Women and Public Policies,* 158–60.

36. Abramowitz, Exit Interview, 13–14.

37. *Public Papers of Jimmy Carter, 1978,* 1643.

38. Laurie Shields, *Displaced Homemakers: Organizing for a New Life* (New York: McGraw-Hill, 1981), 121.

39. Abramowitz to Eizenstat, February 13, 1978, Box HU-14, WHCF, HU1–6, JCL.

40. Tinker, *Women in Washington,* 287–89; Eizenstat to Carter, August 4, 1977, Box FG-207, WHCF, JCL.

41. Jimmy Carter, Memorandum for the Heads of Departments and Agencies, August 10, 1978, Box HU-15, WHCF HU1–6, JCL; Patricia M. Cloherty to Carter, n.d. [December 1978], Box BE-25, WHCF, JCL; Jimmy Carter, Memorandum for the Heads of Executive Departments and Agencies, May 18, 1979, Box FG 297, WHCF, JCL; Tinker, *Women in Washington,* 291–94.

42. Peterson to Costanza, July 13, 20, 1977, Box HU-14, WHCF HU1–6; Susan Schechter, *Women and Male Violence: The Visions and Struggles of the Battered Women's Movement* (Boston: South End Press, 1982), 136.

43. Schechter, *Women and Male Violence,* 137; *Battered Women: Issues of Public Policy. A Consultation Sponsored by the United States Commission on Civil Rights, Washington, D.C., January 30–31, 1978* (Washington, D.C.: U.S. Commission on Civil Rights, 1978); Wandersee, *Women on the Move,* 142.

44. *Battered Women,* 170–80, 649; U.S. Department of Labor, Women's Bureau, Sources of Funding for Battered Women's Programs, January 1978, Box 146, McKenna Files, JCL.

45. Violence in the Family Attendance List, August 24, [1977], Box 2, Costanza Files, JCL; White House Meeting on Violence in the Family with emphasis on the Battered Woman, October 17, 1977, Box 11, Costanza Files, JCL.

46. June H. Zeitlin, "Domestic Violence: Perspectives from Washington," in Tinker, *Women in Washington,* 267; Message to Congress on the Administration's Response to the *National Plan of Action,* Battered Women, Legislation Pending before the 95th Congress, [c. July–September 1978], Box 323, DPS-Eizenstat, JCL.

47. Zeitlin, "Domestic Violence," 268–70; Hartmann, *From Margin to Mainstream,* 147–48; Schecter, *Women and Male Violence,* 146–48; Carter to Donald J. Mitchell, December 5, 1979, Box HU-16, WHCF HU1-6, JCL.

48. Schecter, *Women and Male Violence,* 147–48.

49. Ibid., 186; Valle Jones to Patricia Harris, November 10, 1977, Box 2, Costanza's Files, JCL.

50. Cheryl M. Fields, "Sex-Bias Rules Would Protect Bigtime Football," *Chronicle of Higher Education,* December 11, 1978, 13.

51. Califano, *Governing America,* 263–64.

52. Gelb and Palley, *Women and Public Policies,* 118–20; Cheryl M. Fields, "50 Presidents Ask U.S. to Withdraw Plan to Monitor Sex Bias in Sports," *Chronicle of Higher Education,* June 18, 1979, 12.

53. Doug Barnard to Eizenstat, February 28, 1979, Box FA-11, WHCF, JCL. See also, for example, Jennings Randolph et al., to Califano, March 2, 1979, Box FA-10, JCL.

54. Margot Polivy to Weddington, March 21, 1979, Box 125, McKenna's Files, JCL; Chambers to Carter, March 27, 1979, Box HU-15, WHCF HU1-6, JCL; Weddington to Chambers, March 29, 1979, Box HU-15, WHCF HU1-6, JCL; Chambers to Califano, April 20, 1979, Box 25, Weddington's Files, JCL; Abramowitz to Eizenstat, May 22, 1979, Box FA-10, WHCF, JCL; *New York Times,* April 22, 23, 1979; Califano, *Governing America,* 267–68.

55. Statement by Patricia Roberts Harris, Secretary of Health, Education, and Welfare, n.d. [December 4, 1979], Box 26, Weddington's Files, JCL; Abigail Havens to Weddington, Weddington Files, JCL; Gelb and Palley, *Women and Public Policies*, 121; *New York Times*, December 5, 1979.

56. Carter's only mention of Title IX was in the context of a general report on policy concerning women in September 1979, where he designated "enforcement of all civil rights laws, particularly Title IX," as among "the crucial issues which demand our attention (*Public Papers of Jimmy Carter, 1978*, 1641). Although the 1984 Supreme Court decision in the Grove City case temporarily vitiated Title IX, the Harris guidelines advanced opportunity for women. At least some institutions recognized that Title IX required improving intercollegiate athletics for women, and the numbers of women participating in college sports increased significantly, nearly doubling between 1976 and 1990.

57. See the chapter by Hugh Davis Graham in this volume.

12

Placing Jimmy Carter's Foreign Policy

William Stueck

Where does the Carter administration fit in the history of American foreign relations, especially the era of U.S. globalism from World War II to the present? This chapter addresses that question through an examination of Jimmy Carter's responses to several key issues during his campaign for president in 1976 and his years in office. I argue that Carter ran for and entered the White House intending to alter substantially the foreign policies of his Republican predecessors Richard Nixon and Gerald Ford, but that he wound up changing a good deal less than he had planned and not always in the manner that he had hoped. Yet in part because of his continuation of directions established under his immediate predecessors, in part because of departures from them, his successor, Ronald Reagan, enjoyed an enhanced position from which to compete with the Soviet Union in an intensified cold war. That situation, in turn, led eventually to conditions in which some of Carter's early goals became reachable.

Carter is often portrayed as a man who wanted to be a domestic-oriented president, who in seeking to downscale the imperial aspects of the office sought to reduce the U.S. presence abroad that had been so instrumental in fostering them. Carter the presidential candidate hardly placed foreign policy issues in a secondary position, however; indeed, he declared that the president's "prime responsibility . . . is to guarantee the security of the nation," and a big part of his attack on the Republican administrations of Nixon and Ford centered on their policies toward the outside world, which, he claimed, were highly secretive and partisan, immoral, and overly focused on relations with the Soviet Union.[1] While he cautioned against foreign military intervention "unless our own nation is endangered,"[2] spoke of reducing the defense budget by $5 to $7 billion,[3] and suggested that U.S. troops could be removed from Korea,[4] he rejected any return to isolationism, saw "trimming the fat" rather than canceling weapons systems or cutting manpower as the way to lower spending on the armed forces,[5] emphasized the importance of

244

rebuilding relationships with allies, especially in Western Europe and Japan,[6] and complained that the Soviets had gained more from détente than had the United States.[7] He also advocated a greater degree of multilateralism in American diplomacy—a replacement of "balance of power politics with world order politics" and greater attention to the "common problems of food, energy, environment, and trade"—and an intensive effort to promote human rights abroad.[8] Clearly, candidate Carter had a full and activist foreign policy agenda. It is misleading to position Carter with Woodrow Wilson and Lyndon Johnson as presidents who entered office placing domestic issues in the highest priority but eventually became preoccupied with the international arena largely through inadvertence or events beyond their control.

Although Carter intended to initiate significant changes in U.S. foreign policy, we should not take all of his campaign statements at face value. In 1976, candidate Carter challenged an incumbent president. Public revulsion over the Vietnam debacle and Watergate scandals provided an incentive for Carter to portray himself as an innovator on both the substance and style of American foreign policy. The Republican target was so inviting that, as I. M. Destler, Leslie Gelb, and Anthony Lake remark, Carter attacked from both left and right. From the right, he criticized President Ford for not driving a hard enough bargain with the Soviets on détente, for planning "to give up 'practical' control of the Panama Canal," and for refusing to receive Soviet dissident Alexander Solzhenitsyn at the White House. From the left, Carter promised "no more immoral *realpolitik,* no more Watergate-type secrecy, no more destabilizing CIA interventions."[9]

Yet, as on domestic issues, Carter genuinely desired to move beyond old right-left dichotomies. While his campaign rhetoric did not always represent precise commitments, it did reflect his intention to substantially reform U.S. foreign policy. His administration, historian Gaddis Smith observes, conducted "a fundamental debate about how the United States should behave in international affairs"; it exceeded others' efforts to "relieve the terrible insecurity of the nuclear age through nuclear arms control"; it tried "to think in terms of a lasting world order beneficial to all people rather than to make every decision on the basis of short-term calculation of American advantage over the Soviet Union"; and it sought "to discover and apply an effective combination of morality, reason, and power in the conduct of American foreign policy."[10]

Even so, in many specific areas of foreign policy the Carter administration merely built on patterns already established, especially during the Nixon-Ford years.[11] Initiatives to limit nuclear weapons occurred as far back as the Truman administration, led to major agreements between the United States and the Soviet Union in 1963 and 1972, and verged on another such agreement when Carter entered office. Eight years before, President Nixon had embarked on a course designed to manage at a lower level of intensity the competition with the Soviet Union and to develop a constructive relationship with the People's Republic of China. Nixon initiated a broad reevaluation of the means by which the United States attempted to achieve its foreign objectives, and this produced a substantial reduction in the number of U.S. troops stationed abroad, mostly because of withdrawals from Vietnam but also because of the departure of an army division from Korea.[12] After the Yom Kippur War of 1973 and the Arab oil embargo, Nixon greatly intensified American diplomatic activity directed toward resolving the Arab-Israeli conflict. On the Panama Canal, President Lyndon Johnson had begun the process of attempting to revise the treaty of 1903 only to be derailed by an increasingly recalcitrant Congress and unrealistic demands by the Panamanians. Nixon resumed the effort in 1973, and Ford appeared to be on the verge of success until Ronald Reagan stirred nationalist sentiments in 1976 in the struggle for the Republican presidential nomination. Carter adopted an ambiguous position on the canal in the fall campaign, but by the time he entered office he had accepted the Kissinger-Tack Agreement of February 1974 as the starting point for negotiations with the Panamanian government.[13] In southern Africa, Nixon had shifted Johnson's policy away from support for the British in pressing Rhodesia to move toward black majority rule, but in 1976, in the face of increasing Soviet penetration of Africa, Ford moved dramatically to accommodate the forces for change.[14]

On human rights, Nixon and Ford for the most part lacked initiative, but in 1975 the latter attended a summit of European nations in Helsinki to sign the "Final Act," which included a section on human rights.[15] Although some commentators in the United States regarded this section as meaningless, Ford clearly did not.[16] In 1976, he signed into law a bill establishing a joint executive-legislative commission to monitor compliance, especially among Warsaw Pact countries. Former National Security Council staffers Robert M. Gates and William G. Hyland argue that the "Final Act" provided a major spark for dissent within the Soviet Union and other Eastern bloc countries.[17] Ford signed another bill passed by the Democratic Congress that defined the promotion of "the increased observance of internationally recognized human rights by all countries" as "a principal goal" of U.S. foreign policy. The bill provided that no country should receive U.S. aid if it showed "a consistent pattern of gross violations" of human rights.[18] Gaddis Smith concedes that Carter merely "joined the [human rights] crusade and made it his own."[19]

The simple fact is that Carter ran for and then became president well into, not at the beginning of, a major reevaluation of American foreign policy. The breakdown of the "cold war consensus" in the United States during the 1960s as a result of the war in Vietnam and the increasing strain it and other foreign entanglements placed on American resources had necessitated this reevaluation. Soviet achievement of strategic parity, American devaluation of the dollar in 1971 and 1973, the Arab oil embargo of 1973 and the Western alliance's undisciplined response, and the final fall of South Vietnam in 1975 all reinforced the sense that the United States must adapt to new circumstances. As political scientist David Skidmore has written, "The presidents of the seventies . . . were principally concerned with adjusting U.S. foreign policy to account for declining American power. Their policies were aimed at addressing . . . the growing imbalance between dwindling resources and static commitments."[20] For obvious political reasons, Carter ignored this continuity.

To detect continuity is not to deny the significance of change. Carter did try to reconceptualize American foreign policy, to move the country in directions different from other presidents in the post–World War II era, including Nixon and Ford. At minimum this effort generated shifts in priorities that led to real differences in outcome. Carter also departed in style from his predecessors in ways that often produced substantive results.

Carter is often accused of lacking a coherent worldview, but his first key foreign policy address as president—at the University of Notre Dame on May 22, 1977—belies this charge.[21] Carter began with the assertion that the foreign policy of the United States should reflect "our essential character as a nation": it should be "democratic, . . . based on fundamental values, . . . and [use] power and influence . . . for human purposes." One virtue of such a policy was that the American people could comprehend and support it. Another revealed Carter's classic Wilsonianism: democracy was relevant not just to Americans but to the world at large. "Democracy works," he declared; hence its example "will be compelling" to others if brought "closer" to them. This confidence in democracy at home and abroad would free Americans of "that inordinate fear of communism which once led us to embrace any dictator who joined us in that fear . . . [and to fight] fire with fire, never thinking that fire is better quenched with water." The Vietnam experience had demonstrated the "intellectual and moral poverty" of this approach and helped Americans rediscover their "own principles and values."

Carter proceeded to argue that global change had further compromised the foreign policy constructed by American leaders in the aftermath of World War II. Colonialism had almost disappeared, and nearly a hundred new nations had emerged in its wake. Peoples in these countries were more knowledgeable than before and possessed higher aspirations, including the desire for "justice, equity, and human rights." The old American policy of containing the Soviet Union and seeking "global stability" through an alliance with non-Communist, industrial nations was no longer viable. But the United States need not fear this "new world"; rather, Americans must return to their own primary values in helping "to shape it."

Having provided a foundation for his new approach, Carter outlined "five cardinal principles" that defined "what we have been doing and . . . what we intend to do." First came the "commitment to human rights as a fundamental tenet." This did not entail the "conduct of foreign policy by rigid moral maxims," the limits of which in an "imperfect" world the president insisted he understood. However, the United States must take advantage of "the power of words and of the ideas words embody." The world must come to know that Americans stood "for more than financial prosperity," that their greatest unifying idea, given their boundless diversity, was "a belief in human freedom." To ignore this fact and the "dramatic" increase abroad in "protection of the individual from the arbitrary power of the state . . . would be to lose influence and moral authority." A second and related principle was "to reinforce the bonds among our democratic allies," which he claimed to have furthered recently in NATO meetings in London.

The third principle, which centered on an "effort to halt the strategic arms race," involved relations with the Soviet Union. Carter reaffirmed his desire to move beyond the arms-control goals of previous administrations, to attempt to actually reduce and eventually eliminate altogether the strategic nuclear stockpiles of the superpowers, as well as those of others. Despite his avoidance of the term *linkage,* he hinted at the connection between arms control and other aspects of relations with the Soviets. While acknowledging his belief in détente, he emphasized that "cooperation also implies obligation," that the Soviets needed to work with the United States "in aiding the developing world," and that this included halting their effort to impose their "system of society" on others, "either through the use of direct military intervention or through the use of a client state's military force, as . . . with Cuban intervention in Angola."

Carter's fourth and fifth principles were the continuing search for a "lasting" and "comprehensive" peace in the Middle East and the reduction of "the danger of nuclear proliferation and the worldwide spread of conventional weapons."[22]

The most glaring omission from the speech was any mention of the effort to negotiate treaty revision with Panama regarding control over and operation of the canal, which was central to the president's approach to the "new world" he described.[23] Failure would almost certainly lead to significant unrest in Panama, mounting difficulties in keeping the canal open, and growing, militant anti-Americanism throughout Central America. Indeed, the National Security Council's first Presidential Review Memorandum in January 1977 focused on negotiating the treaties, a reflection of Carter's seriousness in moving away from excessive concentration on Soviet-American relations and on adapting U.S. foreign policy to the postcolonial era.[24]

The determined move of Carter toward treaty revision with Panama and with his early approach to human rights and SALT II negotiations with the Soviet Union provide a window to understanding the shift he brought to American foreign policy. In the first case, Carter initiated little substantive change to the Nixon-Ford policy after 1973, but, in contrast to his predecessors, he elevated the negotiation of new canal treaties and their ratification to the top rungs of his foreign policy agenda. The advancement of human rights and the achievement of a SALT II treaty held similar exalted positions, and in both these areas Carter deviated from Nixon and Ford on important points. In each case, Carter's view of a complex new world to which the United States must adapt helped to produce outcomes different from what would have likely emerged had President Ford continued in office.

On treaty revision with Panama, the *only* way to success was for the United States early on to give the issue a priority second to none. Johnson, Nixon, and

Ford all had come to recognize the explosive nature of the issue in Panama and in Latin America in general, but none of them had committed the political capital necessary to make it viable at home. In Congress, the issue was not strictly partisan, a good sign given the fact that neither party controlled the two-thirds majority of seats in the Senate necessary to ratify a treaty. Nonetheless, in both 1974 and 1975, Senator Strom Thurmond (R.-S.C.) fashioned coalitions of more than one-third of his colleagues to endorse a resolution insisting on the retention of U.S. "sovereign rights" and control over the Canal Zone. A strong majority of the public with an awareness of the issue heartily agreed with the resolution. Without American concessions on sovereignty and control, no agreement with Panama was possible.[25] Carter understood these realities, both at home and abroad, although he failed to comprehend the difficulty of reversing domestic sentiments. He chose the path of seeking the required majorities in the Senate for two treaties acceptable to Panama. After what he later called "one of the most onerous political ordeals of my life," the president won razor-thin victories on both treaties in the upper house during the spring of 1978.[26] William J. Jorden, who worked intensively on the canal issue on the American side through most of the 1970s, remarked later that Carter's decision to put "a spotlight on a North-South problem" represented "a quite remarkable change for . . . newly elected presidents," who long "had focused on East-West aspects of foreign policy."[27]

In all likelihood, the new focus averted very negative consequences in the evolution of U.S. relations with Panama and much of Latin America, but it had its price. Carter used up a huge chunk of capital in the Senate and with the American public. Although he could have done more in the spring of 1977 to involve key senators in the final stages of treaty negotiations with Panama, his larger problem rested in the enormous task, as Newsday observed, of selling the American people on the paradox of "giving up the Canal to save it."[28] Despite the Senate vote, Carter never succeeded in that task, which made the mustering of support from legislators later on for the SALT II treaty all the more difficult. Indeed, eighteen of the senators who supported the treaties paid the ultimate price. Having backed Carter's stance in the face of strong opposition in their constituencies, they lost their bids for reelection in 1978 or 1980.[29] Carter suffered damage as well. His determination on the treaties led him to delay a push in the Senate for passage of a labor reform bill, which gave business groups time to mount an effective resistance. The resulting demise of the bill undermined Carter's already shaky standing with organized labor, a critical constituency in Ted Kennedy's challenge for the Democratic nomination in 1980.[30] Finally, the struggle over the treaties augmented a conservative resurgence in the United States that, along with the Kennedy campaign, proved central in Carter's 1980 defeat at the hands of Ronald Reagan.

At the beginning of his administration, Carter had not ranked Panama Canal treaty negotiations above those on SALT II. In effect, he ranked them as coequal, along with a variety of other measures. During his second week in office, he wrote in his diary, "Everybody has warned me not to take on too many projects so early in the administration, but it's almost impossible for me to delay something that I see needs to be done."[31] This disinclination to establish clear priorities represents one of the most consistent and compelling sources of criticism of his performance in the White House.

Yet the failure to rank SALT II negotiations ahead of those on the Panama Canal did not necessarily mean that the latter would proceed more quickly than the former. Issues remained to be resolved in both areas, but it was Carter's insistence, first, on pushing human rights with the Soviet Union and Eastern Europe and, second, on seeking reductions in strategic weapons rather than adhering to the Vladivostok Accords of 1974 that slowed progress in the SALT II talks. In both cases, the new president's approach clearly departed from that of his predecessor.

To the Soviets, one of the benefits of détente as conceived during the Nixon-Kissinger-Ford era was the de-emphasis on ideological competition, especially insofar as it involved efforts to influence each other's internal affairs. Pressures from the U.S. Congress and the Helsinki Accords threatened to return the human rights issue as an ingredient in superpower relations, but President Ford had refused to push aggressively in this area, much to the dismay of conservatives in both political parties at home. The Helsinki Accords had encouraged dissident activity in the Soviet Union and Eastern Europe, and this activity received considerable press in the United States. Carter took advantage of this trend in his 1976 campaign, attacking the incumbent president for failing to pay more attention to human rights. Whether partly in anticipation of a Carter offensive or purely for internal reasons, the Soviets decided at the end of 1976 to begin a clampdown on dissident contacts with Western officials and members of the press. As Carter entered office, then, the stage was set for a test of wills.[32]

Carter possessed a genuine commitment to human rights rooted most basically in his experience with the African American struggle for equality in the U.S. South. He also recognized that the promotion of "moral principles" abroad could provide a strong foundation "for the exertion of American power and influence," and he hoped that this promotion, especially when directed at the Soviet Union, would curry favor with conservative groups in the United States.[33] While he was not unaware of the complications his human rights campaign might create in relations with the Soviet Union, he anticipated that the issue could be kept separate from arms-control negotiations. After sending a second letter to Soviet leader Leonid Brezhnev during his first month in office, Carter penned naively in his diary that it was important for his counterpart to understand that pressure on human rights did not reflect "an antagonistic attitude of mine toward the Soviet Union."[34] Even more naively, he told an adviser that he hoped during his term "to put our relations with the Soviet Union on the same basis as they are with England."[35]

The Soviets might have largely ignored Carter's moves on human rights had the new president followed the wishes of Cyrus Vance, his secretary of state, for "quiet diplomacy."[36] Some early initiatives were anything but quiet, however, including Carter's response to a letter from Andrei Sakharov encouraging him to continue his effort to promote human rights in the Soviet Union and the president's reception in the White House of recently exiled Soviet dissident Vladimir Bukovsky.[37] This public approach brought a stinging rebuttal from Moscow and helped poison the atmosphere for SALT II negotiations.[38]

Carter's determination at the beginning of those negotiations to advance a proposal that provided for deep cuts in the strategic forces of the two superpowers, especially those of the Soviet Union, eliminated all prospects for early success. The Soviets tried from the start to discourage Carter from abandoning the accord reached at Vladivostok in 1974. As on the human rights issue, the president did not help his prospects for a favorable reception by going public with his initiative prior to laying the groundwork privately with Soviet diplomats. When Vance appeared in Moscow in late March with the new approach in hand, he received a sharp rebuke from his hosts.[39] The Soviets even rejected Vance's backup proposal for an agreement without any provisions regarding the U.S. cruise missile and the Soviet Backfire bomber. Vance wrote years later that "the most serious cost" of the Moscow fiasco was in the United States, where the lead American position became for "anti-SALT and antidétente hardliners . . . the only standard against which to measure the success of the ultimate agreement."[40] In striving for so much so soon, Carter had reduced the possibility of achieving anything at all.

By the time he entered office, détente already was in trouble in the face of growing alarm over the ongoing Soviet military buildup and activities in Africa. The steadier hand of the Ford-Kissinger team, however, probably would have kept SALT II negotiations on track, which could only have reinforced prospects for stable, if not friendly, relations between the superpowers.

Despite the rough going early on in Soviet-American interaction, Carter moved only gradually toward a traditional cold war position. He tried until the fall of 1977 to involve Moscow in negotiations aimed at a comprehensive peace between Israel and its neighbors, which departed from his predecessors' approach both in including the Soviet Union and in seeking an overall rather than a partial agreement. Carter abandoned Soviet participation only in the face of Israel's adamancy and Egypt's flexibility, and these phenomena combined with Syrian intransigence to move him back toward the step-by-step diplomacy of Kissinger.[41] In the face of expanding Soviet intervention in Africa through Cuban proxy forces, Carter moved forward decisively on the normalization of relations with China and abandoned his early pursuit of relations with Angola, Cuba, and Vietnam; however, he refused to give up on SALT, finally concluding an agreement with the Soviets in May 1979. While pushing ahead with the updating of NATO plans and weapons, he canceled the B-1 bomber and deferred deployment of the neutron bomb. His first two defense budgets de-emphasized strategic forces and provided for mere 3 percent increases in overall spending, which represented significant cutbacks from Ford's projections. Although the increase rose to 5 percent in 1979 and his rhetoric toward Moscow toughened from March 1978 onward, it was not until the Soviets invaded Afghanistan at the end of 1979 that he fully adopted a confrontational position.[42]

Carter's early pursuit of a new world featuring U.S. promotion of nonmilitary solutions to problems is well illustrated in his position on human rights. His policy on human rights was selective—never, for example, was it applied to China—and it declined in strength over time.[43] Carter's goal of reducing American arms sales abroad was not achieved—indeed, such sales increased from $12.8 billion in 1977 to $17.1 billion in 1980.[44] Still, the human rights initiatives were by no means inconsequential, and they helped to establish expectations at home that his more conservative successor could not altogether reverse.

We have already seen that Carter's early human rights policy toward the Soviet bloc influenced the SALT negotiations. After the debacle of Vance's March 1977 Moscow visit, Carter toned down his direct, overt pressure on the Soviets in the human rights area until the summer of 1980.[45] Yet this retreat masked a larger, ongoing effort pursued by the Carter administration, first, to covertly distribute dissident literature in Warsaw Pact nations and, second, to greatly increase access of people there to Voice of America, Radio Free Europe, and Radio Liberty programming. National Security Adviser Zbigniew Brzezinski was the most aggressive advocate of such efforts, and he clearly conceived of them as instruments for undermining the legitimacy of the Communist regimes. Although Carter's motives were more complex, there is no doubt that he gave strong support for funding to provide the transmitters necessary to counter Communist efforts to jam airwaves used by Western radios.[46]

The human rights campaign extended well beyond Soviet bloc countries. In his inaugural address Carter declared that "our commitment to human rights must be absolute."[47] He failed to live up to that standard. Unlike Woodrow Wilson, he refused to intervene militarily to advance political reform. Like John F. Kennedy, he often judged U.S. security interests as sufficiently compelling to warrant overlooking flagrant violations of human rights by friendly or potentially friendly regimes.[48] Although he included "the fulfillment of such vital needs as food, shelter, health care, and education" on his list of human rights, he was less aggressive than Kennedy in pushing socioeconomic reform abroad. Stopping short of Kennedy's approach, he declined to identify broad democratization as his fundamental goal.[49] Yet, as political scientist Tony Smith points out, for the first time since Wilson, Carter attempted "to apply his standards for proper government evenhandedly, to friends and foes alike."[50] Some friendly governments averted sanctions but not private remonstrances, and in two major instances, Iran and Nicaragua, Carter resisted the use of force to prop up repressive regimes in countries where American security concerns were at stake.

Any Democrat entering the White House in 1977 would have found it impossible to ignore human rights. Congress was in an assertive mood in the aftermath of the Vietnam debacle and the Watergate scandals, and public revulsion over the latter had led in November 1974 to election of a House of Representatives with a two-to-one Democratic majority. Several of its new members were liberals committed to an aggressive campaign to force the president to take seriously the advancement of human rights abroad. In the next two years, they combined with veterans in their own body and in the Senate to push through Congress legislation establishing a human rights bureaucracy in the State Department and requiring the president to consider the human rights records of foreign governments in granting aid. Liberals in Congress received crucial assistance from private groups. The end of the crusade against the Vietnam War and growing revulsion over the American record under Nixon and Ford, especially in Chile, energized such groups to concentrate broadly on human rights in the Third World.[51]

Despite such pressures, President Ford used loopholes in the wording of legislation to resist compliance with the liberals' desires. His successor could have done the same, although with greater difficulty given his party affiliation. Carter never totally satisfied the liberals, but his actions represented a substantial departure from Ford's. Less than five weeks into Carter's term, Secretary of State Vance announced the intention to reduce aid to Argentina, Ethiopia, and Uruguay because of gross violations of human rights. During the next four years, at least eight, and possibly as many as seventeen, countries lost security assistance on human rights grounds. Seven nations received increased aid because of improvements on human rights.[52]

On occasion Carter took significant risks either in pressing foreign governments for reform or in resisting the temptation to intervene to protect a friendly but repressive regime. In the case of southern Africa, Carter's effective push in Congress for repeal of the Byrd amendment permitting the importation of chrome from Rhodesia was foreshadowed by Kissinger's shift to support for black majority rule in that country before he left office. Nonetheless, it is difficult to imagine a Ford-Kissinger team displaying Carter's persistence in maintaining sanctions against Rhodesia during 1979 in the face of mounting congressional pressure to embrace a racially mixed government cobbled together by Ian Smith. Without such persistence, the free elections of 1980 and subsequent creation of a government dominated by the black majority and friendly toward the United States would not have occurred.[53]

Although few Americans would describe as happy the outcome of Carter's policies toward Nicaragua and Iran, they demonstrate his determination to avoid even covert military intervention in the internal affairs of other countries and, to a lesser extent, his ongoing concern for human rights. U.S. policy toward Nicaragua began to change with Nixon's resignation. Kissinger chose a new assistant secretary of state for inter-American affairs, William D. Rogers, who adopted a course he described as "absolutely neutral both publicly and privately" toward President Anastacio Somoza Debayle and his internal opponents.[54] Yet U.S. aid to the government continued despite protests by liberals in Congress.

The Carter administration devoted little initial attention to Nicaragua, but it did alter the principles behind U.S. policy by linking economic and military assistance to human rights practices. The United States immediately retracted export licenses to Nicaragua for sales of ammunition for sporting weapons. In June 1977, it refused to sign a military aid agreement with Nicaragua unless Somoza instituted reforms on human rights. When in September Somoza halted press censorship and lifted a lengthy state of siege, the United States signed the agreement but delayed its implementation.[55] Most economic aid also continued to be held back.

In May 1978, as a result of pressure from Somoza's friends in Congress, the Carter administration announced its approval, after a year's delay, of $10.5 million in Agency for International Development loans to Nicaragua.[56] In early July, Carter, in an attempt to encourage Somoza to move forward on human rights, sent a letter to the Nicaraguan leader congratulating him on alleged progress already made.[57] By this time, though, a civil war in Nicaragua raged on, and Somoza was less inclined than ever to liberalize his regime.

Although some pressure existed within his administration for action to force out Somoza, for the moment Carter resisted any of the heavy-handed measures so common in past U.S. relations with Latin America. Scholar-participant Robert Pastor likens Carter's approach to Franklin D. Roosevelt's policy of avoiding military intervention and emphasizing mediation, preferably multilateral, with participation by other Latin American states.[58] Thus, in the midst of rapidly escalating violence in Nicaragua in the fall of 1978 and doubts on the part of other governments in the region, Carter proposed mediation—reluctantly joined by the Dominican Republic and Guatemala—between Somoza and the moderate-dominated Broad Opposition Front. The effort led to agreement on the principle of a plebiscite to determine whether Somoza would stay in office, but when he resisted, attempts to assure a fair process of mediation collapsed.

In February 1979, Carter finally imposed sanctions. The U.S. military aid group withdrew, and military assistance that previously had been suspended was now terminated. The only aid that continued was directed at fulfilling "the basic needs of the poor." Carter reduced personnel in the U.S. embassy in Managua by more than half and ordered the withdrawal of all Peace Corps volunteers from the country.[59]

Only in June, as the radical Sandinistas launched their final offensive to remove Somoza by force, did Carter abandon the principle of avoiding direct outside military intervention. Even then he rejected unilateral action, proposing only that the Organization of American States send a "peacekeeping force." When the proposal received no support in the region, Carter again tried mediation, which included a demand that Somoza resign. Carter's objective was to ensure that moderate elements dominated a successor government. The Sandinistas resisted, and, rather than attempting to undermine the new revolutionary government, Carter tried to work with it. In part because of restraints imposed by Congress, in part because of the regime's predisposition, his approach failed.

Although leaders in the region recognized Carter's ploy on mediation as an effort to save the present system in Nicaragua while forcing Somoza's departure, Carter undeniably resisted the temptation to use unilateral military force to prevent the rise of a radical regime in a Central American nation. When the Sandinistas moved decisively toward an alliance with Cuba and the Soviet Union and began to aid a rebellion in El Salvador, Carter expanded arms aid to the brutally oppressive military there and reduced pressure for human rights, but he avoided the direct use of force.[60] Clearly, this represented a break with U.S. presidents since Eisenhower. His refusal to demand Somoza's ouster until the last moment and his insistence on tying military and economic assistance to Somoza's human rights practices also departed from past practice. In all likelihood, a Nixon-Ford team would have intervened earlier to either save Somoza or ease him out, and it would have been far less reluctant to employ unilateral military force. The two presidents who succeeded Carter returned to the previous pattern in Latin America.

Carter also departed from his immediate predecessors on Iran. Although he never denied military or economic aid to the government of Shah Reza Pahlavi on the grounds of human rights violations, Carter created uncertainty in Tehran after eight years of virtually unrestrained bolstering of the regime by Nixon and Ford. The uncertainty derived in part from the Carter administration's frequently expressed concern about human rights. While such utterances may not have had a direct impact on the shah, they did influence the expectations of Iranians, an increasing number of whom became more aggressive in their demands for liberalization. By the time Carter entered the White House, the shah had developed a plan for gradual political liberalization, but in helping to escalate public demands, American efforts probably increased both his discomfort and his sense that he must move forward.[61]

The shah was well briefed on U.S. affairs and thus aware of the growing pressure from Congress to link arms sales and aid to human rights. When, in May 1977, Carter publicized a new policy on arms sales, which imposed severe restrictions on all nations but those with major defense arrangements with the United States and omitted Iran from the privileged group, the shah could not help but be concerned. That concern diminished somewhat in early July when Carter proposed to Congress the sale of seven (rather than the ten requested by the shah) technologically sophisticated AWACS aircraft systems, but it rose again at the end of the month when the president withdrew the request temporarily in the face of resistance on Capitol Hill. The shah reacted sharply, and the issue was resolved in his favor in September only after the administration intervened with key legislators.[62]

Although the president raised the human rights issue with the shah during the latter's visit to Washington in November, Carter, like his predecessors, placed top priority on maintaining friendly relations with a nation positioned on the eastern shore of the strategically vital Persian Gulf. At the end of the year, Carter stopped long enough in Tehran to make his infamous characterization of Iran as "an island of stability" and of its monarch as a leader who received the "respect, admiration, and love" of his people.[63]

Carter's oft-expressed concern about human rights and his reluctance to employ force still worried the shah. During the previous summer, the president had vetoed a proposed Iranian airlift of American arms to Somalia in the face of increasing Soviet and Cuban intervention in the Horn of Africa.[64] In April 1978, a leftist coup d'état occurred in Afghanistan. While no evidence existed of Moscow's complicity, fears arose, in both Tehran and Washington, of expanding Soviet influence. When the shah approached the United States with his concerns, he was advised to recognize the new regime and hope for the best.[65] The Americans did the same, and even continued economic aid in the hope that the outstretched hand would help keep Afghanistan out of the Soviet grasp.[66] Then, in July, Carter approved the bulk of the shah's most recent request to purchase arms but denied him the most advanced wiring equipment for the F-4 aircraft. The shah was, according to National Security Council staffer Gary Sick, "visibly displeased with the decision."[67]

The final train of events leading to the shah's departure from Iran in January 1979 commenced the previous September, when radicals called a general strike, the government declared martial law in several cities, and, in the face of a massive religious-protest rally in Tehran, soldiers fired into a crowd, killing hundreds of citizens and wounding thousands more. Carter responded with a phone call to the shah expressing support.[68] Public statements of support continued into December, but always included denials of any intent to interfere in Iran's internal affairs.[69]

In late October, the shah began seeking U.S. support for a military government. Despite increasing pressure from Brzezinski for this "iron fist" approach, Carter approved only general statements of confidence in the shah's judgment, which usually included compliments of the monarch's initiatives toward liberalization.[70] According to Ambassador William Sullivan, the shah, who for some time had suspected the American CIA of secretly campaigning against him, did not believe he had U.S. support.[71] Whatever the shah's perception, little doubt exists that, as Sick observes, Carter's values "established outer limits to the range of realistic [U.S.] policy options."[72]

The president's frequent clumsiness in dealing with Iran resulted partly from his preoccupation with other issues. During the first three weeks of September 1978, he devoted an extraordinary amount of time to the negotiations between Egypt and Israel leading to the Camp David accords, which combined with the follow-up treaty between the two countries concluded the following spring represented one of Carter's crowning achievements. Some analysts have suggested that Carter paid a high price for his lengthy exercise in personal diplomacy, not only in his diversion of attention from other issues but in his sponsorship of an agreement that left unresolved the questions of Palestinian autonomy and the occupied territories other than the Sinai.[73] However that may be, the approach, both in leaving the Soviets out of the process and in pursuing a partial settlement, reestablished continuity with the policy initiated during the Nixon administration. Although Carter's personal diplomacy, with the possible exception of Woodrow Wilson's efforts in Paris during 1919, was unique for a president in its sustained intensity on a specific issue, it was Secretary of State Kissinger under Nixon and Ford who had initiated this technique—then called "shuttle diplomacy." That approach would have continued had Ford remained in office after January 1977.[74]

Also distracting Carter's attention from Iran, especially at the end of 1978 and early in 1979, was the normalization of relations with China. As with the Egypt-Israeli peace process, full normalization, which was announced on December 15, 1978, represented a major achievement, but one that also probably would have occurred under a Ford administration. While domestic politics, first in the United States and then in both the United States and China, stalled progress in the evolution of Sino-American relations from 1974 through 1977, by 1978 such problems had subsided, and the obvious strategic advantages for both sides of expanded contacts made normalization largely a matter of timing.[75]

It is less clear that a Ford administration would have cast normalization in an anti-Soviet light. The Sino-American rapprochement of 1971–72 occurred simultaneously with an improvement in Soviet-American relations, whereas normalization took place as Soviet-American relations deteriorated.[76] We have already seen that détente with the Soviet Union was in difficulty when Carter entered office, but also that the climate quickly worsened as a result of his human rights policy and his position on SALT, both of which departed from the stance of his predecessor. The most plausible scenario for a Ford administration is that the human rights issue would not have compromised Soviet-American relations, that SALT II would have been completed sometime in 1977 and ratified by the Senate by the spring of the following year, and that Sino-American normalization would have emerged sometime after that, certainly after the congressional elections of November 1978. As it turned out under Carter, normalization delayed the signing of the SALT II treaty for several months, and this delay compromised its ratification by the U.S. Senate.[77]

Yet the United States' relationship with China became a quasi-military alliance only in 1980, after the Soviet move into Afghanistan at the end of the previous year. Only then did the United States commence the sale of military and related equipment to China.[78] Although Soviet action in Afghanistan under a Ford-Kissinger team probably would have occurred in the midst of better overall relations between Washington and Moscow, the event itself certainly would have provoked a sharp U.S. response, including use of "the China card."

Still, Carter's response was extraordinary, ranging from cutbacks in Soviet fishing privileges in U.S. waters, a boycott of the upcoming Moscow Olympics, and an arms embargo on grain sales to the Soviet Union to a withdrawal of the SALT II treaty from consideration by the Senate and announcement of the Carter Doctrine for defense of the Persian Gulf. The Soviet action, he declared, represented "the greatest threat to peace since the Second World War."[79]

Two factors explain this disproportionate reaction to what was largely a defensive move to protect a vital interest. First, Carter's previous naïveté about the Soviet Union compounded his shock and disillusionment when reality set in. Second, the president was entering an election year in which he was not even assured renomination by his party. Afghanistan gave him an opportunity to appear tough in an area where he was often perceived as weak. This consideration was all the more compelling because of the November 1979 seizure of American hostages in Iran, which made Carter appear helpless.

The first of these factors would not have influenced Ford and Kissinger (they had little naïveté to lose), but the second would have. Despite the ongoing presence of the "Vietnam syndrome," with its intense suspicion of military adventures abroad, the late 1970s saw a conservative trend in American politics that included growing hostility toward the Soviet Union.[80] As early as 1976, Ronald Reagan had nearly seized the Republican nomination from incumbent Ford, in part by attacking détente. Reagan would have been back in 1980 even had Ford remained in the White House, and the interest of the latter in the emergence of a moderate successor—in a word, anyone but Reagan—would have forced him to employ tough anti-Soviet rhetoric and stern countermeasures. On the other hand, it is doubtful that Ford would have, as Raymond Garthoff puts it, "mortgaged American policy [toward the Soviet Union] . . . to the continued Soviet military presence in Afghanistan."[81] Thus assuming Reagan's ascendancy in 1981, the final policy of Carter toward the Soviet Union differed less with his successor's hard line than a Ford approach would have.

What does the preceding analysis tell us about the Carter administration's place in the history of American foreign relations? My concluding remarks center on distinguishing between what Carter intended to do and what he actually did, and assessing the impact of his course on the direction of U.S. foreign policy.

Carter wanted to set himself apart from presidents since World War II in de-emphasizing the centrality of the Soviet Union in U.S. foreign policy. He succeeded initially by giving other issues, most notably the Panama Canal treaties, equal priority with SALT II but also by refusing to employ direct military force in the Horn of Africa in the face of what National Security Adviser Brzezinski, among others, considered a Soviet provocation.[82] Although he made no effort to eliminate competition with the Soviet Union and feared the impact on that competition of the fall of the shah in Iran and of Somoza in Nicaragua, Carter declined to use American forces unilaterally, or even to recommend that those autocratic yet friendly rulers adopt the "iron fist" to suppress dissent.

By early 1980, however, the Soviet Union had resumed the central place in U.S. strategy abroad. Striving for a "new world order" had given way to the more traditional goal of containment. In his January State of the Union Address, Carter expanded U.S. military commitments to the Persian Gulf in a manner that departed from the Nixon doctrine emphasizing the primary initial responsibility of America's friends to defend their own security.[83] The Rapid Deployment Force, which had been approved by the president in August 1977 and had entered into the active planning stage after the fall of the shah in early 1979, now gained a high priority in Washington.[84] Carter's defense budget for fiscal 1981 called for a 6 percent increase over the previous year, and his projected defense budget for fiscal 1982 was substantially higher than that. The shift, to be sure, had begun three years earlier, when Carter backed off from his campaign position to cut such spending and proposed a 3 percent increase, but the more dramatic buildup of 1980 reflected, admittedly in part for domestic political reasons, a new assessment of the dimensions of the Soviet threat.[85]

In the end, Carter not only failed to reorient American foreign policy away from the Soviet Union but also abandoned détente and returned to a cold war posture reminiscent of presidents from Truman to Johnson.[86] As Seyom Brown notes, "The Carter administration's new rhetorical and policy preoccupation with the Soviet threat appeared to legitimize the complaints of the unreconstructed cold warriors in the Reagan camp" and helped pave the way for an even more extreme U.S. position in 1981.[87]

Carter also failed to implement major departures from his predecessors by reducing foreign arms sales, and his actions of 1980 in relation to nuclear non-proliferation, human rights, and covert operations limited his achievements in those areas as well. His objective on nonproliferation of eliminating any use by the civilian nuclear industry of materials that could produce weapons already had stalled, first, in the face of domestic opposition and, then, after the passage by Congress in 1978 of the Nuclear Non-Proliferation Act, of foreign resistance to a U.S. effort to change established rules.[88] Finally, in 1980, the renewed concern about security in southwest Asia generated by events in Afghanistan led Carter to approve a major arms package to Pakistan, despite ongoing suspicions about its nuclear program and continued serious infractions in the area of human rights. He followed by agreeing to a large shipment of enriched uranium to India, despite its resistance to international inspection of its nuclear program.[89] Carter also moved sharply away from his previous aversion to covert action abroad, adopting this technique to undermine leftist regimes from western Africa to southern Asia.[90]

Strategically, Carter's most significant contribution to U.S. policy was the full normalization of relations with China and then the initiation of arms sales and technology transfers to the Asian giant. Normalization was consistent with Carter's stated objective before assuming office, but the military dimensions of that process were not, instead representing an outgrowth of his move away from détente with the Soviet Union. Although it is uncertain that the outcome would have been much different had he not entered the White House, there can be little doubt that the evolving Sino-American relationship deeply upset the Soviets and greatly improved the U.S. strategic position in East Asia.[91] Carter's course on China took fire from pro-Taiwan forces on the political right in the United States, including Reagan; however, President Reagan's focus on the Soviet challenge made it imperative that he work with the mainland regime.

Reagan's focus also dictated that he devote attention to human rights, at least in relation to the Soviet bloc. He sharply criticized the treatment of dissidents there and, more than Carter, directly attacked the Soviet system.[92] Yet it was Carter who initiated a truly activist human rights policy toward the Soviet Union. National Security Council staffer Robert Gates, who served U.S. presidents from Nixon to George Bush and directed the CIA under the latter, has written that Carter's human rights campaign and related activities represented an "ideological war on the Soviets . . . [of] a determination and intensity that was very different from his predecessors" and was "sustained and broadened further by his successor." Carter's approach, Gates concludes, "marked a decisive and historic turning point in the U.S.-Soviet relationship."[93]

If Reagan did not need Carter's lead in exploiting the human rights issue in relation to the Soviet bloc, he moved only reluctantly on the matter with non-Communist regimes. Carter's human rights policies in the Third World had faced much criticism from Republicans at home, including Reagan. During Reagan's first year in office, human rights efforts slackened with regard to Chile, South Korea, El Salvador, Argentina, and Brazil. The United States departed from Carter's policy of opposing loans in international financial institutions for governments with poor human rights records. Reagan's first nomination as head of the Bureau of Human Rights in the State Department was Ernest Lefever, who characterized the Carter approach as "a vague romantic optimism with an excessive confidence in the power of reason and good will."[94]

But in the fall of 1981, the Senate refused to confirm the nomination, leading the Reagan administration to recognize the strength of the human rights advocates in Congress and the public.[95] Reagan tried to avoid the "punitive" approach of withholding aid from governments with poor records on human rights, which had had at best mixed results under Carter, and he refused to include an economic/social dimension in his definition of human rights.[96] Nonetheless, from 1982 onward his administration used both public rhetoric and private diplomacy to promote human rights in specific cases involving anti-Communist regimes. By promoting human rights abroad and publicizing the issue on an unprecedented scale at home during the late 1970s, Carter helped produce a domestic atmosphere too powerful for Reagan and his successors to ignore. As Tony Smith concludes, "An abiding concern for human rights abroad is . . . [Carter's] finest legacy to the post–cold war world."[97]

Yet Carter himself failed to transcend the cold war, and it is important to re-iterate the role of his human rights policy in compromising détente. Not only did Carter's early attention to human rights exacerbate strains in Washington's rela-tions with Moscow; the self-imposed restraints created by the concern for human rights in the cases of Nicaragua and Iran conveyed an appearance of weakness to the American public when events developed contrary to U.S. interests. This appearance of weakness increased pressure on the president to develop a hard line toward the Soviet Union.

Although often unappreciated at the time, Carter's most important legacies to his successor were an expanding military machine at home, an absence of new quagmires abroad, a growing security relationship with China, and a strong human rights policy toward the Soviet bloc, all of which provided Reagan dis-tinct advantages in taking the measure of America's primary adversary in the cold war. In helping to put Reagan in a position to eventually end the cold war, Carter departed from much of the framework he had endorsed both as a candi-date and early in his administration. For the long term, however, he set the stage for the emergence of a world in which anticommunism no longer dictated Ameri-can intervention abroad in favor of repugnant regimes, in which relations with a single adversary ceased to shape a large portion of U.S. foreign policy, in which nuclear weapons could be reduced, and in which a well-intentioned former presi-dent could play a significant role as a private citizen in mediating conflicts within nations—in a word, a world not altogether unlike the one Carter had initially envisioned.[98]

NOTES

The author thanks the following for helpful criticisms of earlier drafts of this chapter: Brian Etheridge, Gary Fink, Lloyd Gardner, Peter Hoffer, Robert McMahon, Karl Mechem, K. W. Stroud, Patricia Stueck, Jobie Turner, and Michael Winship.

1. Many of the ideas associated with Carter in this paragraph appeared as early as May 28, 1975, in a speech he made in Japan. See U.S. Congress, *The Presidential Cam-paign 1976*, vol. 1, pt. 1, *Jimmy Carter* (Washington, D.C.: Government Printing Office, 1978–79), 66–70. On the president's prime responsibility, see his May 15, 1976, speech in ibid., 109.

2. See Carter's speech of May 15, 1976, in ibid., 112.

3. See Carter statement of September 18, 1976, in ibid., 695–96.

4. See Carter's speech of June 23, 1976, in ibid., 271.

5. See Carter's statements of September 18, 1976, and in the October 1976 issue of the *Armed Forces Journal* reprinted in ibid., 872–73.

6. See Carter's speech of June 23, 1976, in ibid., 116.

7. See Carter's speech of May 15, 1976, in ibid., 116.

8. See ibid., 113, 118.

9. I. M. Destler, Leslie H. Gelb, and Anthony Lake, *Our Own Worst Enemy: The Unmaking of American Foreign Policy* (New York: Simon and Schuster, 1984), 70.

10. Gaddis Smith, *Morality, Reason, and Power: American Diplomacy in the Carter Years* (New York: Hill and Wang, 1986), 3–4.

11. For two views along this line, the former less extreme than the latter, see David S. McLellan, *Cyrus Vance* (Totowa, N.J.: Rowman and Allanheld, 1985), 36; and John Lewis Gaddis, *Strategies of Containment* (New York: Oxford University Press, 1981), 346–47.

12. On the significance of the shift regarding Korea, see Joo-Hong Nam, *America's Commitment to South Korea: The First Decade of the Nixon Doctrine* (Cambridge: Cambridge University Press, 1986).

13. George D. Moffett III, *The Limits of Victory: The Ratification of the Panama Canal Treaties* (Ithaca, N.Y.: Cornell University Press, 1985), 38–53.

14. For background, see Cyrus Vance, *Hard Choices: Critical Years in America's Foreign Policy* (New York: Simon and Schuster, 1983), 256–61.

15. For the background to and terms of the act, see Raymond L. Garthoff, *Detente and Confrontation: American-Soviet Relations from Nixon to Reagan*, rev. ed. (Washington, D.C.: Brookings Institution, 1994), 527–33.

16. Gerald R. Ford, *A Time to Heal: The Autobiography of Gerald R. Ford* (New York: Harper and Row, 1979), 300–302.

17. Robert M. Gates, *From the Shadows: The Ultimate Insider's Story of Five Presidents and How They Won the Cold War* (New York: Simon and Schuster, 1996), 85–89; William G. Hyland, *Mortal Rivals: Superpower Relations from Nixon to Reagan* (New York: Random House, 1987), 127.

18. Quoted in Smith, *Morality, Reason, and Power*, 50.

19. Ibid.

20. David Skidmore, *Reversing Course: Carter's Foreign Policy, Domestic Politics, and the Failure of Reform* (Nashville, Tenn.: Vanderbilt University Press, 1996), 30–31.

21. For a listing of some of the most important literature in the incoherence school, see ibid., 188n1. Skidmore reflects the opposite view in his statement that "those who argue that the administration lacked a coherent world view fail to distinguish between coherence and complexity" (ibid., 28). See also Jerel A. Rosati, *The Carter Administration's Quest for Global Community: Beliefs and the Impact on Behavior* (Columbia: University of South Carolina Press, 1987). For a broader study that gives Carter credit for considerable coherence early on, see Richard A. Melanson, *Reconstructing Consensus: American Foreign Policy since the Vietnam War* (New York: St. Martin's Press, 1991), chap. 3.

22. *Public Papers of the Presidents of the United States: Jimmy Carter, 1977* (Washington, D.C.: Government Printing Office, 1978), 954–59. Henceforth this source is referred to as *Public Papers of Jimmy Carter*.

23. The omission is understandable given the sensitive stage of negotiations between Panama and the United States in May 1977. See William J. Jorden, *Panama Odyssey* (Austin: University of Texas Press, 1984), chap. 14.

24. For a treatment of the canal issue in historical context, see Gaddis Smith, *The Last Years of the Monroe Doctrine, 1945–1993* (New York: Hill and Wang, 1994), 141–48. For Carter's retrospective account, see Jimmy Carter, *Keeping Faith: Memoirs of a President* (New York: Bantam Books, 1982), 152–85. On the Presidential Review Memorandum, see Zbigniew Brzezinski, *Power and Principle: Memoirs of the National Security Adviser, 1977–1981* (New York: Farrar, Straus and Giroux, 1983), 51.

25. The most detailed account of the entire process of negotiating the treaties and guiding them through the Senate is Jorden, *Panama Odyssey*. Jorden worked on Latin American affairs in the National Security Council from 1972 to 1974, when he became ambassador to Panama. He served in that position through the ratification of the canal treaties. For briefer accounts of the domestic politics of the canal issue prior to 1977, see Moffett, *Limits of Victory*, 41–47, and Walter LaFeber, *The Panama Canal* (New York: Oxford University Press, 1978), 185–91.

26. Carter, *Keeping Faith*, 178.

27. Jorden, *Panama Odyssey*, 341–42.

28. *Newsday*, August 12, 1977, 17, as quoted in Moffett, *Limits of Victory*, 41. On Carter's failure to involve the Senate more in the final stages of the negotiations, see Robert Beckel Interview, November 13, 1981, 23–24, William Burkett Miller Center of Public Affairs, University of Virginia Project on the Carter Presidency Transcripts (hereafter cited as Miller Center), Jimmy Carter Library (JCL). Beckel was deputy assistant secretary of state for congressional relations during the Carter administration.

29. Carter, *Keeping Faith*, 65.

30. Gary M. Fink, "Labor Law Revision and the End of the Postwar Labor Accord," in *Organized Labor and American Politics*, ed. Kevin Boyle (Albany: State University of New York Press, 1998).

31. Carter, *Keeping Faith*, 65.

32. Garthoff, *Detente and Confrontation*, 627–29.

33. Carter, *Keeping Faith*, 143. On the domestic political aspects of Carter's human rights policy, see Joshua Muravchik, *The Uncertain Crusade: Jimmy Carter and the Dilemmas of Human Rights Policy* (Lanham, Md.: Hamilton Press, 1986), 1–7.

34. Muravchik, *Uncertain Crusade*, 218.

35. James Schlesinger, Miller Center Interview, July 19, 1984, 13–14, JCL.

36. On Vance's preference, see Vance, *Hard Choices*, 46. Anatoly Dobrynin, the Soviet ambassador to the United States, indicates that Vance made clear to him in private his own discomfort with the president's approach. See Anatoly Dobrynin, *In Confidence: Moscow's Ambassador to America's Six Cold War Presidents (1962–1986)* (New York: Times Books, 1995), 390.

37. Adam B. Ulam, *Dangerous Relations: The Soviet Union in World Politics, 1970–1982* (New York: Oxford University Press, 1983), 166–67.

38. Dobrynin, *In Confidence*, 389–91. See also former Soviet foreign minister Andrei Gromyko's *Memories*, trans. Harold Shukman (London: Hutchinson, 1989), 291–92.

39. Dobrynin, *In Confidence*, 392; Garthoff, *Detente and Confrontation*, 884–89. For an early and detailed account of the SALT II negotiations under Carter by a journalist with excellent official connections, see Strobe Talbott, *Endgame: The Inside Story of SALT II* (New York: Harper and Row, 1979).

40. Vance, *Hard Choices*, 55.

41. For an account by a scholar-participant that places the Carter administration's policy in historical context, see William B. Quandt, *Peace Process: American Diplomacy and the Arab-Israeli Conflict Since 1967* (Washington, D.C.: Brookings Institution, 1993). For an analysis of the Middle Eastern policies of American presidents from Truman to Reagan, see George Lenczowski, *American Presidents and the Middle East* (Durham, N.C.: Duke University Press, 1990). For Carter's retrospective account, see his *Keeping Faith*, 267–429.

42. Skidmore, *Reversing Course*, 47–51.

43. Victor S. Kaufman, "A Bureau Embattled: The Bureau of Human Rights and Humanitarian Affairs during the Carter Administration" (paper presented at a conference on the Carter administration at the Carter Center, Atlanta, Ga., February 20–22, 1997).

44. Andrew J. Pierre, *The Global Politics of Arms Sales* (Princeton, N.J.: Princeton University Press, 1982), 47, 57.

45. Muravchik, *Uncertain Crusade*, 32–34.

46. Gates, *From the Shadows*, 95–96.

47. *Public Papers of Jimmy Carter, 1977*, 2.

48. As one study concluded, "In Asia, especially Korea and the Philippines, Carter's policies and actions were only cosmetically better than those of his predecessors Richard Nixon and Gerald Ford." See Caleb Rossiter, assisted by Anne-Marie Smith, "Human Rights: The Carter Record, the Reagan Reaction," *International Policy Report* (September 1984), 1. See also Raymond Bonner, *Waltzing with a Dictator: The Marcoses and the Making of American Policy* (New York: Times Books, 1987), chap. 8.

49. Tony Smith, *America's Mission: The United States and the Worldwide Struggle for Democracy in the Twentieth Century* (Princeton, N.J.: Princeton University Press, 1994), 240, 242–44. In a speech on April 30, 1977, which outlined the administration's policy on human rights, Vance placed "civil and political liberties" third and last among the categories of rights to be pursued (see *Department of State Bulletin* 76 [May 23, 1977]: 506). In its list of concerns to be monitored by U.S. missions abroad, the State Department put third in four categories "respect for civil and political liberties, including . . . freedom to participate in the political process" (quoted in Smith, *America's Mission*, 242).

50. Smith, *America's Mission*, 244.

51. Lars Schoultz's *Human Rights and United States Policy toward Latin America* (Princeton, N.J.: Princeton University Press, 1981) concentrates on one region of the world but gives broad coverage to events and organizations that contributed to the rise of the human rights issue in American politics during the 1970s.

52. Muravchik, *Uncertain Crusade*, 44.

53. Vance offers a clear and relatively concise account of the complex story of Zimbabwe's creation in *Hard Choices*, chaps. 12 and 13.

54. Robert A. Pastor, *Condemned to Repetition: The United States and Nicaragua* (Princeton, N.J.: Princeton University Press, 1987), 38–39. Pastor was a National Security Council staffer during the Carter period, specializing in Latin American affairs. His account is sympathetic to Carter administration policy but also places it in historical context.

55. Ibid., 53–56. For an excellent brief account of Carter's policy leading to Somoza's fall, see John H. Coatsworth, *Central America and the United States* (New York: Twayne, 1994), 137–46.

56. Pastor, *Condemned to Repetition*, 65–66.

57. Ibid., 67–71. See also Anthony Lake, *Somoza Falling* (Boston: Houghton Mifflin, 1989), 82–89. Lake headed the Policy Planning Staff in the State Department during the Carter administration. While more favorable toward the Carter administration than most secondary works, these accounts demonstrate a coherence in conception and execution of policy that is missed by historians (see, for example, Smith, *Morality, Reason, and Power*, 118–22, and Walter LaFeber, *Inevitable Revolutions: The United States in Central America* [New York: Norton, 1993], 225–35).

58. Pastor, *Condemned to Repetition,* 78.

59. Ibid., chap. 6.

60. See Coatsworth, *Central America and the United States,* 146–57.

61. Two accounts that have influenced my thinking here are James A. Bill, *The Eagle and the Lion: The Tragedy of American-Iranian Relations* (New Haven, Conn.: Yale University Press, 1988), 226–33; and David C. McGaffey, "Iran: Policy and Practice, Human Rights in the Shah's Iran," in *The Diplomacy of Human Rights,* ed. David D. Newsom (Lanham, Md.: University Press of America, 1986), 69–79. McGaffey was a U.S. consul in Iran during the Carter years.

62. Michael Ledeen and William Lewis, *Debacle: The American Failure in Iran* (New York: Knopf, 1981), 81–82; Bill, *The Eagle and the Lion,* 228–30; Carter, *Keeping Faith,* 434–35.

63. *Public Papers of Jimmy Carter, 1977,* 2221; Carter, *Keeping Faith,* 434–37.

64. Ledeen and Lewis, *Debacle,* 95.

65. Gary Sick, *All Fall Down: America's Fateful Encounter with Iran* (London: I. B. Tauris, 1985), 36.

66. Vance, *Hard Choices,* 384–85.

67. Sick, *All Fall Down,* 44–46.

68. Ibid., 50–53; Bill, *The Eagle and the Lion,* 257–58; William H. Sullivan, *Mission to Iran* (New York: Norton, 1981), chap. 15.

69. See, for example, Carter's statements in press conferences during early December in *Public Papers of Jimmy Carter,* 2172, 2226.

70. See, for example, Carter's statement of October 31 quoted in Sick, *All Fall Down,* 62. On the shah's disappointment at Carter's refusal to advocate military government, see Sullivan, *Mission to Iran,* 172.

71. Vance, *Hard Choices,* 330–31; Sullivan, *Mission to Iran,* 156–58. In his memoirs, the shah complains that Ambassador Sullivan would never confirm in private the Carter administration's public expressions of support. See Mohammad Reza Pahlavi, *Answer to History* (New York: Stein and Day, 1980), 161–62.

72. Sick, *All Fall Down,* 66.

73. See, for example, Lenczowski, *American Presidents and the Middle East,* 184; and Burton I. Kaufman, *The Arab Middle East and the United States: Inter-Arab Rivalry and Superpower Diplomacy* (New York: Twayne, 1996), 114–15.

74. On the "Kissinger legacy," see Quandt, *Peace Process,* 249–51.

75. For accounts of normalization by key players on the American side, see Carter, *Keeping Faith,* 186–211; Vance, *Hard Choices,* 75–83, 113–19; Brzezinski, *Power and Principle,* chap. 6. For brief secondary accounts cast in broad historical perspective, see Warren I. Cohen, *America's Response to China: A History of Sino-American Relations,* 3d ed. (New York: Columbia University Press, 1990), 199–204; Nancy Bernkopf Tucker, *Taiwan, Hong Kong, and the United States, 1945–1992* (New York: Twayne, 1994), chap. 7; Rosemary Foot, *The Practice of Power: U.S. Relations with China since 1949* (Oxford: Clarendon Press, 1995), 78–81, 108–15, 140–42, 227–28.

76. Garthoff, *Detente and Confrontation,* 758.

77. On the broad context for SALT II during 1978–80, see ibid., chaps. 24, 26, and 27.

78. Ibid., 1096–98.

79. Ibid., 1067.

80. See Skidmore, *Reversing Course,* 71–76.

81. Garthoff, *Detente and Confrontation,* 1066.

82. Brzezinski, *Power and Principle,* 178–84.

83. *Public Papers of Jimmy Carter, 1980–81,* 197.

84. Garthoff, *Detente and Confrontation,* 1084–85; Brzezinski, *Power and Principle,* 455–56.

85. For an analysis emphasizing the domestic political dimensions of Carter's shift, see Skidmore, *Reversing Course.*

86. Melanson, *Reconstructing Consensus,* 110.

87. Seyom Brown, *The Faces of Power: Constancy and Change in United States Foreign Policy from Truman to Clinton,* 2d ed. (New York: Columbia University Press, 1994), 384–85.

88. For a brief discussion of Carter's policy on nonproliferation, see Harold Muller, David Fischer, and Wolfgang Kotter, *Nuclear Non-Proliferation and Global Order* (New York: Oxford University Press, 1994), 25–26.

89. Brzezinski, *Power and Principle,* 429, 448; Thomas G. Paterson, J. Garry Clifford, and Kenneth J. Hagan, *American Foreign Policy: A History,* vol. 2, *Since 1900,* 3d rev. ed. (Lexington, Mass.: Heath, 1991), 643.

90. Stansfield Turner, *Secrecy and Democracy: The CIA in Transition* (Boston: Houghton Mifflin, 1985), 84–89; Christopher Andrew, *For the President's Eyes Only* (New York: HarperCollins, 1995), 455.

91. Gates, *From the Shadows,* 123; Foot, *Practice of Power,* 263–65; Garthoff, *Detente and Confrontation,* 1099.

92. Raymond L. Garthoff, *The Great Transition: American-Soviet Relations and the End of the Cold War* (Washington, D.C.: Brookings Institution, 1994), 9, 26.

93. Gates, *From the Shadows,* 96.

94. Quoted in A. Glenn Mower, Jr., *Human Rights and American Foreign Policy: The Carter and Reagan Experiences* (New York: Greenwood Press, 1987), 25.

95. Ibid., 34.

96. Ibid., 38–39; Muravchik, *Uncertain Crusade,* 176–77.

97. Smith, *America's Mission,* 239.

98. For a spirited defense of Carter's foreign policies and the connection between them and his postpresidential efforts, see Douglas Brinkley, "The Rising Stock of Jimmy Carter: The 'Hands On' Legacy of Our Thirty-Ninth President," *Diplomatic History* 209 (Fall 1996): 505–29.

13

The Agenda Continued: Jimmy Carter's Postpresidency

John Whiteclay Chambers II

While Jimmy Carter's postpresidential career has been widely recognized as extraordinary among ex-presidents, the linkage between many of his presidential and postpresidential policies and concerns has received less notice. The continuity in a number of areas is particularly striking. Carter seemed to be taking some of the few acclaimed characteristics of his defeated presidency—his peacemaking and his concern for human rights and for the poor—and making them the focus of a campaign for his own resurrection.

In the nearly two decades since leaving the White House, Carter has traveled around the globe on peacemaking and humanitarian missions, building on areas of concern and strength that he demonstrated in the White House. Earlier chapters in the present volume demonstrate Carter's interest in these programs in the White House: his regard for peacemaking, human rights, and the environment; his attention to Latin America, Africa, and Asia; and his concern for the plight of minorities and the poor in his civil rights, welfare, and urban policies. He has indeed pursued these concerns and even many of these policies in his ex-presidency. So has Rosalynn Carter, who has accompanied him on most of his missions and continued her own special interests in mental health, child immunization, and caregiving—all of which were also areas of interest to her during the Carter presidency.

As Carter has pursued these interests in the years since his 1980 electoral defeat by Ronald Reagan, he has become one of America's greatest ex-presidents. This is an accolade conceded even by many in the media who beleaguered him while he was in the White House. In a cover story on the ex-president, *Time* magazine declared that "despite all his troubles in the White House, Jimmy Carter (yes, Jimmy Carter) may be the best former President America has ever had."[1]

Many have surmised that Carter is driven to vindicate his presidency and counter the rejection of the voters at the polls. But the redemption concept has been overemphasized. It presumes Carter believes he needs to redeem his presidency. He does not. Rather, he is proud of what he accomplished in office and argues that it needs no defense. Like other presidents, he claims the media misunderstood him or condemned him unfairly. He emphasizes his accomplishments and blames largely external circumstances—the performance of the economy and the seizure of American hostages by Iranian militants—for low public approval ratings and his electoral defeat. Recently, however, speaking to a gathering of scholars at the Carter Center, he wistfully declared that "perhaps we tried to do too much."[2] Carter hopes for greater scholarly and public appreciation of his presidency, but it is not redemption of his presidential performance that drives him as an ex-president. Carter takes a longer view and has a larger goal; he wants to ensure a place in history with a legacy that encompasses an extremely long and worthy career in public service: as naval officer, legislator, governor, president, *and* former president.

The press has put forward a paradox in which Carter, an unsuccessful president, becomes a highly successful ex-president. But while containing elements of truth, the paradox is also overdrawn. He was a more successful president than is often remembered, as William Leuchtenburg reminds us earlier in this volume; and as an ex-president, he has not always been as successful as it seems. Of course, no president ever gets everything right, and it should not be assumed that an ex-president would either. Regardless of its other problems, in the areas of foreign policy and human rights the Carter administration certainly took some important steps.[3] And despite his prescience and commitment and several attempts, he has failed as an ex-president to influence a peace settlement in the Middle East. Still, Carter clearly has been a more popular former president than president.[4]

In part this simply reflects Carter's freedom as an ex-president to select the problems he chooses to address. In contrast, modern American presidents have been expected to address all, or at least most, of the pressing major problems on the public agenda. For Carter some of those problems proved insoluble; certainly, many were compounded by deep divisions within the Democratic party and between the Carter administration and the Democratic majority in Congress.[5] But once out of the White House, Carter was no longer expected to resolve critical national problems, nor, of course, did he have to deal with legislators who resented him and his managerial style. The former president could deal directly with chief executives or other top officials.

This ability to select issues may help explain some of the discontinuities between Carter's presidential and postpresidential concerns. Although international conflict resolution, human rights, the environment, and urban poverty were of continuing concern, on education, health insurance, women's equality, or trade and industrial policy little follow-through existed into the postpresidential years. It is unclear whether such discontinuity is a result of Carter's own priorities or his view of the areas in which he can influence policy as an ex-president. A distinct lack of continuity also exists between Carter's advisers in the White House and at the Carter Center, the public policy center the Carters founded in Atlanta. Only one top official at the Carter Center served in the Carter administration—Robert Pastor, director of the Center's Latin American and Caribbean Program, was a member of the National Security Council and a foreign affairs adviser at the Carter White House.[6]

Significantly, Carter has proved much more successful in his relations with the media than he did in office. The media now tends mainly to emphasize his successes, because it is so surprising (thus it is news) that an ex-president can actually determine public policy and influence major events. The press has not given Carter a free ride. He has been criticized by some on the right and sometimes from the left for his negotiations with dictatorial regimes in his attempts to mediate peaceful resolutions to violent or potentially explosive situations, and for making inappropriate remarks, such as telling the Haitian junta that he was "ashamed" of U.S. policy. But on the whole, the media has been favorable to Carter's activities as an ex-president, emphasizing his successful humanitarian and peacemaking activities, sometimes with front-page or front-cover stories, and largely ignoring the efforts of the Carters or the Carter Center that have come to naught.

Carter's more successful media coverage results from the conducive circumstances in which he has found himself as an ex-president. One is the contrast of Carter's activities and reputation with those of other living ex-presidents. Richard Nixon had resigned in disgrace. The press was also critical of former presidents Gerald Ford and Ronald Reagan (before the news that Reagan had Alzheimer's disease) for acquisitive marketing and high living.[7] Their leisure lifestyle contrasted with Carter's energetic public service and fund-raising for public service projects.

It was the foreign policy difficulties of incumbent presidents George Bush and Bill Clinton, however, that gave Carter his greatest opportunities to influence policy and major events. Seen as indecisive and without a coherent foreign policy in the post–cold war world, Bush and Clinton lacked the public support that the Reagan administration had enjoyed. Consequently, Carter acted, building on themes from his presidency and from areas of his strength: peacemaking and his emphasis on democracy, human rights, the environment, and his special attention to Africa, Asia, and Latin America.

The national press began to celebrate the ex-president in 1989 when in Panama he courageously denounced the presidential election of General Manuel Noriega's handpicked successor. Denouncing the election as a fraud, Carter took on the Panamanian dictator, a former American client and an extremely dangerous man, in front of the world media. In truth, Carter's return to Panama was a masterpiece of "guerrilla diplomacy." He used his popularity with the Panamanian people, dating from his achievement of the Panama Canal treaties, to maneuver Noriega into reluctantly accepting the presence of his monitoring delegation, the Council of Freely Elected Heads of Government, which Carter had created through the

Carter Center. To emphasize bipartisanship, he arranged for former Republican president Gerald Ford to accompany the delegation. But Carter ran the show. On his arrival, he used his Spanish speaking ability and access to the local media to urge Panamanians to vote, calculating that a large turnout would overwhelm Noriega's attempts to manipulate the actual voting. On election day, he rushed to spots where shooting or military interference were reported and called for protests to force Noriega to respect the "clear victory" of the challenger, Guillermo Endara. Surveys by the Roman Catholic Church supported Carter's assertion.[8]

Flying back to Washington, Carter briefed President Bush (in a photograph that appeared on the front page of most major U.S. newspapers), who, citing "massive irregularities at the polls" called for international pressure to force Noriega to step aside as military leader.[9] Bush did use U.S. troops six months later, in December 1989, to topple Noriega and install Endara. Widely hailed by the national and international press, Carter's courage and strong moral role in challenging the Panamanian dictator in his own country further enhanced his reputation as a champion of democracy.[10] President Bush understood that his and the nation's interests would be served in this instance by associating with the man he had spent three campaigns ridiculing as a symbol of irresolution and malaise.

Less than a year later, in February 1990, Jimmy Carter achieved an even greater personal and public triumph in monitoring a key election in Nicaragua and persuading the defeated Sandinista president, Daniel Ortega Saavedra, to accept the results and step down. As president, Bush changed Reagan's policy and, in agreement with Congress, supported the idea of peace through new elections in Nicaragua. This gave Carter his opportunity. His administration had played an important role in the fall of the Samoza regime in Nicaragua, and now over a period of months, Carter and his Latin America expert, Robert Pastor, built up a relationship of trust with President Daniel Ortega.[11] As he did in Panama in 1989 when he branded Noriega's claim to victory as fraudulent, Carter once again transformed the traditional role of election observer, previously limited to certifying whether or not an election was honest. In Nicaragua in 1990, Carter went beyond that role and helped to convince the defeated regime to accept the result, thus helping ensure a peaceful transition to democracy.

On the night of the election in February 1990, when it became clear that the Sandinistas had lost the majority and Ortega the presidency, it appeared that the Sandinistas might use force to halt the process and retain their control of the government through fraud.[12] Rushing to Ortega's headquarters, where *commandantes* surrounded the incumbent president, Carter engaged in an incredible conversation in which he shared his own sense of defeat in 1980 with Ortega and explained that his own career showed there could be stature even after defeat. He also provided Ortega with some face-saving statements from the president-elect, Violeta Chamarro, and from U.S. Secretary of State James Baker.[13] Subsequently, Ortega and Chamarro called for a cease-fire and disbanding of the contras, and the Bush administration agreed.[14] Chamorro took office as scheduled on April 25, 1990, and in a gesture of reconciliation retained the former president's brother, General Humberto Ortega Saavedra, as the commander of the country's armed forces.[15]

Once again Carter enjoyed much praise for his skill and integrity, although two conservative columnists, Rowland Evans and Robert Novak, challenged him for making too many concessions, particularly for advocating disbanding of the contras while allowing the Sandinistas to retain control of the army. Conservative criticism made the Bush administration more wary, but it did little to tarnish Carter's burgeoning reputation.[16] Through his actions in Panama and then Nicaragua, the former president contributed to the new idea that foreign observers have a right and responsibility to monitor free elections and certify them to the world as well as the electorate. This concept represented an extension of human rights diplomacy, so much a part of Carter's presidency and now his postpresidency.[17]

Carter thus used his reputation for integrity and as a champion of human rights, as well as a friend of democracy especially in Latin America and Africa, to develop this new role for an ex-president of the United States of election monitoring for democracy. This role helped propel him back into the world spotlight. Carter's spectacular success in helping to cripple Noriega's dictatorship led the press to look again at the ex-president and, in 1989, to provide a series of front-page stories and television programs about his (and Rosalynn's) good work, not simply in election monitoring but in many other humanitarian and democratic activities—from fighting disease in Africa to helping build houses for the poor in America. Panama made it possible for Carter to go public again and to win the acclaim that had eluded him for nearly a decade.

Four years later, in 1993–94, peacemaking diplomacy rather than election monitoring brought Carter back to the front pages in another unprecedented role for a former president. This diplomacy involved mediation of international confrontations concerning the United States in Somalia, North Korea, Haiti, and Bosnia. Once again Carter's opportunity derived from a change in domestic circumstances—this time the election of Democrat Bill Clinton as president and a Clintonian foreign policy combining brinkmanship with indecision, which resulted in crises that gave Carter an opening to come to the rescue of the administration. In all of these he employed the kind of mediation skills he had used in 1979 at Camp David to achieve the Egyptian-Israeli Accords.

During Clinton's first year in the White House, Carter helped the Democratic president disengage from the seemingly hopeless situation in Somalia bequeathed to him by President Bush. The Somalia situation had become worse for the United States because the Clinton administration had moved in 1993 from a U.S./UN humanitarian peacekeeping role to a difficult and dangerous new goal: capturing one of the most aggressive clan leaders, Mohamed Farah Aidid. Although Clinton talked tough, it proved impossible to capture Aidid or impose control over Somalia. Aidid contacted Carter, who had been attempting to mediate an end to a civil war as neighboring Eritrea sought to separate from Ethiopia, and with Clinton's permission the former president began negotiations and obtained Aidid's agreement that he would accept the findings of an independent UN commission investigating responsibility for the killing of UN peacekeepers. Subsequently, the U.S. Air Force flew Aidid to Addis Ababa in Ethiopia to negotiate, thus beginning a process that led to the withdrawal of the American troops in March 1994 and the UN peacekeepers in 1995. Carter not only had eased the crisis but also helped shift U.S. policy away from the military option.[18]

The Georgia native played an even more important and highly publicized role in 1994 in his successful personal diplomacy in North Korea and Haiti. Here again, he built on previous strengths, having established some goodwill in those countries while serving as president. Once again, the indecisive brinkmanship of the Clinton administration provided an opening.

In June 1994, Carter helped defuse a dangerously escalating confrontation between North Korea and the United States over Pyongyang's nuclear program. The immediate issue was Pyongyang's refusal to allow UN inspectors unlimited access to nuclear facilities and the belief in the West that the North Koreans might already have built two atomic bombs. When the Clinton administration responded by breaking off talks and calling for economic sanctions, North Korea declared that the imposition of sanctions would be an act of war. Some Western hawks urged preparation for bombing raids on the nuclear facilities of the "rogue" regime. As president, Carter had sought to ease tensions on the Korean peninsula; now he pressed the Clinton administration to let him accept a long-standing invitation to visit both North and South Korea. In June, Jimmy and Rosalynn Carter visited the two capitals, and in Pyongyang the former president urged open trade and full diplomatic relations. President Kim Il Sung agreed to full UN monitoring of the nuclear sites. Both Seoul and Washington played down Carter's peacemaking effort because of worries that he was overly sympathetic to North Korea. Carter also irritated the Clinton administration by publicly condemning its sanctions policy. Despite a number of subsequent delays, including those resulting from Kim's death, the process of negotiation that Carter had started continued. A preliminary agreement signed in Geneva in October 1994 called for Western aid in exchange for North Korea allowing UN inspection.[19]

The Carters had defused the crisis, moving it from confrontation to negotiation—an achievement widely recognized in the press. Less recognized at the time, the Carters had also given impetus to a long-term change in U.S. policy toward North Korea. The cold war policy of shunning Pyongyang slowly gave way to an active effort to bring it out of its isolation through constructive engagement.[20]

Carter's most highly publicized personal diplomacy came four months later in September 1994 when he led a delegation to Haiti. There, in a weekend-long negotiation, he achieved U.S. goals and successfully headed off an invasion even as airborne paratroopers were on their way to the island. Faced with the stubbornness of the ruling military junta in Haiti, which refused to step down and reinstate the democratically elected president, Jean-Bertrand Aristide, and confronted with a continuing exodus of seaborne impoverished Haitians seeking refuge in the

United States, Clinton had obtained UN economic sanctions on the island and then UN authorization to use military force. In early September 1994, two months before the U.S. congressional elections, Clinton went on national television and ordered the junta to step down or be taken down by American military force.[21]

Despite public bravado in rejecting U.S. demands, the Haitian junta wanted to deal. Prepared for this, Carter knew the administration disliked the idea of sending him to Haiti, so he had contacted two other invasion opponents: General Colin Powell, former chairman of the Joint Chiefs of Staff, and Senator Sam Nunn of Georgia, chairman of the Senate Armed Services Committee. On September 14, he asked Clinton to send them as a mediation team.[22] Despite serious opposition in the Clinton administration to using Carter—especially from Secretary of State Warren Christopher and his deputy Strobe Talbott, who saw the former president as uncontrollable—Clinton agreed to the mission but at the same time prepared for the invasion.[23]

On September 17, a U.S. Air Force plane flew the Carter team to Port-au-Prince, and the negotiators met immediately with the Haitian junta headed by Lieutenant General Raoul Cedras but got nowhere. Carter apparently helped persuade the generals of his nonpartisanship by saying he was "ashamed" of U.S. policy toward Haiti, a remark for which he was later criticized in the United States. He subsequently explained that he meant the U.S./UN embargo had a harmful effect on the health of the poor in Haiti without affecting the junta's power. Carter also told Cedras that he would not be required to go into exile but would have to step down by October 15. In exchange, the Haitian Parliament would declare a *general* amnesty for all members of the military. With news of U.S. paratroopers en route to the island, Haitian officials agreed to the terms Carter had worked out. At 8 P.M., Clinton accepted the agreement and recalled the airborne invasion force. That night Clinton announced the successful mediation in a televised address to the nation—emphasizing that the "Haitian dictators" would go by October 15 and that President Aristide would then be returned to power. The next morning, troops from a naval task force came ashore, and the U.S. military soon took control of the island, pending President Aristide's return on October 15, 1994, the day after General Cedras and his family prudently had departed for Panama.[24]

The mainstream press hailed Carter's—and Clinton's—achievement in obtaining the return of Haiti's first democratically elected president without a massive and potentially bloody U.S. invasion. Noting Carter's fifth nomination for a Nobel Peace Prize, the *New York Times* praised him as a "unique diplomatic resource" and called him "our most useful and perhaps most versatile former President."[25] So did the American public; 68 percent viewed Carter as helpful to the Clinton administration.[26]

•   Still, critics questioned Carter's achievements. Conservatives slammed him for being soft on the Haitian dictators, and many commentators across the political spectrum pointed out that Carter had given the junta a number of face-saving concessions instead of forcing it to step down immediately and face trial for the crimes committed during the military regime. The agreement failed to mention the dictatorship or the deposing of a freely elected president.[27] Even the mainstream press criticized Carter for some of his remarks. In press interviews, he praised Cedras and the junta as honorable men to be treated with respect.[28] Later, he denounced "the basic policy of the State Department" toward Haiti.[29]

Despite the flap over Carter's remarks, the importance of Carter's achievement in September 1994 remained impressive. The ex-president indeed had modified U.S. policy toward Haiti and forced a president anxious to avoid large numbers of American casualties to accept concessions to the junta. As in Korea, Carter helped reverse a dangerous escalation of tensions, and this time he achieved the major objective of the U.S. and the UN—the return of democracy to Haiti.[30]

But Carter's new image lost a bit of luster when, in a 1994 interview following the Haitian mission, the former president revealed that during the 1991 Persian Gulf crisis he had privately written the heads of member nations of the UN Security Council urging them to oppose President Bush's request for UN authorization to use military force to drive Iraq out of Kuwait.[31] Although the Bush administration never responded publicly to Carter's unusual private communication, the former president's attempt to undercut U.S. policy through direct appeals to other governments represented an unprecedented and inappropriate action by a former head of state.

Later in 1994, Carter became involved in a new attempt to end the four-year civil war in Bosnia among ethnic Serbs, ethnic Croats, and Bosnian Muslims. Talks there had broken off in the summer. In December 1994, tensions had escalated as NATO air forces threatened to bomb Bosnian Serb artillery positions shelling cities like Sarajevo. The Bosnian Serbs responded by capturing UN peacekeepers and holding them as hostages. Having resisted earlier pressures to commit U.S. forces, Clinton now agreed to send troops if necessary. Within days, representatives of Radovan Karadzic, the political leader of the Bosnian Serbs, contacted Jimmy Carter, who with Clinton's approval began a series of telephone discussions.[32] On December 14, the ex-president agreed to meet with Bosnian Serb leaders, who said they would make a series of "concessions," including a cease-fire and the freeing of UN peacekeepers held hostage. Until Karadzic's overture to Carter, the Bosnian Serbs had rejected American peace efforts, which they believed were anti-Serb. Although the Clinton administration again divided on whether to use Carter, the president apparently concluded that his Democratic predecessor might achieve a lasting cease-fire in the besieged capital of Sarajevo and perhaps even provide a face-saving opportunity for the Bosnian Serbs to move toward peace.[33]

On December 19, Jimmy and Rosalynn Carter met with Karadzic in the Bosnian Serb capital of Pale, twenty miles from Sarajevo. Carter suggested that the Americans had misunderstood the Serbs. As a result, Karadzic agreed to open peace negotiations based on the international plan he had rejected in July, a plan that proposed an approximately fifty-fifty division of territory instead of about 70 percent that the Bosnian Serbs controlled militarily. The statement signed by

Carter, Karadzic, and Ratko Mladic, military commander of the Bosnian Serbs, also called for a formal, four-month cease-fire, release of UN hostage peacekeepers, and protection of human rights throughout Bosnia. While accepting these provisions, the White House promptly distanced itself from Carter's statement that the American people had heard only one side of the story, reiterating Washington's position that the Bosnian Serbs were the aggressors in the war.[34] In three days of hectic shuttle diplomacy between Sarajevo and Pale, Carter also obtained agreement from the Muslim-dominated Bosnian government. The ex-president thus broke a long deadlock by going directly to the Bosnian Serbs, expressing some sympathy for their position, and offering considerable flexibility in future negotiations. He thus brought the two sides closer to the bargaining table than they had been for six months.[35]

But fighting usually had declined in the winter months anyway, and in the spring of 1995, the Carter-brokered truce ended as the shooting resumed. Carter offered to return to Bosnia to try to restore the cease-fire, but it was not to be, as the fighting escalated through the summer.[36] After the fall of the alleged "safe havens" of Sebrenica and Zepa and reports of large-scale atrocities, the Clinton administration reluctantly decided to use substantial air power against the Bosnian Serbs.[37] The coordination of a massive NATO air campaign with a Croat-Muslim ground attack changed the balance of power on the ground and forced the Bosnian Serbs to the peace table with reduced territorial ambitions. Carter again facilitated the exchange of proposals between Karadzic and the negotiators from the UN and NATO.[38] The Clinton administration brought the three Balkan presidents to Wright-Patterson Air Force Base in Dayton, Ohio, where three weeks of peace talks resulted in their initialing the Dayton Agreements on November 21, 1995. Signed in Paris on December 14, 1995, the treaty ended the civil war and provided for a Bosnian Republic of two "entities" divided 49 percent for the Bosnian Serbs and 51 percent held by a federation of Muslims and Croats.[39]

The Carter Center, essential to the mediating and peacemaking activities the former president carried over into his postpresidency, was founded by Jimmy and Rosalynn Carter in 1982 in partnership with Emory University in Atlanta.[40] By the 1990s, the Carter Center employed at least two hundred full-time and part-time persons, based primarily in the Atlanta headquarters but with field representatives in a number of countries in Africa and Latin America.[41] In Atlanta, more than one hundred graduate and undergraduate students worked as interns with Center programs for academic credit or practical experience each year. In addition, approximately 130 volunteers donated an average of a day of their time each week to the Center. In fiscal year 1994, the Carter Center had an annual operating budget of $28.5 million and an endowment and other assets of $65 million.[42]

The Carter Center aims to combine human and material resources to help resolve conflict and promote democracy, and also to fight disease, hunger, and poverty both at home and abroad. The Center seeks to identify solvable problems and coordinate the efforts of public and private agencies in a task force approach. Two of the Carter Center programs—Global 2000 and Friendship Force—had begun during the Carter presidency but were abandoned by the Reagan administration. Friendship Force, an international program of person-to-person exchanges, helps place Americans for a week in foreign homes and foreign residents for a week in American homes, with an aim of increasing cross-cultural understanding and encouraging world peace.[43]

The Global 2000 environmental program, essentially a world health and environmental task force, is the result of a report commissioned by President Carter in 1977, after the Club of Rome's study on the growing disparity between the earth's limited resources and burgeoning population growth. The report "Global 2000" assessed the future of the world's environment.[44] In his postpresidency, Carter resumed Global 2000 as a private venture. Its Agricultural Program works to end hunger in developing countries by teaching farmers to use high-yielding seeds, fertilizers, and other more productive agricultural practices. Under the Carter Center program, more than two hundred thousand African farmers had learned new techniques by the mid-1990s that could double or triple their grain production.[45]

In its disease eradication projects, Global 2000, working with American pharmaceutical companies and African countries, by 1996 had achieved an imminent victory over guinea worm disease (dracunculiasis), which had afflicted more than 4 million people; it would be only the second disease after smallpox to be eradicated in human history. Program directors also turned their attention to a project against river blindness (onchocerciasis), which plagued 18 million persons in Latin America, Africa, and the Middle East.[46]

In the United States, the Carter Center also encouraged some health programs that the Carters had championed during their White House years. Most dramatic was Rosalynn Carter's twenty-year concern with mental health, her ongoing campaign to help reduce the stigma and provide quality affordable care for people suffering from mental health problems. Continuing the work she had started as First Lady when she assumed responsibility for the creation of the President's Commission on Mental Health in 1977, Rosalynn Carter remains active in both the Task Force on Mental Health and an annual symposium on mental health policy.[47] These programs seek to coordinate consumers, family members, policy makers, and service providers at the state and national levels. Another Rosalynn Carter–inspired program, affiliated with rather than directly originating in the Carter Center, was an attempt to provide vaccinations against disease to infants and preschool children in the United States and around the world.[48]

Jimmy Carter's attitude toward the poor, during both his presidential and postpresidential years, has combined a liberal commitment to social justice for the dispossessed with a conservative suspicion of big government and an emphasis on local efforts and the private sector. As delineated in earlier chapters in this volume on urban policy and welfare reform, Carter's White House policies in these areas in large part reflected his rejection of the idea of an unemployable underclass. He believed people in poverty would work if jobs were available and that these could be best provided through a partnership between government and business. Welfare reform, therefore, could be achieved most effectively through a comprehensive, efficiency-oriented program.

Carter had failed as president to achieve the kind of welfare reform or urban program that he wanted. When, as an ex-president, he again turned to the problem of poverty in the United States, he emphasized many of the same themes he had in the White House. His encouragement of local volunteer programs was nowhere more evident than in his and Rosalynn Carter's support for Habitat for Humanity's self-help, home-building project for the poor. The image of the former president and former First Lady in overalls actually helping the poor build their own homes is irresistible to the press and highly popular with the public. "I think that the most highly publicized thing that Rosalynn and I do is build houses," Carter stated in 1992. "We do it one week a year, but it is something that you can photograph or put on television, and this is a well-known thing."[49]

Carter's White House attitudes on urban policy also continued into his postpresidential career, particularly as he turned his attention to the plight of the urban poor. The Carter administration had rejected large-scale federal urban renewal projects as costly failures; the president's emphasis had been on efficient partnership between the public and private sectors and encouragement of local community redevelopment. These themes continued to guide him in 1991, when at the instigation of Atlanta business leaders he launched an urban program designed to aid the five hundred thousand impoverished persons in the greater Atlanta area. In announcing The Atlanta Project (TAP) to the press, Carter said he had decided to use the approach that brought him success in the Carter Center's projects abroad: to go to the people in charge, enlist their support, assemble a winning team of experts and put them to work, and coordinate projects and organizations and public and private resources. He also sought to give a voice to the people of the local communities and gave them a stake in the outcome. It was, as TAP director and Atlanta planner Dan Sweat put it, "a new paradigm of corporate involvement in urban revitalization . . . partnerships of local neighborhoods and major corporations."[50]

In typical Carter fashion, the former president combined a moral appeal with a voluntaristic, private-oriented approach. He tried to mobilize wealthy and middle-class Atlantans to help their poorer neighbors by sermonizing about two Atlantas: one rich and one poor. With the 1996 summer Olympics being held in Atlanta, Carter tied his program for longer-term goals to the immediate concern of both the public and private sector, which wanted simply a short-term municipal face-lift prior to hosting that prestigious international event.[51] At its most basic level, TAP sought to bring together individual volunteers as mentors, helping in day care centers or in schools in poor areas. It also attempted to simplify forms and standardize government programs. At its most complicated, it tried to use its relatively small annual budget to leverage millions of corporate and foundation donations to help community people and professionals solve problems of teenage pregnancy, juvenile violence, high dropout rates, low immunization rates, lack of affordable housing, and other inner-city problems. TAP sought to create a model partnership among business, academic, and service provider communities and Atlanta's neighborhoods. Atlanta's twenty low-income communities were to form close partnerships with at least one major corporation and institution of higher learning. Loaned executives and volunteers would work with these communities on projects coordinated by local residents.

TAP's ambitious initial focus covered a wide spectrum of concerns: children and families, education, housing, economic development, public safety, and health. TAP residents launched more than four hundred action-filled projects. A massive immunization drive that on one weekend brought together more than seven thousand volunteers who helped identify sixteen thousand preschool children, who in turn received free inoculations or had their vaccination records updated. The TAP into Peace project focused communities' attention on stopping violence. Other major TAP projects included entrepreneurial development and small-business loan funds, simplified forms for applying for social services, and a program for helping teenagers develop strong leadership and life skills.[52] By the mid-1990s, TAP had become the Carter Center's costliest program, accounting for nearly $11 million of the Center's nearly $29 million budget in fiscal year 1994.[53] More than one hundred delegations from other cities visited Atlanta to learn more about the project.[54]

Yet by 1995 it had become increasingly clear that, despite a few successful initiatives, TAP's initial five-year plan for overcoming problems of poverty through community empowerment and public-private partnership had been overly ambitious.[55] Following an internal reassessment, the Carter Center reorganized TAP and downsized it substantially in 1996–97. Four cluster centers, through which the donated resources of TAP's corporate partners would be available, replaced the twenty cluster offices. Carter Center directors then cut TAP's annual budget in half, down to $5.7 million for 1997–2000, and reduced its staff by 20 percent.[56] Jimmy Carter and the Carter Center staff admitted they had been too ambitious in their initial assumptions about community transformation and openly acknowledged that disappointments and even failures qualified the project's successes.[57] Achieving collaboration among service providers—public and private—and obtaining the trust and empowerment of the residents of the impoverished inner-city communities had proved more daunting than anticipated.[58] In 1997, a chastened and downsized TAP began a much less ambitious program entitled Phase II, the more modest goals of which focused on issues relating to quality of life for children, youth, and families. These included immunization of children under two years of age, enrolling more low-income students in Head Start and prekindergarten programs, raising the percentage of high school students graduating on time, and increasing the number of welfare recipients leaving public assistance because of employment or higher incomes. In Phase II, TAP pledged to define clearly partner roles and expectations from the outset.[59] Somewhat akin to the fate of the Carter administration's comprehensive welfare plan in the late 1970s, the Carter Center's initial Atlanta Project of the 1990s had underestimated the obstacles facing its comprehensive plan to transform the impoverished areas of Atlanta.

Carter's domestic programs, as an ex-president, were less successful and certainly attracted less national attention than his international forays dramatically confronting Manuel Noriega or Daniel Ortega. Yet his postpresidential domestic failures are also instructive in evaluating his presidency, for the failure of The Atlanta Project strongly supports Thomas Sugrue's analysis (pp. 137–57) of the inadequacies of Carter's emphasis as president on solving urban problems through relatively inexpensive "place-based" strategies. The low-cost programs built on local initiative and voluntarism failed even in Atlanta, where Carter had so much influence. Similarly, although building housing through Habitat for Humanity is a commendable project for contributors and recipients, it is unlikely to solve the problem of low-cost housing even in a local area, let alone on a national basis. These projects, however, do illustrate the continuity of Carter's basic view of humanitarian effort with a limited role for the federal government, whether considered from the White House perspective or that of the Carter Center. Despite his limited achievements on the domestic scene, Carter's intentions, integrity, and successes in the international arena have provided the luster for his postpresidential career. These successes echo Carter's achievements in his presidency: his emphasis on human rights, democracy, conflict resolution, and, particularly, the Camp David Peace Accord—the high point of his presidency.

Twenty years after his inauguration as president and sixteen years after becoming an ex-president, Jimmy Carter has achieved one of the most memorable postpresidential public service records in American history. Since returning to Georgia, Carter has been ranked with or above even those former chief executives who remained active in public service in their postpresidential careers: John Quincy Adams, who subsequently served with distinction in the U.S. House of Representatives; William Howard Taft, chief justice of the U.S. Supreme Court; and Herbert Hoover, who assisted U.S. relief efforts for refugees after World War II and later headed two "Hoover commissions" on efficiency in the federal government.

Still, the attention and acclaim Carter has received from the press as an ex-president have not altered the media's generally negative view of his presidency, although the more astute commentators have recognized that after 1980 Carter, now as an acclaimed ex-president, continued to pursue many of the same policies he had initiated in the White House. Rather, Carter's enhanced image with the media, particularly since 1989, has been important in aiding him with fund-raising and with the work of the Carter Center. Media acclamation has contributed to Carter's rehabilitation because it has given him worldwide publicity as an international figure with a continuing role in world affairs.

In the process of building a legacy of lifelong public service, including equally the post–White House years, Carter—along with Rosalynn Carter—has redefined the ex-presidency and established a new dimension for the Office of Former President.[60] Carter has done it personally—and, what is less well recognized, has done it institutionally. To the traditional roles of ex-presidents—the retired statesman who simply returned to his home, from which he offered sage advice, or, more rarely, the occasional public servant who ran for office again or accepted a presidential appointment—the Carters have added a third possibility: founding and funding a public policy institute, a center from which both the ex-president and the former First Lady can continue an active public service role.[61]

As of 1997, only the Carters had created such a public policy institute—one that combines financial resources, expertise, and the Carters' leadership—to play an important role and offer a new model for some future former president. This "public policy ex-presidency" represents a unique institutional legacy for Jimmy and Rosalynn Carter, enabling them to continue many of the policies they began in the White House.

NOTES

The author would like to thank Richard M. Pious, and the editors, Gary M Fink and Hugh Davis Graham, for their suggestions; Steven H. Hochman, associate director of programs and senior research associate, and Natasha Singh, program assistant, Office of Public Information, both of the Carter Center, for their assistance; and the late Dan E. Sweat, first director of the Carter Center's Atlanta Project, and especially former President Jimmy Carter for granting him lengthy interviews. Because the Jimmy Carter Library had not opened the postpresidential papers prior to the completion of this chapter, the author relied heavily on published materials supplemented by interviews by the author and documents from the Carter Center.

1. Stanley W. Cloud, "Hail to the Ex-Chief," *Time,* September 11, 1989, 60–63. For similar assessments, see Wayne King, "Carter Redux," *New York Times Magazine,* December 10, 1989, cover, 38–39, 101–9; Kai Bird, "The Very Model of an Ex-President," *Nation,* November 12, 1990, cover, 560–64.

2. Jimmy Carter, "Historical Press Conference," February 20, 1997, the Carter Center, Atlanta, Ga.

3. For a positive assessment, see, most recently, Douglas Brinkley, "The Rising Stock of Jimmy Carter: The 'Hands on' Legacy of Our Thirty-ninth President," *Diplomatic History* 20 (Fall 1996): 505–29; for a more critical view, see Burton I. Kaufman, *The Presidency of James Earl Carter, Jr.* (Lawrence: University Press of Kansas, 1993). On foreign policy, see Gaddis Smith, *Morality, Reason and Power: American Diplomacy in*

the Carter Years (New York: Hill and Wang, 1986); and Richard C. Thornton, *The Carter Years: Toward a New Global Order* (New York: Paragon House, 1991).

4. "How the Public's View Changes as the Presidents Become History," *New York Times,* January 24, 1993, E3.

5. For assessments of Carter's leadership as a president, see Erwin C. Hargrove, *Jimmy Carter as President: Leadership and the Politics of the Public Good* (Baton Rouge: Louisiana State University Press, 1988); Charles O. Jones, *The Trusteeship Presidency: Jimmy Carter and the United States Congress* (Baton Rouge: Louisiana State University Press, 1988); and Herbert D. Rosenbaum and Alexej Ugrinsky, eds., *The Presidency and Domestic Policies of Jimmy Carter* (Wesport, Conn.: Greenwood Press, 1994). Carter's early leadership style has been examined by Gary M. Fink, *Prelude to the Presidency: The Political Character and Legislative Leadership Style of Governor Jimmy Carter* (Westport, Conn.: Greenwood Press, 1980). Two recent books that probe Carter's personality and its relationship to his presidency and also briefly examine his postpresidency are Kenneth E. Morris, *Jimmy Carter: American Moralist* (Athens: University of Georgia Press, 1996), 289–321; and Peter G. Bourne, *Jimmy Carter: A Comprehensive Biography from Plains to Postpresidency* (New York: Scribner, 1997), 474–508. Rod Troester, *Jimmy Carter as Peacemaker: A Post-Presidential Biography* (Westport, Conn.: Praeger, 1996), provides a reference work. A volume by Douglas Brinkley on Carter's postpresidency was scheduled to be published in the fall of 1997.

6. Ellen Rafshoon, "Inside the Carter Center," *Foreign Service Journal* 72 (July 1995): 39.

7. For example, "Jerry Ford, Incorporated," *Newsweek,* May 11, 1981, 28–29; Walter B. Robinson, "Reagan's Legacy Loses Luster during His [First] Year in Retirement," *Boston Globe,* February 12, 1990, 1, 11; Richard Cohen, "The Carter Distinction," *Washington Post,* May 11, 1989, A21; Haynes Johnson, "Out From under Reagan's Spell," *Washington Post,* March 23, 1990.

8. Lindsey Gruson, "Noriega Stealing Election, Carter Says," *New York Times,* May 9, 1989, A1; and William Branigin, "Carter Says Noriega Is Stealing Election," *Washington Post,* May 9, 1989, A1, and "As Observer, Carter Proves Acute," A23.

9. Bernard Weinraub, "Bush Urges Effort to Press Noriega to Quit as Leader," *New York Times,* May 10, 1989, A1.

10. Hendrik Hertzberg, "Mr. Ex-President," *New Republic,* June 5, 1989, 4. See also Richard Cohen, "The Carter Distinction," *Washington Post,* May 11, 1989, A21; and Peter Applebome, "Unofficially, Era of Carter Is Still Here," *New York Times,* May 11, 1989, A9.

11. "Carter, at Sandinista's Urging, Will Monitor Nicaragua Vote," *New York Times,* August 8, 1989, A1, A18; Mark A. Uhlig, "Carter Applauds Nicaraguans on Election-Monitoring Plan," *New York Times,* January 20, 1990, A10; Robert Pear, "End to Official U.S. Observer Role in Managua Vote Raises Debate," *New York Times,* February 9, 1990, A6.

12. Mark A. Uhlig, "Nicaraguan Opposition Routs Sandinistas," *New York Times,* February 27, 1990, A1, A12.

13. Jimmy Carter, interview with the author, May 18, 1992, Carter Center, Atlanta, Ga. The tape and transcript of this interview are to be deposited by the author at the Jimmy Carter Presidential Library, Atlanta, Ga.

14. Mark A. Uhlig, "Ortega, Defeated in Vote, Declares Contra Cease-Fire," *New York Times,* March 1, 1990, A1, A20, A21.

15. Mark A. Uhlig, "Chamarro Takes Nicaragua Helm; Hails a New Era," *New York Times,* April 26, 1990, A1.

16. For an evaluation of Carter's performance in Nicaragua, see Anthony Lewis, "Out of This Nettle," *New York Times,* March 2, 1990, and "Cap in Hand," *Economist,* March 10, 1990, 50.

17. Carter and his group continued to monitor elections in Haiti in 1990; Zambia, 1991; Guyana, 1992; Ghana, 1992; Paraguay, 1993; and Panama, 1994.

18. For subsequent publicity of Carter's role in Somalia, see Michael Kelly, "It All Codepends," *New Yorker,* October 3, 1994, 83–84.

19. David E. Sanger, "North Korea Quits Atom Agency in Wider Rift with U.S. and UN," *New York Times,* June 14, 1994, A1, A12; R. Jeffries Smith, "'Promising' Signs Seen in North Korea," *Washington Post,* June 17, 1994, A1, A20; Andrea Stone, "Citizen Carter, the Statesman," *USA Today,* June 15, 1994, A4; Douglas Jehl, "Carter, His Own Emissary, Outpaces White House," *New York Times,* June 20, 1994, A3; Elizabeth Kurylo, "Agreement Is Feather in Carter's Cap," *Atlanta Journal and Constitution,* June 23, 1994, A12; David E. Sanger, "Who Won the Korea Deal?" *New York Times,* October 23, 1994, E3.

20. "Carter Trip Paves the Way for U.S.–North Korean Pact," *Carter Center News* (Winter 1995), 6, 11.

21. Kelly, "It All Codepends," 85; Sam Howe Vernovek, "Support for Troops, but Policy in Dispute," *New York Times,* September 17, 1997, A8.

22. Kelly, "It All Codepends," 85.

23. John H. Cushman, Jr., et al., "On the Brink of War, a Tense Battle of Wills," *New York Times,* September 20, 1994, A1, A13.

24. Larry Rohter, "Carter in Haiti, Pursues Peaceful Shift," *New York Times,* September 18, 1994, A1, A12; Douglas Jehl, "Haitian Military Rulers Agree to Leave; Clinton Halts Assault, Recalls 61 Planes," *New York Times,* September. 19, 1994, A1, A8; Cushman et al., "On the Brink of War," A1, A13; Thomas W. Lippman, "Once Again Carter Plays Peacemaker," *Washington Post,* September 19, 1994, A17; Eleanor Clift, "A Man with a Mission," *Newsweek,* October 3, 1994, 36–38; Michael Kramer, "The Carter Connection," and Bruce W. Nelan, "Road to Haiti," *Time,* October 3, 1994, 30–38.

25. "Jimmy Carter's Contribution," *New York Times,* September 19, 1994, A16. For a similar analysis, see editorial, "Peacemaker," *USA Today,* September 21, 1994.

26. "Newsweek Poll" in *Newsweek,* October 3, 1994, 36. Results based on Princeton Survey Research telephone poll of 801 adults, September 22–23, 1994.

27. Cushman et al., "On the Brink of War," A14; for criticism, see William Safire, "Jimmy Clinton II," *New York Times,* September 22, 1994, A27; A. M. Rosenthal, "Men of Honor," *New York Times,* September 23, 1994, A35; Joe Klein, "Empathy for the Devil," *Newsweek,* October 3, 1994, 39; "Under the Gun," *Newsweek,* October 3, 1994, 31; Murray Kempton, "The Carter Mission," *New York Review of Books,* October 20, 1994, 71.

28. "Under the Gun," 31, 37.

29. Maureen Dowd, "Despite Role as Negotiator, Carter Feels Unappreciated," *New York Times,* September 21, 1994, A1, A17; Elaine Sciolino, "Carter to Talk to Christopher," *New York Times,* September 24, 1994, A4.

30. Hardly modest, Carter and the Carter Center claimed full credit for it. "Carter Team Visits Haiti to Assess Progress since President Aristide's Return," *Carter Center News* (Summer 1995), 6.

31. Dowd, "Despite Role as Negotiator, Carter Feels Unappreciated," A17. For criticism, see Clift, "A Man with a Mission," 37.

32. Elaine Sciolino, "Carter's Bosnia Effort Provokes Skepticism," *New York Times,* December 16, 1994, A3.

33. Douglas Jehl, "Carter Says He May Travel to Bosnia as Private Envoy," *New York Times,* December 15, 1994, A1, A12; Roger Cohen, "Seeking Carter Visit, Bosnia Serbs Ease Up," *New York Times,* December 17, 1994, A3.

34. Douglas Jehl, "Carter Takes Off for Bosnia on Broadened Peace Mission," *New York Times,* December 18, 1994, A1, A24; Roger Cohen, "Serbs, Meeting with Carter, Agree to Bosnian Cease-Fire," *New York Times,* December 20, 1994, A1, A10.

35. Roger Cohen, "Bosnia Foes Agree to 4-Month Truce, Carter Reports," *New York Times,* December 21, 1994, A1, A14; editorial, "A Little Help from Jimmy Carter," *New York Times,* December 21, 1994, A26; Stephen Kinzer, "Cease-Fire in Bosnia Starts, and Sides Meet on Details," *New York Times,* January 2, 1995, A2; "Carter Center Jump Starts Peace Efforts in Bosnia-Herzegovina," *Carter Center News* (Winter 1995), 1, 3.

36. "Carter Willing to Return to Bosnia to Renew Truce," *New York Times,* April 8, 1995, A5; Rowan Scarborough, "Carter Urges President to Push for Bosnia Talks," *Washington Post,* June 15, 1995, A34.

37. John Darnton, "Allies Warn Bosnian Serbs of 'Substantial' Air Strikes if U.N. Enclave Is Attacked," *New York Times,* July 22, 1995, A1, A4.

38. Roger Cohen, "A NATO Deadline in Bosnia Passes without Attack," *New York Times,* September 15, 1995, 1A, 9A.

39. Elaine Sciolino, "Accord Reached to End the War in Bosnia," *New York Times,* November 22, 1995, A1; Craig R. Whitney, "Balkan Foes Sign Peace Pact," *New York Times,* December 15, 1995, A1.

40. On the origin of the Carter Center, see Steven H. Hochman, "With Jimmy Carter in Georgia: A Memoir of His Post-Presidential Years," in *Farewell to the Chief: Former Presidents in American Public Life,* ed. Richard Norton Smith and Timothy Walch (Worland, Wyo.: High Plains Publishing, 1990), 123–34. For the merger, see Elizabeth Kurylo, "Joining Forces: Emory to Absorb Carter Center," *Atlanta Journal and Constitution,* August 30, 1994, A1.

41. The exact number of staffers varied even in the Carter Center's own materials. For example, the figure is two hundred in the Carter Center *1995 Annual Report,* 6, and three hundred in the Carter Center, *The Carter Center at a Glance* (1996), 5. This discrepancy derived from The Atlanta Project, which at its height in 1995 boosted the Carter Center's total personnel to three hundred (Natasha Singh, program assistant, Office of Public Information, the Carter Center, to the author, March 7, 1997).

42. Carter Center, *1995 Annual Report,* 6, 48–50.

43. Elizabeth Kurylo, "Friendship Force at 20: Still More Personal than Political," *Atlanta Journal and Constitution,* March 16, 1997, F4.

44. Troester, *Jimmy Carter as Peacemaker,* 124.

45. Carter Center, *1995 Annual Report,* 22.

46. "MacArthur Grant Honors Donald Hopkins for Guinea Worm Eradication Efforts," *Carter Center News* (Summer 1995), 5–6; "Carter Center Steps Up Efforts to Control River Blindness and Save Eyesight," *Carter Center News* (Summer 1996), 1, 5–6.

47. Rosalynn Carter, *First Lady from Plains* (Boston: Houghton Mifflin, 1984), 272–77; and Jimmy Carter, *Keeping Faith: Memoirs of a President* (New York: Bantam Books, 1982), 138.

48. "Don't Forget Mental Health," *Atlanta Journal,* March 22, 1994, A10; Rosalynn Carter, "Mental Health Challenges Reach across the Globe," *Mental Health Weekly,* October 9, 1995; Delia M. Rioas, "Former First Lady Is No Second Fiddle," *Ann Arbor News,* October 9, 1995, D1, D2; "Video Offers Help and Hope for People with Mental Illness," *Carter Center News* (Summer 1996), 1, 5. For other projects of Rosalynn Carter, see Carter Center, *1995 Annual Report,* 25, 32–33.

49. Jimmy Carter, interview with the author, May 18, 1992.

50. Dan E. Sweat and Jacquelyn A. Anthony, "The Role of Corporations in Urban Revitalization: The Experience of the Atlanta Project," *National Civic Review* 84 (Summer–Fall 1995): 239. The present account of The Atlanta Project is based on this article, the present author's interview with Dan E. Sweat, May 18, 1992, plus Elizabeth Kurylo, "Going to Bat for Atlanta's Poor: Carter Pledges to Lead Anti-poverty Campaign," *Atlanta Journal and Constitution,* October 25, 1991, A1, 4; Scott Bronstein, "A Pound of Despair: The Baby That Moved President Carter to Tears," *Atlanta Journal and Constitution,* October 26, 1991, A1; Jerry Schwartz, "Carter to Take on Atlanta's Urban Ills," *New York Times,* October 26, 1991, A1, A6; and Ronald Smothers, "Carter's Civic Crusade Tries to Meld Two Atlantas," *New York Times,* April 11, 1992, A6.

51. Jimmy Carter quoted in Kurylo, "Going to Bat for Atlanta's Poor," A1, A4; and Smothers, "Carter's Civic Crusade Tries to Meld Two Atlantas," A6.

52. On some of TAP's accomplishments, see "Computer Registry Ensures Timely Immunizations for Atlanta Children," *Carter Center News* (Summer 1996), 3; "An Experiment in Easing Paperwork: 64 Pages Reduced to 8," *New York Times,* April 19, 1994, A16; Carter Center *1995 Annual Report,* 8–10.

53. Carter Center, *1995 Annual Report,* 50.

54. Ibid., 29.

55. Editorial, "TAP Scales Back, But Its Successes Are Real," *Atlanta Constitution,* October 20, 1995, A16.

56. Creel McCormack, associate director of TAP, to the author, March 7, 1997.

57. Jimmy Carter, "The Power of a Project," *Atlanta Constitution,* October 18, 1995, A11. See also John B. Hardman, executive director of the Carter Center, *The Atlanta Project; Lessons Learned in Phase One* [Atlanta: The Carter Center, 1996], 2–3.

58. Hardman, *The Atlanta Project,* 4–5; Julie K. Miller, "Carter's Project a Dubious Honor," *Atlanta Journal and Constitution,* April 16, 1992, I1.

59. Hardman, *The Atlanta Project,* 6–16; "Atlanta Project Increases Focus on Children and Families," *Carter Center News* (Winter 1997), 6.

60. This is an assertion the author made in an interview on "Former Presidents" on "The Weekend News with Connie Chung," CBS television network, 6 P.M., EST, Sunday, November 19, 1989, transcript, 11. For an account of the evolution of the Office of the Former President, see John Whiteclay Chambers II, "Presidents Emeritus," *American Heritage Magazine* 30 (June/July 1979): 16–25; and the author's testimony, November 7, 1979, in U.S. Senate, subcommittees of the Committees on Appropriations and Govern-

mental Affairs, *Hearing: Cost of Former Presidents to U.S. Taxpayers,* 96th Congress, 1st sess. (Washington, D.C.: Government Printing Office, 1980), 165–200.

61. On the development of the Office of the Former President, including the Carters' public policy institute and its relationship to the presidential libraries and affiliated institutions of other former U.S. presidents, see the author's forthcoming study, *After the White House: The Transformation of the Ex-Presidency.*

Bibliographic Essay

Suzanne Litke

I. JIMMY CARTER

Extensive reference material exists concerning Jimmy Carter, his political career, and his presidency. Primary sources include President and Mrs. Carter's memoirs, administration staff members' memoirs, and the contents of the Jimmy Carter Library. For Carter in his own words, see Frank Daniel, comp., *Addresses of Jimmy Carter, Governor of Georgia, 1971–1975* (Atlanta, 1975); Jimmy Carter, *A Government as Good as Its People* (New York, 1977); Jimmy Carter, *Why Not the Best?* (Nashville, 1977); Jimmy Carter, *The Spiritual Journey of Jimmy Carter, in His Own Words* (New York, 1978); Jimmy Carter, *Keeping Faith: Memoirs of a President* (New York, 1982); Jimmy Carter and Rosalynn Carter, *Everything to Gain: Making the Most of the Rest of Your Life* (New York, 1987); and Jimmy Carter, *Living Faith* (New York, 1996). For Rosalynn Carter's perspective on her husband, see Rosalynn Carter, *First Lady from Plains* (Boston, 1984). For insiders' views of the Carter administration, see Kenneth W. Thompson, ed., *The Carter Presidency: Fourteen Intimate Perspectives of Jimmy Carter* (Lanham, Md., 1990); Walter LaFeber, "From Confusion to Cold War: The Memoirs of the Carter Administration," *Diplomatic History* 8 (Winter 1984): 1–12; Edward R. Kantowicz, "Reminiscences of a Fated Presidency: Themes from the Carter Memoirs," *Presidential Studies Quarterly* 16 (Fall 1986): 651–65; Hamilton Jordan, *Crisis: The Last Year of the Carter Presidency* (New York, 1982); Jody Powell, *The Other Side of the Story* (New York, 1984); Joseph Califano, Jr., *Governing America: An Insider's Report from the White House and the Cabinet* (New York, 1981); Zbigniew Brzezinski, *Power and Principle: Memoirs of the National Security Adviser, 1977–1981* (New York, 1983); and Cyrus Vance, *Hard Choices: Critical Years in America's Foreign Policy* (New York, 1983).

The Jimmy Carter Library in Atlanta, Georgia, is the repository for the Carter White House records and a variety of related materials, including oral histories, audiovisual materials, and books about Carter, his family, and his administration. White House records open for research include the President's Files, the White House Central Files, and Staff Office Files; in aggregate, these records represent the available paper trail for President Carter, his advisers, and the White House staff. The Staff Secretary's File, a subset of the President's Files, includes the Presidential Handwriting File; essentially, this is a record of President Carter's outbox. In these papers, one can find Carter "on the margins"; he, more than any other president in recent history, made handwritten notes and comments on the paperwork crossing his desk each day. Domestic policy papers are more plentiful and are being processed faster than foreign policy papers. An especially useful subset of the Staff Office Files are the Domestic Policy Staff files of Stuart Eizenstat, Carter's assistant for Domestic Affairs and Policy. The holdings of the Carter Library also include extensive oral history records, including exit interviews conducted with more than 160 White House Staff members, and copies of twenty-six oral histories from the White Burkett Miller Center (University of Virginia) Jimmy Carter Project. For additional information about the Jimmy Carter Library, visit the library's Web site at http://gopher.nara.gov:70/1/inform/library/carter or write to 441 Freedom Parkway, Atlanta, GA, 30307.

Biographies of Carter include Peter G. Bourne, *Jimmy Carter: A Comprehensive Biography from Plains to Postpresidency* (New York, 1997); Kenneth E. Morris, *Jimmy Carter: American Moralist* (Athens, Ga., 1996); and Betty Glad, *Jimmy Carter: In Search of the Great White House* (New York, 1980). Works in progress include biographies by Leo Ribuffo, Douglas Brinkley, and Stanly Godbold. For a discussion of Carter's prepresidency, see Gary Fink, *Prelude to the Presidency: The Political Character and Legislative Leadership Style of Governor Jimmy Carter* (Westport, Conn., 1980). For a discussion of Carter's presidency, see Burton I. Kaufman, *The Presidency of James Earl Carter, Jr.* (Lawrence, Kans., 1993); John Dumbrell, *The Carter Presidency: A Re-evaluation* (Manchester, England, 1993); Erwin C. Hargrove, *Jimmy Carter as President: Leadership and the Politics of the Public Good* (Baton Rouge, La., 1988); Charles O. Jones, *The Trusteeship Presidency: Jimmy Carter and the United States Congress* (Baton Rouge, La., 1988); and Garland A. Haas, *Jimmy Carter and the Politics of Frustration* (Jefferson, N.C., 1992). For general discussions of the modern American presidency, including Carter's, see William E. Leuchtenburg, *In the Shadow of FDR: From Harry Truman to Bill Clinton* (Ithaca, N.Y., 1993), and *A Troubled Feast: American Society since 1945* (Boston, 1983); Stephen Skowronek, *The Politics Presidents Make: Leadership from John Adams to George Bush* (Cambridge, Mass., 1993); Robert Dallek, *Hail to the Chief: The Making and Unmaking of American Presidents* (New York, 1996); Alonzo L. Hamby, *Liberalism and Its Challengers: FDR to Reagan* (New York, 1985); James David Barber, *The Presidential Character: Predicting Performance in the White House*

(Englewood Cliffs, N.J., 1985); and Richard E. Neustadt, *Presidential Power and the Modern Presidents: The Politics of Leadership from Roosevelt to Reagan* (New York, 1990).

For a history of American postpresidencies, see John Whiteclay Chambers II, "Presidents Emeritus," *American Heritage Magazine,* June/July 1979, 16–25; and Richard Norton Smith and Timothy Walch, eds., *Farewell to the Chief: Former Presidents in American Public Life* (Worland, Wyo., 1990). For an account of Jimmy Carter's postpresidential activities, see Peter G. Bourne, *Jimmy Carter: A Comprehensive Biography;* Steven H. Hochman, "With Jimmy Carter in Georgia: A Memoir of His Post-Presidential Years," in Smith and Walch, *Farewell to the Chief;* and Kai Bird, "The Very Model of an Ex-President," *Nation,* November 12, 1990, cover and 560–64. For detailed accounts of Carter Center activities, see issues of the *Carter Center News* (published quarterly by the Carter Center, Atlanta) and Carter Center Annual Reports.

II. THE ECONOMY, LABOR, AND INDUSTRIAL POLICY

For a general discussion of the Carter-Reagan debates and the associated economic issues, see Burton I. Kaufman, *The Presidency of James Earl Carter, Jr.* (Lawrence, Kans., 1993); and Garland A. Haas, *Jimmy Carter and the Politics of Frustration* (Jefferson, N.C., 1992). For more recent, more positive reassessments by historians about Carter's ranking in presidential performance surveys, see Ann Mari May, "Fiscal Policy, Monetary Policy, and the Carter Presidency," *Presidential Studies Quarterly* 23 (Fall 1993): 699–712; Erwin C. Hargrove, *Jimmy Carter as President: Leadership and the Politics of the Public Good* (Baton Rouge, La., 1988); and John Dumbrell, *The Carter Presidency: A Reevaluation* (Manchester, England, 1993). Primary sources at the Carter Library include the Domestic Policy Staff files of Stuart Eizenstat; oral interviews with Eizenstat, Alfred Kahn, and James McIntyre; and the papers of McIntyre, including the speech Eizenstat delivered in May 1980 to define the Carter administration's understanding of the economy. For an explanation of the changing economic philosophy during the Carter years, see David Calleo, *The Imperious Economy* (Cambridge, Mass., 1982); Herbert Stein, *Presidential Economics* (New York, 1985); and Sir John Hicks, *The Crisis in Keynesian Economics* (Oxford, 1974). For a discussion of international economic and welfare state reforms, see Gosta Esping-Andersen's *The Three Worlds of Welfare Capitalism* (Princeton, N.J., 1990); Peter Baldwin's *The Politics of Social Solidarity* (New York, 1990); and Paul Pierson's *Dismantling the Welfare State?* (New York, 1994). For statistical and budgetary information on specific U.S. government programs, see *Statistical Abstract of the United States* (Washington, D.C., annual); for similar information for Western European nations, see *National Accounts,* vol. 2, *Detailed Tables, 1979–91* (Paris, 1993).

For a discussion of the relationship between Jimmy Carter and organized labor, see the essays by Taylor Dark and Gary Fink in *The Presidency and Domestic Policies of Jimmy Carter,* ed. Herbert D. Rosenbaum and Alexej Urginsky (Westport, Conn., 1994); Numan V. Bartley, *Jimmy Carter and the Politics of the New South* (St. Louis, Mo., 1979); and Gary M Fink, "F. Ray Marshall: Secretary of Labor and Jimmy Carter's Ambassador to Organized Labor," *Labor History* 37 (Fall 1996): 463–79. For Jimmy Carter's view on his administration's policy toward labor, see Jimmy Carter, *Keeping Faith: Memoirs of a President* (New York, 1982). For an insider's view of the Carter administration's labor policy, see the interview with Ray Marshall in *The Carter Presidency: Fourteen Intimate Perspectives of Jimmy Carter,* ed. Kenneth W. Thompson (Lanham, Md., 1990). A discussion of the administration's stand on labor issues and related economic policy concerns can be found in John Dumbrell, *The Carter Presidency: A Reevaluation* (Manchester, England, 1993); Anthony S. Campagna, *Economic Policy in the Carter Administration* (Westport, Conn., 1994); Burton I. Kaufman, *The Presidency of James Earl Carter, Jr.* (Lawrence, Kans., 1993); and Erwin C. Hargrove, *Jimmy Carter as President: Leadership and the Politics of the Public Good* (Baton Rouge, La., 1988). A history of organized labor in the twentieth century can be found in Melvyn Dubofsky, *The State and Labor in Modern America* (Chapel Hill, N.C., 1994); David Plotke, *Building a Democratic Political Order: Reshaping American Liberalism in the 1930s and 1940s* (New York, 1996); David Brody, *Workers in Industrial America: Essays on the Twentieth Century Struggle* (New York, 1993); and James A. Gross, *Broken Promise: The Subversion of U.S. Labor Relations Policy, 1947–1994* (Philadelphia, 1995). For an explanation of the "politics of productivity," see Charles Maier, "The Politics of Productivity: Foundations of American Economic Policy after World War II," *International Organization* (Autumn 1977). A discussion of the Democratic party's shift from a reform to an economic growth agenda can be found in Alan Brinkley, *The End of Reform: New Deal Liberalism in Recession and War* (New York, 1995); and Nelson Lichtenstein, "From Corporatism to Collective Bargaining: Organized Labor and the Eclipse of Social Democracy in the Postwar Era," in *The Rise and Fall of the New Deal Order, 1930–1980,* ed. Steve Fraser and Gary Gerstle (Princeton, N.J., 1989). For an explanation of the Carter administration's involvement in the Humphrey-Hawkins legislative effort, see Dumbrell, *The Carter Presidency,* and Kaufman, *The Presidency of James Earl Carter.* Primary sources at the Carter Library include Domestic Policy Staff files for Stuart Eizenstat; Miller Center interviews with Jimmy Carter, Eizenstat, Hamilton Jordan, and Ray Marshall; and the papers of Jordan, Marshall, Charles Schultze, Bert Lance, Landon Butler, and Alfred Kahn.

For historical background on American industrial policy prior to and including the Carter years, see Otis L. Graham, *Losing Time: The Industrial Policy Debate* (Cambridge, Mass., 1992); Steve Dreyer, *Trade Warriors: STR and the American Crusade for Free Trade* (New York, 1995); Robert A. Pastor, *Congress and the Politics of Foreign Economic Policies, 1929–1976* (Berkeley, 1980); Herbert Stein, *Presidential Economics: The Making of Economic Policy from Roosevelt to Reagan and Beyond* (Washington, D.C., 1988); and Judith Goldstein, *Ideas, Interests, and American Trade Policy* (Ithaca, N.Y., 1993). For an explanation of economic policy under Jimmy Carter, see Anthony S. Campagna, *Economic Policy in the Carter Administration* (Westport, Conn., 1995). Discussions of American steel policy and the economics of steel can be found in Paul A. Tiffany, *The Decline of American Steel: How Management, Labor, and Government Went Wrong* (New York, 1988); E. Robert Livernash, *Collective Bargaining in the Basic Steel Industry: A Study of the Public Interest and the Role of Government* (Washington, D.C., 1961); and Robert Randall, *The U.S. Steel Industry in Recurrent Crisis* (Washington, D.C., 1981). Primary sources at the Carter Library include Domestic Policy Staff files for Stuart Eizenstat and the oral interview with Lloyd Cutler. Discussions of the international steel industry can be found in Ray Hudson and David Sadler, *The International Steel Industry: Restructuring, State Policies, and Localities* (London, 1989); and Yves Meny and Vincent Wright, "State and Steel in Western Europe," in *The Politics of Steel: Western Europe and the Steel Industry in the Crisis Years, 1974–1984,* ed. Yves Meny and Vincent Wright (Berlin, 1987), 30–31. For an explanation of the product cycle theory, see Ray Vernon, "International Investment and International Trade in the Product Cycle," *Quarterly Journal of Economics* 80 (May 1966): 190–207. A discussion of the responses of segments of American society to the industrial policy debate can be found in Andrew Levison, *The Working-Class Majority* (New York, 1974); David Vogel, *Fluctuating Fortunes: The Political Power of Business in America* (New York, 1989); and Barry Bluestone and Bennett Harrison, *The Deindustrialization of America: Plant Closings, Community Abandonment and the Dismantling of Basic Industry* (New York, 1982).

III. DOMESTIC POLICY: URBAN, WELFARE, CIVIL RIGHTS, WOMEN'S, AND ENVIRONMENTAL ISSUES

For a discussion of urban problems during the 1970s, see Robert A. Beauregard, *Voices of Decline: The Postwar Fate of U.S. Cities* (Oxford, 1993); Jon Teaford, *The Rough Road to Renaissance: Urban Revitalization in America, 1940–1985* (Baltimore, Md., 1990); and Michael B. Katz, ed., *The "Underclass" Debate: Views from History* (Princeton, N.J., 1993). Associated statistical information can be found in John Kasarda, "Urban Change and Minority Opportunities," in *The New Urban Reality,* ed. Paul Peterson (Washington, D.C., 1986), 33–68. For a discussion of urban policy prior to and including the Carter years, see Raymond A. Mohl, "Shifting Patterns of American Urban Policy since 1900," in *Urban Policy in Twentieth-Century America,* ed. Arnold R. Hirsch and Raymond A. Mohl

(New Brunswick, N.J., 1993), 1–45; and Martin Anderson, *The Federal Bulldozer: A Critical Analysis of Urban Renewal, 1949–1962* (Cambridge, Mass., 1964). For an insider's view of the Carter administration's domestic policy formulation process, see Stuart Eizenstat, "President Carter, the Democratic Party, and the Making of Domestic Policy," in *The Presidency and Domestic Policies of Jimmy Carter,* ed. Herbert D. Rosenbaum and Alexej Ugrinsky (Westport, Conn., 1994), 3–16. Discussions of public welfare policy in the twentieth century can be found in Michael B. Katz, *The Undeserving Poor: From the War on Poverty to the War on Welfare* (New York, 1989); James T. Patterson, *America's Struggle against Poverty, 1900–1994* (Cambridge, Mass., 1995); Daniel Patrick Moynihan, *Maximum Feasible Misunderstanding* (New York, 1969); and Frances Fox Piven and Richard Cloward, *Regulating the Poor: The Functions of Public Welfare* (New York, 1971). Primary sources at the Carter Library include Domestic Policy Staff files for Stuart Eizenstat and the oral interviews with Marcia Kaptur. A discussion of community-based politics can be found in Robert Halpern, *Rebuilding the Inner City: A History of Neighborhood Initiatives to Address Poverty in the United States* (New York, 1995). Histories of the War on Poverty can be found in Alan Matusow, *The Unraveling of America: A History of Liberalism in the 1960s* (New York, 1984); and Alice O'Connor, "Evaluating Comprehensive Community Initiatives: A View from History," in *New Approaches to Evaluating Community Initiatives,* ed. James P. Connell (Washington, D.C., 1995), 23–63. For a discussion of the responses of segments of American society to the urban policy debate, see Kevin Phillips, *The Emerging Republican Majority* (New Rochelle, N.Y., 1969); Richard Krickus, *Pursuing the American Dream: White Ethnics and the New Populism* (Garden City, N.Y., 1976); and Jonathan Rieder, "The Rise of the Silent Majority," in *The Rise and Fall of the New Deal Order,* ed. Steve Fraser and Gary Gerstle (Princeton, N.J., 1989). An explanation of the urban policy debate between Sunbelt and Snowbelt interests can be found in Kirkpatrick Sale, *Power Shift: The Rise of the Sunbelt Rim and Its Challenge to the Eastern Establishment* (New York 1975); and Bruce Schulman, *From Cotton Belt to Sun Belt: Federal Policy, Economic Development, and the Transformation of the South, 1938–1980* (New York, 1991).

For an analytical, historical perspective on American welfare efforts, including Carter's, see James T. Patterson, *America's Struggle against Poverty, 1900–1994* (Cambridge, Mass., 1995); and Theda Skocpol, *Social Policy in the United States: Future Possibilities in Historical Perspective* (Princeton, N.J., 1995). For a comprehensive overview of Carter's welfare reform philosophy and initiatives, see Laurence Lynn, Jr., and David Whitman, *The President as Policymaker: Jimmy Carter and Welfare Reform* (Philadelphia, 1982); Erwin C. Hargrove, *Jimmy Carter as President: Leadership and the Politics of the Public Good* (Baton Rouge, La., 1988); Charles O. Jones, *The Trusteeship Presidency: Jimmy Carter and the United States Congress* (Baton Rouge, La., 1988); and Peter G. Bourne, *Jimmy Carter: A Comprehensive Biography from Plains to Postpresidency* (New York,

1997). Sources for welfare statistics and legislative summaries include Gordon Weil, *The Welfare Debate of 1978* (White Plains, N.Y., 1978), and "Welfare Policy," in *Congress and the Nation, 1977–1980* (Washington, D.C., 1981), 679–89. For an insider's view of the Carter administration's welfare reform efforts, see Joseph Califano, Jr., *Governing America: An Insider's Report from the White House and the Cabinet* (New York, 1981). Primary sources at the Carter Library include the White House Central Files; papers of administration officials, including Stuart Eizenstat, Hamilton Jordon, and James Schlesinger; and oral interviews with Eizenstat and Charles Schultze. For the conservative response to Carter's welfare initiatives, see Charles Murray's *Losing Ground: American Social Policy, 1950–1980* (New York, 1984); and George Gilder's "The Coming Welfare Crisis," *Policy Review* 11 (Winter 1980): 25–36. The liberal response can be found in Leslie Lenkowsky, "Welfare Reform and the Liberals," *Commentary* 67 (March 1979): 56–61; and David Whitman's "Liberal Rhetoric and the Welfare Underclass," *Society* 21 (1983), 63–69.

For an analytical, historical perspective on the American civil rights era, see Hugh Davis Graham, *The Civil Rights Era* (New York, 1990). For a discussion of Carter and traditional liberal policy, see Gary W. Reichard, "Early Returns: Assessing Jimmy Carter," *Presidential Studies Quarterly* 20 (Summer 1990): 603–30. For an explanation of the budgetary challenges facing Carter vis-à-vis traditional liberal social initiatives, see John Dumbrell's *The Carter Presidency: A Re-evaluation* (Manchester, England, 1993). The current reactions of civil rights scholars to the Carter presidency can be found in Steven F. Lawson's *Running for Freedom* (Philadelphia, 1991), and in Harvard Sitkoff's *The Struggle for Black Equality, 1954–1992* (New York, 1993); an earlier assessment can be found in M. Glenn Abernathy's "The Carter Administration and Domestic Civil Rights," in *The Carter Years: The President and Policy Making* (New York, 1984), 106–24. For information about affirmative-action requirements in federal agencies, see U.S. Advisory Commission on Intergovernmental Relations, *Regulatory Federalism: Policy, Process, Impact, and Reform* (Washington, D.C., 1984); and Hugh Davis Graham, "Since 1964: The Paradox of American Civil Rights Regulation," in Morton Keller and R. Shep Melnick, eds., *Taking Stock: American Government in the Twentieth Century* (Cambridge, 1998). For information about the problems of EEOC enforcement, see Alfred W. Blumrosen, *Modern Law: The Law Transmission System and Equal Employment Opportunity* (Madison, Wisc., 1993); and Hanes Walton, Jr., *When the Marching Stopped: The Politics of Civil Rights Agencies* (Albany, N.Y., 1988). A critical view of the effects of EEOC enforcement on American business can be found in Herman Belz, *Equality Transformed: A Quarter-Century of Affirmative Action* (New Brunswick, N.J., 1991); a positive view can be found in Blumrosen, *Modern Law*. A discussion of the SBA's "set-aside" program can be found in George R. LaNoue and John C. Sullivan, "Presumptions for Preferences: The Small Business Administration's Decisions on Groups Entitled to Affirmative Action," *Journal of Policy History* 6 (1994): 439–67.

Carter's response to the charges that he was too passive on minority issues can be found in "Minority Business Enterprise," *Public Papers of the Presidents of the United States: Jimmy Carter, 1977* (Washington, D.C., 1978). Fair housing policy under Carter is discussed in Beth J. Lief and Susan Goering, "The Implementation of the Federal Mandate for Fair Housing," in *Divided Neighborhoods: Changing Patterns of Racial Segregation*, ed. Gary A. Tobin (Newbury Park, Calif., 1987); and Douglas S. Massey and Nancy A. Denton, *American Apartheid: Segregation and the Making of the Underclass* (Cambridge, Mass., 1993). For a discussion of the creation of the Department of Education, see Willis D. Hawley and Beryl A. Radin, *The Politics of Federal Reorganization: Creating the U.S. Department of Education* (New York, 1988). On the politics of federal education policy and government reorganization, see Hugh Davis Graham, *The Uncertain Triumph: Federal Education Policy in the Kennedy and Johnson Years* (Chapel Hill, N.C., 1984). For a discussion of bilingual education policy, see Colman Brez Stein, Jr., *Sink or Swim: The Politics of Bilingual Education* (New York, 1986); and Lawrence H. Fuchs, *The American Kaleidoscope: Race, Ethnicity, and the Civic Culture* (Hanover, N.H., 1990). An explanation of the political theory of "disjunction" can be found in Stephen Skowronek, *The Politics Presidents Make: Leadership from John Adams to George Bush* (Cambridge, Mass., 1993). For a discussion of Carter's civil rights policy as governor, see Hunter H. Smith, "'What Does It All Mean': Jimmy Carter and Civil Rights in Georgia" (master's thesis, Georgia State University, 1995).

For a general discussion of women in modern American politics, see Irene Tinker, ed., *Women in Washington: Advocates for Public Policy* (Beverly Hills, Calif., 1983); Susan M. Hartmann, *From Margin to Mainstream: American Women and Politics since 1960* (Philadelphia, 1989); and Joyce Gelb and Marion Lief Palley, *Women and Public Policies* (Princeton, N.J., 1982). Discussions of the women's liberation movement and its political expression include Anne N. Costain, *Inviting Women's Rebellion: A Political Process Interpretation of the Women's Movement* (Baltimore, Md., 1992); Jo Freeman, *The Politics of Women's Liberation* (New York, 1975); Winifred D. Wandersee, *On the Move: American Women in the 1970s* (Boston, 1988); and Myra Marx Ferree and Beth B. Hess, *Controversy and Coalition: The New Feminist Movement across Three Decades of Change* (New York, 1994). For a comprehensive overview of Carter's relationship with his women advisers, see Emily Walker Cook's "Women White House Advisors in the Carter Administration: Presidential Stalwarts or Feminist Advocates?" (Ph.D. diss., Vanderbilt University, 1995). The history of the Equal Rights Amendment (ERA) can be found in Susan D. Becker, *The Origins of the Equal Rights Amendment: American Feminism between the Wars* (Westport, Conn., 1981); Janet K. Boles, *The Politics of the Equal Rights Amendment: Conflict and the Decision Process* (New York, 1979); and Sarah Slavic, ed., *The Equal Rights Amendment: The Politics and Process of Ratification of the 27th Amendment to the U.S. Constitution* (New York, 1982). The history of the ERA in Georgia can be found in Jeffrey G. Jones, "Georgia and the Equal Rights Amendment" (Ph.D. diss., Georgia State University, 1995). For a discussion of Jimmy and Rosalynn Carter's philosophy toward women and the ERA, see Rosalynn Carter, *First Lady from Plains* (Boston, 1984); and Peter G. Bourne, *Jimmy Carter: A Comprehensive Biography from Plains to Postpresidency* (New York, 1997). Related primary sources at the Carter Library include the White House Central Files and the papers of feminist administration officials, including Margaret McKenna, Sarah Weddington, and Midge Constanza. For information on abortion policy during the Carter administration, see Sarah Weddington, *A Question of Choice* (New York, 1992). For a discussion of the emergence of the battered women's movement, see Susan Schechter, *Women and Male Violence: The Visions and Struggles of the Battered Women's Movement* (Boston, 1982).

For historical background on American environmental policy, see Samuel P. Hays, *Beauty, Health, and Permanence: Environmental Politics in the United States, 1955–1985* (New York, 1987); Martin V. Melosi, "Lyndon Johnson and Environmental Policy," in *The Johnson Years*, vol. 2, *Vietnam, the Environment, and Science* (Lawrence, Kans., 1987), 113–49; and John C. Whitaker, *Striking a Balance: Environmental and Natural Resources Policy in the Nixon-Ford Years* (Washington, D.C., 1976). For a discussion of Carter's environmental stance as governor of Georgia and as a private citizen, see Jimmy Carter, *Why Not the Best?* (Nashville, Tenn., 1975); and Jimmy Carter, *Outdoor Journal: Adventures and Reflections* (New York, 1988). An overview of Carter's opposition to federal water projects can be found in Tim Palmer, *Endangered Rivers and the Conservation Movement* (Berkeley, 1986); and Jeffrey K. Stine, *Mixing the Waters: Environment, Politics, and the Building of the Tennessee-Tombigbee Waterway* (Akron, Ohio, 1993). Primary sources at the Carter Library include Domestic Policy Staff files for Al Stern and Stuart Eizenstat, and Margaret Costanza's papers from the Office of Public Liaison. Carter's two major environmental messages to Congress (May 5, 1977, and August 2, 1979) can be found in *Public Papers of the Presidents of the United States: Jimmy Carter* (Washington, D.C., 1977, 1979). An explanation of efforts to reform the Army Corps of Engineers can be found in Daniel A. Mazmanian and Jeanne Nienaber, *Can Organizations Change? Environmental Protection, Citizen Participation, and the Corps of Engineers* (Washington, D.C., 1979); Martin Ruess, *Shaping Environmental Awareness: The United States Army Corps of Engineers Environmental Advisory Board, 1970–1980* (Washington, D.C., 1983); and Jeffrey K. Stine, "Environmental Politics and Water Resources Development: The Case of the Army Corps of Engineers during the 1970s" (Ph.D. diss., University of California at Santa Barbara, 1984). For an explanation of the Corps of Engineers' historic ties to Congress, see John A. Ferejohn, *Pork Barrel Politics: Rivers and Harbors Legislation, 1947–1968* (Stanford, Calif., 1974); Arthur Maass, *Muddy Waters: The Army Engineers and the Nation's Rivers* (Cambridge, Mass., 1951); and Arthur E. Morgan, *Dams and Other Disasters: A Century of the Army Corps of Engineers in Civil Works* (Boston, 1971). A general discussion of the Tellico Dam controversy can be found in William Bruce

Wheeler and Michael J. McDonald, *TVA and the Tellico Dam, 1936–1979: A Bureaucratic Crisis in Post-Industrial America* (Knoxville, Tenn., 1986). The environmentalists' view on the Tellico Dam can be found in "Pork-Barrel Victory," *Atlanta Journal*, September 12, 1979. Then Attorney General Bell's view can be found in Griffin B. Bell, *Taking Care of the Law* (New York, 1982). For a discussion of changes to environmental policy brought about by the Reagan administration, see Ron Arnold, *At the Eye of the Storm: James Watt and the Environmentalists* (Chicago, 1982); and Jonathan Lash, Katherine Gillman, and David Sheridan, *A Season of Spoils: The Reagan Administration's Attack on the Environment* (New York, 1984).

IV. FOREIGN POLICY ISSUES

Carter's foreign policy rhetoric as a presidential candidate can be found in his speeches published in U.S. Congress, *The Presidential Campaign 1976*, vol. 1, pt. 1, *Jimmy Carter* (Washington, D.C., 1978–79). For an analytical, historical perspective on Carter's foreign policy, see Gaddis Smith, *Morality, Reason, and Power: American Diplomacy in the Carter Years* (New York, 1986); and Seyom Brown, *The Faces of Power: Constancy and Change in United States Foreign Policy from Truman to Clinton* (New York, 1994). A discussion of the continuity between Carter's foreign policy and that of his predecessors can be found in David S. McLellan, *Cyrus Vance* (Totowa, N.J., 1985); and John Lewis Gaddis, *Strategies of Containment* (New York, 1981). For insiders' views of the Carter administration's foreign policy, see Cyrus Vance, *Hard Choices: Critical Years in America's Foreign Policy* (New York, 1985); and Zbigniew Brzezinski, *Power and Principle: Memoirs of the National Security Advisor, 1977–1981* (New York, 1983). For Jimmy Carter's view on his administration's foreign policy, see Jimmy Carter, *Keeping Faith: Memoirs of a President* (New York, 1982). For a discussion of the debate concerning the coherence of Carter's foreign policy, see David Skidmore, *Reversing Course: Carter's Foreign Policy, Domestic Politics, and the Failure of Reform* (Nashville, Tenn., 1996); Jerel A. Rosati, *The Carter Administration's Quest for Global Community: Beliefs and the Impact on Behavior* (Columbia, S.C., 1987); and Richard A. Melanson, *Reconstructing Consensus: American Foreign Policy since the Vietnam War* (New York, 1991). A discussion of the Panama Canal treaties can be found in George D. Moffett III, *The Limits of Victory: The Ratification of the Panama Canal Treaties* (Ithaca, N.Y., 1985); and Gaddis Smith, *The Last Years of the Monroe Doctrine, 1945–1993* (New York, 1994). For an explanation of Soviet-American relations from 1960 to the end of the cold war, see Robert M. Gates, *In the Shadows: The Ultimate Insider's Story of Five Presidents and How They Won the Cold War* (New York, 1996); William G. Hyland, *Mortal Rivals: Superpower Relations from Nixon to Reagan* (New York, 1987); and Raymond L. Garthoff, *Detente and Confronta-*

tion: American-Soviet Relations from Nixon to Reagan (Washington, D.C., 1994).
A discussion of SALT II can be found in Strobe Talbott, *Endgame: The Inside
Story of SALT II* (New York, 1979). For a historical account of American foreign
policy in the Middle East, including the Carter years, see William B. Quandt, *Peace
Process: American Diplomacy and the Arab-Israeli Conflict since 1967* (Wash-
ington, D.C., 1993); George Lenczowski, *American Presidents and the Middle
East* (Durham, N.C., 1990); and Burton I. Kaufman, *The Arab Middle East and
the United States: Inter-Arab Rivalry and Superpower Diplomacy* (New York,
1996). For a discussion of American human rights initiatives, see Tony Smith,
*America's Mission: The United States and the Worldwide Struggle for Democ-
racy in the Twentieth Century* (Princeton, N.J., 1994); and Glenn Mower, Jr.,
Human Rights and American Foreign Policy: The Carter and Reagan Experiences
(New York, 1987). A explanation of American policy in Latin America can be
found in Lars Schoultz, *Human Rights and United States Policy toward Latin
America* (Princeton, N.J., 1981); John H. Coatsworth, *Central America and the
United States* (New York, 1994); and Walter LaFeber, *Inevitable Revolutions: The
United States in Central America* (New York, 1993). For a discussion of Ameri-
can policy toward Iran, see James A. Bill, *The Eagle and the Lion: The Tragedy
of American-Iranian Relations* (New Haven, Conn., 1988); Michael Ledeen and
William Lewis, *Debacle: The American Failure in Iran* (New York, 1981); Gary
Sick, *All Fall Down: America's Fateful Encounter with Iran* (London, 1985); and
Mahammad Reza Pahlavi, *Answer to History* (New York, 1980). For a history of
American relations with China, including the Carter years, see Warren I. Cohen,
America's Response to China: A History of Sino-American Relations (New York,
1990); and Rosemary Foot, *The Practice of Power: U.S. Relations with China since
1949* (Oxford, 1995). A discussion of American relations with Taiwan can be found
in Nancy Bernkopf Tucker, *Taiwan, Hong Kong, and the United States, 1945–1992*
(New York, 1994).

V. NATIONAL GOALS

For a discussion of the post–World War II American mind-set, see Sacvan
Berkovitch, *The American Jeremiad* (Madison, Wisc., 1978); Rupert Wilkinson,
The Pursuit of American Character (New York, 1988); and John Kenneth
Galbraith, *The Affluent Society* (New York, 1958). Histories of presidential com-
missions in the twentieth century can be found in Edward D. Berkowitz, "Com-
missioning the Future," *Reviews in American History* 11 (June 1983): 294–99;
Hugh Davis Graham, "The Ambiguous Legacy of American Presidential Com-
missions," *Public Historian* 7 (Spring 1985): 5–26; Elizabeth Drew, "On Giving
Oneself a Hotfoot: Government by Commission," *Atlantic Monthly,* May 1968:
45–49; and Frank Popper, *The President's Commissions* (New York, 1970). The
Eisenhower commission report can be found in President's Commission on Na-

tional Goals, *Goals for Americans* (Englewood Cliffs, N.J., 1960). For a discussion of the activities of the Eisenhower commission, see John W. Jeffries, "The 'Quest for National Purpose' of 1960," *American Quarterly* 30 (Fall 1978): 451–70; Douglas T. Miller and Marion Novak, *The Fifties: The Way We Really Were* (Garden City, N.Y., 1977); William L. O'Neill, *American High: The Years of Confidence, 1945–1960* (New York, 1986); and Charles C. Alexander, *Holding the Line: The Eisenhower Era, 1952–1961* (Bloomington, Ind., 1975). The Carter commission report can be found in *A National Agenda for the Eighties: Report of the President's Commission for a National Agenda for the Eighties* (Englewood Cliffs, N.J., 1981). For a discussion of the Carter commission's work, see Edward D. Berkowitz, "Jimmy Carter and the Sunbelt Report: Seeking a National Agenda," in *The Presidency and Domestic Policies of Jimmy Carter,* ed. Herbert D. Rosenbaum and Alexej Ugrinsky (Westport, Conn., 1994). Jimmy Carter's July 1979 "malaise" speech, "Energy and National Goals: Address to the Nation, July 15, 1979," can be found in *Public Papers of the Presidents of the United States: Jimmy Carter, 1979,* book 2 (Washington, D.C., 1980). For a discussion of the Goals for Georgia program instituted during Carter's governorship, see Mattie S. Anderson, "Governor Jimmy Carter: Idealist or Realist? A Study of Carter's Commitment to Citizen Participation and Planning in the Goals for Georgia Program" (master's thesis, Georgia State University, 1979); and Gary M. Fink, *Prelude to the Presidency: The Political Character and Legislative Leadership Style of Governor Jimmy Carter* (Westport, Conn., 1980).

Contributors

JOHN C. BARROW earned his Ph.D. at Vanderbilt University. He used the resources of the Jimmy Carter Library extensively in completing his dissertation, entitled "A Time of Limits: Jimmy Carter and the Quest for a National Energy Policy."

JOHN WHITECLAY CHAMBERS II is Professor of History and chair of the department at Rutgers University. His many publications include *The New Conscientious Objection: From Sacred to Secular Resistance* (coeditor), *To Raise an Army: The Draft Comes to Modern America,* and *The Tyranny of Change: America in the Progressive Era, 1900–1917.*

MELVYN DUBOFSKY, Distinguished Professor of History and Sociology at the State University of New York at Binghamton, has written extensively on American labor history. His publications include *John L. Lewis: A Biography, We Shall Be All: A History of the IWW,* and, most recently, *The State and Labor in Modern America.*

GARY M FINK, Professor of History at Georgia State University, is the author of *Labor's Search for Political Order: The Political Behavior of the Missouri Labor Movement, 1890–1940; Prelude to the Presidency: The Political Character and Legislative Leadership Style of Governor Jimmy Carter;* and *The Fulton Bag and Cotton Mills Strike of 1914–1915: Espionage, Labor Conflict, and New South Industrial Relations.*

HUGH GRAHAM is the Holland N. McTyeire Professor of History at Vanderbilt University. His book-length publications include *Southern Politics and the Second Reconstruction; The Civil Rights Era: Origins and Development of National Policy, 1960–1972; The Uncertain Triumph: Federal Education Policy in the Kennedy and Johnson Years;* and *Civil Rights and the Presidency.*

SUSAN M. HARTMANN is Professor of History and Women's Studies at Ohio State University. Among other publications, she is the author of *Truman and the 80th Congress; The Homefront and Beyond: American Women in the 1940s;* and *From Margin to Mainstream: American Women and Politics since the 1960s.*

WILLIAM E. LEUCHTENBURG, is the Kenan Professor of History at the University of North Carolina–Chapel Hill. His extensive publications include *Perils of Prosperity; Franklin D. Roosevelt and the New Deal, 1932–1940; In the Shadow of FDR: From Harry Truman to Ronald Reagan;* and *A Troubled Feast: American Society since 1945.*

JAMES T. PATTERSON, Professor of History at Brown University, has written extensively on modern American political history. His *Congressional Conservatism and the New Deal: The Growth of the Conservative Coalition in Congress, 1933–1939,* and *America's Struggle against Poverty, 1900–1994,* are both the standard treatment of their subjects. Professor Patterson won the Bancroft Prize in American history in 1997 for his *Grand Expectations: The United States, 1945–1974.*

BRUCE J. SCHULMAN is an Associate Professor of History at Boston University. His publications include *From Cotton Belt to Sunbelt: Federal Policy, Economic Development, and the Transformation of the South, 1938–1980.* In 1995 he published *Lyndon B. Johnson and American Liberalism: A Brief Biography with Documents.*

JUDITH STEIN teaches at City College of New York and the Graduate School of City University of New York, where she holds the rank of Professor of History. Her list of publications includes *The World of Marcus Garvey: Race and Class in Modern Society* and *Running Steel, Running America: Race and Economy in the United States, 1945 to the Present.*

JEFFREY K. STINE is the Curator of Engineering and Environmental History at the National Museum of American History, Smithsonian Institution. He is the coeditor of *Technology and Choice: Readings from Technology and Culture* and the author of *Mixing the Waters: Environment, Politics, and the Building of the Tennessee Tombigbee Waterway.*

WILLIAM W. STUECK, JR., Professor of U.S. Diplomatic Relations at the University of Georgia, is the author of *The Road to Confrontation: American Policy toward China and Korea, 1947–1950; The Wedemeyer Commission: American Politics and Foreign Policy during the Cold War;* and *The Korean War: An International History.*

THOMAS J. SUGRUE teaches modern American history at the University of Pennsylvania. His publications include *Urban Crisis: Race, Industrial Decline, and Housing in Detroit, 1940.*

ROBERT H. ZIEGER, Professor of History at the University of Florida, has published extensively in modern American labor and political history. Two of his books, *Rebuilding the Pulp and Paper Workers' Union, 1933–1941* and *The CIO, 1935–1955,* have won the Philip Taft Prize in American labor history.

Index